The Demography of Victorian England and Wales

The Demography of Victorian England and Wales uses the full range of nineteenth-century civil registration material to describe in detail for the first time the changing population history of England and Wales between 1837 and 1914. Its principal focus is the great demographic revolution which occurred during those years, especially the secular decline of fertility and the origins of the modern rise in life expectancy. But Robert Woods also considers the variable quality of the Victorian registration system; the changing role of what Robert Malthus termed the preventive check; variations in occupational mortality and the development of the twentieth-century class mortality gradient; and the effects of urbanisation associated with the significance of distinctive disease environments. The volume also illustrates the fundamental importance of geographical variations between urban and rural areas. This invaluable reference tool is generously illustrated with numerous tables and figures, some of the latter being in colour.

ROBERT WOODS is John Rankin Professor of Geography at the University of Liverpool. He is the editor of the *International Journal of Population Geography* and a past president of the British Society for Population Studies. Among his many publications is *The Population of Britain in the Nineteenth Century* (Cambridge, 1995).

Cambridge Studies in Population, Economy and Society in Past Time 35

Series Editors

RICHARD SMITH

Cambridge Group for the History of Population and Social Structure

JAN DE VRIES

University of California at Berkeley

PAUL JOHNSON

London School of Economics and Political Science

KEITH WRIGHTSON

Yale University

Recent work in social, economic and demographic history has revealed much that was previously obscure about societal stability and change in the past. It has also been suggested that crossing the conventional boundaries between these branches of history can be very rewarding.

This series exemplifies the value of interdisciplinary work of this kind, and includes books on topics such as family, kinship and neighbourhood; welfare provision and social control; work and leisure; migration; urban growth; and legal structures and procedures, as well as more familiar matters. It demonstrates that, for example, anthropology and economics have become as close intellectual neighbours to history as have political philosophy or biography.

For a full list of titles in the series, please see end of book.

The Demography of Victorian England and Wales

ROBERT WOODS

University of Liverpool

CAMBRIDGE UNIVERSITY PRESS

PUBLISHED BY THE PRESS SYNDICATE OF THE UNIVERSITY OF CAMBRIDGE
The Pitt Building, Trumpington Street, Cambridge, United Kingdom

CAMBRIDGE UNIVERSITY PRESS
The Edinburgh Building, Cambridge CB2 2RU, UK   www.cup.cam.ac.uk
40 West 20th Street, New York, NY 10011-4211, USA   www.cup.org
10 Stamford Road, Oakleigh, Melbourne 3166, Australia
Ruiz de Alarcón 13, 28014 Madrid, Spain

First published 2000

Printed in the United Kingdom at the University Press, Cambridge

Typeface Adobe Palatino 10/12 pt.   *System* QuarkXPress™   [SE]

A catalogue record for this book is available from the British Library

ISBN 0 521 78254 6 hardback

To the memory of my grandmother
Hannah Maud Nettleton (née Garner)
born Liverpool 1882 – died Birmingham 1984

Contents

Figures

List of figures

Tables

Preface

A preface should certainly apologise and acknowledge, but it must also consider expectations, both the readers' and the author's. This is a demographic study written by a geographer. It describes and offers some interpretations of the course of demographic change in England and Wales during the Victorian era, 1837–1901. It is especially concerned with changes and variations in nuptiality, fertility and mortality, but it has relatively little to say directly on the subject of internal migration although it does devote a chapter to the consequences of urbanisation for the pattern of national mortality trends. There is no intention to make the study a comprehensive survey in which each demographic component receives equal attention. For example, childhood mortality is given an especially prominent place not only because of its interest to contemporaries especially in the early years of the twentieth century, but also because of its contribution to variations in life chances and its possible influence on reproductive behaviour. The book is not preoccupied exclusively with one period and place. The Victorian era, whilst being remarkable for the development of new statistical sources and for its position at the origin of several secular trends, cannot be treated in isolation. Much needs to be said about the early years of the nineteenth as well as the eighteenth century and the analysis will not be halted arbitrarily in 1901 or 1911. Similarly, the borders of England and Wales will be crossed when to do so would seem to enrich the account either by allowing the experiences of other regions to be 'borrowed' so that gaps may be filled by analogy or where other places offer illuminating contrasts. No one theory will be tested or methodology employed, although a critique of the demographic transition concept is bound to occupy an important position and demography amounts to very little if it cannot quantify vital events, or their absence.

The Demography of Victorian England and Wales has a clear and distinctive focus. It is concerned with space as well as time: with the ways in which nuptiality, fertility and mortality varied and changed during sixty or seventy years. It uses a common set of 614 districts based on the registration districts defined by the General Register Office, London, to chart these changes. Whilst it has been obvious for some time that a country as small as England and Wales was nonetheless far from homogeneous in economic, social or even political terms, it has taken far longer to establish the extent of demographic diversity and especially the importance of local variations. These may only be charted when districts or sub-districts are employed in preference to the 45 registration counties. Although this geographical perspective is obvious, there will be occasions on which it will need to be complemented or replaced by other approaches. For example, compared with several other European countries, the decline of marital fertility in England and Wales does not lend itself to ecological analysis since such change was not sufficiently geographically differentiated. Similarly, it will be important to show the way in which the life chances of people engaged in different occupations and the members of social groups or classes improved in the late nineteenth century regardless of where they lived. However, the spatial perspective will prove of particular value for an analysis of marriage and of the pattern of mortality, its age components and causes of death.

This book also presents powerful arguments for the consideration of joint effects in demographic studies. Nuptiality and overall fertility need to be treated together as do fertility and childhood mortality, for instance. Although it has proved necessary to deal with these themes in separate chapters, they are also brought together in the notion of demographic regimes which is defined and discussed in chapter 10.

Authors are obliged to make certain assumptions about their readers. I shall assume that those using this book have at least a basic knowledge of demographic terms and analytical concepts. If this is not the case then reference may be made to my *Population Analysis in Geography* (Longman, 1979) and *Theoretical Population Geography* (Longman, 1982). If a short, non-technical introduction to Victorian demography is required then *The Population of Britain in the Nineteenth Century* (Cambridge University Press, 1995) should serve the purpose.

Studies of this nature are written and assembled over a protracted period, twenty years in this case, and they require the financial support of several organisations as well as the assistance of many individuals. The Nuffield Foundation provided a Research Fellowship in the Social Sciences in 1985; the Wellcome Trust's History of Medicine Panel supported research on infant mortality (chapter 7) and occupational mortality (chapter 6); the Economic and Social Research Council funded work on mortality and cause of death (Grants R-000-23-3373 and R-000-23-4824) which led to the publication of *An Atlas of Victorian Mortality* (Liverpool University Press, 1997) and contributed to chapter 8 here; and, finally, a grant (F/25/BD) from the Leverhulme Trust for the period 1996–98 allowed the book to be completed. The following individuals have made their own important contributions as students, assistants, colleagues or advisors and to them I owe a special debt of gratitude: Michael Anderson, Chris Galley, Eilidh Garrett, Bill Gould, David Grigg, Michael Haines, Andy Hinde, Violetta Hionidou, Clare Holdsworth, Gerry Kearns, Dick Lawton, Paul Laxton, Sandra Mather, Graham Mooney, Bob Schofield, Sally Sheard, Nicola Shelton, David Siddle, Chris Smith, Richard Smith, Simon Szreter, Patti Watterson (now Tomlinson), Paul White, Naomi Williams, Paul Williamson, Chris Wilson, John Woodward and Tony Wrigley. Even though they will surely find aspects with which they disagree, I hope that in general they will think the job well done. Alison, Rachel and Gavin like the figures.

17 September 1999

1

Bricks without straw, bones without flesh

Demographers are more akin to hedgehogs than foxes. They possess a particular unifying principle and relate everything to a single central vision. The foxes, on the other hand, think in a diffuse fashion: they move on many levels collecting objects and experiences without seeking to fit them into any form of all-embracing scheme.[1] Demographers are like hedgehogs in another sense: they tend to rely on one highly effective strategy for survival against which the cunning of foxes will usually fail. The unifying principle is the notion of the demographic system and transition, while the survival strategy involves quantification within an empiricist-positivist methodology.

Although this caricature cannot do justice to the contributions of demographers, it nonetheless highlights certain important characteristics about the way questions are asked and answers attempted. Philosophical introspection is rarely indulged in and thoughts on what might be an appropriate epistemology for demography are not aired. Even among historical demographers, at least some of whom have been drawn from the ranks of history and geography where disciplinary self-doubt has been rife,[2] there is a quiet contentment with very specific lines of enquiry in which the first step invariably involves the measurement and description of a certain set of events: birth, marriage, death, migration. This is usually followed by the search for some form of demographic order, pattern recognition and modelling. Finally, explanation or interpretation is attempted although this may take many forms varying from formal hypothesis testing to 'thick description'. Whatever the finer points of the approach there is always a sense in which it is better to practise, to engage with the materials of demography, than to

---

[1] Berlin (1953). Of course Berlin was not thinking of demographers as such when he drew this distinction.   [2] See, for example, Evans (1997).

enter the methodological and ideological debates.[3] This account of the demography of Victorian England and Wales will be no exception. It follows the lead given by *The Population of India and Pakistan*, *The Population of Japan* and *The Demography of Tropical Africa*[4] in that it will provide a detailed description via demographic measures of changes and especially variations in nuptiality, fertility and mortality. It will also offer some lines of interpretation based, as far as is possible, on the available empirical evidence. There will be a place for speculation and conjecture where, as often happens, the evidence appears unsound or there simply is none. The approach adopted is also multi-disciplinary; no single perspective dominates although in places there are contributions which statisticians, economists, sociologists, geographers and epidemiologists, as well as several branches of history, would certainly recognise as their own. It is true that our understanding of nineteenth-century demography is still in a state of flux. There are many unanswered questions especially relating to the causes of change whether economic and technological, social and cultural; the extent to which Victorians gained more control of their everyday lives must be set against the increasing role of the state, both national and local, and its power to intervene and regulate, to initiate change through public policy. Similar tensions and confusions exist in attempts to set the forces for integration and conformity against those which encouraged diversity and variation – for example, those that exacerbated inequalities among social groups and between places in terms of poverty, health and mortality.

Before returning to a discussion of that unifying principle in demography, the notion of system and transition, two further points must be made. First, it is tempting to view England and Wales in isolation and the reconstruction of its demography as an end in itself. But England and Wales was part of several far larger spheres in terms of the so-called European marriage pattern; the Western system of applied scientific knowledge, engineering and medical science included; and the international flows of capital, goods and people, to give three obvious examples. There are two other senses in which neither the place nor the period will be treated in isolation in this study. The demographic experience of other societies will be used to plug gaps in our knowledge when direct evidence is lacking. This is a device well known among historical demographers who often have resort especially to the Scandinavian model of demographic change, occasionally with unfortunate consequences. Further, there are even today populations in

---

[3] This tradition is now subject to healthy criticism and challenge, for example, Kertzer and Fricke (1997).

[4] Respectively, Davis (1951), Taeuber (1958) and Brass *et al.* (1968).

Africa and Asia with relatively high fertility and mortality. Studies of their characteristics may prove of value in our attempt to understand Victorian society just as the 'lessons from the past' argument has been used to draw analogies between the historical experience of the West, but mainly western Europe, and the way in which matters are likely to progress among non-European populations. Secondly, Victorian scientists, especially the medical statisticians, knew a great deal about the demography of their society both from the published tabulations and surveys, and from first-hand experience. Sir Edwin Chadwick, William Farr, Sir Arthur Newsholme, Seebohm Rowntree and Charles Booth established the British tradition of empirical social enquiry. Their findings, even their surmises, must not be overlooked otherwise they are likely merely to be discovered again.

One unifying principle with two distinct parts has tended to dominate the thinking of scholars working especially on the demography of past societies: the Malthusian demographic system and the demographic transition model. These will be considered in their turn as frameworks for our present account of the Victorian period. But first we must say a little by way of introduction about the empirical nature of these enquiries.

True facts

English historical demographers have been justly applauded for their ability to make bricks without straw whilst at the same time being criticised for failing to put sufficient flesh on their statistical skeletons.[5] Although it sometimes appears that social historians are energetic in showing us the flesh and blood of real people whilst eschewing the deeper demographic structures and generalities that give the behaviour of their subjects some wider meaning, no one could accuse the nineteenth-century statisticians and actuaries in this regard. For them the search for 'true facts' was of prime importance and without them their work would be meaningless, just theory. Those who campaigned for legislation to establish a regular population census and an accurate system for the registration of births, deaths and marriages had several motives, but the need to keep human accounts for the sake of efficient

---

[5] J. D. Chambers took 'Bricks without straw: the course of population change in the eighteenth century' as the title of one of his chapters in *Population, Economy, and Society in Pre-industrial England* (Chambers, 1972), while Wrigley *et al.* (1997) have used an alternative analogy to 'bones without flesh' when they talk about 'laying the foundations and erecting the main fabric of a house, but leaving its finishing and furnishing to another day' (p. 5).

administration would surely have been one of their foremost concerns. Another would have been rather more intellectual: to determine the true course of population growth in the eighteenth century.[6] With the establishment of the regular decennial census in 1801 and the introduction of civil registration in 1837 it might be supposed that the controversy that fuelled their campaign would have come to an end, but it has not been until recent decades that we have finally secured reliable estimates of the size of England's population before 1801 and of trends in the major demographic indices prior to 1837. With these materials we are now in a position to place the nineteenth century and especially the Victorian age in context.[7]

Figure 1.1 helps us to see at a glance why the Victorian period was so important as a turning point in England's longer population history.[8] It shows that life expectancy at birth in years (e_0), perhaps the best single number measure of mortality, varied between 30 and 40 in the seventeenth and eighteenth centuries. It was around 40 years early in the nineteenth century and stayed at about that level until the third quarter of the century when the secular decline of mortality began. Life expectancy at birth has doubled in the past 150 years. In figure 1.1 fertility has been measured by the total fertility rate (TFR), that is, the number of children a woman might expect to have had on passing through the reproductive ages 15–49. Until the middle of the eighteenth century,

---

[6] See Glass (1973).

[7] Wrigley and Schofield (1981), Wrigley *et al.* (1997) and Wrigley (1997, 1998) summarise the Cambridge Group for the History of Population and Social Structure's project to fully analyse Anglican parish registers for the period 1538–1837. The 1989 reprint of Wrigley and Schofield (1981) also contains a chapter entitled 'The debate about *The population history of England*: an introductory note' (pp. viii–xxxiv) which offers a reply to some criticisms, including the standing of the back projection estimates, and a useful list of reviews and reactions. Although these estimates are obviously not above criticism, they not only provide measures far superior in quality and detail to any previously available, but also ones that are unlikely to be bettered. See especially Wrigley *et al.* (1997), pp. 515–44, on 'Reconstitution and inverse projection', but also Levine (1998) and Razzell (1998).

[8] The measures used to construct figures 1.1 and 1.2 have been derived from Wrigley *et al.* (1997), table A9.1, pp. 614–15, up to 1840 and from the Registrar General's *Annual Reports, Decennial Supplements* and *Annual Statistical Reviews* thereafter. The 31 decades 1581–90 to 1981–90 are shown for England and Wales. Although, strictly speaking, the estimates for the decades prior to 1841 are for England, it has been assumed that they can reasonably stand for England and Wales as a whole. The reported gross reproduction rate (GRR) has been inflated by 2.05 to give the total fertility rate (TFR). For the 1840s to the 1930s TFR has been estimated; see Office of Population Censuses and Surveys, *Birth Statistics: Historical Series of Statistics from Registrations of Births in England and Wales, 1837–1983*, Series FM1 No. 13 (London: HMSO, 1987), table 1.4, and also table 4.2 below. The quality of Victorian civil registration is considered in chapter 2, and life expectancy at birth and the childhood mortality rate are reported and further discussed in table 9.3.

TFR varied from about 3.75 to 4.50; thereafter it rose substantially to peak at 5.75 in the early decades of the nineteenth century. A long decline then set in, although this appears to have been temporarily halted during the 1850s and 1860s. From the fourth quarter of the nineteenth century fertility was apparently in free fall, only ending its decline in the 1940s. Clearly the Victorian era was above all one of demographic change in which the secular declines of both mortality and fertility began, and by 1901 new, lower than previously experienced levels had been reached. Figure 1.2 captures this sense that the people of England and Wales were entering a new demographic age during Victoria's reign in an even more striking fashion. It shows the timepath for fertility–mortality again for the 31 decades used in figure 1.1. It also indicates, using Model West, the levels of TFR-e_0 that would be necessary to generate rates of natural population growth of 0 and 2 per cent per year.[9] Before the middle of the nineteenth century, population growth in England and Wales was largely the result of fluctuations in fertility; variation along the vertical axis of figure 1.2 is substantially greater than along the horizontal, but in or by the 1870s fertility and mortality set off together on a new, joint downward course into previously uncharted demographic territory.

The Model West, referred to above, comes from Coale and Demeny's *Regional Model Life Tables and Stable Populations*, first published in 1966.[10] This single work more than any other symbolises efforts to utilise to the full demographic data from the nineteenth century and to draw parallels between that largely European experience of high mortality and conditions in much of Africa, Asia and Latin America today. Coale and Demeny's models have established a framework within which the quality of historical European mortality statistics may be evaluated as well as allowing the estimation of vital rates for populations which, while regularly enumerated, lacked effective registration systems. Of the 326 life tables selected for analysis, 113 related to periods prior to 1918 and of these 86 were European in origin. From the set of 326 empirical life tables, Coale and Demeny identified four distinct age patterns of mortality which they labelled North, South, East and West thereby signifying the regions of Europe from which the constituent tables were principally drawn. For example, the life tables underlying the North model were: Sweden, 1851–90 (4 tables); Norway, 1856–80 and 1946–55

---

[9] Model life tables, of which West is one, will be used at various points throughout this book. They offer a convenient device for representing the various age profiles of mortality in terms of life expectancy at birth and of illustrating what population age structures will look like given certain levels of mortality and fertility.

[10] Coale and Demeny (1966).

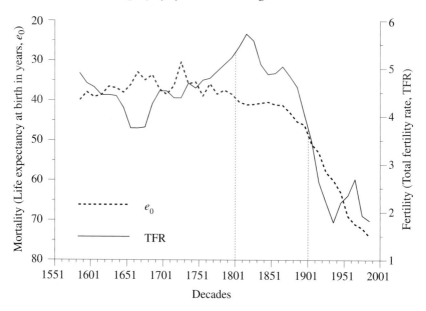

Figure 1.1. Long-run trends in mortality and fertility in England and Wales
Note: The axis showing life expectancy at birth has been reversed to illustrate
the decline of mortality.
Source: See text for explanation.

(4); and Iceland, 1941–50 (1). Model West, on the other hand, represented a residual category once the North, South and East patterns had
been removed. Here the underlying tables were drawn mainly from
England and Wales, France, the Netherlands, Denmark, Canada, the
USA, Australia and New Zealand.[11] Model life tables were estimated for
each of the four families using life expectancy at birth as the reference
for defining levels of mortality, and these in turn became the basis for
stable population models with various constant rates of population
change.

These regional model life tables have been used extensively by
English historical demographers as devices for checking the quality of
data, for estimating mortality rates for which empirical data are entirely
missing, and as a general reference tool, providing co-ordinates in
demographic space. As such, they have proved of exceptional value.
However, in recent years there has come to be an uncritical over-

---

[11] In passing, it is interesting to note that Coale and Demeny (1966), p. 12, excluded from
further consideration life tables for periods prior to 1870 for England and Wales, France
and the Netherlands because they had 'irregular patterns that appeared to arise from
faulty data', although 11 for England and Wales 1871–1959 were used.

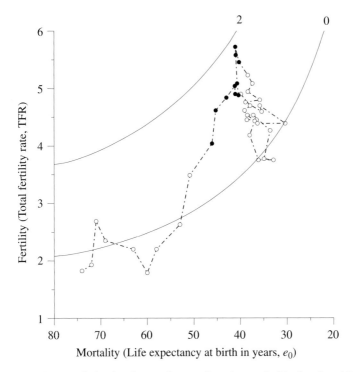

Figure 1.2. Timepath for fertility and mortality change in England and Wales, decades 1580s to 1980s
Note: The axis showing life expectancy at birth has been reversed to illustrate the decline of mortality. The curves labelled 0 and 2 indicate 0 and 2 per cent per year natural growth rates in Model West. The decades of the nineteenth century have been emphasised.

dependence on the reliability and comprehensive nature of these models which their creators could not have envisaged. Where they are perhaps at their most vulnerable is when one section of the age-specific mortality curve, usually adult mortality, is to be inferred from another, infant and child mortality.[12] There has also been the tacit assumption, for example, that because the third English Life Table for 1838–54 matches rather closely level 10 of Model North, England's historical mortality experience can, in broad terms, be represented by the North pattern.[13] However, Coale and Demeny also comment on the 'unusual

---

[12] See Woods (1993).

[13] Wrigley and Schofield (1981), p. 110 and appendix 14. Naturally, they are sensitive to the problems this is likely to cause for their back projection. See Wrigley *et al.* (1997), pp. 515–44.

incidence of tuberculosis' in North and that 'Model tables incorporating this experience would be suitable only for populations with a high endemicity of tuberculosis.'[14] If this assertion did indeed prove to be valid it would have important implications for epidemiological studies of the early modern period. But more detailed recent work with a larger number of family reconstitution studies has tended to cast doubt on the wisdom of making such broad generalisations linking mortality experience to one family over such a long period. Wrigley *et al.* have confirmed that as far as infancy and early childhood are concerned:

> mortality in the early modern period did not conform either to model West or to model North, though edging closer to model North pattern in the late eighteenth and early nineteenth centuries. Indeed, mortality in infancy and childhood in the English historical past does not appear to have resembled the patterns found in any of the families of tables which were extrapolated from more recent data in the Princeton tables.[15]

Presumably Model West is still appropriate for England and Wales post-1871.

The use of the Princeton model life tables epitomises the problems faced by historical demographers, even those working on the nineteenth century. Bricks may be created without straw, but they are bricks of perhaps uncertain quality which will not necessarily make the soundest foundations for a new residence.

A variation on the same theme can also be illustrated by the Princeton European Fertility Project of which Ansley J. Coale was the guiding spirit. In order to chart the progress of fertility decline among the provinces of nineteenth- and early twentieth-century Europe it was necessary to develop a set of indices that not only captured the general level of fertility, but also made it possible to differentiate the contributions of legitimate and illegitimate fertility as well as the effects of fertility within marriage compared with the influence of nuptiality itself. In normal circumstances this problem would have been solved by using the total period fertility rate and the total marital fertility rate or some modification of the gross and net reproduction rates. But many countries, including Great Britain, whilst possessing a system for civil registration lacked data on the age of mother at the birth of her children. Age-specific total or marital fertility rates could not be calculated, therefore. Coale's solution to this problem involved the development of a set of four indirectly standardised measures: I_f, the index of overall fertility; I_g, the index of marital fertility; I_h, the index of illegitimate or non-

---

[14] Coale and Demeny (1966), p. 12. Figure 8.2 illustrates what this means especially for mortality in the age group 15–34.   [15] Wrigley *at al.* (1997), p. 263.

marital fertility; and *Im*, the index of proportion married.[16] These measures have several characteristics which make them especially important. First, they require relatively little empirical data: at minimum the numbers of legitimate and illegitimate live births, and the numbers of currently married and single women distinguished by five-year age groups 15–19 to 45–49. The births could be found from civil registration and marital condition from population censuses.[17] This usually meant that local and regional as well as national patterns could be charted. Secondly, the four measures are age-standardised and therefore avoid the problems of distortion associated with the use of the crude birth rate or even the general fertility rate. Thirdly, the indices are related one to another in a way that has certain useful properties for representing changes and variations in the joint effects of marital fertility and nuptiality on overall fertility. Since

$$If = Ig \bullet Im + Ih(1 - Im) \qquad (1.1)$$

if *Ih* is zero, or at least very low, then overall fertility can be said to be the product of marital fertility and proportion married ($If = Ig \bullet Im$).[18] Fourthly, and of particular significance, in choosing a standard age-specific marital fertility schedule Coale was careful to select a population with what has come to be known as natural fertility, that is fertility that was not being limited in a parity-specific way. His choice of the especially well-documented Hutterite population and, in particular, the fertility experienced by the 1921–30 first marriage cohort meant that *Ig* not only measured marital fertility, but it also set the level of fertility against that achieved by the Hutterites for whom *Ig* was by definition 1.0.[19] Further analysis of a range of *Ig* values suggested to Coale that if the index was found to be greater than 0.6 it was likely to indicate the presence of natural fertility and thus the absence of deliberate family limitation behaviour.[20]

---

[16] Coale (1967).

[17] In fact Wilson and Woods (1991) offer a method for deriving these measures based on Wrigley and Schofield's (1981) back projection results for England in the parish register era before 1837.

[18] This property has been used extensively in several figures in chapters 3 and 4. For example, figure 3.6 shows the *Ig-Im* timepath for England and Wales, while figure 4.18 illustrates the changing pattern of variation among districts.

[19] Eaton and Mayer (1954), table 1, p. 84. The Hutterites were, of course, a most unusual population. The total marital fertility rate for those women married in the 1920s was 12 and only 3.4 per cent of all marriages were childless representing an exceptionally low level of natural sterility. Eaton and Mayer also speculate that whilst contraception was not used, coital frequency may have declined rapidly once a woman reached her late thirties (p. 24).

[20] The matter of identifying the presence or absence of certain forms of family limitation behaviour has proved to be far more complicated in practice, see pp. 124–40.

In reality, however, our account of demographic change and variation, even for England and Wales in the second half of the nineteenth century, cannot be made out of true facts as the Victorian actuaries might have wished. Rather, it has to employ estimates and approximations, use subjective judgement, and be selective and at times partial. This point may be illustrated just as effectively when we turn to the unifying principle of demography which has guided our understanding of population history: the concepts of demographic system and demographic transition.

Systems

The concluding chapter of *The Population History of England, 1541–1871* outlines a systems model designed to capture the dynamic relationship between population and environment in early modern England.[21] At its centre the model contains a diagrammatic representation of the ways in which the two checks to population outlined by T. R. Malthus in his *An Essay on the Principle of Population* are capable of exerting regulatory influences on the size of a population. The model is illustrated here in figure 1.3. In the outer circuit we have the positive check which works by raising mortality if and when real incomes are depressed because food prices have increased as a consequence of too rapid population growth. The preventive check occupies the inner circuit. Here the effect of falling real incomes will be to reduce nuptiality which will consequently lead to lower fertility and a reduced rate of population growth. These two routes, the first emphasised by Malthus in his 1798 *Essay* in terms of famine, disease and war, and the second in the 1803 and subsequent editions of the *Essay*, particularly as moral restraint operating via prudential and especially delayed marriage, offer alternative paths. If the preventive check is firmly in place and working effectively then there may be no need for the positive check, misery and vice may be avoided to a large extent, and there may even be positive economic benefits in terms of higher real incomes and higher living standards in general.[22] On to this essentially Malthusian, self-regulating negative feedback system, dominated by what the biologists term 'homeostasis', Wrigley and Schofield have bolted a number of additional sub-systems, endogenous and exogenous factors.[23] The first of these involves what

---

[21] Wrigley and Schofield (1981), pp. 454–84.

[22] Wrigley (1988) provides a more elaborate statement of some of the economic–demographic arguments.

[23] Wilson and Airey (1999) offer an interesting discussion of the application of homeostatic arguments in demography.

they call the system of ecological niches. Now mortality is not only negatively linked to population size to represent the positive check, but it is also positively linked to nuptiality. In certain forms of largely agrarian society, access to a secure livelihood on the land will require the inheritance of property. If for some reason mortality increases this may free up access to land which will in turn remove the need for marriage to be delayed. By this means a population suddenly affected by an exogenous mortality shock will be able to recover quite rapidly through increased fertility. The second inserts the effect of net migration linking real income with population size in a positive fashion. If real incomes increase, people will be drawn in, but if they decline then emigration will be a possible response with the same effects as the positive and preventive checks. Finally, an additional economic sub-system dominated by positive feedback is associated with real incomes to allow for the effects that rising incomes will have on the demand for consumer products and services, and in turn the demand for labour which will produce wage inflation. This sub-system is also linked via urbanisation to mortality. Assuming the presence of a sharp urban–rural mortality gradient, the demand for manufactured goods and services which will stimulate urban growth and urbanisation is likely to increase average mortality levels as more people crowd into the unhealthy towns. The completed model, with the addition of exogenous influences affecting the demand for labour and mortality, is shown as the top panel of figure 1.3.

The model works rather well until the beginning of the nineteenth century when the positive link between population size and food price ceases to have an influence, with population growth continuing apace without adversely affecting the price of food and thus real income. Representations of the model for England in both the seventeenth and sixteenth centuries give special emphasis to this link and the preventive check circuit in general, whilst relegating to negligible significance the role of the positive check and the negative link between real income and mortality. This new emphasis has led to a radical revision of our understanding of the demography of the early modern period in England.[24] It has diverted attention away from mortality and towards fertility as the prime initiator of long-run population growth and has been especially damaging to the arguments of those who see the stabilisation and eventual disappearance of demographic crises as the initiating factor in mortality decline. It has also encouraged considerable discussion of the possibility that, in England in particular and western Europe in general,

[24] See Wrigley and Schofield (1989), pp. xiii–xxxiv.

The full demographic system

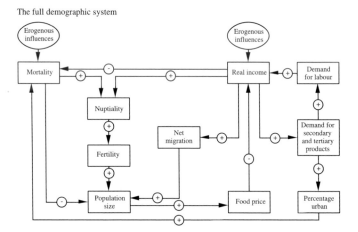

England in the early nineteenth century

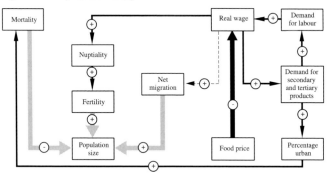

England towards the end of the nineteenth century

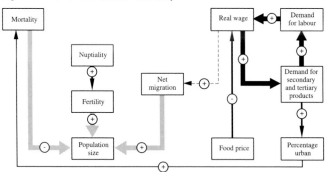

Figure 1.3. Examples of demographic systems models for England and Wales
Source: Redrawn from Wrigley and Schofield (1981), figures 11.5, 11.8 and 11.9.

the lower level of fertility together with its capacity to adjust to economic circumstances via the preventive check gave the region some initial demographically inspired economic advantage – an advantage that encouraged consumer-led economic growth and laid favourable preconditions for industrialisation. England could take advantage of its beneficial low-pressure demographic system, while China, to use an example popular with Malthus, was locked into a high-pressure system at the mercy of the positive check.[25]

The debate about *The Population History of England* has tended to focus on the following issues: the reliability of the demographic estimates and especially back projection; the mechanism of economic–demographic change, but particularly the absence of an endogenous positive check in England, the lagged response of nuptiality to real wages (including the credibility of the real wage series used), and the need to decompose nuptiality into proportion marrying and age at marriage; and, in general, whether 'dilatory homeostasis' is an appropriate device for modelling the early modern experience. On all of these matters a good deal of progress has been made.[26] But there are two further points which, although occasionally mentioned, have failed to attract sustained attention. The first is the matter of regional and local variations, and the second relates to the question of how demographic change in the nineteenth century might be modelled when homeostasis was no longer even dilatory.

Finally, the functioning of the national aggregate will never be well understood unless analyses or relations that appear to characterise the national entity are paralleled by similar work on a local scale. Only in this way can those aspects of English demographic and economic history in which there was homogeneity of behaviour throughout the country be distinguished from those where the national aggregate reflects an average condition that may prove to have been true of few individual communities, and that may therefore tend to lead to misguided conclusions about the relations between demographic and economic behaviour in the past.[27]

---

[25] There are frequent references to misery and vice in China in Malthus's first *Essay* (1798) while the second *Essay* (1803) has chapter 12 of book 1 devoted to the subject. See also Wrigley and Schofield (1989), p. xxiv, and Wrigley *et al.* (1997), p. 549. We shall return to a comparison of the demographic regimes of England and China in chapter 10.

[26] Much of this has been summarised by the contributors to Rotberg and Rabb (1986), but see also Wrigley and Schofield (1989), pp. xiii–xxxiv, and Schofield (1989) which brings the role of welfare policy, especially the Poor Law, into the equation particularly in the late eighteenth century. The nuptiality question is considered again in chapter 3 (pp. 107–9).

[27] Wrigley and Schofield (1981), p. 482. Wrigley *et al.* (1997) do not, in general, take this point further; indeed, it would be difficult to do so with family reconstitutions for at maximum 26 parishes and for some periods as few as eight (see chapter 3, 'Representativeness'). As Wrigley and Schofield point out, they come closest to taking up their own challenge in the analysis of crisis mortality among the 404 parishes in appendix 10.

The problem is one of level, trend and variation. It may well be that as far as nuptiality is concerned most parishes trended together, but that the variation between parishes was not insubstantial and that it increased over time. In the case of mortality there was certainly a wide difference between the urban and rural parishes, but also among the latter between those in the marshes and fens, and those located in more salubrious regions. And what of real wages? These would certainly have had strong regional and local components in their trends and, like mortality, their distributions would probably have become more skewed as time progressed, although not necessarily in the same way.

As far as the nineteenth century is concerned, even weak homeostasis appears to offer little potential as the basis for modelling demographic change and variation. Figure 1.3 also shows Wrigley and Schofield's models for the early and late nineteenth century. The three logical demographic links between mortality, fertility, net migration and population size are illustrated in grey while the other significant links are represented by lines of varying thickness. In the model for the early nineteenth century there is still a strong positive link between real wages and nuptiality, but by the end of the century this has all but disappeared. The positive link between percentage urban and mortality has weakened, but not disappeared, although links between the consumer demand and demand for labour sub-systems which drive urbanisation have strengthened.[28] In neither nineteenth-century model are there links between population size and food price, and between real wages and mortality. The former is regarded as having become redundant in or about 1806 while the latter only appears as a weak negative link in the model for the sixteenth century. Similarly, the ecological niche link between mortality and nuptiality is only shown in its weakest form in the models for the sixteenth and late seventeenth centuries. Had the model been taken on a further hundred years from the 1870s to, say, the 1970s virtually all of its non-logical links would have disappeared. Nuptiality would no longer be linked to fertility, except via divorce; the demand for secondary and tertiary products would not be linked to percentage urban or even the demand for labour; and the link from food prices to real wages would have become much weaker.

Clearly, all would agree that a dynamic systems model founded on the principle of homeostasis is not the best way to represent the demo-

---

[28] Wrigley and Schofield (1981) remark of the late nineteenth century that 'Even the link between urban growth and mortality was of much reduced importance. The gap between urban and rural death rates had begun to close, and in the early decades of the twentieth century disappeared entirely.' (p. 476) As we shall see in chapter 5, matters were in fact not quite so simple.

graphic experience of nineteenth-century England and Wales.[29] How, then, should we proceed? Let us take four steps. First, it must be appreciated that demographic change, and especially the secular decline of mortality and fertility, cannot be understood simply in terms of the relationship between population and resources, population and the economy. Many other factors are involved including the application of scientific knowledge in public policy and the often only boundedly rational behaviour of individuals with respect to their own reproduction. Secondly, population growth and redistribution can be seen to act as a stimulus to economic development, social and cultural change; it need not always be taken as a red light, a warning to rein back. Thirdly, whilst there is much to be learned by modelling the processes that regulate animal numbers, especially as this may be assisted by laboratory experiment and is sufficiently simple to allow considerable mathematical sophistication, there are many dangers in its application to even the least developed human societies.[30] Fourthly, there is the need to recognise the importance of chance, fortuitous coincidences and unforeseen consequences in both their temporal and spatial senses. Jenner and cowpox, the Irish potato famine and the Bradlaugh–Besant trial each had important, although very different, effects on demographic change in the nineteenth century, as also did the reform of Parliamentary democracy and the demands it placed on politicians to concern themselves with public opinion and its management.

Transitions

It might be argued that the 'ideal type' model proposed by Wrigley and Schofield can offer a new and superior way of envisioning the first

---

[29] Wilson and Airey (1999) ask the key question without answering it in respect to demographic transition theory.

[30] The story of the development of the models proposed by Wrigley and Schofield is of interest in its own right. The influences of Malthus, Darwin, Wynne-Edwards and Lee are clear and often mentioned, but the way in which their ideas were combined, applied and especially represented in diagrammatic form is of fundamental importance. The following appear to mark significant points in the course of the story: Wrigley (1967, 1969), Schofield (1976, 1986) and Lee (1986, 1987). Bideau (1980) offers a sceptical review of the early work by historical demographers. In anthropology, Wynne-Edwards's thesis was not taken up thanks, undoubtedly, to a critique delivered in 1966 by Mary Douglas (1966). The central idea of V. C. Wynne-Edwards's *Animal Dispersion in Relation to Social Behaviour* (1962) is that in certain cases special forms of animal behaviour have evolved that give information on population density, thereby helping to make territoriality a more effective demographic regulator, and that, in general, group self-regulation of population size developed through the course of evolution. These views were always controversial among zoologists and were ultimately also rejected by their originator.

pre-industrial stage in the classic demographic transition model, that second part of demography's central unifying principle. But this could prove damaging to the model as a whole because it would raise nuptiality to the key position and would undermine the role of mortality decline as the initiator of rapid population growth. It would also require the model and its accompanying theory to be made more flexible so that a number of different routes to low mortality and fertility could be accommodated. These substantial revisions could easily be justified, however. Before attempting such a major revision, it is necessary to consider the origins of the demographic transition model and theory in rather more detail.

Figure 1.4 illustrates three early versions of the demographic transition diagram for England and Wales. The top panel shows C. P. Blacker and D. V. Glass's representation of John Brownlee's figures for the crude birth and death rates.[31] It is probably the first attempt to give diagrammatic expression to the now familiar time-series. The middle panel shows the same graph, but now it is in a form so much simplified that it can for the first time be called a model.[32] Although the Political and Economic Planning Report was published anonymously, it seems likely that the identification of the four stages in the model owed much to C. P. Blacker's influence.[33] Finally, the bottom panel of figure 1.4 reproduces a version of the model from a medical textbook of the 1960s.[34] This appears to have been the only occasion on which Thomas McKeown ventured to render the long-run population history of England and Wales in diagrammatic form.

It is now generally accepted that Brownlee's estimates of the crude birth and death rates for decades before the 1800s are seriously flawed.[35]

---

[31] Blacker and Glass (1936), figure 1, p. 7, cite as the source of their data Brownlee (1916), table XI, p. 232. Blacker and Glass note in their figure caption that 'The figures after 1876 are accurate.'

[32] Political and Economic Planning (1955), figure III, p. 108. The Blacker and Glass diagram is also reproduced as figure II, but no reference is made to Brownlee's original estimates.

[33] Blacker (1947).

[34] McKeown and Lowe (1966), figure 2, p. 6. Again, no mention is made of Brownlee, although McKeown and Brown (1955) do refer to his estimates with approval (pp. 134–35).

[35] See Wrigley and Schofield (1981), especially pp. 144–52 and 577–86. Brownlee based his estimates on data drawn from the Parish Register Abstracts compiled and published by John Rickman in the early nineteenth century. All their users, including William Farr, have appreciated their shortcomings, but until the new collection of parish register material (co-ordinated by members of the Cambridge Group) and the development of back projection these could not be overcome. The following table gives a very simple summary of the differences between Brownlee's estimates and those by Wrigley *et al.* (1997), table A9.1.

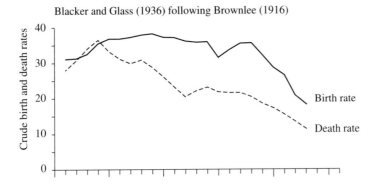

Blacker and Glass (1936) following Brownlee (1916)

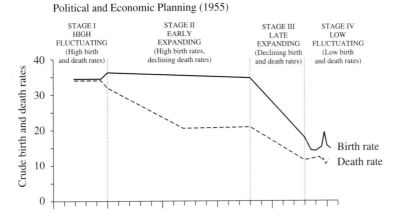

Political and Economic Planning (1955)

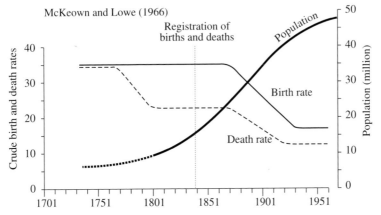

Figure 1.4. Three early diagrammatic representations of the demographic transition in England and Wales

The picture of long-term changes in fertility and mortality are better captured by using the total fertility rate and life expectancy at birth, measures which are not vulnerable to shifts in the age structure of a population. That is, figures 1.1 and 1.2 have been substituted for figure 1.4. But, as Szreter has recently argued, 'the principal virtue and function of the idea of demographic transition has always been in providing a graphic metaphor that summarily describes – and predicts – a long-term emergent pattern of change'.[36] It is this 'graphic metaphor' that persists in the demographic transition model, now more a pedagogic device than an explanatory tool.

However, there is still considerable debate about the existence of a global demographic transition and whether the various processes involved may be expressed in the form of a general theory. Although Warren S. Thompson and Adolphe Landry are widely credited with the identification of different demographic patterns in terms of population growth potential, it was Frank W. Notestein who in the 1940s and early 1950s offered the first coherent statement of what could be called a theory of the demographic transition.[37] To oversimplify, Notestein's theory can be reduced to the following four propositions.

1. The demographic transition is initiated by the secular decline of mortality.
2. Mortality decline is caused by the cumulative influences of the agricultural, the industrial and the sanitary revolutions which, respectively, lead to better food supplies, an improvement in the factors of production and the standard of living in general, and improvements in public health.
3. Rapid population growth is the result of the temporal lag between the decline of mortality and that of fertility.
4. Fertility decline eventually occurs because the social and economic supports to high fertility are removed. The materialism and

footnote 35 (*cont.*)

		1701–10	1751–60	1801–10
Brownlee	CDR	31.6	30.3	23.9
	CBR	28.6	36.9	37.5
Wrigley *et al.*	CDR	26.0	25.2	23.9
	CBR	30.3	32.4	37.8

There is a remarkable match between the estimates for 1801–10, but there the similarity ends.   [36] Szreter (1993), quoted from p. 692.
[37] Landry (1934 also 1909), Thompson (1929), Notestein (1945, 1953). Of the three, the work of Adolphe Landry (1874–1956) has been rather neglected although he coined the phrase 'le régime démographique'. See Sauvy (1956).

individualism associated with the urban way of life give impetus to the rational control of fertility by means of contraceptive practices.[38]

Notestein's 1953 paper offers some additional points of emphasis for the theory. For example, although 'it is evident that urbanization provides no mystical means for the reduction of fertility' it seems likely that the particular pressures of urban-industrial life created the conditions for the weakening of old ideas and beliefs, and the establishment of a new small family size ideal. The principal factors involved were probably as follows: 'the growing importance of the individual rather than the family, and particularly the extended family group; the development of a rational and secular point of view; the growing awareness of the world and modern techniques through popular education; improved health; and the appearance of alternatives to early marriage and childbearing as a means of livelihood and prestige for women.'[39] But perhaps of greater importance, the 1953 paper also gives some of Notestein's arguments on historical precedents: Europe as model. 'An understanding of their experience [Europe and the industrialised countries of the New World] gives us considerable information about the kinds of processes likely to be found in other parts of the world as technological development gets under way.'[40] And, 'Both the Japanese experience and the different course of events produced by a different sort of economic development in such areas as Ceylon, Formosa, and Puerto Rico tend to confirm the hypothesis that the principles drawn from the European demographic transition are widely applicable throughout the world.'[41] 'But in the densely settled regions of Asia the initial conditions are strikingly different from those of Europe a century ago.'[42] There it is less likely that

[38] See Woods (1982a), p. 161, for a more detailed discussion of Notestein's ideas; also Chesnais (1992), especially pp. 1–28, Jones *et al.* (1997) and Dupâquier's introduction to Bardet and Dupâquier (1998), pp. 7–17.   [39] Notestein (1953), p. 18.

[40] Notestein (1953), p. 15.

[41] Notestein (1953), p. 21. See also Notestein (1945), figure 4, p. 47, where the similarities between CDR and CBR trends in England and Wales, 1881–1939, and Japan, 1921–41, are illustrated.

[42] Notestein (1953), p. 21. Notestein concludes his paper by proposing a list of policies to speed the process of social change because of the difficulty of relying on the sort of economic development which automatically produces the socio-economic change required for the transition to low mortality and fertility. Examples of the policies are: lifting the age at marriage; promoting community education; communicating information on the practice of birth control; weakening the support system provided in the extended family by providing some element of basic economic security. See also Notestein (1948) written at a time when Notestein was not only Director of the Office of Population Research at Princeton University, but also Consultant-Director of the United Nations Population Division.

without policy interventions events will follow the course they have taken in Europe.

Although Notestein's theory has been elaborated, revised and criticised it still retains, even after fifty years, relevant arguments about the nature of demographic change as the response to socio-economic development, the possibility of drawing and applying lessons from the European past, and the justification for policy interventions when economic development has stalled or failed to induce rapid modernisation.[43] From the perspective of Europe's population history, and especially the experience of England and Wales in the nineteenth century, Notestein's theory of the demographic transition fits only some of the facts. First, and as will already be obvious from figure 1.1, the demographic transition in England and Wales was not initiated by the secular decline of mortality, but rather the modern rise of population was launched by a cyclical upswing in fertility after which mortality and fertility declined together. Secondly, nuptiality variations did not play a prominent part in the theory although the western European experience appears to have been influenced by the presence of a distinctive form of marriage pattern, one which had dominated for several centuries in place of the extended family norm. Thirdly, although England might be described as the first industrial-urban nation, the processes of industrialisation and urbanisation cannot be said to have initiated demographic change in any simple way. Indeed, urbanisation probably worsened the life chances of the working population during the eighteenth and nineteenth centuries. However, the decline in marital fertility probably was, as Notestein argued, very much a matter of changed attitudes, a new small family size ideal formed in the setting created by improved education, secularisation and the enhanced bargaining power of women.

Although it must be acknowledged that only a small part of Notestein's version of demographic transition theory applies to nineteenth-century England and Wales it nonetheless provides a valuable point of departure; a framework against which to set empirical experience so far as it is now known, and one to which reference will be made on several occasions in the chapters that follow. But there are other approaches, rather less well formalised perhaps, which attempt to con-

---

[43] These criticisms and revisions are far too numerous to list, but Greenhalgh (1995), pp. 3–28, in particular raises important issues in relation to the limitations of modernisation theory, the need to combine concepts of structure and agency, the dangers of Eurocentrism, and the importance of gender and culture. It is also important to appreciate that there are several parallel transition theories, for example Omran (1971) on epidemiology and Zelinsky (1971) on mobility.

sider both change and variation at the same time. Let us now turn to examples of these by way of conclusion to this introductory chapter.

Time and space

So far, we have mainly been concerned with change over time and not with geographical variations or the ways in which geographical variations may themselves change. This concern reflects the emphasis of most demographic enquiries, especially those dealing with population history, and this despite the warning given by Wrigley and Schofield, for example, mentioned above. However, there have been a small number of important exceptions to this general rule.[44] Three will be considered here. The first identifies geographical differences before tracing their origins. The second uses variations to explore the correlates of change. The third charts the reduction of differentials as a device for identifying the causes of decline.

Hajnal's paper 'European marriage patterns in perspective' is widely regarded as one of the most influential contributions to historical demography in recent years.[45] Although the main theme of his paper is also the principal topic especially of Malthus's second *Essay*, Hajnal was perhaps the first to spell out the particular characteristics and the geographical extent of the distinctive north-west European marriage pattern.

The marriage pattern of most of Europe as it existed for at least two centuries up to 1940 was, so far as we can tell, unique or almost unique in the world. There is no known example of a population of non-European civilisation which has had a similar pattern.

The distinctive marks of the 'European pattern' are (1) a high age at marriage and (2) a high proportion of people who never marry at all. The 'European' pattern pervaded the whole of Europe except for the eastern and south-eastern portion.

The European pattern extended over all of Europe to the west of a line running roughly from St Petersburg to Trieste.[46]

To the east and south of this line, and elsewhere in the world, a non-European marriage pattern prevailed, with early and universal marriage, especially among females, linked to the joint family system. But to the west and north, the stem system (a variant of the nuclear system, but with the eldest son remaining in the parental household after marriage) and not the joint or extended system was the dominant type, with

---

[44] Setting aside, that is, important work on migration and geographical mobility. Pooley and Turnbull (1998) provide an excellent recent survey of this work.
[45] Hajnal (1965).   [46] Hajnal (1965), p. 101.

independent households being formed at marriage between partners of similar ages. The research available to Hajnal allowed him to establish the broad outlines of his generalisation for 1900 and to push the origins of the European marriage pattern back to at least the seventeenth century, if not before.

Of course these broad generalisations have not gone unchallenged. The absence of the joint family system among the general population has been found to coincide with a number of variations on the late marriage, high proportion of celibate adults, nuclear or stem family theme especially in Italy and Iberia. For example, not all men may marry, but if they do it will not be until their late twenties and then to young women in their late teens. It has also been observed that the joint family system often acts as an ideal, that even in areas where the ideal holds sway the progress of the developmental cycle will necessitate the break-up of extended family living arrangements, and thus at any one time most households will not be of the joint, multi-generational type. These and other points led Hajnal to revise and elaborate the propositions outlined in his 1965 paper, and to identify the north-west European marriage pattern with a distinctive household formation system.[47] North-west Europe is taken to comprise Scandinavia, the German-speaking area, the Low Countries, the British Isles and northern France, but not Finland, the Baltic states, Italy, southern France and Iberia. In north-west Europe the simple household system dominated while outside this area the joint household system prevailed. In the former, most individuals spent their lives in a household with only one married couple, while in the latter a majority of people passed at least some time living in a household with two or more married couples. Hajnal's rules for the formation of these two household systems are reproduced in table 1.1.

Of these rules Hajnal gives special emphasis to 1c in north-west Europe where, in the seventeenth and eighteenth centuries, servants represented at least 6 per cent, and usually more than 10 per cent, of the total population. They lived as part of their master's household, were unmarried and were usually aged between 10 and 30. For a substantial proportion of young people, being in service for a few years was a normal life-cycle stage. Indeed, the circulation of servants between households was an essential feature of the north-west European household system. Hajnal takes his point one further stage by arguing that:

the institution of service played an important role in the demography of pre-industrial north west Europe. For it constituted part of the much discussed

[47] Hajnal (1982).

Table 1.1. *Hajnal's rules for the formation of household systems in pre-industrial societies*

1	North-west Europe, simple household formation rules
1a	Late marriage for both sexes (mean age at first marriage for females over 23 and for males over 26).
1b	After marriage a couple are in charge of their household as a separate housekeeping unit (the husband is head of the household).
1c	Before marriage young people often circulate between households as servants.
2	Formation rules common to joint household systems
2a	Earlier marriage for males and rather early marriage for females (mean ages at first marriage are under 21 for females and under 26 for males).
2b	A young married couple often start life together either in a household of which an older couple is and remains in charge or in a household in which an unmarried older person (such as a widower or a widow) continues to be head. Usually the young wife joins her husband in the household of which he is a member.
2c	Households with several married couples may split to form two or more households, each containing one or more couples.

Source: Hajnal (1982), p. 452.

mechanism that, by varying the age at and extent of marriage, adjusted fertility and thus population growth in response to the economic conditions. It was probably because of service that north west Europe could operate with a balance between birth and death rates established at a lower level than prevailed in other pre-industrial societies.[48]

Societies with joint household systems that relied on family labour rather than non-kin servants lacked this adjustment mechanism.[49]

Although Hajnal did not intend his rules for north-west Europe to be applied to the nineteenth century, rules 1a and 1b are probably still applicable, but what of rule 1c? As far as we can tell, the percentage of the population of England who were servants declined from perhaps 11–14 per cent in the seventeenth and eighteenth centuries to about 7 per cent in rural and 3 per cent in urban areas in 1851. The proportion of the population who were heads of households, their spouses or their children remained constant at about 80 per cent.[50] While these figures clearly support the argument that England was dominated by the simple household system, they also suggest that, by the middle of the nineteenth century, service was much less likely to have had national

---

[48] Hajnal (1982), p. 478.
[49] See Goody (1996) for a challenging review of Hajnal's rules, and more recently, Skinner (1997). [50] Wall (1983), see table 16.3, p. 498.

demographic significance with less than 6 per cent of the total population. However, it is very likely that the concentration of large numbers
of female domestic servants in certain areas will have had a profound
effect on the nuptiality patterns of those places and that the continuing
demand for domestics would also have had an important bearing on
migration patterns, age at marriage and even the possibility of social
copying. Further, Kussmaul's work has shown the importance within
the process of agrarian change of the reorganisation of the labour
supply so that wage labourers were substituted for servants in husbandry especially in the south and east of England where arable
farming dominated.[51] This upheaval in the rural labour supply occurred
mainly in the late eighteenth and early nineteenth centuries and had a
distinctly regional aspect. It meant the transformation of service as an
institution: whereas in early modern England most servants worked
outdoors looking after animals, by the Victorian era most were young
women working indoors looking after people. The demographic consequences of this transformation may prove to be as important as Hajnal's
claims for the role of the institution itself in the seventeenth and eighteenth centuries.

The second example of a consciously geographical study in which
variations are used to identify the correlates of change is the Princeton
European Fertility Project.[52] The first objective of the project was to chart
the variations in fertility among 579 European provinces in the late nineteenth century using the indices If, Ig, Ih and Im. Using this material it
was possible to map variations in 1870, 1900, 1930 and 1960; to establish
a pre-decline plateau level for Ig from which the control of marital fertility could be measured; to construct time-series for countries and
provinces; and to consider the joint distribution of Im and Ig as If
declined. This database has made it possible for Coale to draw the following conclusions.[53] Outside France and the French-speaking areas of
Europe, and excluding the case of Ireland, the decline of marital fertility took about 50 years and was most obvious between 1891 and 1931.
During this time, fertility was increasingly restricted by the adoption of
parity-specific family limitation – that is, stopping behaviour – as
married couples reduced childbearing by using contraception or

---

[51] Kussmaul (1981), especially figure 7.2, which shows that nearly three-quarters of the
farm servants in England in 1851 lived north and west of a line from the Wash to the
Exe via the Severn Estuary; most of the remainder were in Kent. See also Kussmaul
(1986, 1990) where she uses seasonality of marriage data for the 404 English parishes to
illustrate the spread of commercial and industrial activities in the rural economy.
[52] Some of the project's findings, together with the principal descriptive database, are
reported in Coale and Watkins (1986), and Watkins (1991). See also Tilly *et al.* (1986).
[53] Coale and Watkins (1986), pp. 1–79.

resorted to induced abortion. Although nuptiality had an important bearing on the level of overall fertility prior to the secular decline of marital fertility, *Im* remained largely unchanged before 1940 as *Ig* declined. The pattern of *Im* among provinces in 1870 illustrates the 'remarkable validity' of Hajnal's St Petersburg–Trieste line drawn to distinguish the European marriage pattern.[54]

The monographs that summarise the findings for individual countries invariably use ecological correlation in conjunction with some form of multiple regression analysis as their principal method of enquiry. Spatial variations in the Princeton fertility indices or the date by which *Ig* had declined to 90 per cent of its pre-transition value are taken as the dependent variables and these are related to both variations and changes in a variety of measures reflecting demographic, economic, social and cultural conditions. Questions commonly asked are: Was a prior decline in infant mortality necessary for fertility decline? Were variations in the pattern of industrialisation and urbanisation related to the level of *Ig*? Was the rise of female literacy an important prior condition? How did cultural areas defined by language, religion and ethnicity affect the pattern of variation and its change? Since these questions are principally directed to providing statistical explanations of the timing of fertility decline, the most interesting results obtained have tended to highlight anomalous provinces: those that were precocious or tardy. For example, in Belgium there were striking differences between the early decline of *Ig* in the French-speaking districts and in the Flemish districts to the north. In Germany marital fertility stayed highest in the predominantly Catholic districts, and especially in the south-east of the country these were also the areas in which infant mortality was particularly high because breastfeeding was not routinely practised.[55] But in the case of England and Wales this search for leading and lagging populations proved disappointing for, as Coale has pointed out: 'the transition from high to low *Ig*, while extensive, occurred at nearly the same time in almost all the [45 registration] counties', and 'a series of small ellipses [summarising the *Im/Ig* pattern] shows how uniform the change both in marital fertility and proportion married was in the counties of England and Wales, although the change in both was quite large'.[56]

---

[54] Coale and Watkins (1986), p. 48. No reference is made to Hajnal (1982).

[55] Lesthaeghe (1977), Knodel (1974).

[56] Coale and Watkins (1986), pp. 49 and 73. The ellipses for 1871, 1901, 1931 and 1961 are shown in figure 2.12, p. 65. Although Coale's point is broadly correct, the 45 registration counties of England and Wales offer a relatively poor framework for the analysis of what were essentially local demographic patterns. The *Ig/Im* distributions for 614 districts in 1861, 1891 and 1911 are illustrated in figure 4.18 and discussed in chapter 4 of this volume.

It might have been assumed that, at its end, the Princeton European Fertility Project would have provided some firm conclusions about the causes of fertility decline and its differential timing, but more than 20 years on from its final stock-taking conference there is still much uncertainty and not a little apprehension about what lessons for policy, if any, might be learned. For instance, Watkins has speculated as follows.

Although relatively modernized provinces usually began the transition earlier, those with relatively high infant mortality and illiteracy and relatively low levels of industrialisation and urbanization followed within a few decades, well before they had reached the same threshold of social and economic change as the pioneers.

It would appear that the new ways of living adopted by some change the landscape for all.[57]

This can be set alongside the conclusion to one of the most recent re-analyses of fertility decline for a European country.

Religion is by far the most important indicator of fertility level [in Prussia, 1875–1910], followed by ethnicity and proportion of miners. None of the other variables is significantly associated with fertility level. However, changes in religion, ethnicity, and proportion of miners contribute little to the explanation of fertility decline.

Our analysis of fertility decline is more interesting theoretically than the analysis of fertility level. Our results strongly support expectations derived from socio-economic models of fertility decline, and suggest that inferences drawn from previous research have resulted in unwarranted rejection of the importance of structural economic factors. The increase in the number of women employed in non-traditional occupations, growth of financial institutions, development of transport and communication infrastructure, reduction in infant mortality, and improvement in education are the forces that drove fertility decline in nineteenth-century Prussia.[58]

This last passage raises several interesting points about the problems encountered in dealing with variations and changes together. First, Galloway *et al.* indicate that as far as Prussia was concerned those factors most responsible for the former had little effect on the latter. And, secondly, they are particularly critical of research which stresses the importance of the social and cultural over the economic, but especially the modernisation of the economy and the transformation of its labour force.[59] However, there are other matters on which Galloway *et al.* are remarkably silent. No mention is made of the methods Prussians may have chosen to limit their fertility, nor is the importance of

---

[57] Coale and Watkins (1986), p. 449.   [58] Galloway *et al.* (1994), quoted from pp. 157–59.
[59] Galloway *et al.* (1994), p. 158, who take their inspiration from Notestein (1953), single out Knodel and van de Walle (1986) and Cleland and Wilson (1987) for special mention in this regard.

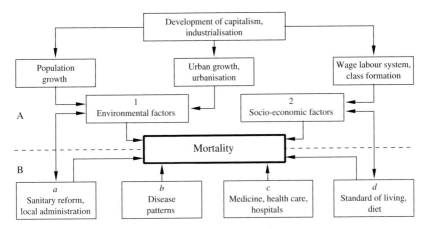

Figure 1.5. A simple model of the factors affecting mortality levels

simultaneous infant mortality decline emphasised despite its significance in their results.[60] In short and despite the obvious technical superiority of an analysis thoroughly grounded in econometrics, one using 407 rather than 30 geographical units, we still lack a full understanding of the causes of fertility decline in Prussia. What can be said of Prussia may certainly be claimed for Europe as a whole.

Our third, and final, example of research that marries time and space involves the study of mortality differentials and their causes. Figure 1.5 shows a simple model to illustrate the factors that are likely to have created mortality differentials both between places and among social groups (A); together with four possible ways in which mortality decline may have been promoted and differentials reduced especially in the nineteenth and early twentieth centuries (B).[61] The top half of the diagram focuses on the different effects of environmental (1) and socio-economic factors (2) although, as far as Victorian England and Wales was concerned, both would have been heavily influenced by the development of industrial capitalism. The former were made especially prominent by the growth of population and its increasing concentration in large urban centres, so that the consequences of the urban–rural mortality differentials which had existed in Europe for several centuries were exacerbated by urbanisation.[62] The crowding together of people

[60] Knodel (1974) devotes an entire chapter to this connection.
[61] Figure 1.5 is based on figure 15 in Woods (1982b); it has been elaborated upon in figure 1 of Luckin and Mooney (1997).
[62] The background to this problem has been discussed in detail by de Vries (1984), Schofield *et al.* (1991) and Williamson (1990).

affected disease patterns, especially those of infectious diseases; it created a more lethal sanitary environment; and it also led to new, higher and more concentrated levels of air pollution.[63] These hazards were faced by all those living in cities, but there were other problems – those associated with poverty and type of employment, with housing and diet – whose effects were borne differentially depending on one's social group or class. These effects were given further geographical expression by the process of socially selective migration that accompanied suburbanisation.[64] There are, however, further arguments concerning the nature of socio-economic factors which draw distinctions between material conditions, individual behaviour in respect to health and knowledge of best health care practice. For example, since access to and the ability to use knowledge are both socially differentiated it has become a point of debate whether public health or personal hygiene was of greater significance in the late nineteenth century once germ theory had gained acceptance by the medical profession.

Broadly speaking it appears that the environmental factors were of most importance in Victorian England and Wales, but that there were also significant differences between the life chances experienced by adult males influenced by their occupations and that these in turn established what, since 1911, have been termed social class mortality differentials. Several recent studies have attempted to flesh out this complicated distinction between the effects of geography and class, and the way the balance changed over time. Using especially detailed data for Sheffield in the early 1870s and the example of infant mortality, Williams has been able to show that although changing one's social class might reduce infant mortality by 17 per cent, changing the environment of one's residence would have a 25 per cent effect, and changing both together might have a 35 per cent effect, thereby reducing the infant mortality rate from 204 to 133.[65] In a similar vein Reid has also concluded that 'the largest differentials in infant and child mortality were associated with where a child lived', and that, as was the case in Sheffield, 'class did, however, retain some effect, especially in the "worst" environments, where the children of the higher classes were advantaged in terms of health'.[66] These two ingenious studies using very different sources exemplify quite admirably the additive nature of the environmental and socio-economic effects on health and mortality in the Victorian period.

[63] These issues are taken up in chapter 8.   [64] See Pooley and Turnbull (1998).
[65] Williams (1992).
[66] Reid (1997), quoted from p. 151. See also Reid, 'Infant and child mortality from the 1911 census', chapter 3 of Garrett *et al.* (forthcoming).

The lower half (B) of figure 1.5 focuses explicitly on the ways in which mortality might have declined, or have been made to decline, in the second half of the nineteenth century. It borrows from Thomas McKeown's account of the causes of mortality decline his four distinct, although not mutually exclusive, possibilities.[67] The secular decline of mortality may have been initiated by improvements in all four, but although it is necessary for *a*, *c* and *d* to combine for very low levels of mortality to be secured and sustained it is unlikely that each would have had the same impact. For example, Preston has shown that in terms of international variations in life expectancy at birth since 1930, substantial increases have occurred despite only modest improvements in living standards (*d*) and that these can be accounted for largely in terms of *c* and *a*: basic health care measures, imported drug technology, improved water supply.[68] Before 1930 it is unlikely that, apart from smallpox vaccination, *c* would have had an important bearing on the evident decline of mortality. This is the first aspect of McKeown's argument; it is followed by his emphasising *d*, *a* and *b* in that order. We shall return to consider the McKeown interpretation at greater length in chapter 8; here it is sufficient to note that, unlike our other examples in this section, McKeown made no reference to spatial variations in the decline of mortality and this despite his emphasis on the importance of material well-being, especially the benefits of the sanitary revolution and its impact on the water- and food-borne infectious diseases.

Each of the six factors illustrated in figure 1.5 as having a direct bearing on mortality changed its contribution in time and varied its contribution in space during the nineteenth century. But it appears likely that before the 1930s, variations were more substantial than changes in terms of the pattern of mortality. The reasons for mortality decline cannot be offered unless its variability is also appreciated.

This first chapter has introduced the principal themes and questions to be considered in the remainder. Chapter 3 takes up the matter of the preventive check and nuptiality in general as a preliminary to the re-examination of fertility decline in chapter 4. Since, as we now know, changes in nuptiality were responsible for initiating the modern rise of population in England, it seems appropriate to consider marriage and childbearing before mortality. Chapter 5 acts as an introduction to the

---

[67] McKeown (1976).
[68] Preston (1975). Although this finding is still valid, it is now appreciated that relative income distribution may have an important influence on national life expectancies and that mortality cannot be sustained at very low levels without the high investment in health care that is only possible when living standards and per capita incomes are also high.

analysis of mortality variations by examining the 'laws of mortality' as defined by the nineteenth-century actuaries and medical statisticians. Chapter 6 considers the mortality of adult males and especially the role of occupation and social group (A2 in figure 1.5) while chapter 7 searches for the origins of the secular decline in childhood mortality. Disease environments and McKeown are the subject of chapter 8 (A1 and B). The demographic effects of internal migration and especially urban growth and urbanisation are assessed in chapter 9 as a means of drawing together some of the more general consequences of economic growth and environmental deterioration characteristic of the Victorian age. Chapter 10 brings us back to Landry and Hajnal, to the unifying concept of demographic regimes, to the place of England and Wales in north-west Europe, and of Europe in global demographic space. Finally, chapter 11 offers by way of conclusion an assessment of our current understanding of the demography of Victorian England and Wales. But first we must consider in more detail what is known of the true facts.

2

Vital statistics

Any study of the demography of Victorian England and Wales must owe a substantial debt to the establishment in 1837 of a system of civil registration for births, deaths and marriages. This new system operated alongside the old ecclesiastical registration of baptisms, burials and marriages which had been in operation for 300 years. Although far from perfect, especially in its early years, civil registration had a number of important advantages over its ecclesiastical counterpart. First, it was concerned with the registration of vital events – births and deaths in particular – and not ecclesiastical ceremonies – baptisms and burials. Marriages were registered in both systems, but civil registration allowed for legal marriage outside the established church. Secondly, vital events were formally certified by the issue of birth, death and marriage certificates. Certification gave proof that the event had taken place, but it also allowed copies of the certificates to be assembled centrally, processed, filed and stored for future reference. Compared with the Anglican parish registers or the nonconformist registers, which were completed locally and retained in the parish or district, the national system of certification had very important advantages in terms of consistency of practice and ease of access.

Thirdly, civil registration required the creation of an effective system of local and national administration. At the local level, registrars and superintendent registrars were appointed on a part-time basis, usually from among the ranks of the Poor Law officials or the legal profession, to register and certify the vital events, and to forward material to the General Register Office in London. The post of Registrar General was established in 1836 partly for the organisation of the decennial population censuses, but the introduction of a continuous system of civil registration also required the appointment of more staff and the establishment of a permanent office within the home civil service. It also necessitated the appointment of technically competent professionals whose role it became to manage the registration system and the population censuses, and also to analyse and report on those trends and variations that could be identified from the wealth of new statistics. The appointment of a Compiler of Abstracts, Compiler of Statistics or, as the post was eventually titled, Statistical Superintendent, under the nominal supervision of the Registrar General, helped to create a new cadre of professionals specialising in medical statistics. These Statistical Superintendents proved to be men of great influence not only as administrators and scientists, but also as advocates for public health reform.

Fourthly, the development of the local apparatus for civil registration and the establishment of the General Register Office also had a beneficial effect on the conduct of the decennial population censuses. From 1841 these became both more efficient and more complicated. There was a greater emphasis on the reporting of age, marital status and occupation, all of which were needed in the analysis of civil registration data. Finally, the process of reporting via the Registrar General's *Annual Reports* and his *Decennial Supplements* to those *Reports*, with their accompanying tables, commentaries and topical letters from the Statistical Superintendent, placed in the public domain an enormous body of statistical material carefully standardised to allow a high degree of comparison year-to-year, decade-to-decade and area-to-area. It is these *Reports* and *Supplements* which now provide the basis for any demographic study of Victorian England and Wales.

This chapter focuses on the contents of these *Annual Reports* and *Decennial Supplements* as a way of assessing the qualities of Victorian vital statistics and thus the scope they offer for demographic reconstruction and empirical knowledge. Others have provided valuable user-guides to the population census and histories of the General Register Office, especially in terms of its administrative development and its contribution to the formulation of state policy.[1] Here we shall be concerned with the uses to which the material in the *Reports* has and could be put, how its several qualities and limitations must shape our understanding. Since there is as yet no comprehensive guide to the *Reports* it may prove useful to begin with a brief introduction to their contents and the principal interests of their creators, the Statistical Superintendents.[2]

---

[1] On the censuses, see Wrigley (1972), Lawton (1978), Higgs (1989). On the GRO, see Nissel (1987), Szreter (1991) and Higgs (1996). Issue 48 (1987) of *Population Trends* also contains several articles tracing developments in the census and celebrating the GRO's 150th anniversary.

[2] The appendices to Woods and Shelton (1997) provide a list of the locations of the *Reports* in British Parliamentary Papers (BPP) together with some brief notes on their contents, especially in relation to mortality statistics.

Contents of the Annual Reports

To begin at the weakest point: neither the population censuses nor the civil registration system provided an adequate means of measuring migration in the nineteenth century. Place of birth was recorded in the censuses, and since the entries for individuals survive in the census enumerators' books it is possible to analyse origins and, with the aid of nominal record linkage, to trace movers within relatively small areas. It is also possible to estimate net migration rates in counties, for instance by finding the difference between actual inter-censal population change and natural change (births − deaths). This may even be treated in an age-specific way. There have also been attempts to measure emigration and even to approximate trends in net international migration.[3] However, the absence of a continuous system for the registration of normal place of residence or even the absence of data on normal place of residence at a given period prior to census day means that migration is a dark area as far as Victorian demography is concerned. This will also have implications for attempts to check the quality of birth and death registration, and the census counts particularly for small areas in which population turnover may have been a substantial component of demographic change. The *Annual Reports* largely ignore migration; it even occupies a relatively minor position in the *Census Reports*.

Marriage takes a far more prominent place in the *Reports*. The civil registration system recorded and reported the number of marriages per year; whether spinsters, bachelors, widows or widowers were involved; whether those marrying had reached the age of 21; whether they could sign the marriage register; how the marriage was solemnised. The arrangements for registering marriages also provided, therefore, a means of assessing the level of literacy among brides and grooms and of measuring the extent to which civil marriage was increasing in popularity.[4] The population censuses regularly reported current marital status in an age-disaggregated fashion so the proportion of the population married or ever-married can be easily found, but ages at marriage were not regularly published with the result that such important variables as mean age at marriage, first marriage, etc. cannot be calculated directly.[5] It is also the case almost by definition that civil registration was

---

[3] See Baines (1985) on the problems to be encountered in this exercise. Further references to migration are to be found in Mills and Pearse (1989), Woods (1995), pp. 20–25 and 60–62, and Boyer and Hatton (1997). Pooley and Turnbull (1998), pp. 11–19, offer a critical assessment of our current state of knowledge on internal migration in Britain.

[4] Haskey (1980, 1987).

[5] See Wrigley *et al.* (1997), pp. 154–60, on the problems of using data in early *Annual Reports* to measure age at marriage. Table 3.1 provides an interesting special exception.

at its most accurate in the reporting of marriage since without a certificate the union could not be regarded as legal. However, it was also
quite likely that many partners in consensual unions would have
declared themselves married on the census return and, in order to avoid
a child being recorded as illegitimate, mothers may also have named the
father as their husband when registering the birth of a child. Divorce
was extremely unusual in nineteenth-century England and Wales,
although under certain circumstances marriages could of course be
annulled.[6]

The registration of live births is always said to be the weakest area of
Victorian civil registration. It was certainly the case that, compared with
mortality, the birth rate was of only very minor interest to the Statistical
Superintendents before the turn of the century.[7] Partly for this reason
birth registration between 1837 and 1874 was kept very simple. Local
registrars were required to register all live births, their gender and legitimacy, and where the birth occurred, within 42 days of its having taken
place. In 1874 the responsibility for the registration was transferred to
the infant's parents and a fine of 20 shillings was introduced for non-
compliance within 21 days. But it was not until after the 1938 registration (Statistics) Act that any attempt was made to record the age of
mother, the child's parity and the mother's birth history in general.[8]
Victorian civil registration made no effort to record stillbirths; these
were only registered after the Births and Deaths Act of 1926.[9] The rudimentary nature of birth registration in England and Wales, and for that
matter most of western Europe, means that the study of fertility patterns
and their causes has been severely restricted. None of the age-specific
fertility measures, such as the total fertility rate or the gross reproduction rate, can be calculated directly. Only the crude birth rate, the

[6] See Rowntree and Carrier (1958), especially table 2, p. 201, and Stone (1990). Between
1861 and 1865 the number of divorce decrees per year in England and Wales averaged
226; by 1906–10 it averaged 808.
[7] William Farr has left us some notes on the duties of the Statistical Superintendent. These
included: '1. Knowledge of Medicine and the Collateral Sciences. 2. Practical Mathematical Knowledge of some range. 3. A fair acquaintance with at least the French,
Italian and German languages.' See Glass (1973), p. 168.
[8] During the first year of civil registration in Scotland (1855), age of mother was recorded,
but the practice was rapidly abandoned. The Registrar General's *Statistical Review for
1938 and 1939* (London: HMSO, 1947), pp. 203–6 and 236–37, describes an ingenious
method for distributing the registered births to mothers. Age-specific fertility and
marital fertility rates are derived thereby. See chapter 4, p. 130.
[9] The registration of stillbirths (born dead after 28 weeks' gestation) began on 1 July 1927,
but there had been some informal registration since 1918. See Registrar General's
Statistical Review for 1927 (London: HMSO, 1929), pp. 128–31, Sutherland (1949) and
Wrigley (1998).

general fertility rate or indirectly standardised measures like the Princeton or Coale's indices *If*, *Ig* and *Ih* are available;[10] parity progression ratios and cohort fertility analysis are not. The under-registration of births will be considered in a later section.

The registration of deaths was the shining star of Victorian civil registration. It was to this area that most attention was given and from which the greatest detail was sought. Before 1874, when the onus of responsibility was transferred to the relatives or friends of a deceased person, the local registrars were required to register, within five days of the death, the gender of the deceased, his or her age and occupation, the cause of death and the place of death. Since without a death certificate a body could not be disposed of legally it has been assumed that the number of deaths registered in any particular period or place was largely correct, although this assumption has not been applied to the other recorded characteristics, especially cause of death and even age at death.[11] As we shall see, the system was probably at its weakest when a live born infant died before its birth could be registered. Despite certain deficiencies, death certification allowed the Statistical Superintendents and other medical statisticians to describe the mortality patterns of England and Wales in great detail, to calculate full and abridged life tables based on the 'true facts' for the first time and, in general, to monitor the health of the nation. However, no adjustment was made to those deaths that occurred in institutions, especially hospitals and workhouses, so that they could be reallocated to the deceased's normal place of residence. This may have had an important bearing on the levels of mortality apparently experienced by certain urban areas.[12]

Something of the level of interest in this particular area of vital statistics, almost to the exclusion of all others, comes from the writings of Dr William Farr, the first Statistical Superintendent (1838–80), whose great compendium of published works, suitably entitled *Vital Statistics*, was

[10] These measures are considered at length in chapters 3 and 4. See also Werner (1987).

[11] The problems encountered in measuring occupational mortality will be considered separately in chapter 6, while the recording of cause of death is dealt with more fully in Woods and Shelton (1997) and in chapters 7 and 8 below (see tables 7.1 and 8.1, for example). Glass (1973), p. 128, reproduces a handbill, dated February 1850, giving warning from the Registrar General to those concerned with the burying of bodies not to pass off live born children as still-born. The warning was occasioned by a sexton being found guilty of burying the bodies of two infants born alive, but who died within several hours.

[12] See, for example, Guy (1856). Guy gives a map of the London registration districts showing the location of the principal hospitals (pp. 16–17). Mooney et al. (1999) provide the most recent and thorough attempt to solve this problem.

edited by Noel A. Humphreys and appeared in 1885. *Vital Statistics* runs to 536 pages of printed text organised in six parts. 'Population' occupies 11 per cent of the space; 'Marriage' 3 per cent; 'Births' 4 per cent; 'Deaths' 62 per cent; 'Life tables' 10 per cent; and a final part called 'Miscellaneous' occupies 10 per cent. The contents and even the title of Sir Arthur Newsholme's influential textbook, which was also first published in the 1880s – *The Elements of Vital Statistics in their Bearing on Social and Public Health Problems* – are also preoccupied with mortality and health; fertility and nuptiality play minor roles.[13] These concerns not only reflected the dominant demographic problem of the day, but they also represented the intellectual interests of the first five Statistical Superintendents – William Farr, William Ogle, John Tatham, T. H. C. Stevenson and Percy Stocks – all of whom were medically qualified and, with the exception of Farr, had served as public health professionals. However, it was Farr who in his four decades at the General Register Office established the precedents for reporting vital statistics, setting its working agenda which his successors normally followed.[14]

Finally in this section it is necessary to make some observations about the size of the registration task faced by the staff of the General Register Office, the choice of age groups and the nature of the geographical units used to report vital events.

By the mid-1840s the registration system was dealing with as many as 1 million events per year, rising to 1.7 million in the early decades of the twentieth century. In 1841 the population census enumerated nearly 16 million persons in England and Wales and in 1911 the figure was 36 million. Considering the detail of reporting and the standard of accuracy obtained, this was a very considerable achievement, especially so before the 1880s when few other countries could boast such a comprehensive registration system.[15]

---

[13] Newsholme (1889). In 1889 Newsholme was Medical Officer of Health for Brighton; in 1893 he was considered for the post of Statistical Superintendent at the GRO; he subsequently became Medical Officer to the Local Government Board in 1908.

[14] It is impossible to study the demography of the Victorian period without fully appreciating Farr's contribution as a statistical innovator. His influence will be met at every turn. See Eyler (1976, 1979, 1980), also Newsholme (1923). Office of Population Censuses and Surveys, *William Farr, 1807–1883, The Report of a Centenary Symposium held at the Royal Society on 29 April 1983*, OPCS Occasional Paper No. 33 (London: HMSO, 1983) also celebrates Farr's contribution. While it is not possible to catalogue the contents of all the *Annual Reports*, some idea of their coverage can be obtained by comparing two of Farr's early contributions: the Registrar General's *Fifth Annual Report for 1841* (BPP 1843/XXI) and the *Eighth Annual Report for 1845* (BPP 1847–48/XXV). Both are substantial and remarkable documents for their time.

[15] Even the Swedish and French registration systems of this period were not without their problems and in terms of death registration, there were no serious rivals. See, for example, Bonneuil (1997).

The choice of age groups for reporting both census data and age at death can have an important bearing on the use to which those data may be put as well as the possibility of detecting errors, especially the presence of age-misreporting. The conventional age groups adopted in the *Annual Reports* and their *Decennial Supplements* were as follows (in completed years): 0–4, 5–9, 10–14, 15–19, 20–24, 25–34, 35–44, 45–54, 55–64, 65–74, 75–84, 85 and over. Often the age group 0–4 was further broken down into 0 and 1–4 or even into single years: 0, 1, 2, 3 and 4; and there were even certain periods during which age at death was given in months under one year of age. Sometimes the upper age group was set at 75 and over.

The definition of geographical units for the collection and reporting of vital events is also of crucial importance. The basic building block in use between 1838 and 1911 was the registration district. Many of the most populous urban districts were further divided into registration sub-districts which, although important for the administration of civil registration, were not used consistently as the principal reporting units particularly for data distinguished by age groups. The registration districts were further grouped into 45 registration counties (two for Wales and 43 for England including Monmouthshire) and eight registration divisions. The 626 registration districts were based initially on the unions defined by the Poor Law Commission under the Act of 1834. Since these Poor Law unions were defined without reference to the county boundaries, the registration counties do not coincide with the ancient counties although they share the same names and are equal in number.[16] The registration districts were finally abandoned as collection and reporting units in 1911 when local government administrative areas were adopted. Between 1838 and 1911 there were many revisions to registration district boundaries. Often this meant the division of an existing district because of population growth, but occasionally more radical solutions were adopted and new combinations of districts were created. These revisions were particularly important in certain parts of the country, especially the West Riding of Yorkshire around Leeds and Bradford, and in the London division. Since these 600-odd registration districts represent the basic reporting units – and certainly the smallest areas for which age-specific data are available – considerable attention has been given to the creation of a common set of comparable districts which can be used to analyse variations in nuptiality, fertility and mortality measures as well as to explore changes between census years

---

[16] Farr, *Vital Statistics* (1885), pp. 8–9, comments on this matter (taken from the *Census Reports* for 1851 and 1871).

or decades. The solution adopted here involves the definition of 614 districts for England and Wales including 25 for London.[17] These districts are shown with simplified boundaries in figure 2.1. They provide the basic units for much of the demographic description and interpretation in succeeding chapters. However, they are not perfect units for geographical comparison being unequal in size and extent of internal heterogeneity. For example, some contain a mixture of urban and rural areas while others are entirely urban in environment. But they are superior in virtually all respects to the registration counties.

The quality of registration

An assessment of the quality of the Victorian system of civil registration is far from straightforward. Important assumptions are required and there are usually too many unknown factors. For example, take the basic demographic equation

$$P_{t+1} = P_t + b_{t,t+1} - d_{t,t+1} + i_{t,t+1} - e_{t,t+1} \qquad (2.1)$$

where P_{t+1} and P_t are enumerated populations at times $t+1$ and t; $b_{t,t+1}$ is the number of live births registered between times t and $t+1$; d is the number of deaths; i is the number of immigrants (in-migrants); and e is the number of emigrants (out-migrants); with the number of net migrants ($nm_{t,t+1}$) given by $i - e$. If we simply consider the single unit of England and Wales then P will be provided by the decennial censuses, b and d by civil registration, but e can only be judged from passenger embarkation lists and i is virtually unknown. Net migration has usually been found in the following way:

$$nm_{t,t+1} = (P_{t+1} - P_t) - (b_{t,t+1} - d_{t,t+1}). \qquad (2.2)$$

This assumes that the population enumerations are broadly correct and that births and deaths are fully registered. However, if nm can be assumed to be negligible or at least of minor relative importance, and if death registration is assumed satisfactory, then a new estimate of b (*b) may be found by rearranging equation 2.1 and adjustment factors derived (*b/b):

[17] This solution is neither unique nor ideal. It involves the estimation of demographic measures for a small number of districts, but it does have the considerable advantage of allowing local variations in demographic behaviour to be observed at a level of detail far superior to what would be possible using only the 45 registration counties. However, it must be emphasised that many districts were still mixed in nature containing perhaps a small town surrounded by a rural area. See Lawton (1968) for an early use of registration district data, and Woods and Shelton (1997), maps A, B and C, for more detailed maps of the 614 districts.

0   50   100 km

N

Figure 2.1. The 614 districts of England and Wales
Note: London districts are shown in the inset.

0   10 km

$$*b_{t,t+1} = (P_{t+1} - P_t) - d_{t,t+1}. \qquad (2.3)$$

Suppose now that we have reason to doubt not the enumeration of the total population in the census but the reporting of its constituent age groups then we might compare the age profiles from adjacent censuses and derive therefrom census survival factors ($^aS_{t,t+1}$, where a denotes that the measure is age-specific) which can then be compared with model schedules in order to establish age group-specific population adjustment factors:

$$^aS_{t,t+1} = {}^aP_{t+1}/{}^aP_t. \qquad (2.4)$$

And finally, consider the possibility that the component registration counties of England and Wales have experienced differential birth under-registration, as well as variable net migration rates, some of which may be far from negligible. The procedure summarised in equation 2.3 will then need to be repeated on an area-by-area basis while nm is also allowed for.

Lee and Lam have focused on the problem of age-misreporting in the population censuses using a more sophisticated form of the procedure outlined above as equation 2.4.[18] They do not question the total count and deal mainly with the female population in ten-year and five-year age groups enumerated in 1841 to 1931, but also with the male population in 1861 and 1871 and the female population in 1821. Their results suggest that there was a high degree of regularity in the pattern of age distortion, but their adjustment factors are only in excess of plus or minus 10 per cent for age groups over 80. Females in their early twenties are over-represented while those in their late fifties are under-represented, as are those in the 0–4 age group. In general the adjustment factors for all but one of the age groups tend towards unity as one approaches the twentieth century. The exceptional age group is again 0–4 which for females at least appears to increase in its level of under-enumeration up to the 1890s and decline thereafter. Lee and Lam express particular concern about the level of age distortion in the 1841 census.

Undoubtedly the most influential assessment of the quality of birth registration is the investigation undertaken by Glass and published in 1951.[19] Glass's approach represents a development of equation 2.3 and in this it appears to follow Farr's own efforts to estimate the level of birth under-registration.[20] Assuming that birth registration after 1880 is largely correct, Glass makes estimates of the population aged 2–4 which he compares with the enumerated population for that age group to derive birth inflation factors for 1861 onwards, the entire five-year age group 0–4 being used for 1851 and the 5–9 age group for 1841–45. Although Glass's method deserves close attention in its own right, the assumptions he is obliged to make are of even greater interest.

The assumptions are:

1. that the influence of migration upon the age group 0–4 years need not be taken into account;

[18] Lee and Lam (1983).
[19] Glass (1951), also Glass (1973), pp. 181–205, and Wrigley and Schofield (1981), appendix 8.
[20] Farr, *Vital Statistics* (1885), pp. 89, 522–24 (*Thirty-fifth* and *Thirty-ninth Annual Reports*). Farr does not make clear exactly how he derived his birth inflation factors, but they are: 1841–50 1.069; 1851–60 1.030; 1861–70 1.018; and for 1837–76 1.050 (revised estimate).

2. that it was birth registration, and not death registration, which was incomplete;
3. that the census returns accurately represent the populations alive at the various census dates.[21]

Glass argues that: 'The first assumption has to be made because, given the poor quality of the migration statistics for nineteenth-century England and Wales, it is not possible to take migration into account in any satisfactory way.'[22] The second assumption 'is also made because there is not enough direct evidence on which to base any other assumption' as is the third: 'the assumption of complete enumeration is also made because there is no direct evidence to the contrary, and because indirect estimates would involve arguing in a circle'.[23]

Glass's estimates of birth inflation factors for the quinquennia 1841–45 to 1876–80 are illustrated in figure 2.2 where they are also compared with his, Farr's and Teitelbaum's estimates for decades.[24] Teitelbaum was concerned to estimate birth inflation factors for each of the 45 registration counties of England and Wales for the decades 1841–50 to 1901–10 as part of the wider Princeton European Fertility Project. His approach benefited substantially from the availability of Coale and Demeny's *Regional Model Life Tables and Stable Populations* (1966) which were themselves a by-product of the Princeton Project. With the aid of Model West, Teitelbaum was able to select an appropriate model life table for each county and to project backwards the population age 0–9 from each of the censuses 1851–1911 in order to derive an estimate of the number of births in each decade which could then be compared with the actual number of births registered.[25]

Again, the assumptions necessary to make these estimates are

---

[21] Glass (1951), p. 74.   [22] Glass (1951), p. 74.

[23] Glass (1951), pp. 75–76. Glass also quotes from the *Second Annual Report* to the effect that death under-registration may be of the order of 2 per cent, and from the *Thirty-eighth Annual Report* (Farr, *Vital Statistics* (1885), p. 527) to the effect that few deaths escaped civil registration and that the chief defect was the 'want of accuracy in the information supplied'.

[24] The second order polynomial fitted to Glass's estimates and shown in figure 2.2 has the equation: $y = 0.044x^2 - 166.118x + 157623.035$ (where y is birth inflation factor x 1,000) and may be used to approximate factors for individual years (x). Teitelbaum (1974) and (1984), pp. 56–74. Wrigley and Schofield's (1981), pp. 631–37, birth inflation factors for the 1840s agree with Glass's, but are slightly higher for the 1850s and 1860s.

[25] Teitelbaum (1974), pp. 330–31 and (1984), pp. 58–59 used the age-specific death rate $_5M_0$ to select a model life table (the rate for 1851–60 was also used for 1841–50 since county-level $_5M_0$s could not be calculated directly for that decade) and the ratio $l_0/_{10}L_0$ was used for the reverse projection. Adjustments were also made to allow for growth in the number of births during a decade and for net migration. The latter was found using equation 2.2 and then applied as a deflation factor to the number of births found from reverse projection (2.5 times the annual rate of net migration). The Princeton model life table system is described in Coale and Demeny with Vaughan (1983).

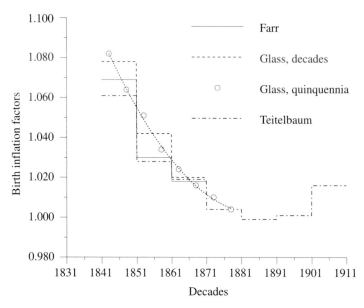

Figure 2.2. Estimates of birth inflation factors for England and Wales by Farr,
Glass and Teitelbaum
Source: Glass (1951), table 9 and p. 85; Teitelbaum (1974), table 1.

particularly interesting. First, it must be assumed that the enumerations
of children aged 0–9 in the censuses are correct and, secondly, that childhood mortality will not be severely under-estimated if based on deaths
aged 0–4 and enumerated population aged 0–4 since it was the childhood death rate that was used to select the most appropriate model life
table for each county. Figure 2.2 suggests that Teitelbaum's method of
deriving birth inflation factors makes civil registration appear the most
effective when compared with those of Farr and Glass. However, it is
also clear that Farr and Teitelbaum are in close agreement for the 1850s
and that all of the factors derived for the 1840s are prone to considerable
error, although Farr's is the happy average. During the first decade of
civil registration in England and Wales, births appear to have been
under-registered by between 6 and 8 per cent.

The most important feature of the exercise undertaken by Teitelbaum
is that it offers the possibility of considering geographical variations in
birth under-registration. Figure 2.3 shows the relationship between
Teitelbaum's birth inflation factors for the 1850s and those for the 1840s
among the 45 registration counties (see table 2.2). While for a majority
of the counties with low factors (less than 1.050) there is a fair degree of

stability between the decades, there are others with high and changing factors. The most interesting of these divide into two geographical groups: the Home Counties around London, and Wales with Shropshire. For London, Teitelbaum comments on the apparent over-registration of births in decades from the 1860s to the 1900s and in so doing discusses the possible reasons for substantial under-registration in the surrounding counties, but especially Middlesex, Surrey and Essex. The first explanation, and the one favoured by Teitelbaum, is that a number of births registered in London are due to mothers normally resident in the Home Counties being confined in London institutions or homes. Given the very small number of beds available in lying-in hospitals in the nineteenth century it seems rather unlikely that this would have been a major factor, especially as such institutions catered mainly for the high-risk cases where a fatality was more likely to occur. However, it is quite possible that the very wealthy would have preferred to have their babies at their London homes where access to specialist obstetricians would be assured. But such families would be rather few in number and might be expected to return to any and every corner of Britain after the confinement. Teitelbaum's second explanation emphasises the effects of suburbanisation; it 'would mean that larger proportions of births would take place in London than would be represented in the child population under ten at the time of the following census'.[26] Given the known massive expansion of London's outer metropolitan area throughout the nineteenth century, together with the commonly observed W-shaped pattern of age-specific migration (in which the most mobile section of the population is invariably young adults who are also the most fertile), it would seem entirely reasonable that selective migration could be responsible for distortions to the enumerated age-profiles of counties like Middlesex, Surrey and Essex.[27] Unfortunately for Teitelbaum's census-based method, 'If the adjustment factors arise entirely from births to women resident outside London being registered in London, the adjustment factors truly represent the magnitude of registration errors. If, on the other hand, the adjustment factors arise from rapid rates of net out-migration of children aged 0–9, the adjustment factors do not represent true errors but rather the flow of migration.'[28]

The case of North and South Wales and Shropshire is equally interesting, but rather more difficult to explain. Here it may well be that civil

[26] Teitelbaum (1974), p. 338.
[27] See Lawton (1968), Pooley and Turnbull (1998), pp. 93–146, and chapter 9 below, especially figures 9.8 and 9.9 on the outward expansion of London.
[28] Teitelbaum (1974), p. 340, and (1984), p. 73.

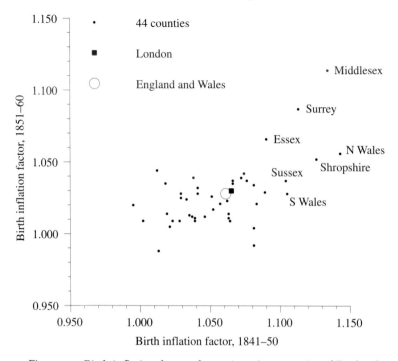

Figure 2.3. Birth inflation factors for registration counties of England
and Wales, 1851–60 against 1841–50
Source: Teitelbaum (1974), table 1.

registration encountered some early difficulties which were not only
restricted to birth registration, but affected the registration of deaths as
well.[29] Figure 2.4 helps to place the two Welsh registration counties in
context. If birth registration was genuinely poor in Wales during the
1840s, one would expect Teitelbaum's birth inflation factors to be initially high and to decline rapidly to some acceptably low average level.
This is exactly as the factors appear, so although the factor for North
Wales is higher than that for Middlesex in the 1840s, by the 1850s it is
substantially lower and continuing to decline. However, one would also
anticipate that the trend of decline should be relatively smooth (as both
Teitelbaum's and Glass's estimates prove to be); that is, there should be
no suddenly exceptional decades. But figure 2.4 shows that for South
Wales the 1860s and for North Wales the 1890s were exceptional
decades for which Teitelbaum's method produces lower inflation

---

[29] Woods and Shelton (1997), pp. 38–46.

factors closer to those for London than for England and Wales as a whole. Lancashire in the 1840s also appears out of line, perhaps for similar reasons. Teitelbaum's estimates suggest that births were underestimated by 1.2 per cent in the 1840s, but by 4.4 per cent in the 1850s (for neighbouring Cheshire the percentages are 8.1 and 2.4). The figure for Lancashire in the first decade of registration seems implausibly low; if it did prove to be correct it would signify a truly remarkable achievement on the part of the local registrars who, in the towns of Liverpool and Manchester, were having to deal with the effects of rapid population growth not least through Irish immigration.[30] It is far more likely that Lancashire in the 1840s was simply displaying an extreme form of the London problem. Births were registered to parents who by the time of the 1851 census had taken their children away out of the county, even out of the country.[31]

There appears to be sufficient *prima facie* evidence to doubt some of Teitelbaum's estimated birth inflation factors for particular counties. The key problem, as Teitelbaum readily acknowledges, is that of having to use census enumerations for a particular age group when, as Lee and Lam found for England and Wales as a whole, that age group was subject to under-enumeration and, in terms of county variations, was undoubtedly one of the most mobile. But the importance of Teitelbaum's approach, and to a lesser extent that of Glass, lies not only in his method of estimating birth inflation factors which in itself is an interesting intellectual exercise, but also in his willingness to apply those factors to correct the number of births and to use the corrected births in the calculation of crude birth rates and the Princeton fertility measures.[32] This has special significance in the case of Teitelbaum's contribution to the European Fertility Project because the Project's principal analytical approach relies on ecological correlation and the implied significance of variations in the level of fertility between geographical units, which in Britain's case means registration counties. The matter is somewhat different in Glass's case because his birth inflation

---

[30] Neal (1998) provides a vivid account of the impact of Irish migration to such places as Liverpool; see especially chapter 5, 'Liverpool and the Irish fever'.

[31] The particular circumstances affecting Lancashire probably meant that births were under-registered in relation to the census enumerated population which may itself have been under-counted. Lancashire contained 13 per cent of registered births in England and Wales in the 1840s, the highest by registration county.

[32] Teitelbaum (1974) presents tables of corrected CBRs while *The British Fertility Decline* (1984) gives I_f, I_g, I_h and I_m. These corrected indices were also used in the wider Princeton European Fertility Project; see Coale and Watkins (1986), pp. 164–65, although uncorrected registered births were used for Scotland, 1861–1931 (p. 169). However, it should be noted that the Princeton indices were not calculated for England and Wales in the 1840s.

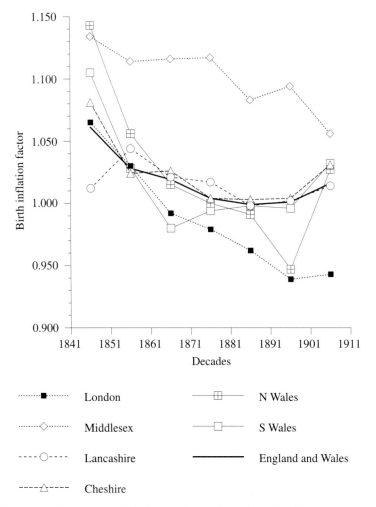

Figure 2.4. Trends in birth inflation factors for selected registration counties
Source: Teitelbaum (1974), table 1.

factors have simply been used to create a new time-series for the crude birth rate, one which suggests that fertility did not increase as substantially as formerly supposed between the 1840s and the 1870s.[33] The detection of errors and their correction are clearly very different matters.

[33] Glass (1951), p. 85, table 12.

Detection without correction

In attempting to evaluate the acceptability of his estimates of birth under-registration Glass also considered the implications of his revised estimates for the sex ratio at birth and the infant mortality rate.[34] We shall also follow that precedent here, but before doing so it may prove useful to look in a little more detail at the annual number of births, marriages and deaths as registered.

Figure 2.5 shows the number of births, deaths and marriages registered each year in England and Wales between 1838 and 1913, together with the numbers enumerated in the decennial censuses from 1801 onwards. Apart from the obvious increase in the volume of events that the registration system had to cope with, it is also clear that the annual numbers registered followed rather different patterns. Births rose continuously until the early 1870s and then began to stabilise; deaths showed sharper year-on-year fluctuations; and the number of marriages displayed a continuous steady increase with interesting short-run oscillations.[35]

The difference between the numbers of births and deaths gives an annual natural increase; this series is shown in comparison with emigration in figure 2.6.[36] If it could be assumed that the annual series for births (b), deaths (d) and emigrants (e), as well as census enumerations of the total population (P), are broadly correct then we could rewrite equation 2.1 to provide a means of estimating the unknown component: the number of immigrants (i). Thus:

$$i_{t,t+1} = (P_{t+1} - P_t) - b_{t,t+1} + d_{t,t+1} + e_{t,t+1}. \qquad (2.5)$$

Of course, as we have already seen, these would be unreasonable assumptions, but the resulting estimates especially of net migration ($nm_{t,t+1} = i_{t,t+1} - e_{t,t+1}$) should prove of interest as well as offering a further means of testing the registration and census systems.

The result of solving equation 2.5 and of combining immigration and emigration to give net migration is illustrated in figure 2.7. But figure 2.7 also shows what would happen if the number of births corrected by

[34] Glass (1951), p. 84, table 10. Farr (1865) also focused on infant mortality and the enumeration of children.
[35] The short-run fluctuations in the number of marriages has been analysed in Southall and Gilbert (1996).
[36] The series for the number of emigrants leaving England and Wales per year running from 1825 to 1950 is taken from Carrier and Jeffery (1953), table C(1), pp. 92–93; they are also used in Baines (1985), appendix 4, pp. 301–3. Strictly speaking, these figures relate to the movement between England and Wales and extra-European countries. This is of course a serious drawback because it ignores the considerable flows between Ireland and Scotland, and England and Wales.

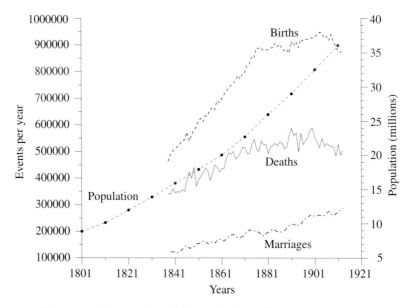

Figure 2.5. The number of births, deaths and marriages registered per year, 1838–1913, and the enumerated population, 1801–1911, England and Wales

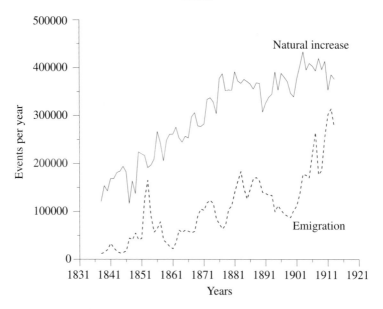

Figure 2.6. Natural increase (births − deaths) and emigration per year, England and Wales, 1838–1913

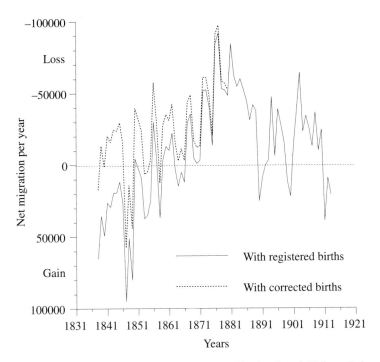

Figure 2.7. Estimates of net migration per year, England and Wales, 1838–1913

Glass's method were to be substituted for registered births.[37] The estimated number of immigrants would be reduced and the level of net out-migration increased thereby. The effect of correcting birth registration is in fact sufficiently great that whereas the middle decades of the nineteenth century formerly appeared to be ones of net in-migration, they now show longer periods of net out-migration from England and Wales. The late 1840s now appear even more exceptional, although it should also be noted that the census years 1851, 1861, 1871 and 1881 also stand out, but for the opposite reason. Table 2.1 summarises these estimates by quinquennia for 1838–1913.

To what extent should the figures shown in table 2.1 be taken to represent the true state of affairs and which are the most reliable? We cannot know the answer to this question. It seems most likely that the registration of deaths (but not necessarily their characteristics) was the most reliable, followed by the enumeration of the total population, the registration of births and the emigration count. Ideally, we would wish

[37] The equation for estimating Glass's birth inflation factors for individual years is given in footnote 24.

Table 2.1. *The balance of population change, England and Wales, 1838–1913*

Period	Population growth	Registered deaths	Registered births	Corrected births	Emigration	Implied net migration A	Implied net migration B
1838–40		1,041,431	1,458,664	1,603,178	46,372		
1841–45	1,001,390	1,746,110	2,641,506	2,861,768	100,844	105,994	–114,268
1846–50	1,071,965	2,023,286	2,847,230	3,034,386	198,726	248,021	60,865
1851–55	1,142,540	2,087,236	3,121,736	3,278,754	482,650	108,040	–48,978
1856–60	1,213,115	2,123,479	3,349,934	3,473,902	243,409	–13,340	–137,308
1861–65	1,283,690	2,331,957	3,624,851	3,718,792	236,838	–9,204	–103,145
1866–70	1,354,265	2,462,541	3,875,245	3,941,436	368,329	–58,439	–124,630
1871–75	1,424,840	2,572,749	4,158,676	4,201,950	545,015	–161,087	–204,361
1876–80	1,495,415	2,605,562	4,430,106	4,456,583	425,552	–329,129	–355,606
1881–85	1,565,990	2,585,156	4,464,398		760,124	–313,252	
1886–90	1,636,565	2,659,606	4,425,840		788,940	–129,669	
1891–95	1,707,140	2,785,391	4,539,266		617,869	–46,735	
1896–1900	1,777,715	2,789,984	4,615,887		478,042	–52,781	
1901–05	1,848,290	2,671,569	4,723,269		772,428	–203,410	
1906–10	1,918,865	2,577,208	4,604,940		1,103,106	–108,867	
1911–13		1,519,727	2,635,765		894,007		

Notes:

Population growth has been derived from census enumerations smoothed to allow for inter-censal increase. Corrected births have been inflated using Glass's (1951) birth inflation factors. Implied net migration A uses registered births and deaths while B uses corrected births.

Source: Emigration is from Carrier and Jeffery (1953), table C(1), pp. 92–93, and relates to movement between England and Wales and extra-European countries. Estimates of the true level of emigration would need to consider flows between Ireland, Scotland, England and Wales as well as the extent of permanent resettlement.

to adjust all of these series and, following Teitelbaum's example, do so in a geographically disaggregated fashion. But the difficulties are too numerous and too substantial, and the corrections may introduce new biases of which we may have little understanding.

Glass used the sex ratio at birth (registered live male births per 1,000 female births, SRB) as a means of considering the acceptability of the registration system. He noted that there was a decrease in the SRB between 1841–45 and 1876–80, that it was especially low in the 1870s, that his calculations suggested 'there was a slightly greater deficiency of registration for female than for male births', and that this was 'not inherently improbable in a society which placed considerably greater emphasis on males than on females'.[38] Figure 2.8 shows the annual SRB series together with Glass's SRB using corrected births. The corrected births SRBs are certainly lower than the registered births SRBs, but not substantially so. For example, in the 1850s the former was 1044 while for registered births it was 1046 for England and Wales. Figure 2.8 also illustrates, in a way that Glass's series cannot, the apparent anomaly that SRB was declining while the quality of birth registration was improving, that SRB reached its lowest point in the 1890s and began to increase thereafter (see also figure 2.10). A complementary way of considering the problem would be to examine variations in SRB among the registration counties. Taking the 45 registration counties in the 1850s, the mean SRB for registered births was 1047, the median 1046 and the standard deviation 9 (see table 2.2). In general, the distribution was very close to the normal, but there were six counties with SRBs greater than one standard deviation above the mean (Northumberland and Suffolk (over 2 standard deviations), Durham, Norfolk, Westmorland and Oxfordshire), and seven with an SRB less than one standard deviation below the mean (Surrey, Berkshire, Middlesex, Buckinghamshire, Somerset, Gloucestershire and Rutland). There appears to be no strong evidence to suggest that at the county level there were abnormally high or low SRBs in the 1850s. Certainly there is little sign that there were regions in England and Wales where SRB was especially low (less than 1029) which might suggest the systematic non-registration of female births, but baby girls do appear to be less well represented in some of the Home Counties where Teitelbaum's estimated birth inflation factors were relatively high.

---

[38] Glass (1951), pp. 83–84. Parkes (1976), p. 93, suggests that the sex ratio at conception probably varies from 1070 to 1240. When the SRB is 1050 (commonly taken as a reasonable guide among demographers) the sex ratio at conception is likely to be 1150. By Parkes's estimates, if the SRB is as low as 1035 then the sex ratio at conception would be 1135 and still within tolerable range.

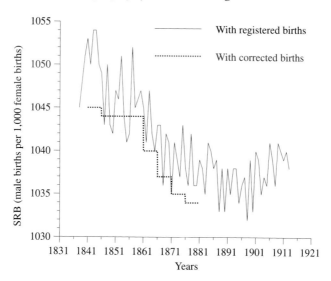

Figure 2.8. Annual sex ratio at birth (SRB), England and Wales, 1838–1913

So far we have only considered the total number of births without regard for legitimacy, but since it is believed that illegitimate births made up from 4 to 7 per cent of the total and that the infant mortality rate among illegitimates was approximately twice as high as among legitimates, it is possible that some of the early problems of birth registration owe more to the neglect of bastards regardless of gender.[39] However, it is not clear exactly what our expectations should be: are the numbers of illegitimate births more likely to be under-registered if the local registrar or the baby's mother has the responsibility for ensuring that it is registered? Figure 2.9 shows the annual series for registered legitimate and illegitimate births, together with the percentage of all births that were illegitimate. Perhaps it would be unwise to make too much of the apparent turning point in 1875 after which the number of illegitimate births registered per year moved into a short period of temporary increase, but this could represent one of the effects of the new Registration Act. Coincidentally the 1870s was also the turning-point decade for marital fertility decline.

There are substantial differences between the experiences of the nineteenth and twentieth centuries in terms of SRB; these are traced by figure 2.10.[40] Since the 1940s the legitimate SRB has stabilised at about

---

[39] Woods *et al.* (1988, 1989), especially (1988) table 2, p. 353. However, the differential was greater in post-neonatal mortality than neonatal.

[40] Figure 2.10 uses the SRBs reported in Office of Population Censuses and Surveys, *Birth Statistics: Historical Series of Statistics from Registrations of Births in England and Wales, 1837–1983*, Series FM1 No. 13 (London: HMSO, 1987), table 1.1, p. 19.

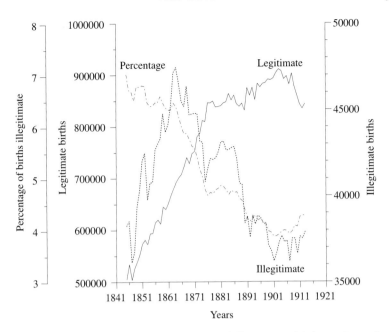

Figure 2.9. The number of legitimate and illegitimate births registered
per year, England and Wales, 1845–1913

1060 with illegitimate SRB a little lower although more volatile.
Between the second quinquennium of the twentieth century and the
Second World War the two SRBs move together, but for earlier periods
the series appear to be out of phase. Apart from the anomalous 1870s
there are signs of an inverse relationship. One possible interpretation of
these trends and apparent differentials would be that the registration of
births in the nineteenth century was adversely affected by the relatively
high level of infant mortality, especially mortality in the first few hours
and days. Among the most vulnerable, baby boys were especially at
risk, for while more males were born than females early age mortality
among males was also substantially higher.[41] Just as the increase in SRB
in the first half of the twentieth century reflects the decline of infant

[41] Table 2.2 illustrates the point using the sex ratio among neonatal deaths for the registration counties of England and Wales in 1839–44. While the SRB was 1052 in the 1840s,
the neonatal deaths sex ratio was 1372. Johansson and Nygren (1991) show long-run
changes in the sex ratio among live and stillbirths for Sweden. In the case of the former,
the average SRB in the nineteenth century was between 1040 and 1060 while for the
stillbirths it was between 1250 and 1350, but declined to 1100 by 1950 (p. 38). The experiences of England and Wales and Sweden appear to be sufficiently close to one another
and to the expected for us to conclude that there is insufficient evidence of large-scale
and systematic gender bias in registration and probably treatment. In China in the
1980s, SRB among parity one children averaged 1066, but for parity three and above it
was 1197.

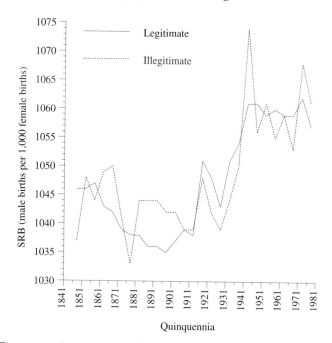

Figure 2.10. Long-term trends in the sex ratio at birth (SRB), England and Wales, 1846–51 to 1976–80

mortality, so the higher illegitimate SRB in the nineteenth century could indicate an even greater degree of discrimination against girls.

The sex ratio at birth is probably not an ideal device for the detection of problems in the registration of births. For example, it is difficult to know which norm to select for comparative purposes. If 1060 were to be chosen, then the SRBs for every year and virtually every county would be substantially below expectations. What would be the cause? Too few females because of differential treatment and discrimination or too few males because of higher early age mortality among baby boys? The latter would seem more likely, but cannot be fully demonstrated.

Glass's second way of assessing the acceptability of his birth inflation factors was to consider the effect of their application on the infant mortality rate (IMR). Since the IMR is based on the ratio of infant deaths to live births it will be reduced by the revision upwards of the base at-risk population. For example, in the 1850s IMR would be reduced from 154 to 148 by the application of Glass's birth inflation factors. For the single quinquennium 1841–45 Glass also inflates the number of infant deaths by 2 per cent in order to adjust upwards what he regards as an unreasonably low IMR for the period, thereby changing the estimate from 136 to 147.[42] This process of double correction poses particular problems for the calculation of IMRs in the early years of civil registration.

If 1,000 live births were registered in a town in a particular year together with 200 infant deaths, the IMR would be calculated as 200. With our favoured birth inflation factor of 1.080 and our infant death inflation factor of 1.020, births would be 1,080 and deaths 204, giving an IMR of 189 (5.5 per cent lower). Also, suppose that there are, in addition, an unknown number of babies who, although technically live born, die in a matter of hours and are treated as though still-born and go entirely unregistered. If there were 15 of these cases then the number of births would be 1,095 and the number of infant deaths 219, giving an IMR back at 200.[43]

Farr also encountered these problems, and several others, in defending the reporting of age in the 1861 census against William Lucas Sargant's attack.[44] The Statistical Superintendent argued that: 'The ages of deceased children are registered deliberately; and, upon the whole correctly, by instructed registrars; and under 1 or 2 years ages are stated in weeks or months: all the births are not registered.'[45] That: 'During the last of these ten years [1851–60] the registration approached nearer, than it did in the first, to the actual number of births; and of unregistered births a certain number are never registered as deaths – but are buried probably still-born; these should be struck off both sides of the account.'[46] And in his conclusion Farr also made the following important admission: 'The variation in the practice of returning the ages of children is great in different towns; and so is necessarily any defect in the registration of births. And furthermore it is impossible to pass by one general ratio from the births in a town to the numbers surviving at a census; as the deaths in infancy are differently distributed in every town

---

[42] Glass (1951), tables 10 and 11, pp. 84–85.

[43] In 1931–35 for every 1,000 live births there were 43 stillbirths. Given the prevailing level of neonatal mortality in Victorian England a figure of up to 60 stillbirths per 1,000 live births would not be unreasonable (see table 7.2). Farr, *Vital Statistics* (1885), p. 107 (from *Thirty-eighth Annual Report for 1875*), speculated that 'In England the proportion of still-born children to total births is supposed to be about 4 per cent, but this is uncertain.' Karl Pearson (1897), p. 38, reports several studies which give ratios of still to total births from 3.9 to 6.9 per cent. This would suggest that rates of 40 and perhaps up to 60 (stillbirths per 1,000 live births) would be appropriate for the Victorian period. Pearl (1939), pp. 88–89, reports a rate of 38 (per 1,000 total births) for the USA in 1932. Wrigley (1998) gives the decline of stillbirths a special place in the story of fertility increase in the late eighteenth century.

[44] Sargant (1864, 1865). Farr (1865) made a spirited but, as Glass (1951), p. 72, remarks, not entirely convincing reply in the light of his own views on birth under-registration.

[45] Farr (1865), p. 132.

[46] Farr (1865), p. 134. As we have seen, this 'striking off' will not be appropriate if one wishes to calculate IMR.

and year, according as this or that form of disease is prevalent: convulsions kill the infant of the first month; measles, scarlatina, whooping cough, kill him later, or in the tenth, eleventh, and twelfth month.'[47]

Modern demographers, as the examples of Lee and Lam, Glass and Teitelbaum illustrate, still resort to birth survival techniques to check censuses and reverse survival from enumerations to assess registration, but there are now also certain devices which by considering the structure of early age mortality rates may offer an additional means of isolating deficiencies in birth and death registration. Jean Bourgeois-Pichat's method of distinguishing between endogenous (deaths associated with congenital defects and the trauma of birth) and exogenous (deaths attributable to the post-natal environment) mortality in infancy by relating the cumulative mortality rate under 365 days (y) to age in days (x) has proved especially popular among historical demographers working with family reconstitution material derived from parish registers.[48] Bourgeois-Pichat observed that the following straight line regression equation could be fitted to the relationship between y and x once x had been transformed:

$$y = b[\log(x+1)]^3 + a .\qquad(2.6)$$

By this means the constant a would provide an estimate of endogenous mortality while the difference between a and the infant mortality rate would give exogenous mortality. If the curve fitted to observations for 1, 3, 6, 9 and 12 months is not reasonably straight, or if a is found to be small and endogenous mortality unreasonably low, then these may give grounds for concluding that the registration system is in some way defective. Although it is now common practice to fit a quadratic equation to the relationship in order to improve the fit, the points about linearity and the magnitude of a still hold.

In their analysis of family reconstitution material for 26 English parishes Wrigley *et al.* compare the early age mortality curve for 1825–37 with others for selected registration districts in 1841–46.[49] They argue that: 'If the Registrar-General's returns are trustworthy it is difficult not to conclude that the reconstitution-derived endogenous rates are also reliable', and that 'The very close similarity of the endogenous rates from the 1870s to those of the 1840s tends to enhance the claim of the latter to reliability, and therefore indirectly to underwrite the reconstitution mortality estimates.'[50] The second strand of their argument rests on

[47] Farr (1865), pp. 136–37.
[48] Wrigley (1977) and Galley *et al.* (1995). The Bourgeois-Pichat technique is not without its problems, some of which are discussed by Galley and Woods (1998).
[49] Wrigley *et al.* (1997), pp. 224–35.
[50] Wrigley *et al.* (1997), pp. 234–35. It seems most likely that Wrigley *et al.* following Wrigley (1977), footnote 26, p. 299, have incorrectly ascribed the contents of table M (p.

the close correspondence between curves for England and Wales in 1841–46 and 1875. It is assumed, following Glass, that the registration of births and deaths was full and accurate by the 1870s or 1880s. Wrigley *et al.* also make the following interesting speculation: 'a low endogenous mortality of about 20–35 per 1,000 prevailed generally in England by the mid-nineteenth century, whatever the overall level of infant mortality'.[51]

Figure 2.11 illustrates the Bourgeois-Pichat transformation for selected populations. It shows the age pattern of mortality between birth and age five years for two of Farr's most important early life tables – the third English Life Table for 1838–54 (ELT 3) and the first Healthy Districts Life Table for 1849–53 (63 HDs) – together with two equivalent curves for 11 urban counties and 16 rural counties of England and Wales in 1905.[52] Figure 2.11 also shows mortality curves for ages one to five from Model North when life expectancy at birth is 30, 40 and 50 years.[53] Since the two 1905 curves match those for the 1840s rather well, it would seem reasonable to allow the three curves from Model North together

xlix) in the *Thirty-eighth Annual Report for 1875* to that year, whereas the data reported actually relate to England and Wales in 1838–54, to selected healthy districts of England and Wales in 1849–53 and to Liverpool in 1839–46. This can be shown by comparing the age structures of the labelled data in table N with those of table M. Regrettably, there are no data for 1875. However, their argument is still valid that if A is sound and its accuracy is acceptable; then the form and structure of B is sufficiently close to A to make it too appear sound; while C, although derived from a different source to B and A, is also sufficiently close in form and structure to B to allow it to be considered reliable, and thus C takes on the qualities of A. In the absence of 1875 we shall take 1905 to stand for A.

51 Wrigley *et al.* (1997), p. 233. Their analysis indicates that endogenous mortality varied between 75 and 90 between 1580 and 1750, but fell to 33.3 by 1825–37 when IMR was 144.1 (table 6.4 and figure 6.4).

52 The construction of the full Third English Life Table (ELT 3) is described in Farr (1864) and the first Healthy Districts Life Table for 63 registration districts (63 HDs or HDLT 1) with crude death rates less than 17.5 in Farr (1859). In both cases the published life tables only cover single years of age, but in their construction Farr also considered the age structure of mortality during the first year of life. For ELT 3, see Farr (1864), tables VI and VII, pp. xxii–xxiii, and Farr, *Vital Statistics* (1885), p. 189; and for the Healthy Districts Table, Farr (1859), table C, and Farr (1885), p. 200. These two life tables are considered in greater detail in chapter 5, pp. 178–85. The data for 1905, which will be assumed to be of the highest quality, are taken from Registrar General's *Sixty-eighth Annual Report for 1905* (BPP 1906/XX), tables O and P, pp. cxxviii–cxxxi. The *Supplement for 1891–1900* to the *Sixty-fifth Annual Report*, Part I (BPP 1907/Cd. 2618), table D, p. cvii, also gives a life table in months for 1905. The urban registration counties are: London, Middlesex, Staffordshire, Warwickshire, Nottinghamshire, Lancashire, West Riding, East Riding, Northumberland, Monmouthshire and Glamorgan. The rural counties are: Buckinghamshire, Oxfordshire, Huntingdonshire, Cambridgeshire, Suffolk, Norfolk, Wiltshire, Cornwall, Somerset, Herefordshire, Shropshire, Rutland, Lincolnshire, Westmorland, South Wales (excluding Glamorgan) and North Wales.

53 Coale and Demeny with Vaughan (1983), p. 37. Model North seems to provide the best fit to the mortality structure of mid-nineteenth-century England and Wales, although West is perhaps more suitable in the second half of the century.

with ELT 3 and 63 HDs to act as guidelines against which the experiences of other periods or sub-populations can be compared.[54] In this case the Bourgeois-Pichat transformation has been extended up to age 1,826 days to allow comparison with the model life tables and to provide a means of highlighting potential problems in the reporting of age at death, especially round 12 months. Figure 2.11 also departs from convention by logging the vertical axis. This has been done to assist the comparison of experiences at very early ages and especially differences in estimates of endogenous mortality.

Alongside ELT 3 and 63 HDs, figure 2.11 also shows observations for England in the periods 1725–49, 1800–24 and 1825–37 drawn from the combination of family reconstitution results reported by Wrigley *et al.*[55] The second quarter of the eighteenth century has been selected because it appears to have been one of high infant mortality (190.8) combined with moderately high endogenous mortality (80.5) and high exogenous mortality (110.3). In each case, including ELT 3, 63 HDs, and 1905, endogenous mortality has been estimated by fitting a quadratic equation to the 1, 2, 3, 6, 9, 12 months experience while the full curve (birth to 1,826 days) has been described using a fourth order polynomial. It is these seven curves that are shown in figure 2.11. As we have already seen, on the basis of this evidence and the assumption that ELT 3 and 63 HDs are sound, Wrigley *et al.* conclude that the material they use and combine to construct their period averages is also sound.

There are various ways in which these arguments may be taken further. We shall only develop two here. The first makes use of Farr's local life tables for 1841, while the second involves a wider analysis of variations in estimated levels of endogenous mortality among the registration counties in a way that would parallel Teitelbaum's efforts to derive birth inflation factors.

The Registrar General's *Fifth Annual Report for 1841* contains, among many other statistical innovations, abridged life tables for the metropolis, the extra-metropolitan registration districts of the county of Surrey and the registration district of Liverpool based on deaths registered in the year 1841 and the population enumerated in the census of

---

[54] In fact the urban and rural curves for 1905 lie neatly between ELT 3 and 63 HDs under 12 months, but thereafter the lower levels of early childhood mortality, in the early twentieth century make the cumulative mortality curve rise less steeply than the ones for the 1840s.

[55] Wrigley *et al.* (1997), tables 6.1 and 6.4, pp. 215 and 226. Table 6.4 reports mortality rates under age 1 together with endogenous infant mortality, while table 6.1 gives infant and early childhood mortality for ages 1 to 4 which has been disaggregated using ELT 3 to give mortality rates for the second to the fifth years of life.

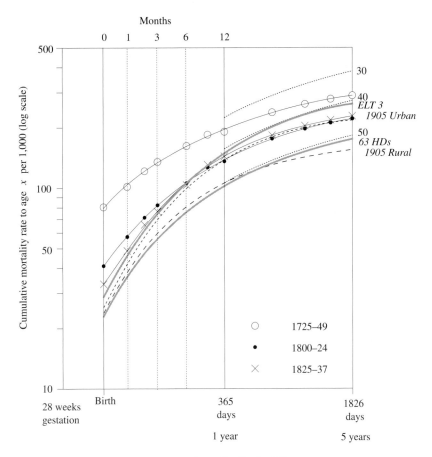

Age *x* in days transformed by [log(*x*+1)]³

Figure 2.11. Comparison of early age mortality curves for England,
1725–49, 1800–24 and 1825–37, with the Third English Life Table (ELT 3) for
1838–54, a Healthy Districts Life Table (63 HDs) for 1849–53, and England and
Wales urban counties (1905 Urban) and rural counties (1905 Rural) for 1905
Note: See text for explanation and figures 2.12 and 2.14 for comparison.

that year.[56] These three life tables are of particular interest in their own
right, but here they will simply be used as a basis for the generation of
early age mortality curves in the anticipation that these will reflect on
various qualities of the registration system. The tables as calculated by
Farr only give mortality for single years of age from 0 to 5, so the

[56] Registrar General's *Fifth Annual Report for 1841* (BPP 1843/XXI), pp. xxiv–xxviii.

Registrar General's returns themselves must be used to disaggregate mortality by month during the first year.[57] The curves for Liverpool, London and Surrey in 1841 are illustrated in figure 2.12. The curve for Surrey appears unexceptionable; it simply parallels the experience of the 63 Healthy Districts Life Table at a slightly lower life expectancy at birth. But Liverpool and London are different cases. Neither performs especially well between 365 and 1,826 days compared with Model North, at least not as well as ELT 3 and 63 HDs. At ages under 365 days the Liverpool curve is perhaps more concave than one might expect while that for London shows especially low endogenous mortality even compared with the experience of the Healthy Districts. Could it be that insufficient neonatal deaths have been registered in London and too few live births in Liverpool?

There is sufficient evidence in figure 2.12 for us to suspect that all may not have been well with the registration of infant deaths and their ages in some areas. This is sufficient to encourage a closer examination of infant death reporting among the registration counties. Table 2.2 lists the 45 registration counties of England and Wales and compares a number of measures which may prove indicative of the quality of registration. In columns A and B it repeats Teitelbaum's birth inflation factors for the 1840s and the 1850s while in columns C and D it reports sex ratios at birth for 1839–44 and 1851–60. The sex ratio among neonatal deaths is given in column E again for 1839–44, allowing comparison with the SRB in column C.[58] The last four columns also focus on the years 1839–44 and the pattern of variations among the counties of various measures of early age mortality. Column F gives endogenous infant mortality estimated by fitting the quadratic form of equation 2.6, while columns G and H show neonatal mortality rates for under 1 month and the infant mortality rate, respectively. Only registered births and infant deaths have been used to calculate the measures in columns C to H. But column I illustrates what would happen to the IMRs in column H if the birth inflation factors from column A were applied and if infant deaths in all counties were to be increased by 2 per cent.

The measures in table 2.2 offer several opportunities to examine the

---

[57] The Registrar General's *Eighth Annual Report for 1845* (BPP 1847–48/XXV) gives tables of deaths at the following ages: under 1 month, 1, 2, 3, 6, 9, 12 months for the individual years 1838–44 for registration counties and districts. The figures for 1841 have been used to supplement Farr's reported life tables. See also Farr, *Vital Statistics* (1885), pp. 200–1, on Liverpool.

[58] Data for 1839–44 are summarised in the Registrar General's *Eighth Annual Report for 1845* (BPP 1847–48/XXV), especially p. 282. Data for these six years should provide a useful summary of civil registration in its early years and before the effects of various disruptions in the late 1840s.

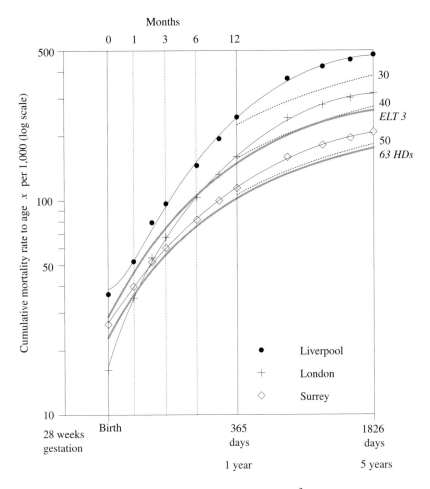

Age *x* in days transformed by [log(*x*+1)]³

Figure 2.12. Comparison of early age mortality curves for Liverpool, London and Surrey in 1841

possibility of defective infant death registration. For example, figure 2.13 shows the relationship between neonatal and endogenous mortality and the infant mortality rate and endogenous mortality among the registration counties. For the first-mentioned pair there is a strong although not perfect positive association, but between IMR and endogenous mortality the association is far weaker and barely significant.[59]

[59] Between neonatal and endogenous mortality the r² is 0.712, but between IMR and endogenous mortality it is only 0.275.

Table 2.2. *Birth inflation factors, sex ratios and infant mortality measures for the registration counties of England and Wales*

Registration counties	A	B	C	D	E	F	G	H	I
1 London	1.065	1.030	1047	1040	1340	18.9	36.4	152.1	155.3
2 Surrey	1.113	1.087	1036	1032	1446	20.7	35.8	113.2	103.8
3 Kent	1.029	1.028	1047	1049	1325	22.0	39.8	133.8	132.6
4 Sussex	1.104	1.037	1073	1046	1455	26.0	41.1	122.2	112.9
5 Hampshire	1.062	1.023	1057	1047	1345	19.8	35.4	116.3	111.7
6 Berkshire	1.072	1.039	1021	1030	1260	22.5	38.8	124.1	118.0
7 Middlesex	1.134	1.114	1036	1034	1393	16.9	38.2	141.5	127.3
8 Hertfordshire	1.041	1.032	1035	1042	1420	28.1	49.8	142.4	139.5
9 Buckinghamshire	1.033	1.024	1050	1036	1449	30.1	49.5	140.9	139.1
10 Oxfordshire	1.037	1.012	1043	1064	1367	30.7	48.4	138.6	136.4
11 Northamptonshire	1.023	1.009	1039	1046	1353	37.7	55.8	148.5	148.1
12 Huntingdonshire	1.002	1.009	1014	1049	1361	37.3	55.8	152.8	155.5
13 Bedfordshire	1.039	1.009	1050	1043	1554	36.4	62.1	158.2	155.3
14 Cambridgeshire	1.021	1.005	1059	1048	1402	29.6	54.8	170.4	170.2
15 Essex	1.090	1.066	1030	1045	1269	23.3	43.2	134.4	125.8
16 Suffolk	1.035	1.113	1058	1068	1413	26.2	45.6	132.2	130.3
17 Norfolk	1.064	1.009	1060	1061	1338	26.7	54.6	161.3	154.6
18 Wiltshire	1.046	1.012	1036	1041	1375	24.6	36.7	118.0	115.1
19 Dorset	1.063	1.011	1052	1051	1487	20.8	34.7	106.7	102.4
20 Devon	1.074	1.042	1039	1051	1268	19.1	31.8	110.5	104.9
21 Cornwall	1.081	1.004	1069	1053	1355	16.6	30.4	108.0	101.9
22 Somerset	1.038	1.039	1048	1037	1290	23.9	40.1	128.3	126.1
23 Gloucestershire	1.041	1.028	1052	1037	1381	20.2	41.2	144.6	141.7
24 Herefordshire	1.018	1.035	1053	1042	1371	23.8	44.6	128.1	128.3

		A	B	C	D	E	F	G	H	I
25	Shropshire	1.126	1.052	1.063	1050	1426	25.7	47.7	136.6	123.8
26	Staffordshire	1.066	1.035	1.056	1046	1340	32.5	52.5	152.0	145.5
27	Worcestershire	1.066	1.037	1.050	1040	1416	30.0	52.3	164.7	157.6
28	Warwickshire	1.089	1.029	1.044	1039	1353	24.9	47.0	167.5	156.8
29	Leicestershire	1.052	1.017	1.054	1053	1431	35.9	58.5	164.8	159.7
30	Rutland	1.019	1.014	1.010	1031	1294	23.2	45.4	133.4	133.5
31	Lincolnshire	1.057	1.021	1.059	1043	1353	29.4	57.3	151.5	146.2
32	Nottinghamshire	1.083	1.021	1.060	1039	1365	31.8	55.7	164.8	155.2
33	Derbyshire	1.039	1.011	1.052	1047	1369	32.8	52.8	150.5	147.7
34	Cheshire	1.081	1.034	1.066	1053	1383	28.9	51.0	175.4	165.5
35	Lancashire	1.012	1.044	1.052	1047	1394	34.8	50.6	190.2	191.7
36	West Riding	1.063	1.014	1.052	1041	1430	42.4	58.9	160.2	153.7
37	East Riding	1.029	1.025	1.048	1053	1391	28.0	59.8	176.8	175.3
38	North Riding	1.013	0.988	1.056	1043	1328	31.0	47.0	114.9	115.7
39	Durham	1.076	1.037	1.070	1058	1329	39.2	58.0	151.1	143.2
40	Northumberland	1.051	1.026	1.057	1067	1344	36.1	49.4	135.5	131.6
41	Cumberland	1.028	1.009	1.061	1041	1319	31.0	44.4	125.1	124.1
42	Westmorland	0.995	1.020	1.051	1058	1352	27.6	38.9	102.6	105.1
43	Monmouthshire	1.081	0.992	1.054	1052	1379	26.5	43.0	152.3	143.7
44	South Wales	1.105	1.028	1.060	1054	1345	23.9	36.8	112.5	103.8
45	North Wales	1.143	1.056	1.063	1055	1338	24.5	40.2	116.0	103.5
	England and Wales	1.061	1.028	1.052	1046	1372	25.1	46.4	150.1	144.3

Notes:

A and B: Teitelbaum's birth inflation factors for 1841–50 and 1851–60; C and D: sex ratio at birth 1839–44 and 1851–60;
E: sex ratio among neonatal deaths 1839–44; F: endogenous mortality 1839–44; G: neonatal mortality 1839–44;
H: infant mortality rate 1839–44; I: corrected infant mortality rate 1839–44 (births corrected by the birth inflation factors in
column A and infant deaths by the factor 1.020).

Source: Columns A and B – Teitelbaum (1974), table 1, p. 333, and (1984), table 3.3, p. 63.

Figure 2.13 also shows that there are several counties with endogenous mortality less than 20 or greater than 35, that if IMR is about 150 then endogenous mortality could be as low as 20 (18.9 for London) or as high as 40 (39.2 for County Durham), and that there are several interesting geographical clusters at the extremes of the endogenous mortality range. Devon and Cornwall (20, 21) and London and Middlesex (1, 7) are examples. Figure 2.14 selects Cornwall and Middlesex for comparison with the West Riding of Yorkshire (36) and Lancashire (35), two counties at the higher end of the endogenous mortality or IMR ranges. In Cornwall and Middlesex endogenous mortality was very low, perhaps too low? This may suggest the under-reporting of deaths in the first days. In the cases of Lancashire and the West Riding, which might have been expected to have had similar early age mortality experiences, the curves cross, but should this be taken to signify irregularities?

Finally in this chapter, let us come full circle and reconsider the problem of age reporting, especially as it affected census enumerations, but also the registration of age at death. The problem was well known to staff at the General Register Office who were often wary of publishing data on enumerated populations by single years of age, preferring to use five- or ten-year age groups.[60] However, the 1911 population census does offer an opportunity to examine the self-reporting of age in some detail and in a way that can be compared with the registration of age at death for that same year. Figure 2.15 illustrates the phenomenon of age-heaping as it appears in the male and female enumerations and the sex ratio. Age 20 is not popular but 21 is, as are 30, 40, 50 and 60. There is also a short-fall in the number of young children aged one year. The sex ratio suggests that there are some small differences in the choice of ages among males and females aged 30 to 70 although these do not appear at other ages. The sex ratio also reflects the general surplus of females, but this is especially evident in the early twenties and must reflect to some extent the absence of males on military service overseas. The 1911 census allows the detailed age profile for married, widowed and single persons to be identified. These patterns are shown in figure 2.16 for ages 0 to 50.

One would anticipate that the same pattern of age-heaping evident in census enumerations would also appear in the reporting of age at death. Figure 2.17 shows that for 1911 this was in large measure the case, but the relative emphasis on ages with terminal digit 0 and the avoidance of 1 was if anything even more pronounced in the census

---

[60] See Farr (1865), p. 127, also Drake (1972), p. 44. As we shall see in chapter 5, the first full English Life Tables applied various interpolation devices to age group data in order to estimate rates for single years of age.

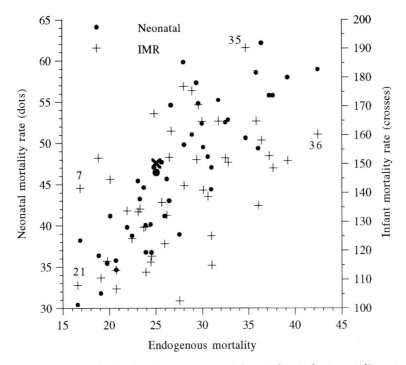

Figure 2.13. The relationship between neonatal mortality, infant mortality rate and endogenous mortality among the 45 registration counties of England and Wales, 1839–44

Note: England and Wales neonatal is shown by a large dot and IMR by a diagonal cross. Middlesex (7), Cornwall (21), Lancashire (35) and West Riding (36) are identified. Only registered births and deaths are used in the calculation of the three measures.

Source: Table 2.2, columns F, G and H.

than in the civil registration system. Since the census involved the reporting of individuals in household units, whereas death registration dealt with individuals in their own right, this should not be too surprising.[61] However, it might have been anticipated that the local registrars would have been more critical of the ages of deceased persons offered to them by their informants. All those who died in 1911 aged 70 or less and who were born in England and Wales would have had birth certificates. Apparently the existence of these certificates did not

[61] Work with the census enumerators' books has often shown that perhaps as many as 40 per cent of the mid-Victorian population were incapable of ageing themselves 10 years between censuses. See, for example, Tillott (1972).

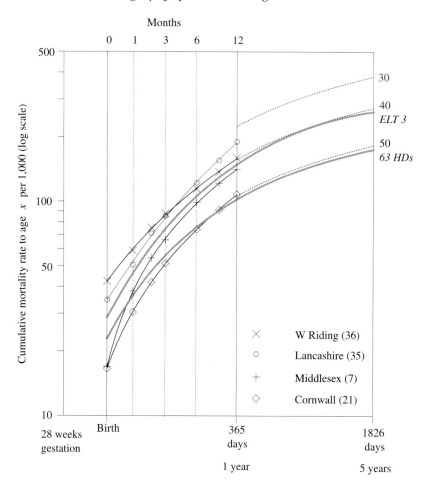

Figure 2.14. Comparison of early age mortality curves for the West
Riding, Lancashire, Middlesex and Cornwall, 1839–44
Note: See table 2.2 and figure 2.13.

necessarily mean that age at death would be remembered and recorded
precisely.

Another way of checking the various qualities of the 1911 census age
structure involves comparing it with the number of registered births.
Broadly speaking, those aged 60–69 in 1911 would have been born in the
1840s. It will be possible, therefore, to take the numbers born in each
year since 1837 and to calculate the probabilities of their surviving to

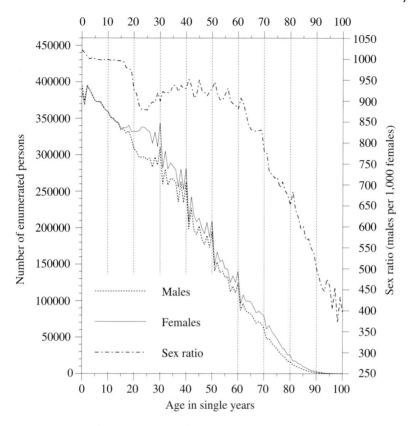

Figure 2.15. Number of males and females enumerated by single years of age in the 1911 census, England and Wales

1911, although this exercise will not take account of additions and losses due to migration and will not, therefore, measure the true extent of survival. The result is illustrated in figure 2.18 which also includes the survival curve from the eighth English Life Table (ELT 8) for 1910–12.[62] Once again the effects of age clumping are clearly evident in the curve for birth cohorts, although the life table curve which has been calculated using the 1911 census age structure and the mean of deaths registered in the three years 1910–12 has been smoothed. The two curves in figure

---

[62] The Registrar General's *Decennial Supplement for 1901–10*, Part I (BPP 1914/XIV) contains ELT 7 (1901–10) and ELT 8 together with notes on their derivation and accompanying appendices compiled by the actuary George King. The survival curve (l_x/l_0) from ELT 8 in figure 2.18 combines males and females using the 1911 census sex ratio for exact ages.

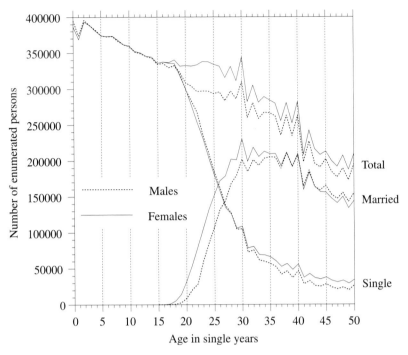

Figure 2.16. Number of single and married males and females enumerated by single years of age 0 to 50 in the 1911 census, England and Wales

2.18 are, of course, not directly comparable. One is a sophisticated expression of the actuary's art while the other reflects both the quality of Victorian civil registration and the great nineteenth-century legacy of census-taking together with the risks of dying during the seven decades covered by this book.

In conclusion, it will be obvious that the Victorian civil registration system was far from perfect. To begin with, there were problems with the registration of births and, to a lesser extent, infant deaths. Clearly many people did not know their own or their relatives' ages, or at certain times in their lives they deliberately gave false ages. Even in the 1840s these defects were not sufficient to invalidate the civil system which was, even at its worst, far superior to its predecessor in every respect. But the demographer who wishes to use these data is still faced with an important problem: given that several of the defects can be detected, should they be corrected for and if so how? In the chapters that follow no corrections have been made to the registered births and deaths used to calculate demographic measures. The principal reasons

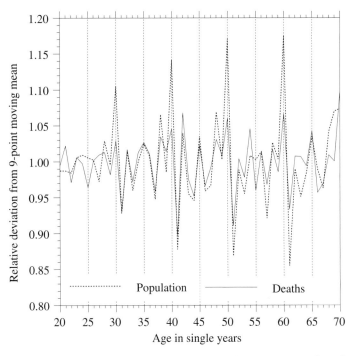

Figure 2.17. Relative deviations from trend by enumerated total population and registered deaths, England and Wales, 1911

are as follows. First, with the possible exception of the under-registration of births in England and Wales as a whole, there is no clear consensus on what the correction factors should be, although there is a view that by the 1880s the accuracy of civil registration was acceptable. Our illustration of age-reporting in 1911 demonstrates that even then the characteristics of the numbers enumerated or reported dying were not precisely accurate even if the global totals were. Secondly, the various methods discussed above for detecting errors all require important assumptions to be made about the quality of other data. Figure 2.7 provides perhaps the most interesting illustration of this problem. The revision upwards of the number of births affects estimates of net migration unless, that is, the statistics on emigration are not revised downwards to compensate. The potential for circular argument, as all commentators acknowledge, is ever present. Thirdly, perhaps the most important theme to be developed in this book involves the deliberate geographical disaggregation of nuptiality, fertility and mortality patterns so that local variations may be recognised. In this respect,

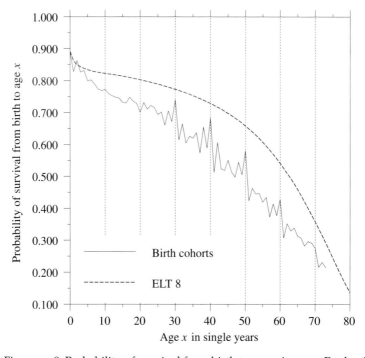

Figure 2.18. Probability of survival from birth to age *x* in 1911, England and Wales
Note: ELT 8 is the English Life Table for 1910–12. The potentially distorting effects of age-specific migration have been ignored. See text for explanation.

Teitelbaum's effort to derive birth inflation factors for the registration counties offers a cautionary lesson, particularly since we would wish to use the 614 districts shown in figure 2.1 as our basic units rather than the 45 counties. Fourthly, chapters 6 and 8 will consider, respectively, the mortality of occupations and local variations in cause of death patterns. In these cases it is even more difficult to detect the presence of systematic errors in the reported additional characteristics of death registration. In short our motto will be: use the available materials with care, but do not build elaborate explanations in circumstances where the specific qualities of the data are unknown and unknowable.

3

Whatever happened to the preventive check?

There are several reasons why this title may seem to pose an eccentric question. By the second half of the nineteenth century England's pre-industrial demographic regime had largely been transformed. External forces had removed the links between population growth and food prices, and between real wages and nuptiality. The balancing mechanism provided by these links, which had been so important in seventeenth-century England, was no longer needed. Economic growth had a momentum of its own, unhindered – perhaps encouraged – by population expansion. The preventive check concept therefore appears redundant by 1850, let alone by 1900. Yet Malthus's highly effective notion of the way that moral restraint, when applied to the postponement of marriage, can not only depress overall fertility in the long term in such a way that the balance between population and resources is made more favourable, but also act as a relatively short-run break when times have been hard, may prove to be more complex than had once been thought. The preventive check combines the effects of age at marriage and the proportion marrying. Both variables influence the level of nuptiality in ways that are only just beginning to be understood, especially among non-European populations.[1]

Even when one treats the preventive check in its original, less complicated form (bearing in mind that homeostatic population ecology was not so relevant to the nineteenth century), nuptiality rates still varied over time and between regions in ways that would certainly have

---

[1] See chapters 1 and 10 for general discussions of the European marriage pattern (pp. 21–23) and its significance when compared with the Asian demographic regime (pp. 382–89). The Malthusian 'total demographic system' is also outlined in figure 1.3 as it might apply to the nineteenth century. Wrigley and Schofield (1981), chapter 11, and Wrigley *et al.* (1997), chapter 5 on 'Nuptiality', pp. 121–97, provide important analyses and interpretations of the significance of nuptiality before the mid-nineteenth century.

influenced the general level of fertility and thus the rate of population growth. Herein lies a clue to the importance of the question in the chapter title. For while Wrigley and Schofield have focused on long-term fluctuations in the time-series of population growth, fertility, mortality and wages, it would seem that nuptiality's role in influencing fertility during the late nineteenth century was related to its geographical variation rather than any substantial change in the national level that may have occurred during the period. One can easily imagine why the late nineteenth century might have been particular in this regard, yet there would have been significant regional differences in the form and function of the nuptiality effect or preventive check even before the expansion of great industrial cities.

This chapter examines some of these points more closely in a variety of ways. First, the influence of nuptiality and the preventive check on fertility are reviewed in a wider European context for the nineteenth century. Secondly, temporal and spatial variations in nuptiality patterns are analysed for England and Wales between 1861 and 1911 using the districts shown in figure 2.1. Thirdly, geographical variations in nuptiality are explored in greater detail, especially with regard to the effects of urbanisation, differential migration and occupational specialisation. Fourthly, the influence of nuptiality on illegitimate fertility rates is discussed partly as a way of reconsidering the supposed positive association between non-marital fertility and delayed marriage, but also as an introduction to chapter 4 on family limitation.

The European marriage pattern in the nineteenth century

There is still much controversy over the form, even the occurrence, of a demographic revolution in nineteenth-century Europe. The difficulty stems partly from the differential supply of long-run demographic series for European regions. The Scandinavian series, in which the incidence of catastrophic demographic crises subsides to be followed by secular decline of mortality, and after a period of accelerated population growth, the decline of fertility, do not appear directly relevant to other parts of western Europe. Yet because these northern European data run from the 1730s or 1750s they have repeatedly provided the basis for transition models. France and England almost certainly differed substantially from the northern European pattern. In England there were perhaps two 'demographic revolutions'. The first took place in the mid-eighteenth century when the preventive check switched from one that was influenced mainly by the extent of celibacy to one in which nuptiality was also affected by age at marriage. In the late nineteenth and early twentieth centuries marital fertility came to be controlled in a parity-specific way, thus ending the dominance of nuptiality as the most important demographic regulator in England.[2] Mortality also declined during this period, as we have seen in figure 1.1, but before the decline of early childhood mortality from the 1860s – and especially infant mortality at the end of the century – life expectancy at birth increased relatively slowly. Internal migration led to massive shifts in the distribution of population which in itself appears to have had important side effects for both mortality and, via nuptiality, fertility patterns in general.

Demographic transition models dependent on northern European data fail to capture the complex nature of demographic change in England over the past 300 years, just as the theories with which the models have become inextricably linked fail to provide adequate explanations for the observed changes. The reasons for this failure of theory are quite clear. First, it is now accepted that the dominant form of marriage played a central role in European historical demography. The distinctive European marriage pattern provided the context for a low-pressure demographic system in which fertility variations could play a leading part even when marital fertility remained relatively constant over time. Secondly, the notion of sequential demographic stages is inappropriate. Even when stages can be identified, they do not follow the exact sequence indicated by classical demographic transition theory. Thirdly, demographic change in the nineteenth century was not simply a matter of response to agricultural, industrial or sanitary revolutions or an after-effect of social modernisation. The set formula is rarely an effective device for predicting either the timing or the sequence of change. In western Europe the move to low fertility and high life expectancy at birth was set against the background of a marriage pattern which persisted throughout the nineteenth century. What effects did that pattern have on other elements of demographic change?

The aspect of this question most widely debated in recent years, yet having its origin in Malthus's 1803 *Essay*, concerns the influence of the European marriage pattern on levels of overall fertility.[3] Lesthaeghe has provided a useful summary statement.

In the European historical experience, nuptiality patterns played a very significant role in the development of low fertility. Late marriage and widespread celibacy provided one of the mechanisms by which age-specific fertility rates

[2] See the discussion of figure 3.5 which follows, and for a broader outline Wrigley (1988), especially chapter 2, and Wrigley (1987), especially chapter 9. Marital fertility is considered at length in chapter 4.

[3] See chapter 1, especially pp. 21–24, and table 1.1 for Hajnal's important account of the north-west European marriage pattern.

were brought to low levels in the populations of Western Europe. In Eastern and Central Europe, on the other hand, where marriage customarily occurred earlier and was more nearly universal, a somewhat slower fertility transition was achieved through a reduction in marital fertility – without any drastic accompanying nuptiality change.[4]

The implications for contemporary population growth in the Third World are clear: 'changes in nuptiality are able to produce the same effects as those brought about by serious changes in marital fertility and can, therefore, add as much or more to the reduction of population growth, especially since their effects become apparent sooner'.[5]

The specific mechanisms involved varied widely in nineteenth-century Europe. In Norway Malthus, Eilert Sundt and, more recently, Drake found a demographic regime in which marriage for bachelors and especially spinsters was late; where the taboo on pre-marital sexual intercourse was generally weak so that bridal pregnancy and illegitimacy were common; and where marital fertility was high.[6] Factors such as rigid control of access to land exerted by landlords together with the system of farm service, low levels of industrialisation and urbanisation, and an active fishing and merchant marine all served to restrict the opportunities for household formation in a society where both the nuclear family system and the need for independent economic means were dominant. Despite the rigour of the preventive check, figure 3.1 shows that between 1735 and 1974 Norway's population was rarely stationary, and then only for short periods due to demographic crises. Between the 1820s and the 1920s natural growth rates varied from 1.0 to 1.5 per cent per year. The surplus population was supported partly by agricultural improvements, but increasingly large numbers of Norwegians sought relief via emigration.

In spite of the evidence of contemporary observers and family reconstitution studies it is tempting to describe figure 3.1 in terms of the positive check establishing low rates of growth through the action of mortality crises. An alternative interpretation would re-emphasise the importance of the preventive check, but would also impose upon the system frequent massive demographic crises of the subsistence and epidemic disease varieties, which were both exogenous to the prevailing demographic system and dependent upon Norway's marginal agricultural environment. Where marriage is delayed and especially where celibacy is high, mortality crises will serve to replenish the supply of economic niches thereby stimulating short-run fluctuations in the birth

[4] Lesthaeghe (1971), quoted from p. 415.   [5] Lesthaeghe (1971), p. 424.
[6] Malthus visited Norway in 1799; see James (1966). Sundt (1980) and Drake (1966, 1969) outline the population history of Norway.

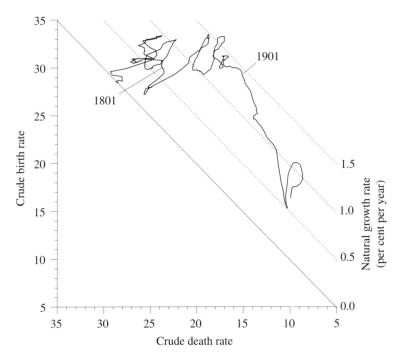

Figure 3.1. Timepath for change in the annual crude birth and death
rates, Norway, 1735–1975
Note: A 9-point moving mean has been applied to the time-series.
Source: Drake (1969), appendix 1; Mitchell (1981), table B6.

rate consequent upon similar fluctuations in the timing of marriages. In
eighteenth-century Norway the preventive check did not serve to stave
off the positive check, rather it helped to generate low growth in the
long term and to encourage rapid recovery in the short term. The two
checks need not be inversely related as Malthus argued.[7]

Although there were demographic divisions in Norway – town and

---

[7] The 1806 and subsequent editions of Malthus's *Essay on the Principle of Population*
contain the following passage: 'The sum of all these preventive and positive checks,
taken together, forms the immediate check to population; and it is evident that, in every
country where the whole of the procreative power cannot be called into action, the preventive and positive checks must vary inversely as each other; that is, in countries
either naturally unhealthy, or subject to a great mortality, from whatever cause it may
arise, the preventive check will prevail very little. In those countries, on the contrary,
which are naturally healthy, and where the preventive check is found to prevail with
considerable force, the positive check will prevail very little, or the mortality be very
small' (Malthus (1989), volume I, p. 19).

country, élite and peasantry, south and north, coast and interior – they would prove minor by comparison with Austria-Hungary. Demeny's study of the Habsburg empire in the 1880s and 1900s reveals an important new dimension: the inverse relationship between nuptiality and marital fertility.[8] In Austria nuptiality tended to be low, but marital fertility was high, while in Hungary the positions were reversed. The argument constructed to account for these observations runs as follows: early and universal marriage generates population pressure when there is some decline in infant mortality, but the importance of economic aspirations, especially the desire to retain and if possible accumulate land, will lead to the early decline of marital fertility in a peasant society even when socio-economic modernisation is absent. Hungary provides the example. In Alpine Austria the late marriage, high celibacy, high out-migration, high seasonal migration, but also high marital fertility regime proved relatively effective in limiting overall fertility, as did its equivalent in Norway.[9] Thus, parity-specific control of marital fertility came later in those areas where the preventive check was most effective. This argument has important limitations when translated beyond Austria-Hungary, but even there Demeny failed to emphasise the importance of illegitimate fertility in Hungary and its contribution with marital fertility to the level of overall fertility. Just because the provinces of Austria-Hungary appear to show an inverse relationship between nuptiality and marital fertility, the association need have no wider application.

Nineteenth-century Spain provides further examples of regional differences in the combination of nuptiality and marital fertility.[10] Figure 3.2 shows the changing regional pattern of nuptiality and marital fertility for five dates: 1787, 1797, 1887, 1900 and 1910. It uses the number of married women aged 16 to 50 per 100 women in the same age group as the nuptiality rate and the estimated number of legitimate live births per 1,000 married women aged 16 to 50 as the marital fertility rate. In Spain as a whole, the nuptiality rate did not vary greatly but marital fertility appears to have declined during the period. The most interesting aspect of figure 3.2 is the diversity of movement. The most distinctive regions are Catalonia in the north east and Galicia with Asturias in the north west. The latter are also typical of northern Portugal. In Galicia one finds late marriage, fragmented land holdings

[8] Demeny (1972).
[9] Viazzo (1989) outlines the complex and varied Alpine fertility regime in which restricted nuptiality and migration play an important part. Viazzo (p. 89) gives an example of the 'Austrian' model in which I_f is 0.34, I_g 0.70, I_m 0.40, I_h 0.10, while in the 'Swiss' model I_m is also 0.40, but I_g is 0.90 and I_h 0.01.   [10] Livi Bacci (1968).

and endemic migration, but marital fertility is not exceptional. In Catalonia marital fertility appears to have declined throughout the nineteenth century, but since nuptiality was at a higher level than in Galicia, overall fertility was probably higher in Catalonia before 1900. Catalonia's position is partly related to Barcelona's role as an urban-industrial centre with important international links, especially with France. There are also differences among the other Spanish regions, but in most general fertility rates were reduced after 1887 by the combined effects of declining nuptiality and marital fertility.[11]

Returning to northern Europe, Denmark is an example of a small country with good demographic data in which there was relatively little regional diversity but important differences between the capital, the provincial towns and rural areas.[12] Figure 3.3 uses Coale's fertility indices, first developed in the 1960s for the Princeton European Fertility Project and introduced in chapter 1, to pick out the trend of If by plotting Ig against Im, marital fertility against nuptiality, with the curved isolines tracing overall fertility. Since the series extends to the late eighteenth century one can see how nuptiality was responsible for fixing If at the relatively low level of 0.3 and of maintaining it at about that position for over a century. The same system of preventive check, but mixed with acute demographic crises, probably operated throughout the early modern period. Before 1900 the regime had changed to one dominated by the decline of marital fertility, with the result that during the 1920s If fell below 0.2 and has remained there since. In the capital and provincial towns marital fertility began its secular decline from 1880, but in the rural areas the peak level of Ig was not reached until 1900. Copenhagen not only had a lower Ig than the towns, but a significant minority of its inhabitants may have been limiting their fertility throughout the late nineteenth century.

The Danish case is important for two additional reasons. The percentage of the population living in towns at least doubled between 1840 and 1911; the 'urban influence' on fertility therefore grew rapidly. Also, nuptiality tended to increase slightly as marital fertility fell, and there is some evidence to suggest that Ig was likely to fall earlier where Im was lower.

More recently Weir has made estimates of the long-run change in Ig and Im for France from 1741–45 to 1931–35.[13] These are shown in figure 3.4. The stability of Im over 200 years is quite remarkable in the French case especially when compared with the almost continuous decline in Ig.

---

[11] Reher (1997) provides an important recent account of Spain's population and family history which takes full account of the substantial inter-regional variations.
[12] Matthiessen (1985).   [13] Weir (1994).

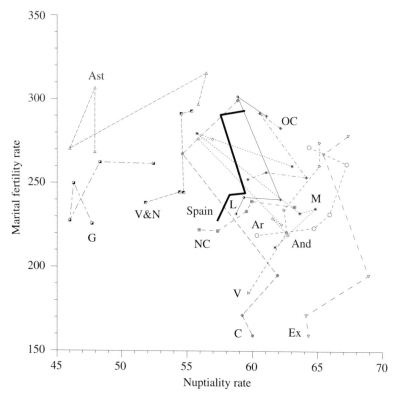

Figure 3.2. Regional timepaths for change in marital fertility and
nuptiality, Spain, 1787, 1797, 1887, 1900 and 1910
Note: Nuptiality rate is percentage of women aged 16–50 who are married;
marital fertility rate is estimated live births per 1,000 married women aged
16–50. And-Andalusia, Ar-Aragon, Ast-Asturias; NC-New Castile, OC-Old
Castile, C-Catalonia, Ex-Extremadura, G-Galicia, L-Leon, M-Murcia,
V-Valencia, V&N-Vascongadas & Navarre. The code for the region has been
placed towards the 1910 end of the timepath.
Source: Livi Bacci (1968), tables 9 and 15.

The examples of Norway, Austria-Hungary, Spain, Denmark and
France can be used to illustrate five important points. First, the significance of Lesthaeghe's observations is reaffirmed. That the timing, extent
and duration of marriage played critical roles in creating a distinctive
demographic regime in pre-industrial western Europe is beyond doubt,
but the particular forms of the marriage pattern and their precise effect
on demographic regulation varied widely. Secondly, even within the
same country there were regional or urban–rural differences which cut

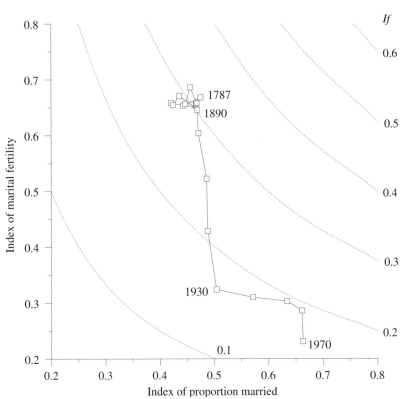

Figure 3.3. Timepath for change in marital fertility (*Ig*) and nuptiality
(*Im*), Denmark, 1787–1970
Note: The timepath link observations for 18 census years.
Source: Matthiessen (1985), table 2.1.

across national patterns. Norway, Alpine Austria and Galicia provide interesting cases of similarly mountainous and remote environments conditioning and constraining economic, social and cultural relationships in ways that are in their turn responsible for similar forms of demographic behaviour. Thirdly, there appears to have been a trade-off between nuptiality and marital fertility: where the former is low the latter can remain high, where the former is high the latter will be lower than usual, when the latter declines the former may increase. Fourthly, there are conflicting examples of the role of nuptiality in the secular decline of marital fertility. In Hungary high nuptiality appears to encourage the development of low marital fertility and its decline, while in Denmark marital fertility was at its lowest level and showed

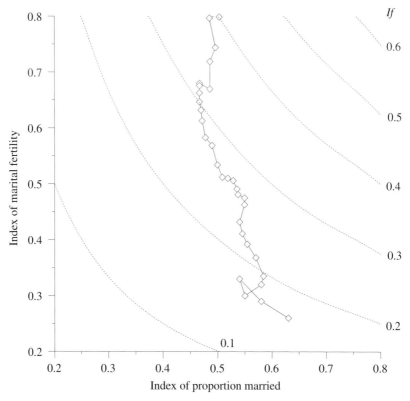

Figure 3.4. Timepath for change in marital fertility (*Ig*) and nuptiality
(*Im*), France, 1741–45 to 1931–35
Note: The timepath link observations for 39 quinquennia.
Source: Weir (1994), table B3.

signs of early decline where nuptiality was also low. In France nuptiality appears not to have had an important influence in changing overall
fertility between the 1730s and the 1930s, although its role may have
been of regional significance. Fifthly, the 'urban effect' was certainly
important in Denmark and Catalonia; it may have been locally significant in other parts of Spain, Norway and Austria-Hungary.

   The problem of family form and household formation rules must also
be raised in passing since the various types of family structure are connected with the prevailing marriage pattern and the extent of nuptiality. It is also the case that the ages of bachelors and spinsters at marriage
varied widely. In Norway brides were often several years older than
their grooms whereas in most of Spain brides tended to be much

younger than their husbands. The matter of family form is a complicated one and will not be examined at length here save to say that there
has been a tendency for the nuclear or elementary form to be associated
with delayed marriage and high levels of celibacy. This still appears to
be a broadly reliable generalisation for north-west Europe, although
subject to some local variation especially where migration affects
nuptiality or where marital fertility is high but child survival is poor. In
southern and eastern Europe there are well-known regional complications linked with the tendency in the former for women to marry young
if they are going to marry at all, and in the latter for more complex
household types to exist alongside or as a developmental stage from the
more simple nuclear structure.[14]

These various observations provide the introduction to a more
detailed examination of the form and influence of the preventive check,
and nuptiality in general, in nineteenth-century England. It has already
been noted that the research of historical demographers who work
mainly with parish registers has emphasised the long-term role of the
preventive check in England, but what of the late nineteenth century?
From what is known about the European marriage pattern and from the
five examples already described, one would expect Britain, especially
England and Wales, to be dominated by the effects of urban-industrial
growth, but to display a residual pattern in its rural areas reminiscent of
the eighteenth century and earlier.

Nuptiality patterns in England and Wales

Schofield's illustration of the joint effects of celibacy and age at marriage
on the level of fertility in early modern England provides an appropriate starting point for our consideration of nuptiality in Victorian
England and Wales. Figure 3.5 uses his diagram as a base, but it also continues the timepath using the proportion of women ever-married by age
45–49 and their singulate mean age at marriage (SMAM) for the census
years 1851 to 1931.[15] It shows that by the middle of the nineteenth
century the position of England in what might be called 'nuptiality
space' had not only stabilised after the movement of earlier decades but

---

[14] See table 1.1 and its outline of Hajnal's household formation rules. Wall *et al.* (1983)
provide a number of important European examples.

[15] Weir (1984), Schofield (1985), especially figure 1, p. 11, and Schofield (1989), especially
figure 8.8. SMAM is a measure of mean age at marriage derived by John Hajnal for use
on age-specific marital status data commonly available in population censuses. It is a
substitute for the true mean age which can be calculated directly from the ages given
on marriage certificates or in family reconstitution studies where age at marriage may
be determined by linking entries in baptism and marriage registers. See Hajnal (1953).

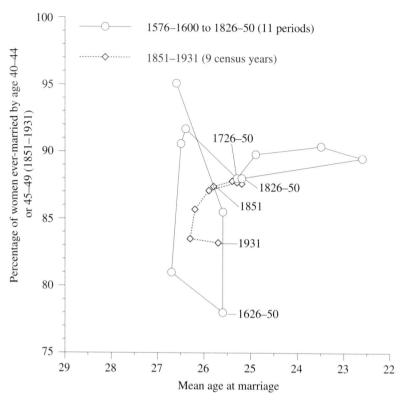

Figure 3.5. Timepath for the relationship between proportion married and mean age at marriage, England 1576–1600 to 1826–50, and England and Wales 1851–1931
Source: Teitelbaum (1984), tables 5.1 and 5.2.

had also returned to a position typical of the third quarter of the eighteenth century: 88 per cent of women were married by about their mid-forties and the mean age at marriage was just over 25 years. Only after 1901 did the percentage ever-married increase somewhat, and not until after 1931 did the mean age fall to the low twenties and the percentage of women who were married at some time in their reproductive years rise substantially. In this sense, figure 3.5 makes the late eighteenth and the early decades of the nineteenth century appear even more like a wayward temporary excursion in which new highs were reached, but not sustained.

Victorian civil registration allows the direct calculation of Coale's fertility measures only for the years after 1851, unlike its Danish equivalent in figure 3.3, but by using Wrigley and Schofield's estimates of general fertility (since *If* must parallel the gross reproduction rate, GRR)

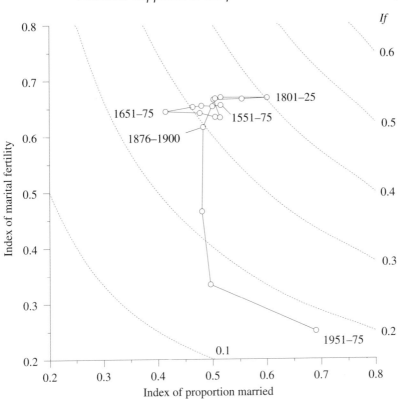

Figure 3.6. Timepath for change in marital fertility (*Ig*) and nuptiality
(*Im*), England, 1551–75 to 1951–75
Note: The timepath link observations for seventeen 25-year periods.
Source: Wilson and Woods (1991), appendix table.

and Laslett's of illegitimacy, Wilson has been able to derive long-run
series for all four of Coale's fertility indices.[16] Those for *Ig* and *Im* in
combination are shown in figure 3.6 using seventeen 25-year periods
rather than quinquennia as in figure 3.4. From the third quarter of the
nineteenth until during the second quarter of the twentieth century,
changes in overall fertility were dominated by changes in marital fertility. Before 1850 cyclical changes in nuptiality held sway, probably to a
far greater extent in England than they did elsewhere in western Europe
if the experiences of Denmark and France are any guide.

    Figure 3.6 illustrates particularly clearly what is by now a rather com-
monplace point, although this would not have been accepted as such

---

[16] Wilson and Woods (1991). Wrigley (1998) argues that there was also an increase in
marital fertility in the eighteenth century (associated with the decline of the stillbirth
rate) which suggests that estimates of *Ig* should be revised upwards.

even in the 1970s, but it only shows one small part of the story. Figure 3.7 introduces another theme, the extent of regional variations in nuptiality even in the late nineteenth century, and prompts further questions about the significance of those regional as opposed to temporal variations for aggregate national fertility levels before the nineteenth century. Unfortunately, most of these questions cannot be tackled yet, but their relevance may be explored directly during the civil registration period.[17]

The most interesting feature of figure 3.7 is its suggestion of regional variation. County Durham in the north-east of England, Sutherland in the north-west of Scotland, and London are three extreme areas. London has particularly low marital fertility (Ig was less than 0.6 even in 1851) while in Durham and Sutherland Ig was, and in the latter case remained, high throughout the late nineteenth century. In other respects County Durham and Sutherland were quite different. Durham achieved normal nuptiality levels which were in keeping with those of Spain and parts of eastern Europe, while the extreme form of the preventive check was displayed by Sutherland, where Im was usually only a little higher than in Ireland and equivalent to areas in Norway, Sweden, the Alps and north-west Spain.[18] England and Wales and Scotland fell into the middle ground.

Although it appears that the influence of nuptiality on overall fertility was largely confined to regional or local rather than temporal variations, the former are of great significance and interest in their own right. Figure 3.8 (colour section, page *a*) compares the distribution of Im by districts in England and Wales in 1861, 1891 and 1911.[19] By itself figure 3.8 provides important clues to the factors that influenced marriage patterns. The first and most remarkable point relates to the pattern's stabil-

[17] Teitelbaum (1984) briefly considers nuptiality in chapter 5. The celibacy and age at marriage (SMAM) averages used in figures 3.5 and 3.10 are from tables 5.1 and 5.2. Coale and Treadway (1986), appendix A, pp. 80–152, give estimates of the four fertility indices for the provinces of Europe (registration counties in the case of the British Isles). Table 2.2 (p. 62) and the accompanying discussion outlines the various problems encountered by Teitelbaum and others in evaluating the quality of birth registration in the registration counties.

[18] Anderson and Morse (1993) place Sutherland within the Scottish context as far as Im and Ig are concerned, and Guinnane (1997), especially chapter 7, distinguishes variations in the Irish marriage pattern.

[19] Coale's fertility indices were calculated for the 614 districts shown in figure 2.1 for three points in time – 1861, 1891 and 1911 – by taking the mean of births in the years 1861–63, 1891–93 and 1909–10, respectively, in conjunction with age and marital status data from the 1861, 1891 and 1911 censuses. Registration districts were abandoned as the geographical units for reporting civil registration data in 1911. The remaining fertility indices are illustrated in the colour section as follows: *If* figure 4.16 (page *f*); *Ig* figure 4.17 (page *g*); and *Ih* figure 4.12 (page *c*).

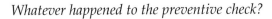

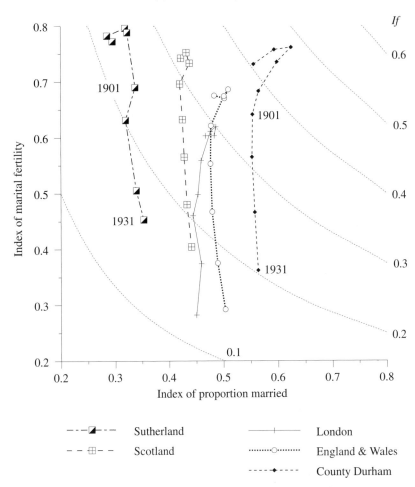

Figure 3.7. Examples of regional variations in the timepaths for change
in marital fertility (*Ig*) and nuptiality (*Im*), Scotland, 1861–1931, England and
Wales, 1851–1931
Source: Coale and Watkins (1986), appendix A, pp. 80–152.

ity. South-west Wales and the northern Pennines had persistently low
female nuptiality as did many of the towns in southern England and
especially the south coast resorts. Female nuptiality remained high
especially in the coalfield districts, but also in parts of East Anglia and
the East Midlands. In rural England and Wales, the further one moved
towards the west and north the lower *Im* was likely to be, while among
urban districts low levels were found towards the south and east away

Table 3.1. *Mean age at first marriage for selected occupations, England and Wales 1884–85*

Husband's occupation	Bachelors	Spinsters
Miner	24.06	22.46
Textile hand	24.36	23.43
Shoemaker, tailor	24.92	24.31
Artisan	25.35	23.70
Labourer	25.56	23.66
Commercial clerk	26.25	24.43
Shopkeeper, shopman	26.67	24.22
Farmer or farmer's son	29.23	28.91
Member of the professional or independent class	31.22	26.40

Source: Ogle (1890), table F, p. 274.

from the urban-industrial centres of the North. The changes that occurred between 1861 and 1891 are particularly tantalising, for it seems that most of the south-east of England together with the south Midlands had high *Im*s, apart, that is, from London and that area of the Home Counties directly under London's expanding influence. Further, most of those other high *Im* districts which fell outside the south-eastern region were affected by concentrations of mining populations in 1861. One is tempted to speculate on the antecedents of the 1861 pattern. Was the late eighteenth- and early nineteenth-century rise in nuptiality, and thus the mid-nineteenth-century fall, a phenomenon associated not only with the rapid expansion of northern industrial centres on or by the coal-fields, but also with the reorganisation of labour supply in those south-eastern districts specialising in arable farming? At the moment, this must remain a plausible speculation beyond clear demonstration.

William Ogle's special analysis of those marriages that took place in England and Wales in 1884–85 may help us to see more clearly just how important occupations were in influencing the ages at which marriages were contracted and how they differed between brides and grooms.[20] Table 3.1 reproduces Ogle's tabulation of the mean age at first marriage of bachelors engaged in a selection of occupations as well as the means for their brides.

The index of proportion married (*Im*) may be accused of concealing as much as it reveals since age at marriage and the extent of celibacy are

[20] Ogle (1890), tables F and G, p. 274.

expressed by a single number which in any case only relates to the marital condition of women. It is important to confirm that, in the late nineteenth century, female celibacy and the mean age at marriage were positively related and thus that average *Im*s were not the result of women who married doing so at an early age while a significant proportion of women never married at all. The point is well illustrated by figure 3.9 which uses Knodel's data for German administrative areas in 1880.[21] The percentage of women never married and aged 45–49 is plotted against the singulate mean age at marriage (SMAM) for women, but the scatter is further classified by level of *Im*. In Germany there was a positive yet weak relationship between celibacy and age at marriage. Celibacy could vary considerably when age at marriage was only at an average level, but the two variables do, nonetheless, tend to support one another in their influence on *Im*.[22] Figure 3.9 also confirms suspicions that *Im* is not a precise tool; it appears more sensitive to small variations in the timing than the extent of marriage. The same class of *Im* may cover wide variations in celibacy and there is overlap within the scatter between classes. Figure 3.10 offers an additional perspective principally using Danish data, but also including some for England and Wales. At the foot of the graph it shows time series for *Im* which it compares with four other measures of the extent of marriage among women: the mean age at first marriage, the proportions ever- and currently married at age 50, and the proportion marrying each year aged under 21.[23] In this case both the proportion ever-married and the mean age at first marriage are in decline, but the effect of the latter on the steady increase in *Im* is obviously greater than that of the increase in celibacy. The index *Im* is certainly capable of distinguishing broad differences in nuptiality levels in circumstances where age at marriage and celibacy complement one another, but it also seems likely that of the two *Im* will be rather more sensitive to age at marriage in nineteenth-century Europe.

---

[21] Knodel (1974), especially appendix table 2.1, and Knodel and Maynes (1976), especially appendix table A.1.

[22] The correlation between the two variables in figure 3.9 is $r^2 = 0.122$. Here $Im = -0.041 SMAM + 1.537$ ($r^2 = 0.652$) and if the mean age of marriage were to be 23 (lowest English mean age at marriage from figure 3.5) then *Im* would be 0.594 which is consistent with the estimate for England in 1801–25 shown in figure 3.6.

[23] See Wrigley *et al.* (1997), pp. 154–60, on the difficult process of matching family reconstitution data which are capable of distinguishing age at marriage with the Registrar General's early returns which largely ignore age (apart from age of majority at 21). Series *a* in figure 2.10 are taken from table 5.3 (p. 134) with the addition of a figure for the mean age at first marriage for females in England and Wales in 1846–48 estimated by Wrigley *et al.* from material in the *Annual Reports* and reported in table 5.9 (p. 156).

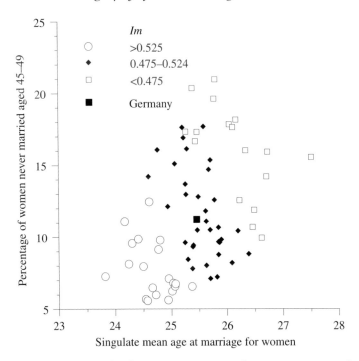

Figure 3.9. Relationship between percentage of women never married aged 45–49 and the singulate mean age at marriage for women, distinguishing categories of *Im*, German administrative areas in 1880
Source: Knodel (1974), appendix table 2.1, p. 274; Knodel and Maynes (1976), appendix table A.1, pp. 162–63.

Data equivalent to those used in figure 3.9 are not available for English and Welsh registration districts. We must therefore rely on *Im* to a greater extent than may be desirable, but this can be supplemented in certain circumstances by individual level data drawn from the census enumerators' books and considered in the form of local case studies later in this chapter.

The effects of urbanisation, migration and occupational specialisation on nuptiality

In broad terms the level of nuptiality must be influenced by the availability of eligible partners, the propensity to enter into formal marriage contracts rather than informal consensual unions, and the form of financial provision that is necessary before a new household and/or

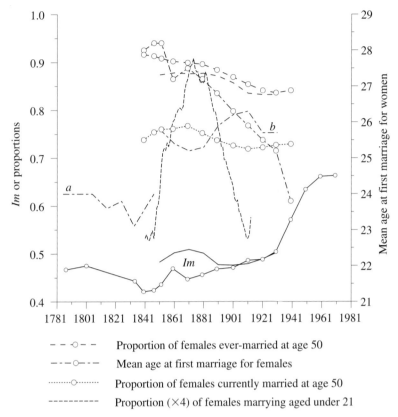

Figure 3.10. Time-series for *Im*, the mean age at first marriage for females, the proportion of females marrying aged under 21, and the proportions of females ever-married at age 50 and currently married at age 50, Denmark and England and Wales in the nineteenth century

Note: Denmark is shown by open circles; the remaining series are for England and Wales or England. Series *a* relate to mean age at first marriage, but *b* are SMAMs derived from censuses.

Source: Denmark – Matthiessen (1985), tables 2.1 and 2.6; England and Wales – Wrigley *et al.* (1997), tables 5.3 and 5.9; Registrar General's *Annual Reports*; Teitelbaum (1984), tables 5.1, 5.2 and 5.3.

reproductive unit can be established. Nuptiality levels will appear low if there is a serious imbalance among partners or if formal, legally binding marriage contracts and thus ecclesiastical or civil marriage ceremonies are spurned, or the financial requirements for independent household formation are prohibitively high. The extent to which marriage is a matter of choice for the principals concerned or their relatives also has significance.[24] In Victorian England one is dealing with free choice, or at least the power of veto, and new independent households are generally formed at or about the time of marriage. Since *Im* only measures the nuptiality of women it will be relatively low where there is a surplus of eligible young women and where terms of employment preclude formal marriage, as was the case among domestic or farm servants.

The high degree of stability in the pattern of *Im* together with the definitional nature of some of the hypothetical associations mentioned above suggest that it should be possible to develop formal statistical models to account for geographical variations in *Im* taken as a dependent variable.[25] Table 3.2 defines a number of variables which can be used to measure the demographic and social setting of districts for which there are adequate data. Let us begin by supposing that the following functional relationship held:

$$Im(\text{date}) = f(-\text{SR}, -\text{S}, -\text{FE}, \text{PD}, \text{A}, \text{C}).$$

This implies that female nuptiality was low where there was a high percentage of eligible women in the population, where there were female domestic servants, and where female non-domestic employment was available, but that it was high where population density was high and where agricultural labourers or coal miners represented significant proportions of the adult male population.

There are several problems to be solved in operationalising models of this form which appear to lend themselves to multiple regression analysis and thus ultimately the general linear model. First, many of the relationships one may wish to explore are precluded by the absence of information. The variables defined in table 3.2 are drawn from population censuses, but mainly the one for 1861 which provides detailed occupational statistics for registration districts not available for 1891 or 1911. In this particular case the variables were chosen to reflect a variety of influences which emphasise occupational specialisation or demographic imbalance in terms of age or geographical distribution. Secondly, the variables are themselves interrelated. For example, coal-mining communities tended to have little employment for women, few domestic servants and a sex ratio biased towards men. Yet the variable for coal miners has proved useful in the study of variations in marital fertility and, since it symbolises a particular form of closely knit, male-

---

[24] See Reher (1997), figure 6.3, p. 172, for a formalised version of a similarly structured model for use with Spanish data.

[25] See Anderson (1976) and Woods and Hinde (1985) for earlier attempts to build models to account for spatial variations in nuptiality.

Table 3.2. *Definitions of variables used in multiple regression analysis of* Im

Variable	Definition
Population density (PD) (date)	Log persons per square kilometre for various dates
Sex ratio (SR) (date)	Percentage of 20–24-year-olds who are female for various dates
Female servants (S)	Percentage of females aged 20 and over employed as domestic servants in 1861
Agricultural labourers (A)	Percentage of males aged 20 and over employed as agricultural labourers in 1861
Female employment (FE)	Percentage of females aged 20 and over in non-domestic employment in 1861 (i.e. excludes domestic servants and housewives)
Coal miners (C)	Log percentage of males aged 20 and over employed as coal miners in 1861
Im (date)	Index of proportion married for various dates

oriented, semi-urban society, it is also likely to prove of value for the analysis of nuptiality variations. Thirdly, the techniques used to operationalise models of the form outlined above also impose their own restrictions and require particular interpretation. The techniques of multivariate analysis enable us to assess the statistical association between groups of independent and single dependent variables. Stepwise multiple regression analysis in particular enables one to explore the strength and sign of the relationship between dependent and independent variables when the latter are combined in a sequence that allows increasing amounts of the former's variance to be explained.

Table 3.3 summarises one attempt to develop multivariate models in which *Im* is the dependent variable; the independent variables are defined in table 3.2. In the three models the five independent variables each make significant contributions, but they do so in combinations which vary in their overall effect (measured by the coefficient of multiple determination, R^2) and in order of priority, which also varies from model to model. For example,

$$Im1861 = f(-S, -FE, -SR1861, PD1861, A, C) \quad R^2 = 70 \text{ per cent}$$
$$Im1891 = f(-SR1891, PD1891, -S, A, -FE, C) \quad R^2 = 71 \text{ per cent}$$
$$Im1911 = f(-SR1911, PD1911, -S, -FE, A, C) \quad R^2 = 66 \text{ per cent}$$

Table 3.3. *Summary of results for stepwise multiple regression analysis on variations in the index of proportion married (Im) for 590 districts, England and Wales, 1861, 1891 and 1911*

Variable	b	beta	t	R^2 at each step
Im1861				
Female servants (S)	−0.00906	−0.50117	−17.418	0.32048
Female employment (FE)	−0.00163	−0.29483	−10.595	0.55496
Sex ratio (SR) (1861)	−0.00396	−0.30988	−11.911	0.59533
Population density (PD) (1861)	0.04151	0.38379	13.238	0.63220
Agricultural labourers (A)	0.00143	0.37130	11.528	0.68277
Coal miners (C)	0.02473	0.17196	5.909	0.70069
Constant	0.72074		41.517	
Im1891				
Sex ratio (SR) (1891)	−0.00578	−0.44390	−16.269	0.45227
Population density (PD) (1891)	0.04565	0.43990	15.219	0.53995
Female servants (S)	−0.00674	−0.33969	−11.492	0.61650
Agricultural labourers (A)	0.00137	0.32337	10.075	0.66194
Female employment (FE)	−0.00094	−0.15442	−5.704	0.69073
Coal miners (C)	0.02486	0.15745	5.452	0.70573
Constant	0.73750		37.195	
Im1911				
Sex ratio (SR) (1911)	−0.00458	−0.41973	−15.156	0.28928
Population density (PD) (1911)	0.04791	0.50290	16.118	0.48591
Female servants (S)	−0.00625	−0.32233	−10.668	0.57528
Female employment (FE)	−0.00097	−0.16381	−5.856	0.62236
Agricultural labourers (A)	0.00100	0.24281	7.083	0.63492
Coal miners (C)	0.03274	0.21226	6.866	0.66223
Constant	0.66698		36.245	

Notes:
The variables are defined in table 3.2, the dependent variables (*Im*) are shown in figure 3.8 and the residuals in figure 3.11. All values of *t* are significant at the 0.0001 level at least. London is one unit.

gives the three models in functional form with signs and order of inclusion. Each of the models provides a high level of statistical explanation for the variation in nuptiality levels, over 70 per cent in two cases, but a certain amount of the variance still remains unaccounted for. The relative contribution of each independent variable does change, but *Im*1891 and *Im*1911 are very similar. The models confirm the supposed signs of the association with high sex ratios and higher proportions of female servants and women in employment generally serving to depress *Im*, while higher relative levels of the other variables tend to be associated with higher levels of *Im*. It should be remembered that this is, of course, an ecological analysis in which the geographical variation in one variable is being assessed in terms of its associated co-variation with a number of other variables. It is also the case that the units of analysis – the districts – although numerous are far from homogeneous in terms of population distribution, economic and social characteristics. The implications for temporal variations must be considered separately and need not be directly implied.

A more detailed consideration of the relative contribution of individual independent variables suggests the following points. First, the sex ratio among 20–24-year-olds holds a key position in influencing the level of nuptiality.[26] It is most likely that this variable is in its turn affected by age- and sex-selective migration which concentrates men in the urban-industrial centres and women – as domestic servants – in the urban service centres, while the age structure of the population in the rural areas is influenced by net out-migration in which both sexes may take an active part. The chances of finding an eligible partner are thus linked to the consequences of migration, which are much conditioned by the concentration of production at a restricted number of locations.[27] Secondly, the population density variable helps to draw the distinction between urban and rural districts, but it does so in a crude fashion which ignores both differences between types of urban or rural places and the distortions created by variable district boundaries. Yet the population density (PD) variable does make a consistently significant and substantial positive contribution to the three models, which confirms the general point that the more urbanised places tend to have higher levels of nuptiality, while the low density rural districts have considerably lower levels of *Im*. This association with urbanisation is first and foremost a characteristic of the nuptiality pattern; it is not necessarily a causal relationship. Thirdly, wage labour among women has an adverse effect on nuptiality. It is quite clear why this should be so in the case of domestic servants, but the opportunities for women to find non-domestic employment also served to delay age at marriage. The most important instance of this phenomenon occurred in the textile districts where mill employment among young women represented a distinct and nearly universal stage in the life cycle. Fourthly, the two remaining variables included in the models represent agriculture and

---

[26] See also figure 2.15 (p. 67) which shows the age-specific sex ratios for England and Wales in 1911.

[27] Pooley and Turnbull (1998) are able to illustrate in considerable detail the various patterns of internal migration in nineteenth-century Britain.

coal mining. The agricultural labourers variable (A) distinguishes between systems of labour organisation operating on the arable farms of the east and south east, and those tied to animal husbandry in the west and north west. In the late nineteenth century these broad regional variations were still in evidence, but the system of farm service was in decline even in the north and west, so the effects on demographic behaviour of systems of agricultural labour organisation were very much more muted by 1914 than they had probably been even a hundred years earlier.[28] The coal-mining variable (C) also makes a consistently positive contribution to the models, but its effects are somewhat diluted by the inclusion of sex ratio and urbanisation variables through which the demographic influence of the peculiar social structure of mining communities operated to increase female nuptiality.[29]

Although the models described in table 3.3 are relatively successful in terms of R^2, both the distortions resulting from strong inter-correlations between variables and the possibility of clustering among residuals cannot be ignored. Figure 3.11 (colour section, page *b*) addresses the last point. It shows the distribution of positive ($>+1$) and negative (<-1) standardised residuals from the three models. In those districts with positive residuals, the level of *Im* has been under-predicted by the regression model while the negative residuals locate districts where the actual level of *Im* was lower than predicted by the model. While there are certain areas with consistently positive or negative residuals, in neither case do they display the same characteristics. For example, the negative residuals in south-west Wales and the northern Pennines are most likely the consequence of distortions to the age structure caused by selective out-migration typical of the extreme north and west of the British Isles, but the negative residuals in south Lancashire and parts of west Yorkshire stem from the effects on demographic behaviour, especially in terms of delayed marriage, of the textile industry. Similarly, the positive residuals pick out the coalfields, but also a diverse group of districts scattered throughout England and Wales with apparently little in common.[30] The general impression given by the distribution of residuals is that there are few clear patterns; where there are spatial clusters they tend to be small in size and relate especially to the extremes of the residual distribution which are unlikely to be predicted by a

---

[28] Kussmaul (1981, 1990) shows that to the north and west of the Tees–Exe line English parishes were more likely to be pastoral or industrial while to the south and east they were predominantly arable with some industrial.

[29] Coal-mining populations have been shown repeatedly to have distinctive demographic characteristics; see Friedlander (1973) and Haines (1979).

[30] Lawton (1986), compare figures 2.28–2.31 and 2.32–2.35 for marriage and migration by counties of Great Britain, and see also Pooley and Turnbull (1998).

nationwide model based on 590 units. The inclusion of additional variables could improve the models, but they would need to refer to local circumstances in ways that would detract from the more generalised forms of the models presented here.

Despite the obvious limitations of this ecological approach, a plausible account of the likely reasons for local variations in nuptiality patterns can be provided – one in which the effects of migration and occupational specialisation appear to be both influential and relatively stable in terms of their spatial manifestations.

Local studies

Local circumstances were especially important in conditioning and constraining the choice of marriage partners – circumstances which can only be described fully by considering the workings of the marriage market in particular places. The most interesting will doubtless prove to be those in which the dominant form of labour organisation posed an effective form of opposition to marriage and where non-domestic employment offered alternative means of support, at least for a few years before marriage and motherhood. There can have been few places in England and Wales as extreme as western Ireland where the emigration of young men and the scarcity of viable tenancies prolonged celibacy, especially among women. There were, however, parts of the highland zone north of a (far from straight) line between the rivers Tees and Exe in which out-migration combined with the labour demands of a largely pastoral form of rural economy to discourage marriage even in England and Wales.

Merely because of its size (3.8 million people in 1891) the local circumstances of London had national significance. There the inner city and the suburbs, the East and West Ends showed rather different levels of nuptiality, as they did in so many other social and demographic respects. The London Registration Division can be divided into 25 units, registration districts or combinations of registration districts, which enable one to consider not only geographical variations, but also changes over time, in rather more detail than is often possible for the other large British cities. In the case of nuptiality, again measured by the index of proportion married, there are clear and important differences among the districts. Figure 3.12 shows for the 25 districts the Ig/Im variations for 1861, 1891 and 1911, with the timepath for the whole of London (1851–1931) also illustrated. It has been noted in figure 3.7 that London was somewhat precocious in terms of lower nuptiality and marital fertility, but it is obvious from figure 3.12 that even in terms of

Colour Section

between pages 96–97

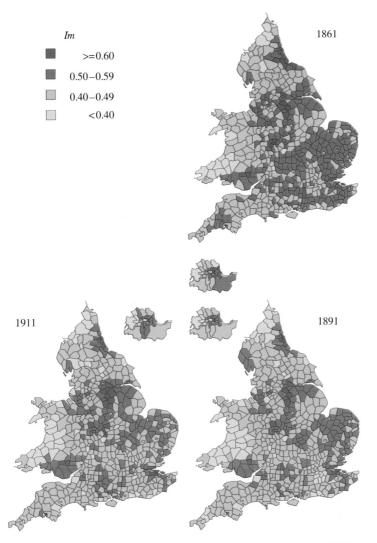

Figure 3.8. Variations in *Im* among the districts of England and Wales,
1861, 1891 and 1911

a

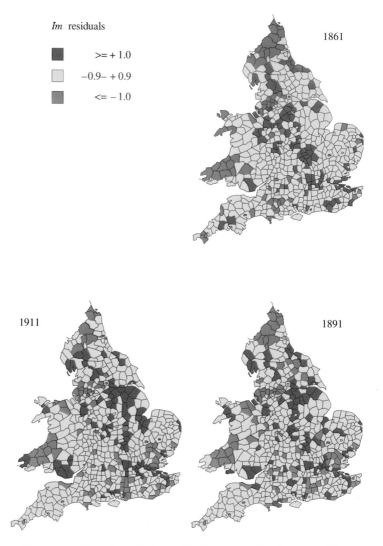

Im residuals

- ■ >= + 1.0
- □ −0.9– + 0.9
- ■ <= − 1.0

1861

1911

1891

Figure 3.11. Variations in *Im* residuals among the districts of England and Wales, 1861, 1891 and 1911

b

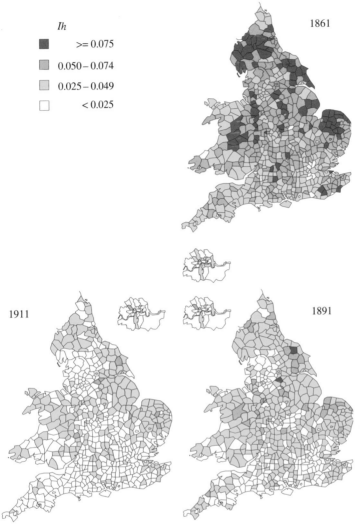

Figure 4.12. Variations in *Ih* among the districts of England and Wales, 1861, 1891 and 1911

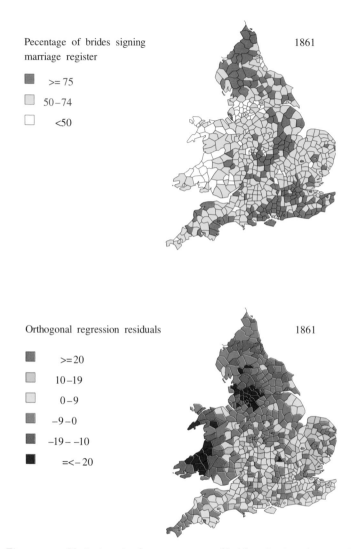

Figure 4.14. Variations in the percentage of brides signing the marriage register and literacy residuals among the districts of England and Wales, 1861

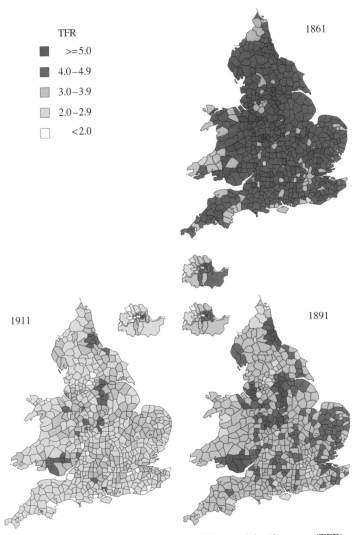

Figure 4.15. Variations in estimates of the total fertility rate (TFR) among the districts of England and Wales, 1861, 1891 and 1911

e

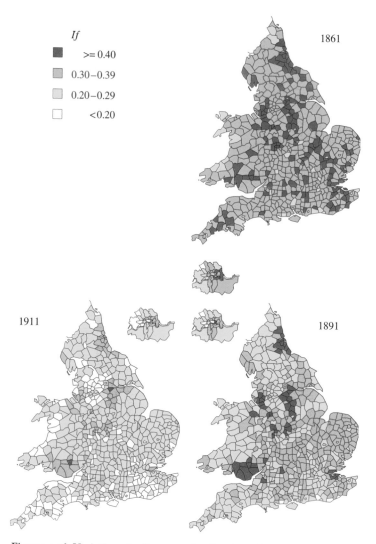

Figure 4.16. Variations in *If* among the districts of England and Wales, 1861, 1891 and 1911

f

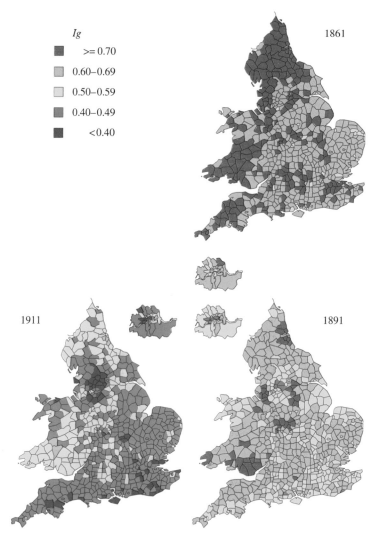

Figure 4.17. Variations in *Ig* among the districts of England and Wales, 1861, 1891 and 1911

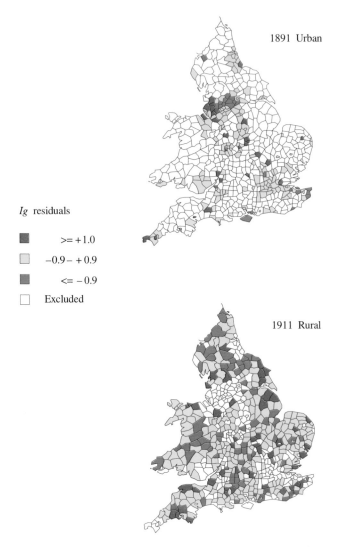

1891 Urban

Ig residuals

■ >= +1.0
☐ −0.9 − +0.9
■ <= −0.9
☐ Excluded

1911 Rural

Figure 4.20. Variations in *Ig* residuals among the districts of England and Wales, 1891 urban and 1911 rural

h

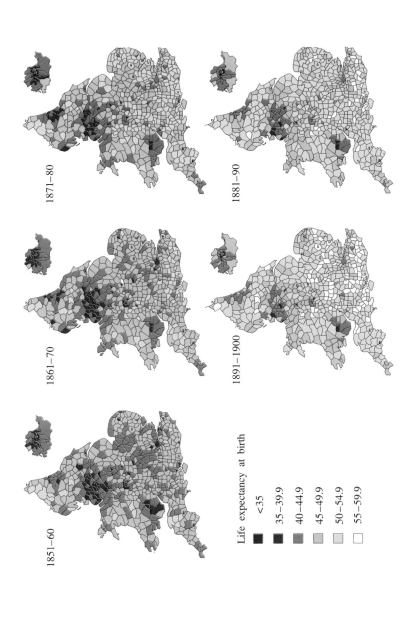

Figure 5.17. Variations in life expectancy at birth in years (e_0) among the districts of England and Wales, 1851–60 to 1891–1900

1871–80

1881–90

1861–70

1891–1900

1851–60

Life expectancy at birth

<35
35–39.9
40–44.9
45–49.9
50–54.9
55–59.9

i

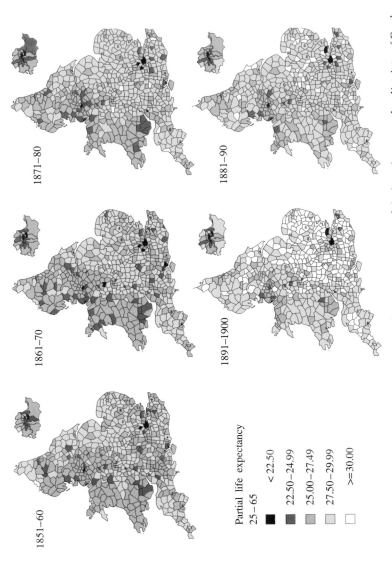

Figure 5.18. Variations in partial life expectancy in years between ages 25 and 65 (e_{25-65}) among the districts of England and Wales, 1851–60 to 1891–1900

1851–60

1861–70

1871–80

1881–90

1891–1900

Partial life expectancy
25 – 65

< 22.50

22.50–24.99

25.00–27.49

27.50–29.99

>= 30.00

j

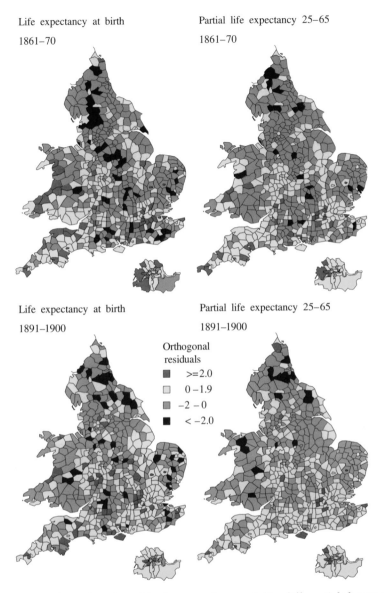

Life expectancy at birth
1861–70

Partial life expectancy 25–65
1861–70

Life expectancy at birth
1891–1900

Partial life expectancy 25–65
1891–1900

Orthogonal
residuals

▪ >=2.0
□ 0–1.9
▨ −2–0
■ < −2.0

Figure 5.19. Variations in residuals expressing mortality differentials between males and females among the districts of England and Wales, 1861–70 and 1891–1900

k

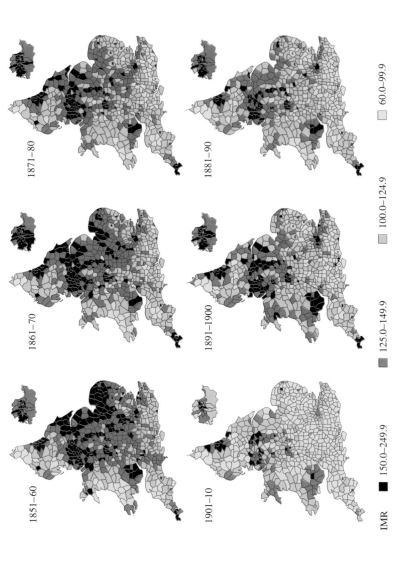

Figure 7.5. Variations in the infant mortality rate (IMR) among the districts of England and Wales, 1851–60 to 1901–10

1851–60   1861–70   1871–80

1901–10   1891–1900   1881–90

IMR   ■ 150.0–249.9   ■ 125.0–149.9   ■ 100.0–124.9   ■ 60.0–99.9

l

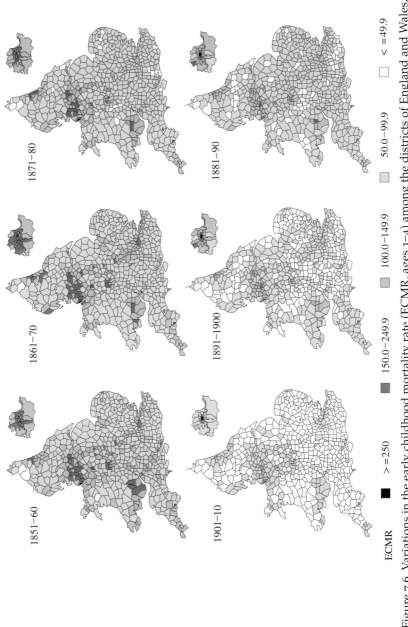

1851–60   1861–70   1871–80

1881–90

1891–1900

1901–10

ECMR   ■ >=250   ■ 150.0–249.9   ▨ 100.0–149.9   ▨ 50.0–99.9   □ < 49.9

Figure 7.6. Variations in the early childhood mortality rate (ECMR, ages 1–4) among the districts of England and Wales, 1851–60 to 1901–10

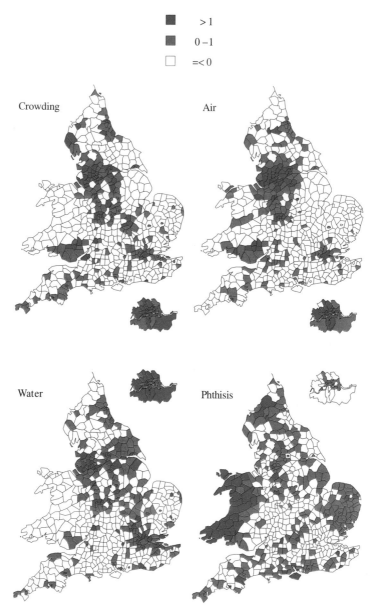

Figure 8.13. Variations in disease Z-scores among the districts of England and Wales

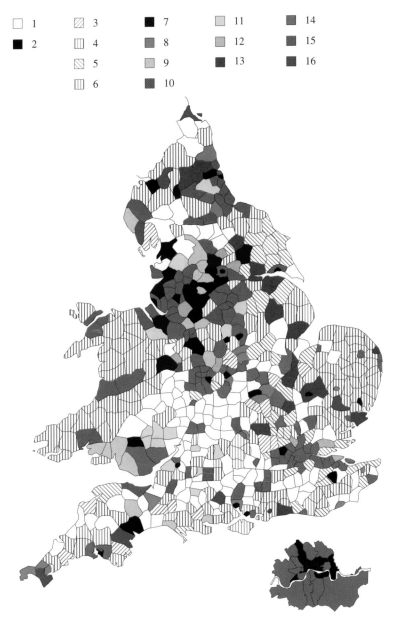

Figure 8.15. Classification of disease environments, English and Welsh districts

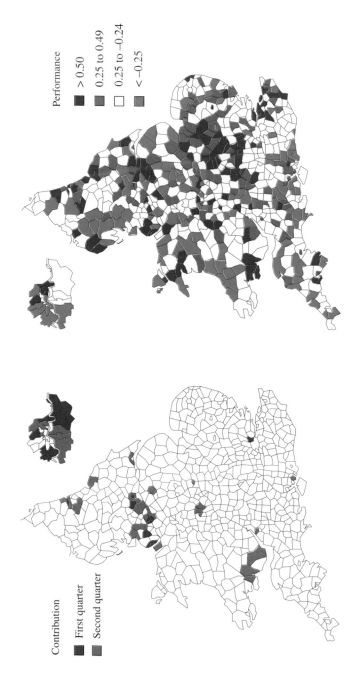

Figure 8.18. The location of the 53 districts contributing in sum 50 per cent of the decline in deaths from Diarrhoea & Typhus (Contribution) and residuals from the regression of proportionate contribution to decline on proportion of population of England and Wales in each district (Performance)

Performance

■ > 0.50
■ 0.25 to 0.49
□ 0.25 to –0.24
■ < –0.25

Contribution

■ First quarter
■ Second quarter

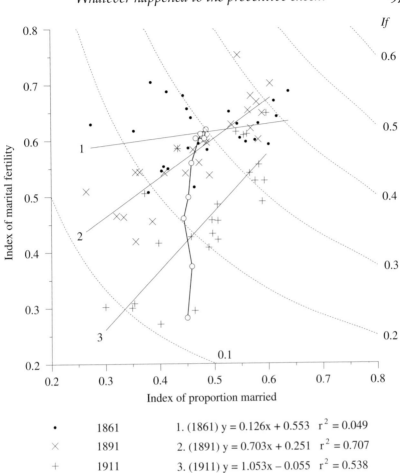

Figure 3.12. Changing relationship between marital fertility (*Ig*) and nuptiality (*Im*), London districts, 1861, 1891 and 1911
Note: The timepath for London runs from 1851 to 1931, see figure 3.7.

Im, and certainly for *Ig,* the metropolis contained highly diverse demographic worlds.[31]

London demonstrates the clear importance of domestic service. Among the 25 districts there is an almost perfect inverse relationship (r[2] is 93.4 per cent) between *Im* and the percentage of the female population aged 20 and over employed as domestic servants in 1861. There can be no doubt that in those districts occupied predominantly by the

---

[31] Woods (1984) offers a fuller account of nuptiality and fertility variations in London.

servant-keeping classes, female nuptiality will appear lower merely because many young spinsters are resident there. When servants marry, most will leave the area to be replaced by other spinsters. The resident population of servant employers may also marry rather later, as the mean ages at first marriage in table 3.1 suggest, but this will tend to be obscured by aggregate statistics. There is also a consistent and, as would be expected, inverse relationship between the distribution of servants and the extent of poverty, as estimated by Charles Booth in the late 1890s, but the link is not a perfect one. The most poverty-stricken areas had the highest levels of nuptiality and the highest levels of fertility, both marital and thus overall. Outside London one would also expect to find the rather stark patterns of urban social segregation reflected in levels of nuptiality, but this cannot always be seen in the demographic measures that are available, most of which cover entire towns rather than particular communities with distinct social profiles.

Research undertaken using the census enumerators' books can help us to tackle this problem of disaggregation in a rather different way. The work of Chris Smith on Sheffield (West Riding of Yorkshire), of Eilidh Garrett on the textile town of Keighley (West Riding of Yorkshire) and of Andy Hinde on the four rural communities of Mitford (Norfolk), Bakewell (Derbyshire), Pateley Bridge (North Riding of Yorkshire) and Atcham (Shropshire) has shown how nuptiality may vary with local cir-cumstances.[32] Bakewell and Pateley Bridge are both Pennine districts whose population was affected by rural out-migration in the nineteenth century. Mitford and Atcham represent contrasting agricultural economies; Mitford in the arable east and Atcham in the mixed farming or pastoral west where servants in husbandry still had an important role even in the late nineteenth century. Table 3.4 illustrates some of the more obvious differences in nuptiality patterns between these five popula-tions using the proportion ever-married by age 30 for 1861 and *Im* for 1861, 1891 and 1911. The figures for 1861 summarise samples drawn from the census for that year, while the *Im*s are for the population of the entire registration district from which the samples were drawn. Places are ranked in terms of the proportion of women ever-married by age 30, and since the mean age at marriage is normally two or three years younger for women than for men, the proportion ever-married by age 30 is likely to be higher for women than for men. Keighley is an exception which merits further enquiry. The range of experience in terms of the timing of marriage is quite substantial, with the steel town and the arable agricultural area at one extreme and the pastoral area and the

---

[32] Woods and Smith (1983), Hinde (1985, 1989) and Garrett (1990).

Table 3.4. *Percentage ever-married by age 30 in 1861 and* Im *for 1861, 1891 and 1911, selected English districts*

| District | Percentage ever-married by age 30 | | Im | | |
	Males	Females	1861	1891	1911
Sheffield with Ecclesall-Bierlow	83	85	0.594	0.573	0.581
Mitford	75	81	0.499	0.516	0.522
Bakewell	65	72	0.491	0.436	0.455
Pateley Bridge	62	72	0.491	0.466	0.471
Keighley	75	69	0.456	0.450	0.453
Atcham	54	65	0.439	0.416	0.425

Note:
The districts are registration districts, but the percentages are for sample populations drawn from the 1861 census enumerators' books for the district.

textile town at the other. The two Pennine populations are very similar and occupy the middle ground.

Of these six cases, Keighley is undoubtedly the most complex and thus the most interesting.[33] In the nineteenth century the economy of the town was dominated by textile manufacture, and a period of employment in the mills became a stage in the life of all but a handful of young adult women. It is often supposed that the Victorian convention obliged women to leave paid employment outside the home once they got married or became pregnant for the first time, but figure 3.13 shows clearly that among married women aged 20 to 44, between a quarter and a half regarded themselves as engaged in textile work when the 1861 census was taken. In the same age group, some half to three-quarters of unmarried women were so employed. If the distributions illustrated by figure 3.13 had remained constant for any length of time, then only 15 per cent of all women would have avoided working in textiles at some time in their careers. Obviously, the difference between the curves for married and unmarried women reflects both the interplay between the marriage and job markets and the local social conventions which established the bounds of respectability for the behaviour of married women.

This small number of rather selective local studies helps us to complement the broader generalisations which are possible using time-series,

[33] For a fuller account of the economic and social history of Keighley, see Garrett (1987).

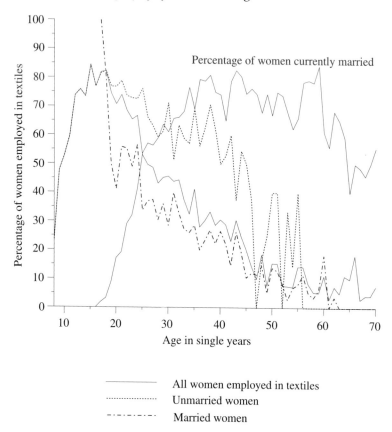

Figure 3.13. Relative age distribution of unmarried and married women employed in textile manufacture, Keighley, West Riding of Yorkshire, 1861
Source: Garrett (1987).

timepath and ecological approaches. The story is a consistent one for Victorian England and Wales. The mean age at marriage for women was about 25.6, somewhat younger if only first marriages are counted, and about an eighth of all women had not been married before their late forties. However, there were important local variations in the country which were created by a combination of the effects of age- and sex-selective migration and occupational specialisation. It is not so much that the pattern of nuptiality variation was a simple one – indeed local demographic and economic differences seem to have established a complicated patchwork of variations – but it was rather predictable and stable.

The influence of marriage patterns on illegitimate fertility

Malthus's idea of a preventive check operating via moral restraint – 'the restraint from marriage which is not followed by irregular gratifications' – will be effective in demographic terms if births only occur within marriage and if pregnancy is not the reason for marriage.[34] The relationship between illegitimate or non-marital fertility and nuptiality is not only an intriguing one in terms of what it may reveal of prevailing social values and the way in which women are regarded, but it may also be important in demographic terms. Irregular gratifications may undermine the effectiveness of the preventive check. It is reasonable to assume that where women marry young and there are few spinsters, illegitimate fertility will also be extremely low, indeed marriages for teenage brides may be contracted with the very aim of avoiding the risk of pre-marital sexual relations or pre-marital birth once sexual intercourse has taken place. Where virginity is highly prized, bastardy will be feared and marriage will be early, although it may not be universal. However, it is unreasonable to assume that where marriage is delayed and a significant minority of women remain spinsters then illegitimate fertility will necessarily be high. The most important intervening variables will be the extent of the taboo on sexual intercourse outside marriage, the effectiveness with which society polices that taboo and the retribution which it exacts on those who have clearly broken the social rules (they may be obliged to abandon their children, for example).

Figure 3.14 illustrates the relationship between illegitimate fertility and nuptiality in a very simple fashion using *Im* and Coale's index of non-marital fertility, *Ih*.[35] The line passing through A and B represents the hypothetical negative association. Populations falling in the area of A will have extremely low illegitimate fertility. Arranged early marriages may be used to ensure the bride's virginity, and women will marry in their teens or early twenties even if their husbands are older and sexually experienced. The preventive check will be of great significance for populations at B, but the weakly enforced or non-existent taboo on pre-marital sexual intercourse will give rise to higher levels of illegitimate fertility. In terms of the relationship sketched in figure 3.14, populations C and D are both marginal cases. At C nuptiality is low and

---

[34] Malthus (1989), volume I, p. 18, of the 1803 *Essay* continues, 'Promiscuous intercourse, unnatural passions, violations of the marriage bed, and improper arts to conceal the consequences of irregular connexions, clearly come under the head of vice.' In this way some of the preventive checks may involve both misery and vice whereas moral restraint will only involve some perhaps temporary misery.

[35] We shall return to consider other aspects of the distribution of *Ih* in chapter 4 where it will be dealt with alongside *Ig*.

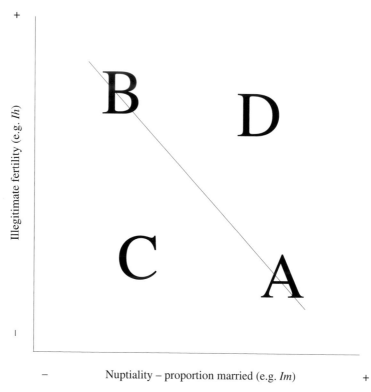

Figure 3.14. Hypothetical relationship between illegitimate fertility and nuptiality

illegitimacy is also kept low by means which may include the use of birth control. But for the forms of historical societies with which we are most concerned here, this is more likely to involve fierce social penalties for unmarried couples engaging in sexual intercourse, and also rigid economic constraints on the opportunity to marry. Populations falling in or near D are likely to have both high illegitimacy and nuptiality, although neither the former nor the latter is generally as high as at B or A.

Figure 3.14 is merely a very crude device with which to focus on some interesting hypothetical relationships. It has most value in allowing the isolation of particular complexes that lie at the extremes of the distributions. As we shall see, Victorian England and Wales offers few examples of these extremes compared with other parts of Europe, even Scotland, and Asia.

One way to examine the relationship a little more closely is shown in

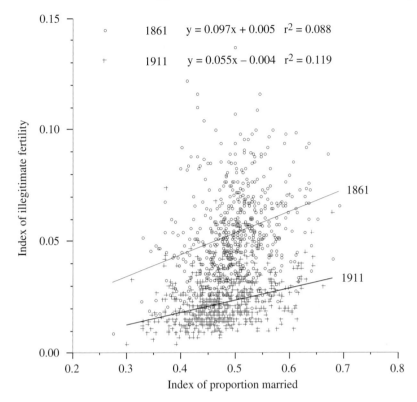

1861 $y = 0.097x + 0.005$ $r^2 = 0.088$

1911 $y = 0.055x - 0.004$ $r^2 = 0.119$

Figure 3.15. Relationship between illegitimate fertility (*Ih*) and nuptiality (*Im*) among English and Welsh districts, 1861 and 1911

figure 3.15 where *Ih* is plotted against *Im* for the registration districts of England and Wales in 1861 and 1911. Clearly there was no strong inverse relationship in the late nineteenth century, rather there are some signs of a weak positive association (C–D in figure 3.14). At mid-century at least, there is a tendency for those districts with higher levels of *Im* also to have higher *Ih*, although the association cannot be said to be as regular as the statistical textbooks often require.

Timepaths for change in illegitimacy–nuptiality can also be quite revealing. Those for Denmark and England are shown in figure 3.16. Here too there is a sense in which C–D seems to be more important than A–B, and certainly A is under-represented.

Figures 3.15 and 3.16 raise the obvious question: why in Europe are A and B relatively under-represented and C and D over-represented? There are two principal answers. First, it is actually unreasonable to

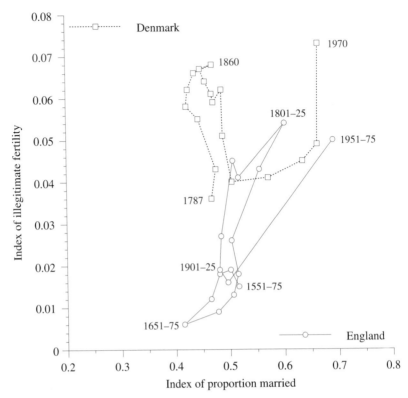

Figure 3.16. Timepaths for change in nuptiality (*Im*) and illegitimate fertility (*Ih*), Denmark, 1787–1970, and England, 1551–75 to 1951–75
Source: Matthiessen (1985), Wilson and Woods (1991).

assume that just because marriage is delayed the opportunity for pre-marital sexual activity will be encouraged. Rather, those social rules which helped to make the preventive check so effective in Ireland and northern Europe were probably also capable of restricting sexual activity among the young or of forcing couples to marry shortly after conception had been confirmed. Secondly, if one were also to show the estimated location of 'traditional rural' China in the early 1930s, its location would immediately remind one how eccentric Europe's demographic position was in relation to the rest of the world since it is China that is by far the best example of A (figure 3.17).[36] The extreme position

[36] The data for China are taken from Barclay *et al.* (1976), table 9. The following estimates are given for China in 1929–31: *If* 0.446; *Ig* 0.510; *Im* 0.874; *Ih* 0.002; SMAM for females 17.52 and for males 21.32. See also figure 10.3 and, in general, Lee and Wang Feng (1999a, 1999b).

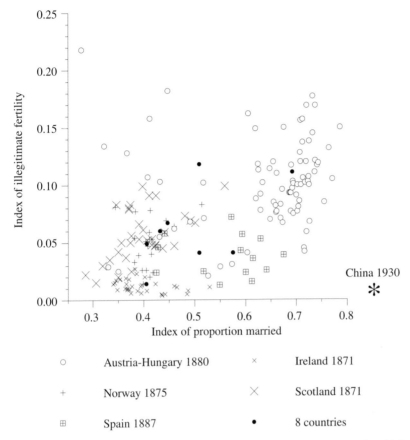

Figure 3.17. Relationship between illegitimate fertility (*Ih*) and nuptiality (*Im*), selected countries of Europe

of China makes Hungary's location in D more obvious, for although *Im* was high by European standards, *Ih* could also be high because many women clearly were not married in their early twenties and teenage brides were uncommon. There was thus more scope than might have been anticipated for non-marital fertility.

Two additional points require emphasis. Figure 3.17 also shows the inter-regional distributions for Norway, Spain and Austria-Hungary, as well as Ireland and Scotland. The Norwegian distribution captures the northern European range, but also gives examples of *Ih* as low as those for Irish counties. The Spanish distribution has no particular focus and displays a substantial degree of diversity ranging from type A to C. The distribution for Austria-Hungary is quite remarkable since it contains examples of all four types. These three regional patterns establish beyond doubt the internal heterogeneity of the European experience even in the late nineteenth century; the various demographic regimes were no respecters of political boundaries or of hypothetical relationships.

The second point relates once again to the difficulties of using *Im* as a measure of nuptiality. Although age at marriage and celibacy are related, there may be circumstances in which those women who marry do so at a young age while their sisters are exposed to the risks of pregnancy pursuing their careers as spinsters. It may be that parts of Austria and Hungary tended to conform to this pattern.

Figure 3.17 indicates that the demographic position of England and Wales in 1871 was also intermediate between the far north and west of Europe and the south. In Scotland there were regional examples in the north-east and the south-west where relatively high levels of illegitimate fertility were tolerated.[37]

Three distinct lessons can be learned from this brief consideration of the relationship between illegitimate fertility and nuptiality. First, there was no particular association between these two variables as measured by *Ih* and *Im*, and certainly no inverse relationship is apparent among and within nineteenth-century European countries. If anything, a slight positive association was more likely. Secondly, the range of experience among European regions whilst startling in one sense, even within countries, tended to display what by non-European standards were always far lower levels of nuptiality and far higher levels of illegitimacy. World regions may therefore conform more closely to an A–C–D distribution in which C and D are particularly dominated by European examples. Thirdly, the relative absence of examples of B in Europe points to an unsuspected severity in the social control of sexual morality which belies the often-reported laxity of north Europeans. The most likely reason for this peculiarity is the widespread acceptance of bridal pregnancy as a means of legitimising the illegitimate. Disregard for virginity should not be confused with acceptance of bastardy.

Returning to the preventive check and moral restraint, it seems that the population of England and Wales did practise the latter, by and large, or if it did not then pregnancy was a clear cue for marriage. The preventive check was therefore effective in depressing fertility in general, although this clearly varied from locality to locality.

---

[37] See Morse (1988) and Blaikie (1994).

The Victorian marriage pattern and its antecedents

Since the broad outlines of the Victorian marriage pattern may be charted with some accuracy and in considerable detail – at least in terms of *Im*, SMAM and proportion ever-married, their temporal and geographical variations – it is tempting to use this evidence to speculate on the process of change in earlier periods. In particular, it would be interesting to know whether the decline in mean age at marriage in the late eighteenth and early nineteenth centuries, which had such an important influence on nuptiality in general, overall fertility and thus population growth rates, was a phenomenon universal to every district of England and Wales, and if so how this might be reconciled with the ecological models described earlier.

Figure 3.18 uses family reconstitution data for ten English parishes to illustrate trends in the mean age at first marriage for women and men separately from the second half of the sixteenth century to the first half of the nineteenth.[38] In the upper panel for females, nine of the ten show the anticipated fall in age at marriage into the nineteenth century (Hawkshead in Cumbria is the exception), and five have virtually indistinguishable patterns of change. The parishes that do not conform exactly are: Bottesford and Terling at the extremes of the range, and Aldenham and Hartland. Of course, just because the populations of nine of these ten parishes appear to be behaving in the same fashion should not convince us that all of England was the same. It should also not persuade us that male nuptiality was behaving in the same fashion; indeed, the lower panel of figure 3.18 demonstrates quite clearly that in five of the parishes the mean age at first marriage actually remained unchanged or increased between the late eighteenth and nineteenth centuries. But the series in figure 3.18 do demonstrate that it was not merely the rapidly urbanising places or those where male in-migration had created a shortage of women who could marry and marry younger where nuptiality was increasing, although this may well have happened to an even more marked degree in the industrialising districts. It suggests that there was a widespread and relatively rapid lifting in the restrictions on marriage imposed by the system of organising agricultural labour, but especially among women. The ties that bound farm servants in the late eighteenth century were loosened as young men became agricultural labourers left to fend for themselves on an hourly

---

[38] Wrigley (1982), especially table 1, p. 221–22, but see also Wrigley *et al.* (1997), table 5.18, pp. 184–85, and figure 5.5, pp. 192–93. The villages are: Alcester, Aldenham, Banbury, Bottesford, Colyton, Gainsborough, Hartland, Hawkshead, Shepshed and Terling; see Wilson and Woods (1991), pp 408–9, for their location.

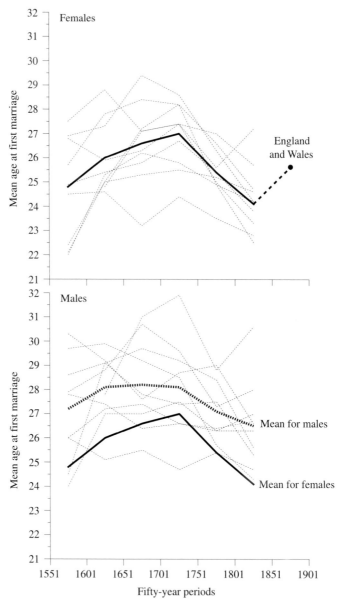

Figure 3.18. Variations in mean age at first marriage among ten English parishes, 1551–1837
Note: The last period for which parish data are shown is 1801 to the start of civil registration in 1837.
Source: Wrigley (1982), table 1.

wage, but without restrictions as to their remaining single, and young women were left to the marriage market. In the early nineteenth century, and certainly during the post-1815 depression, harsher economic circumstances retightened the rural marriage market and these constraints persisted throughout the nineteenth century. In the towns there were opportunities to marry early, but especially in those places with a shortage of women – the coalfields and male-oriented manufacturing centres. Restrictions on domestic servants, and alternative opportunities for textile workers, tended to encourage the postponement of marriage, although not its rejection.[39]

It was this unique combination of high and rising urbanisation, accelerating industrialisation and commercialisation, and the reorganisation of agricultural labour which so quickly, substantially and generally reduced the mean age at marriage, especially for women, and thus increased fertility in the late eighteenth and early nineteenth centuries. The preventive check was not being abandoned – as Malthus might have feared from his Surrey vantage point – merely temporarily relaxed. It was still working well, although perhaps more geographically diverse, towards the middle of Victoria's reign when fertility began to be controlled directly within marriage.

---

[39] The most detailed discussions of these issues are to be found in Schofield (1985), pp. 15–19, and Schofield (1989), especially figure 8.8, p. 297. The brief outline provided here chimes well both with Schofield's interpretation and the *Im* models presented earlier, but it also helps to clarify the importance of gender differences in the organisation of labour to which, of course, measures such as *Im* would be especially sensitive. It may also help us to see more clearly why the single-sex proletarianisation model proposed by Goldstone (1986) remains unconvincing since it only deals with males and sees the fall in age at marriage as a function of the creation of a regularly employed proletariat. If the evidence of figure 3.18 is to be believed, a full explanation of the increase in nuptiality and thus fertility must start with the experiences of rural women although it could, of course, include those of proletarian men.

4

Family limitation

In broad terms, demographers and social historians have adopted two forms of approach in their efforts to explain the origins and causes of the historical fertility transition. The first attempts some test of theory, however conceived or executed. The second approach is more empirically oriented; it seeks to identify regularities or patterns and to make generalisations therefrom. The application of these approaches to the study of family limitation has led to a plethora of published pieces each yielding their own particular insights. But in many respects we seem to be no closer to solving the various problems involved than was David Glass when he took up the challenge more than sixty years ago.[1] Why should this be so?

As a preliminary to detailed considerations of individual approaches in the remainder of this chapter, some general observations are in order. First, it now appears clear that England and Wales did not display the pattern of demographic change illustrated in classical transition models. This much at least was established in chapter 1. Rather, fertility increased in the late eighteenth and early nineteenth centuries and declined thereafter until the 1940s with only a short interruption in the 1850s and 1860s. Mortality declined slowly during the first half of the nineteenth century, but the pace of change quickened, especially when infant mortality began its rapid secular decline from 1899/1900. The protracted fertility transition was influenced by two rather different processes. In the first period, up to the 1870s, variations in overall fertility rates were mainly affected by changes in nuptiality, which have already been described in chapter 3, but in the second period marital

---

[1] Glass (1938). Glass rather than T. H. C. Stevenson, Sidney Webb or Sir Arthur Newsholme because he was one of the first to have the opportunity to view the marital fertility transition in its entirety. As far as the different approaches are concerned, compare Coale and Watkins (1986), in the demographers' corner, with Gillis *et al.* (1992), for the social and cultural historians. The former are short on theory while the latter avoid any quantitative description of the extent of the revolution.

fertility itself was reduced by the direct application of family limitation methods. The two periods were quite distinct, although this is not apparent when general fertility measures, such as the total fertility rate (TFR) or the index of overall fertility (*If*), are inspected. The fertility transition was not, therefore, simply one sequence of demographic change with one set of processes involved.[2]

Secondly, England and Wales were not alone in western Europe in experiencing secular decline of marital fertility during the last decades of the nineteenth century. Although the precise timing varied from country to country and region to region, permanent changes of a similar magnitude occurred in many areas within a relatively short time-span. Whatever influenced marital fertility decline in England and Wales after the 1870s may also have been important in other parts of Europe. Individual countries or regions cannot be considered in isolation. For example, there will be little to gain by emphasising the importance of industrialisation and urbanisation merely because they were relatively advanced in England and Wales, when it is clear from the case of France that neither was sufficient or necessary to establish low and apparently controlled marital fertility.[3]

Thirdly, the vital registration systems of most European states were concerned with mortality and public health. Considerable effort and expense went into recording cause of death by age, sex, place of death and occupation, but until the turn of the century there was relatively little interest in births, mothers and fertility. Certainly in England and Wales, a mother's age at the birth of her children was not regularly recorded, let alone her parity or her husband's characteristics, except whether or not she was married. This means that age-specific marital fertility rates, the essential raw materials of most discussions of fertility control, cannot be calculated directly and one is left, as was Glass, to estimate TFR or the gross reproduction rate (GRR) indirectly, to rely on Coale's fertility indices which can be calculated directly, or to use some form of proxy for completed family size – children ever born per woman, for example. Needless to say, none of these measures is entirely satisfactory; indeed, the lack of age-specific marital fertility rates hinders conclusive resolution of the fundamentally important 'starting-spacing-stopping' problem.[4]

Fourthly, although it is known that marital fertility did decline in

---

[2] Wrigley and Schofield (1981) and Wrigley *et al.* (1997), especially chapter 7 on 'Fertility'.

[3] See figure 3.4 and Wrigley (1987).

[4] Although age of mother at the birth of her children was not routinely recorded in England and Wales until 1938, the Registrar General's *Statistical Review for 1938 and 1939* (London: HMSO, 1947), pp. 203–6 and 236–37, contains an ingeniously derived set of estimates of the age-specific marital fertility rates for census years 1851–1911, 1922 and 1933. See table 4.2.

England and Wales as elsewhere in Europe towards the end of the nineteenth century, it is not known how this was accomplished. How did
sexually active couples prevent conception? Did pregnant women have
recourse to abortion in any considerable number? Was this a contraceptive revolution with new technology, as in the 1960s, or merely old
methods used to better effect? There is insufficient evidence with which
to answer these questions directly and convincingly for Victorian
England.

Finally, the absence of crucial and convincing evidence appears to
have encouraged speculation and loose theory; similarities have
become differences, and coincidences have turned into causes, in the
effort to achieve slight advances in understanding. In the case of the
fertility transition, hypothesis has run far ahead of description to the
detriment of interpretation.

This chapter is also, of course, a victim of these problems. What arguments can also be sustained by evidence in terms of the timing of the
fertility transition in Victorian England?

Transition theory

Frank W. Notestein's original attempt to develop a theory for the demographic transition remains influential but is dated and rather battered.[5]
It is a comfortable old hat: much loved, often used, but no longer
shapely or weather-proof. Fertility decline responds only slowly to
modernisation after the fall of mortality, for while mortality is high,
fertility must compensate. According to Notestein, 'All such societies
are therefore ingeniously arranged to obtain the required births. Their
religious doctrines, moral codes, laws, education, community customs,
marriage habits, and family organisations are all focused toward maintaining high fertility.'[6] And, 'Birth rates were reduced largely by means
of contraception, but in response to drastic changes in the social and
economic setting that radically altered the motives and aims of people
with respect to family size.'[7] The setting for change was provided by the
rise of urban-industrial society, and the motives were related to growing
individualism and the decline of family responsibilities, many of which
were taken over by schools, employers or the State. Large families
became 'progressively difficult and expensive' undertakings. 'In short,

---

[5] Notestein (1945). This is the first clear and elaborate statement of demographic transition theory, see chapter 1. For a recent account of the intellectual history of transition
theory see Szreter (1993). Mason (1997) offers a general over-view of the problems of
developing fertility transition theories.   [6] Notestein (1945), p. 39.
[7] Notestein (1945), p. 40.

under the impact of urban life, the social aim of perpetuating the family gave way progressively to that of promoting the health, education, and material welfare of the individual child; family limitation became widespread; and the end of the period of growth came in sight.'[8]

These are highly perceptive remarks, but they over-emphasise the roles of industrialisation and urbanisation. The emergence of an urban-industrial society in Victorian Britain does not appear to have altered the setting sufficiently on its own to change individuals' motives; indeed, the possibility of non-agricultural employment for men is likely to have reduced both the mean age at first marriage for women and the proportion of spinsters in their thirties and forties, thus increasing the level of overall fertility.[9] Even in late nineteenth-century England, whether a place was urban or rural was not especially relevant for marital fertility. The differences between the East End and West End of London were as great as any to be found between provincial urban and rural places. As we shall see, marital fertility tended to remain higher longer among workers in the heavy industries and among coal miners than in most other sections of the population. The fertility transition in England and Wales appears not to have been directly dependent upon the urban-industrial revolution in a way that is consistent with Notestein's ideas; rather, the beginnings of this particular revolution in the eighteenth century is more likely to have been at least partially responsible for the dramatic increase in fertility and thus the origins of the modern rise in population. We shall also see that geographical and occupational variations in the level of marital fertility in England and Wales tell a different story to the one envisaged by Notestein. All of which suggests that Notestein's account of the process of long-term demographic change need not apply to all cases, although it may prove an accurate explanation in some.

Since 1945 there have been several attempts to revise transition theory. One of the most valuable has come from Kingsley Davis in the form of his concept of 'multi-phasic demographic responses'.[10] These responses include the following: emigration, rural–urban migration, restrictions on marriage, and the control of marital fertility. Since their individual effects are in some senses similar, they might be regarded as interchangeable as reactions to the rapid population growth resulting from a sharp fall in mortality. Friedlander has attempted to apply this notion, with some amendments, to Victorian England and Wales.[11] Societal strains are seen to be the major determinants of demographic

---

[8] Notestein (1945), p. 41.   [9] See chapter 3.   [10] Davis (1963).
[11] Friedlander (1983).

responses. The former occur when there is 'a widening discrepancy between the current welfare of a large proportion of families or individuals, and that which could be achieved (or is aspired to) under a changed pattern of behaviour, demographic or otherwise'.[12] Recourse to arguments about popular welfare, whilst plausible in a general sense, may offer little help if they are required to be empirically verified. The threat to mass welfare accentuated by rapid population growth is a very familiar theme, and the fact that the popular response could be recourse to family limitation is also unexceptionable. But why should the fear of economic strain have produced such a rapid change in mass behaviour at roughly the same time in much of western Europe, especially when absolute living standards appear to have been improving? Davis's theory is a special example of the broader 'negative stimulus leads to behavioural response' argument. In this case the negative stimulus is actual present or anticipated future worsening of individuals' economic circumstances. Should family limitation be seen in this rather crude deterministic way?

Social diffusion

The originality of the family limitation phenomenon is central to the theory of relative economic pressure and social diffusion proposed by J. A. Banks as the first element in his tripartite analysis of the Victorian family and parenthood.[13] His argument takes the following form: 'the decline in family size commenced as an upper- and middle-class phenomenon at some time during the 1860s and 1870s. It was not until sometime later that the new reproductive habits began to spread amongst the less privileged social groups.'[14] The behaviour of the middle-class innovators is influenced by changes in their standard of living, but particularly changes in attitude to well-being and the level of material aspirations. Faced with the rising costs of hiring domestic servants and of education to permit their children to compete for status-conferring employment, and with greater attention paid to child care and the ever-rising expectations for consumption standards, middle- and upper-class couples were prompted to restrict their fertility. They

---

[12] Friedlander (1983), p. 250.
[13] Banks's tripartite analysis is to be found in Banks (1954, 1981) and Banks and Banks (1964). In fact Notestein and before him the French demographer A. Dumont in 1890 had emphasised the importance of social diffusion. For example, Notestein (1953), p. 16: 'A trend toward birth restriction started in the urban upper classes and gradually moved down the social scale and out to the countryside.'   [14] Banks (1954), p. 5.

substituted small numbers of high-quality children for larger numbers of low-quality ones. Economists describe this process as the 'relative income compression phenomenon'.[15]

Banks has presented sufficient evidence to make this first aspect of his argument – the reasons for innovation – seem plausible for the Victorian middle classes, but the mechanism by which the 'new reproductive habits' spread down the social hierarchy to other members of the community requires closer scrutiny. The mechanism most obvious to Banks 'is that of direct diffusion through, perhaps, simple copying of family limitation practices, as desirable, by those sections of the population most closely associated with the upper and middle classes'.[16] The crucial link is provided by the experience of female domestic servants whose personal, intimate experience of the way of life of the pioneers of family limitation may have convinced them of the need for such practices when they themselves formed their own families later in life. Banks reinforced his point with respect to servants in the following way:

[B]y that time [post-1870] the lesson had been learned, at least in the sense that some of the middle-class standards and aspirations had been adopted by the working class. It is not suggested here that they learned to use birth control from being employed in the middle class families. So far as it is possible to tell, working class birth control is a twentieth-century practice, on the whole, and there seems to have been a 'conspiracy of silence' on the issue on their part long after the Victorian age had come to an end.[17]

This second part of the argument, concerning the diffusion and adoption of new reproductive ideals – not the means to implement them – by three-quarters of the Victorian population (i.e. those who were not middle or upper class), is difficult if not impossible to substantiate. There were more than 1 million domestic servants in England and Wales in 1861, most of whom were spinsters. Had all of these women adopted the attitudes of their masters and mistresses the effects could have been considerable, but there is still no firm evidence to suggest that the reproductive patterns of married women who had been domestic servants were significantly different from those who had not. Indeed, what we do know of the differences in fertility levels between occupations provides a far from clear picture. The 1911 *Census of Fertility* offers the opportunity to illustrate some of these points for social groups and a substantial selection of individual occupations. It can also be used to sketch out the general pattern of marital fertility decline – expressed in terms of children ever born per married couple – related to mother's age

---

[15] See Leibenstein (1974, 1975).   [16] Banks (1981), p. 107.
[17] Banks (1968), quoted from p. 287; see also Banks (1973), especially p. 115.

and the duration of her marriage.[18] For example, figure 4.1 shows the number of children born, that is average parity (a), and the number of surviving children (b) per married couple where the wife is 45 or over at the time of the 1911 census. It distinguishes the date of marriage and the age at marriage of the wife and mother (15–19 to 40–44). For those women who married in their twenties or early thirties – the over-whelming majority in Victorian England – figure 4.1 shows the continuous decline of marital fertility among successive marriage cohorts from at least the 1850s onwards. For those married aged 20–24 the number of children ever born fell from 7.4 for the pre-1851 marriage cohort to 5.1 for the 1891–96 cohort, and for those married aged 25–29 the decline was from 5.9 to 3.3 between the same marriage cohorts. But the lower panel of figure 4.1 also indicates what happens when effective fertility is considered and the number of surviving children is used to chart fertility changes.[19]

However, complications arise when one attempts to consider social groups or individual occupations. For example, Szreter has demonstrated that five of the eight 'Social Classes' defined in 1911 for the purposes of reporting social variations in fertility and mortality were remarkably heterogeneous in terms of the average parity of their component occupations.[20] Table 4.1 describes the 'Social Classes' as defined for the reporting of fertility and illustrates variations in average parity for women who were aged 20–24 and 25–29 when they married. It is by now conventional to point out that these average parities appear to reflect a distinct social hierarchy in terms of the level of marital fertility running from V to I, high to low, and from working class to middle and upper class, and that this holds even when one standardises for age at

---

[18] The 1911 Census of Fertility was published in three parts: as an appendix to volume X of the *1911 Census of Population* (BPP 1914–16/LXXI, *Classification of Occupations*); in volume XIII on *Fertility of Marriage, Part I* (BPP 1917–18/XXXV, tables on fertility by duration and age at marriage); and *Fertility of Marriage, Part II* (OP. 1100.20.2), published in 1923 giving a substantial *Report* and details of fertility by occupation. See also Registrar General's *Seventy-fifth Annual Report* for 1912 (BPP 1913/XVII), especially pp. xvii–xxxvi. Material in *The Fertility of Marriage, Part II* has been extensively used, but it is not without problems in terms of the effects of differential sample size for different marriage cohorts, the effects of recall and the potential distortions which the various selection processes may entail. These problems are discussed at length and the material analysed in detail in the following: Stevenson (1920), Innes (1938), Banks (1954, 1981), and most recently Szreter (1996), Garrett and Reid (1996), Anderson (1998a, 1998b), and Garrett *et al.* (forthcoming).

[19] When infant and childhood mortality remains constant the chances of survival will be affected by the length of the period from birth to reporting in 1911, but early childhood mortality was in decline for all the cohorts captured in figure 4.1 and infant mortality declined rapidly in the ten years prior to the census. The mortality-related element of child survival is therefore a complicated one during this period. See chapter 7 on infant and childhood mortality.   [20] Szreter (1996), pp. 285–309.

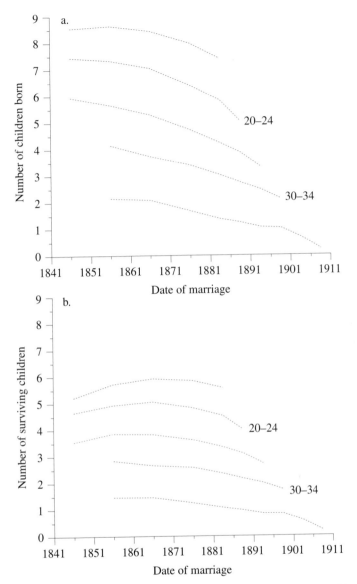

Figure 4.1. Fertility of women aged 45 and over in 1911 disaggregated by date of and age at marriage, all married couples, England and Wales: (a) children born per married couple (average parity), (b) surviving children per married couple
Source: 1911 Census, Fertility of Marriage, Part II (1923), table XLIV.

Table 4.1. *Average parities for 'Social Classes', England and Wales*

	'Social Classes'								
	All	I	II	III	IV	V	VI	VII	VIII
Wife's marriage age 20–24									
Date of marriage									
1886–90	5.1	*3.8*	*4.4*	*5.1*	*5.2*	*5.8*	4.5	6.6	6.0
1881–85	5.9	4.4	5.1	5.9	6.0	6.5	5.4	7.4	6.8
1871–80	6.5	5.2	5.9	6.5	6.5	7.0	6.0	7.7	7.1
1861–70	7.2	6.3	6.9	7.2	7.2	7.5	6.8	8.1	7.5
1851–60	7.5	6.7	7.4	7.5	7.3	7.8	7.1	8.2	7.9
Pre-1851	7.6								
Wife's marriage age 25–29									
Date of marriage									
1891–95	3.4	*2.6*	*3.1*	*3.4*	*3.4*	*3.4*	3.0	4.4	4.2
1886–90	3.9	3.0	3.6	4.0	4.0	4.5	3.5	5.2	4.8
1881–85	4.3	3.5	4.0	4.3	4.4	4.7	3.9	5.4	5.1
1871–80	4.8	4.2	4.7	4.9	4.8	5.1	4.4	5.6	5.4
1861–70	5.4	5.0	5.4	5.5	5.4	5.6	5.0	6.3	5.7
1851–60	5.8	5.2	5.9	5.8	5.9	6.0			6.0

Note:
The 1911 'Social Classes' were defined in the following way:
I. Upper and middle class
II. Intermediate class (excluding scholars)
III. Skilled workmen
IV. Intermediate class
V. Unskilled workmen
VI. Textile workers
VII. Miners
VIII. Agricultural labourers
III–VIII. Working class.
Only the average parities for those married women aged 45 or over at the census of 1911 are given as are those for groups of 100 couples or more. Those shown in italics may represent incomplete fertility. 'All' refers to all couples where the husband is occupied and can therefore be classified.
Source: 1911 *Census of Fertility, Fertility of Marriage, Part II* (1923), table XLIV.

and duration of marriage. Although this is an interesting and general finding it does not help us consider directly Banks's argument that not only were there differentials in fertility level, but rates of change were patterned in a class-specific fashion such that pioneers and followers in the adoption of fertility control could clearly be identified.

Haines concludes his analysis of fertility differentials with the following observations.

It appears, for England and Wales, the United States, France, and Norway, at least, that fertility decline was 'led' by the middle and upper classes. Social and economic elites apparently did act as leader in modifying this most basic of activities – human reproduction. In contrast, the agrarian population was slower to change. It must be borne in mind that at least some fertility decline characterised almost all social classes from the earliest marriage-duration cohorts measurable from the retrospective [1911] census reports analysed here. This is, in itself, not unusual, but it was the middle and upper classes that adjusted more rapidly.[21]

Haines's difficulty is neatly illustrated in figure 4.2 which draws from table 4.1 the social groups I, V, VI and VII to show average parities and surviving children for women who married at the age of 20–24. Each of the social groups shows fertility decline from marriage cohort to cohort, but the differences in average parity were greater among those women who married in the early 1880s than among those who married in the 1860s. The gap between the family sizes of couples in the middle and upper classes (I) and those in which the husband was employed as a miner (VII) had certainly increased, but this, as Haines says, is a matter of speed of adoption; it need not imply that the former are pioneers while the latter are followers, that one group innovates while the other merely copies.[22]

The point may be emphasised further by selecting a small group of occupations to see how they behave relative to one another. Figure 4.3 considers the fertility of members of the medical profession (from I); farmers and graziers (from II); and coal and shale miners working at the face (from VII). Once again, average parities are shown and only the fertility of wives aged 45 and over in 1911.

These simple analyses of the 1911 *Census of Fertility* suggest, in summary, several important points. First, there were, as one would expect from Banks's argument, clear differences between occupations at each of the four marriage durations, with mean parities generally lower for the higher status occupations. Secondly, marriage in the late twenties tended to reduce the average parity by about one child. Thirdly, when one considers effective average parity – surviving children per married couple – the range is narrowed and the status-fertility ranking is less obvious, although levels remain at their highest among farmers and miners. The slow rate of change with duration of marriage, and thus period, in effective average parity among coal miners almost certainly reflects a persistently high rate of childhood mortality; a theme which is taken up in chapters 6 and 7. Fourthly, fertility declined in

---

[21] Haines (1989), quoted from p. 322. See also Szreter (1996), pp. 306–7.
[22] Consider the case of two strangers who get off a bus together. Their destination is the same, but one walks more quickly than the other. The slower of the two will appear to be following the faster if their locations are compared at regular intervals.

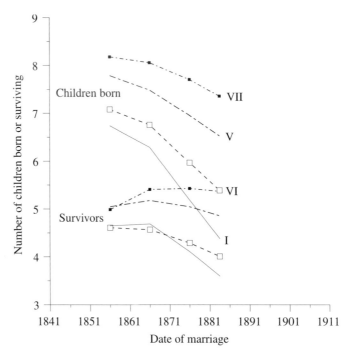

Figure 4.2. Fertility of married women with husbands in selected
'Social Classes', England and Wales
Note: All women were aged 45 and over in 1911 and only those aged 20–24 at
marriage are considered.
Source: See table 4.1.

successive marriage cohorts in all the occupations and social groups
illustrated. This last point is potentially the most damaging for the
social diffusion hypothesis, since it appears from figures 4.1 to 4.3 and
table 4.1 that a substantial proportion of couples in all occupations were
behaving in a similar fashion at roughly the same time by practising
some form of family limitation, although the proportion of laggards
may have varied in different occupations, thus affecting the rates of
change. Either the process of social diffusion occurred so rapidly that its
demographic effects cannot be observed in the results of the 1911 *Census
of Fertility* or the status-fertility range was much narrower for those
married in the 1840s, and the process of fertility decline began much
earlier in certain social groups than trends in national aggregates would
suggest. Neither possibility is very likely. The decline in marital fertility
affected all occupational groups at the same time, but the occupation-
specific, and thus social group-specific, effective average parities that

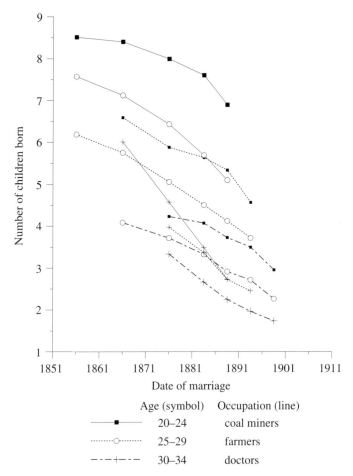

Figure 4.3. Children born per married couple in three occupational
groups: physicians, surgeons and registered practitioners; farmers and
graziers; and coal and shale miners at the face, England and Wales
Note: Only women aged 45 and over in 1911 and three marriage age groups
(20–24, 25–29 and 30–34) are considered.
Source: 1911 Census, Fertility of Marriage, Part II (1923), table XXXV.

resulted were influenced by differences in pre-decline levels, nuptiality
patterns and child survival. There was no social diffusion, but there
were social differences in every element of the demographic matrix.

The 1911 *Census of Fertility* has its limitations. Table 4.1, for example,
has been constructed from data given in table XXXV of *Fertility of
Marriage, Part II*, which deals only with the self-reported fertility of

women aged 45 and over who were currently married in 1911, arranged by husband's occupation. Table XLIV provides equivalent information for the five 'Social Classes' and three distinct occupational groups. Most criticisms of these materials relate to the new definition of social class created by the combination of men's occupations,[23] but the occupation-specific data are themselves subject to the distortions of differential sample size; the over-emphasis on male employment and occupational labels reported late in life; and the need for both partners to survive until 1911 for the couple's fertility to be recorded. It may be unwise, therefore, to place too much reliance on this one source of material alone, however rich it may seem. For example, Szreter's very detailed analysis of data from the published tables has led not only to his rejection of the 'professional model' which led T. H. C. Stevenson to propose the classification of occupations on the basis of some form of skill hierarchy, but also to his arguing the case for more significance to be given to 'employership or proprietorship status' and especially the 'affiliation to a given industrial sector' which is likely to be geographically concentrated in particular localities and will therefore condition the behaviour of certain communities.[24]

The occupational data of 1911 has conventionally been considered to support the notion of a single, socially graded and unified national event, 'the fertility decline'. However, the patterns actually revealed by the 1911 census . . . are much more complex and clear-cut than that. The overall picture to emerge is one of multiple falling fertilities in Britain: an essentially fractured and fissured set of relatively independent processes, occurring in different ways over a period of nearly a century in different locations and communities.[25]

Szreter is surely correct to warn us about the unitary approach and the importance of independent processes, but in doing so he may also have failed to avoid perhaps the greatest trap set for analysts of the 1911 *Census of Fertility*, namely the temptation to dwell on small differences in fertility levels when the most striking observation is undoubtedly the way in which average parity could more than halve in most occupations in a matter of forty years.

Contraceptive revolution?

Had there been a contraceptive revolution in the late nineteenth century, the timing and pace of the secular decline of marital fertility would have been far easier to understand. New birth control techniques developed, disseminated, adopted and used effectively by a population

---

[23] Szreter (1984), pp. 522–46, also Szreter (1996), pp. 239–82.
[24] Szreter (1996), especially pp. 360–66.   [25] Szreter (1996), p. 364.

only too willing to restrict its fertility would certainly provide a ready explanation.[26] Yet the bulk of what little evidence there is suggests that Banks is correct in his view that effective appliance methods of birth control were not available at prices accessible to the working population until well into the twentieth century. If this is so, what means were being used to limit family size before 1911? The most likely candidates are *coitus interruptus*, abortion and sexual abstinence. Although there is anecdotal evidence for the use of these methods, there exists no means by which to judge their general usage, effectiveness in preventing conception or relative contributions.[27] For example, there has been considerable debate over the extent of induced abortion in Victorian England. Seccombe argues that 'The rate of induced abortion (relative to live births) seems to have risen substantially in the late nineteenth and early twentieth centuries . . . It seems reasonable to conclude that a rise in the abortion rate made a considerable contribution to the decline of the birth-rate prior to the widespread use of contraceptive devices in marriage.'[28] But there is little direct evidence to support this and similar claims regarding the manner in which family size was limited. This is the most important stumbling block to any full understanding of the origins of the secular decline of marital fertility in the nineteenth century. Demographers and social historians simply lack basic information about the means of family limitation used.

Even in those cases where there is exceptionally detailed information about the behaviour of individual married couples there are still problems for interpretations of the history of events and yet more difficulties for our appreciation of motivations. The case of Mary Pierce Poor offers

---

[26] Ideally, one would wish to replicate Westoff and Ryder's (1977) account of the American contraceptive revolution of the 1960s and 1970s in which a new, more effective, female-oriented contraceptive was developed, came on to the market and was rapidly adopted by eager consumers for whom the Pill meant sexual freedom and minimal risk of pregnancy.

[27] Roberts (1984), especially pp. 93–103, provides interesting evidence on the use of *coitus interruptus* and abstinence, while Lewis-Faning (1949) sheds some light on the behaviour of the pre-1910 marriage cohort, where the use of appliance methods of birth control appears to have been slight. There is a considerable non-demographic literature on the 'birth control question', for example McLaren (1978) and Soloway (1982), and sexual knowledge, for example Porter and Hall (1995). Most of these discussions focus on pamphlet and other neo-Malthusian publications, and are not able to consider coital frequency or contraceptive use. Only Peel (1963) offers any empirical evidence on the high price and limited availability of appliance methods of contraception before the First World War.

[28] Seccombe (1990), quoted from p. 154. Seccombe is here relying on Sauer (1978), but Sauer (p. 92) admits that 'Evidence of abortion is even scantier than that of infanticide. There were no statistics of prevalence, but all observers agreed that abortion was more frequent than infant murder.' See Woods (1992) and Szreter (1996), pp. 424–31, who are also sceptical about the importance of abortion.

an excellent example.[29] Mary Poor spent all her life in New England or New York; she was born in 1820 and married at 21 in 1841 a man eight years her senior. Between 1842 and 1863 she had seven children (when Mary was 22, 24, 28, 33, 35, 40 and 41) and two miscarriages (at age 31 and 43). Mary was both fecund and sexually active for a period of 27 years between 1841 and 1868. Within Mary Poor's birth history there are three periods of 43, 45 and 41 months in which she did not conceive, but was sexually active throughout even in the middle of her menstrual cycle at about the time of ovulation. There is no evidence, therefore, of sexual abstinence, but clearly some form of contraception was in use. There is some sign from her diary that Mary frequently resorted to vaginal douching and that she extended the duration of breastfeeding to 13–16 months for the higher parity births, although menstruation resumed after 5–10 months. There is no other direct evidence about how the Poors managed to achieve such long birth intervals. Henry Poor may have used condoms or *coitus interruptus*, but this cannot be known. Until the birth of their sixth child, when Mary was 40, it appears that the Poors were attempting to space their children. Thereafter it is clear that Mary wanted no more pregnancies – the Poors turned from being 'spacers' to 'stoppers' for reasons of age and health as much as parity.[30]

Of course Mary Poor was exceptional in many ways – the detail of her diary, for instance – but her fertility was not untypical of middle-class America or Britain, nor was her desire for contraception to control the number of pregnancies, her obvious love for and continuing sexual intimacy with her husband, and her ignorance of the true 'safe period'. While telling us so much about sexuality, emotions and behaviour ultimately Mary Poor still leaves us guessing about the means of contraception adopted.

Coale and Trussell: *stopping or spacing?*

Since the pioneering work of Louis Henry in the 1950s demographers have been encouraged not only to elaborate his concept of 'natural fertility' in a variety of subtle ways and to attempt the quantification of its various manifestations, but also to select standard fertility schedules against which to measure its absence.[31] In the case of model fertility schedules, the work of Coale and Trussell has defined the field of

---

[29] Brodie (1994), especially chapter 1, 'A story of love and family limitation: "X" for sexual intercourse'.

[30] Of the seven children born, only four survived to adulthood: the third child died at 9 months, the fourth at 19 years and the seventh at 7 years.

[31] See, for example, the work of Knodel (1977a, 1978, 1983).

research both in terms of the identification of regular patterns in age-specific marital fertility and in the measurement of the extent of deliberate fertility control via a small number of parameters.[32] They used both the concept of 'natural fertility' and the regularity in marital fertility curves if voluntary birth control is not practised in a parity-specific way (i.e. no stopping behaviour) to define the following model:

$$r(a)/n(a) = M \exp (m \bullet v(a)) \tag{4.1}$$

where $n(a)$ is a schedule of natural fertility given by age-group (a) specific marital fertility rates, this being the standard for the model against which the fertility of other populations is compared; $r(a)$ is the fertility schedule for just such a population; M is a scale factor expressing the ratio $r(a)/n(a)$ at some arbitrarily chosen age; m is a constant expressing the extent of voluntary fertility control (index of family limitation) although it may also be given in the form of an age-related function ($m(a)$); and the function $v(a)$ 'expresses the tendency for older women in populations practising contraception or abortion to effect particularly large reductions of fertility below the natural level'.[33]

Of course, Coale and Trussell realised that if a standard fertility schedule could be chosen for $n(a)$ and one for $r(a)$ then by setting $M = r(20-24)/n(20-24)$ and letting $m = 1$, a further standard for $v(a)$ could be derived as follows:

$$vS(a) = ln \, [rS(a)/(M \bullet nS(a))] \tag{4.2}$$

where S has been inserted to denote a standard schedule so that $nS(a)$ represents natural fertility, $rS(a)$ reflects controlled fertility, $vS(a)$ gives the logarithmic departure of $rS(a)$ from $nS(a)$, M captures the general level of fertility and m the extent of fertility control.

So far so good, but to extend the scope of the model so that M and m may be estimated for particular non-standard populations ($r(a)$ varies, but $nS(a)$ and $vS(a)$ are retained), the following seven problems have to be resolved.

1. A standard natural fertility schedule ($nS(a)$) needs to be selected. Coale and Trussell derived their $nS(a)$ by averaging 10 of the 13 fertility schedules reported by Henry as reflecting natural fertility.[34] The range is shown in figure 4.4 together with $nS(a)$.
2. A standard schedule of voluntarily controlled fertility ($rS(a)$) also has to be selected. Again, Coale and Trussell solve this problem by averaging 43 selected empirical age-specific marital fertility schedules,

---

[32] Coale and Trussell (1974, 1975, 1978). See also Okun (1994) and Xie and Pimental (1992).
[33] Coale and Trussell (1974), p. 188.   [34] Henry (1961), table 1, p. 84.

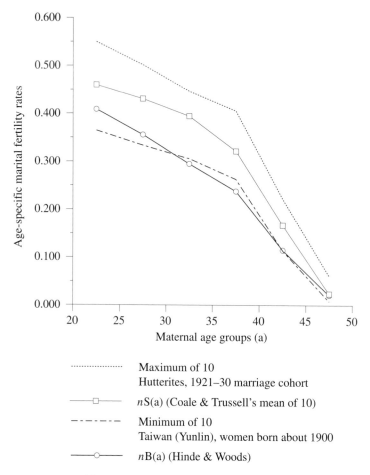

Figure 4.4. Examples of natural fertility

this time drawn from the United Nations *Demographic Yearbook* for 1965. Although the resulting *r*S(a) clearly reflects a high degree of fertility control, a number of the 43 schedules from which it was derived are far closer in shape to the curve for Taiwan shown in figure 4.4, including that for the Republic of Ireland in 1961. In other words, *r*S(a) is not an average of only non-natural fertility schedules in the way that *n*S(a) is an average of only natural fertility schedules.

3. The standard schedule expressing departure from natural fertility (*v*S(a)) is also needed, but this can be estimated from equation 4.2 once *n*S(a) and *r*S(a) are known and M has been assumed.

4. The scale factor M is normally found from $rS(20\text{–}24)/nS(20\text{–}24)$, but M may also be estimated by least squares linear regression.
5. A means of estimating m must be found. Coale and Trussell suggest three possibilities, but only two will be considered further here.[35] One method is to find M as in 4 and to substitute its value in:

$$m(a) = ln\ [r(a)/(M \bullet nS(a))]/vS(a). \tag{4.3}$$

The values of $m(a)$ may then be averaged to give a single number estimate of m. A second possibility, and the one preferred by Coale and Trussell, is to use equation 4.1 in the following form:

$$ln\ [r(a)/nS(a)] = ln\ M + (m \bullet vS(a)) \tag{4.4}$$

as the basis for a regression model $(y = c + (m \bullet x))$ in which $ln\ [r(a)/nS(a)] = y$, $ln\ M = c$ and $vS(a) = x$. Now both M and m are found by means of regression, and the former is not a fixed ratio as in 4.
6. It is also necessary to determine upon a statistic for expressing goodness of fit between the $r(a)/nS(a)$ discrepancy and $vS(a)$. Coale and Trussell recommend the mean square error calculated over the age groups 20–24 to 40–44.
7. If it is intended to use the model to assess fertility control, it will also be important to consider whether there are critical values of at least m which would establish that $r(a)$ is sufficiently different from $nS(a)$ that it may be judged the result of reproductive behaviour consistent with voluntary fertility control. Coale and Trussell suggest that 'any value of m less than 0.2 can be taken as evidence of no control', this with their $nS(a)$ and $vS(a)$ as defined in 1 and 3, respectively. But Guinnane *et al.* argue that 'the Coale–Trussell method cannot be used to distinguish pretransition populations with a minority of birth controllers from those in which birth control is absent. Moreover, even a substantial increase in m from near-zero levels cannot be interpreted safely as the introduction of a *new* behaviour.'[36]

It is important to emphasise that decisions on each of these seven points must be made before the model can be deployed. This being so, it may be something of a surprise that the Coale and Trussell model has achieved such widespread acceptance as a device for identifying populations beginning to control their fertility.

[35] Coale and Trussell (1978), p. 203.
[36] Guinnane *et al.* (1994), quoted from p. 13. Figure 4.6 shows that when m is 0.2, Ig is likely to be about 0.6. It has also been suggested that levels of Ig greater than 0.6 are likely to indicate the absence of deliberate fertility control within marriage. These problems are also considered in Guinnane (1997), especially chapter 8. Guinnane appears to be willing to use an Ig reduction of greater than 10 per cent as an indicator of significant fertility decline (p. 251).

In Hinde and Woods's development of the model they sought to define a particular standard natural fertility schedule, one that would be of special value in the analysis of British historical fertility patterns.[37] They specified a British standard ($nB(a)$) using age-specific marital fertility estimates derived from English family reconstitution studies for the parish register period (in this case especially 1650–1799) in combination with a schedule for Scotland in 1855. The principal reason for adopting this new $nB(a)$ was that by continental European standards England probably experienced an especially low form of natural fertility up to the last quarter of the nineteenth century and that to adopt Coale and Trussell's $nS(a)$ would have been to set British fertility an unreasonably high level standard from which to decline. The point is illustrated in figure 4.4 where $nB(a)$ is shown to lie close to the lowest of the ten schedules averaged by Coale and Trussell. The logic of this argument still appears impeccable even though far more is now known about legitimate fertility in England in the sixteenth, seventeenth and eighteenth centuries.[38] The revised basis for 1 still holds.

In order to pursue the development of a new model it was also necessary to define a new $rB(a)$ to indicate the pattern of voluntarily controlled fertility towards which marital fertility in England and Wales might be reduced. Somewhat counter to the spirit of the Coale–Trussell model, Hinde and Woods originally solved problem 2 by using schedules for just one country – Denmark. They summarised the Danish fertility transition between 1860–64 and 1940–44 in such a way that data for Copenhagen, urban non-metropolitan Denmark and rural Denmark were given equal weight. The resulting $r(a)$ showed a pattern of fertility which one might expect to have found in Britain in the early decades of the twentieth century. Fertility decline was evident compared with $nB(a)$, but compared with Coale and Trussell's $rS(a)$, fertility reduction still had some way to go.[39]

It now seems appropriate to reconsider Hinde and Woods's choice of $rS(a)$. Ideally, what is required is a fertility schedule that reflects strong voluntary control in the English population itself. Unfortunately, this is not a simple matter since we lack the ability to calculate directly age-specific marital fertility rates for England and Wales as a whole before 1938, and after the Second World War legitimate fertility passed through a series of cyclical phases in which, although the fertility of women aged 35 and over continued to decline, that of women in their twenties and

[37] Hinde and Woods (1984). See also Anderson (1998a), especially pp. 11–12, for a detailed discussion of the relative merits of the Coale–Trussell and British standards.
[38] Wilson and Woods (1991), Wrigley *et al.* (1997), pp. 354–511, and Wrigley (1998).
[39] See the Ig/Im timepath for Denmark shown in figure 3.3.

early thirties was often higher than it had been in the 1930s.[40] Any $rS(a)$ chosen from schedules for England and Wales in, for instance, the early 1960s would display accentuated concavity with high M and $m(a)$, but especially $m(40-49)$. In these circumstances the most obvious choice for $rB(a)$ would be England and Wales 1938. Age-specific marital fertility schedules for this year follow closely those for the 1930s in Sweden and Denmark; they avoid the effects of the war years and the post-war oscillations which were accompanied by increasing skewness in the distribution of maternal ages. Indeed, 1938 might be said to represent the end of the fertility transition in Britain, and for that matter Europe as a whole.

Table 4.2 gives the age-specific marital fertility schedule for England and Wales in 1938 as $rB(a)$ along with $nB(a)$ as originally defined by Hinde and Woods and the new $vB(a)$ estimated via equation 4.2.[41] These are also shown in figure 4.5. The new $vB(a)$ has the following advantages over that proposed in Hinde and Woods: its derivation is clear and obvious since $rB(a)$ is defined simply and is not an average of international experiences or of time periods; and it represents non-natural fertility effectively at the end of the process of fertility transition and before the start of substantial fertility swings and distortions due to the aftermath of the Second World War and the late-1940s baby boom.

The standards proposed in table 4.2 have the accompanying $M = 0.648$ and $m = 1.0$ values, but their calculation requires the solution of problems 4 and 5. In this case M is simply given by its ratio form, namely $r(a)/nB(a)$, and this is the general procedure recommended here in conjunction with the use of equation 4.3 to derive m from the average of $m(25-29)$ to $m(40-44)$. The regression method in equation 4.4 is rejected because it has the tendency to be especially susceptible to the influence of aberrant values for individual age-groups and because M found by the ratio method is both simple to calculate and easy to interpret compared with e^c from equation 4.4.

Problem 6 may be resolved not by using the mean square error, but by reviewing the variance of $m(a)$ over the four age-groups used to derive m. Again, this is a simple solution but one that deflects attention from the goodness of fit problem since it remains unclear what a poor

---

[40] It is interesting that Farr paid very little attention to fertility, but in one of his last publications read before the Royal Society on 29 January 1880 he turned to the question of age-specific fertility rates: 'It is to be regretted that the mother's age at the birth of her child is not yet included in the particulars recorded in the English birth registers' (Farr, 1880, p. 281).

[41] Office of Population Censuses and Surveys, *Birth Statistics: Historical Series of Statistics from Registration of Births in England and Wales, 1837–1983*, Series FM1 No. 13 (London: HMSO, 1987), table 3.2, p. 55.

Table 4.2. *British standard fertility schedules and age-specific marital fertility rates for England and Wales*

Maternal age groups (a)	British fertility standard nB(a)	England & Wales 1938 rB(a)	vB(a)	England 1600–1824	England 1800–24	1851	1861	1871	Farr's estimate for 1871	1881	1891	1901	1911	1922	1933
20–24	0.409	0.265	0.000	0.411	0.425	0.426	0.426	0.428	0.396	0.424	0.418	0.408	0.402	0.365	0.275
25–29	0.356	0.171	−0.301	0.366	0.381	0.367	0.363	0.367	0.367	0.361	0.345	0.320	0.294	0.247	0.178
30–34	0.295	0.110	−0.552	0.313	0.311	0.306	0.300	0.308	0.316	0.298	0.271	0.241	0.206	0.163	0.108
35–39	0.238	0.059	−0.959	0.246	0.255	0.249	0.239	0.249	0.257	0.237	0.208	0.173	0.135	0.098	0.059
40–44	0.115	0.020	−1.322	0.130	0.142	0.120	0.112	0.120	0.149	0.112	0.096	0.076	0.053	0.033	0.020
45–49	0.021	0.002	−1.946	0.021	0.019	0.018	0.018	0.018	0.042	0.016	0.012	0.008	0.006	0.004	0.002
TMFR (20–49)	7.17	3.14		7.44	7.67	7.43	7.29	7.45	7.64	7.24	6.75	6.13	5.48	4.55	3.21
M		0.648	1.000	1.005	1.039	1.042	1.042	1.046	0.968	1.037	1.022	0.998	0.983	0.892	0.672
m		1.000		−0.073	−0.072	0.010	0.052	0.013	−0.181	0.052	0.171	0.338	0.586	0.843	1.036
Ig				0.666	0.668	0.675	0.670	0.686		0.674	0.621	0.553	0.467	0.375	0.292

Notes:
The derivation of $nB(a)$ is given in Hinde and Woods (1984); $rB(a)$ is the age-specific marital fertility schedule for England and Wales, 1938 from Office of Population Censuses and Surveys (1987), table 3.2, p. 55; and $vB(a)$ is estimated by equation 4.2. TMFR is the total marital fertility rate for ages 20–49. M and m are estimated using the British fertility standard.

Sources: England – Wrigley et al. (1997), table 7.1, p. 355; 1851–1933 for England and Wales – estimates from Registrar General's *Statistical Review for 1938 and 1939* (London: HMSO, 1947), table 4b, p. 237; and Farr 1871 – Farr (1880), p. 285. See text for explanation. The sources for lg are: England – Wilson and Woods (1991), appendix table; England and Wales – Teitelbaum (1984), table 6.1, p. 115. lgs for 1921 and 1931 are shown.

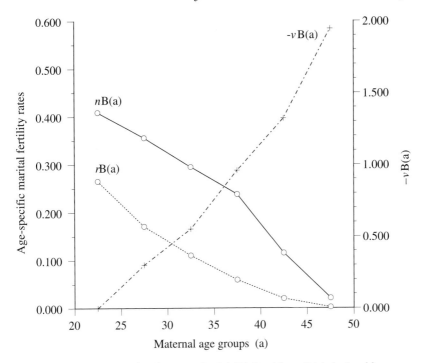

Figure 4.5. British fertility standard (nB(a)) with $-v$B(a) derived by letting rB(a) be the age-specific marital fertility schedule for England and Wales, 1938
Source: See table 4.2.

fit actually signifies other than that a particular r(a) has a distinctive shape, the result of period effects and for exceptional reasons.

Finally, problem 7 requires some attention. It would be useful to have a critical value for m even if, as Coale and Trussell argue, that value is taken as evidence of *no* control rather than of sufficient control for r(a) not to reflect natural fertility. When time-series of r(a) are available then the beginning of a continuous upward trend in m is probably all that is required, but when r(a)s for populations of occupations, social classes or places are being compared on a cross-sectional basis then considerable care is required if one wishes to determine a level of m that signifies fertility control. Also, as Okun has recently pointed out, m may not be especially sensitive if only a minority of married couples are controlling their fertility.[42] However, since this is an especially important problem some guidance on the approximate equivalence between

[42] Okun (1994), p. 222.

fertility control measures may be of value. Figure 4.6 provides a very general and rather over-simplified graphical guide to the correspondence between m, Ig and the percentage of married women practising contraception.[43] In broad terms one would expect the three measures to be related: as the percentage of married women practising contraception increases so the extent of family limitation will increase and marital fertility will decline. But the associations are not perfect. Figure 4.6 is only a rough guide to the correspondence, therefore. For example, if Ig is about 0.6 then it might be expected that m would be approximately 0.3 and the percentage practising contraception perhaps 35 assuming, of course, that the Swedish and Thai experiences upon which figure 4.6 is based were representative.

Alongside the British fertility standard, table 4.2 also reports age-specific marital fertility rates for England 1600–1824 and 1800–24 derived from family reconstitution data together with estimates of marital fertility rates for England and Wales 1851–1933, including Farr's estimates for 1871.[44] It shows the total marital fertility rate (TMFR), M, m and Ig.

We are now in a position to consider the changing pattern of marital fertility based on the Registrar General's estimates and a number of other examples drawn from family reconstitution studies. For instance, Reay has calculated the age-specific marital fertility rates for three Kent parishes.[45] He gives these by four marriage cohorts – 1800–34, 1835–49, 1850–64 and 1865–80 – and estimates M and m in the conventional way outlined by Coale and Trussell. He also makes adjustments for non-marital fertility. Table 4.3 gives Reay's $r(a)$s, his unadjusted Ms and ms together with the Ms and ms that would be found by using $nB(a)$ and $vB(a)$. Reay follows Knodel's advice that 'steady rises in the value of m . . . are almost certainly indications of increasing practice of family limitation even though each successive increment was often small in size' and argues on the basis of rising m and M that 'the early stages of the transition to fertility control were carried out in these rural parishes

---

[43] Figure 4.6 is based on the experience of Sweden (m and Ig) and Thailand (m and percentage contracepting). It also charts what may have been the experience of England and Wales as summarised by the measures in table 4.2. See van de Walle and Knodel (1980), figures 6 and 9.

[44] See Wrigley *et al.* (1997), p. 355; Registrar General's *Statistical Review for 1938 and 1939* (1947), p. 237; and Farr (1880), p. 285. Since the Registrar General's estimates only deal with female births they have been inflated by 2.04 to allow for the sex ratio at birth. They are heavily influenced by the schedule for Scotland 1855, but Farr chose to use Norway 1871–72 as his guide for the reallocation of legitimate births to married women arranged by age groups, although he did compare Scotland with Norway, Sweden and Denmark.   [45] Reay (1994, 1996), chapter 2.

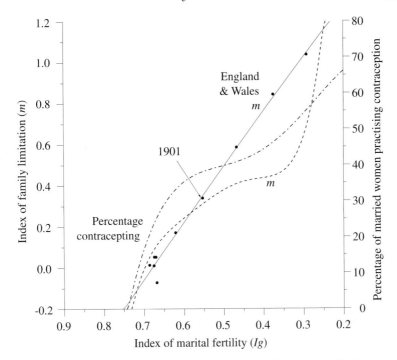

Figure 4.6. Generalised relationships between the index of family
limitation (*m*), the percentage of married women practising contraception, and
the index of marital fertility (*Ig*), based on the experiences of Sweden and
Thailand
Note: The experience of England and Wales in the nineteenth and early
twentieth centuries is also shown for *m* against *Ig*.
Sources: Sweden and Thailand – van de Walle and Knodel (1980), figures 6 and
9; England and Wales – table 4.2.

. . . in the face of an increasing natural fecundity'.[46] The use of *n*B(a) and
*v*B(a) tells a different story, or no story at all. The overall level of marital
fertility did increase a little in these Kent parishes in the nineteenth
century as judged by *M*, and *m* did increase a little, but compared with
the British standard this was still probably natural fertility (see table 4.3
and figure 4.7). Figure 4.7 also shows age-specific marital fertility rates
for the 1647–1719 marriage cohort of Colyton, Devon,[47] and the 1875–99
marriage cohort of fourteen German villages in combination.[48] In
neither case and when compared with *n*B(a) is there strong evidence for

---

[46] Reay (1994), pp. 102 and 107, Knodel (1978), p. 489.
[47] Wrigley (1987), table 10.4, p. 250, as well as Wrigley (1978).
[48] Knodel (1988), table 10.2, p. 257.

Table 4.3. *Age-specific marital fertility schedules (r(a)) for three Kent parishes*

Maternal age groups (a)	r(a) for marriage cohorts			
	1800–34	1835–49	1850–64	1865–80
20–24	0.429	0.474	0.481	0.506
25–29	0.412	0.380	0.361	0.413
30–34	0.355	0.334	0.315	0.316
35–39	0.275	0.282	0.260	0.205
40–44	0.184	0.154	0.162	0.112
45–49	0.038	0.017	0.020	0.018
M	0.93	1.03	1.05	1.10
m	−0.08	0.26	0.33	0.41
Adjusted m	−0.19	0.11	0.22	0.26
M using $r(20–24)/nB(20–24)$	1.049	1.159	1.176	1.237
m using $nB(a)$	−0.249	0.046	0.152	0.258

Source: Reay (1994), tables 3, 5 and 7; Reay (1996), table 2.7.

voluntary family limitation of a parity-specific kind consistent with the absence of natural fertility. The same could also be said of the fertility of the British Quakers recently considered by Vann and Eversley.[49] In each of these four cases the presence of natural fertility is confirmed by employing more realistic $nS(a)$ and $rS(a)$s. This conclusion must still hold even if one accepts that there may have been a minority of fertility controllers in each of the populations.[50]

By now there may be reason to think that the Coale–Trussell model has outlived its usefulness and even that the very concept of natural fertility needs to be abandoned in the light of its failure to distinguish those populations in which birth-spacing is practised as a deliberate means to family limitation; those in which birth-spacing is an indirect consequence of prolonged lactation, for instance; and those perhaps transitional populations in which birth-spacers are mixed up among parity-specific birth controllers. How low may age-specific marital fertility rates be before they fail to reflect natural fertility? Is there a dis-

---

[49] Vann and Eversley (1992), pp. 178–85.

[50] See Guinnane *et al.* (1994), also Friedlander and Okun (1995, 1996) who tackle the same problem using *Ig*. Friedlander and Okun (1996) argue on the basis of the distribution of *Ig* among registration districts that 'a substantial proportion of districts experienced pretransition variations in marital fertility that were so large that they are suggestive of deliberate fertility control'. (p. 1) But as figures 4.18 and 4.19 will indicate, a more realistic interpretation would emphasise the variability of natural fertility in England and Wales in the 1850s and 1860s rather than the presence of deliberate control.

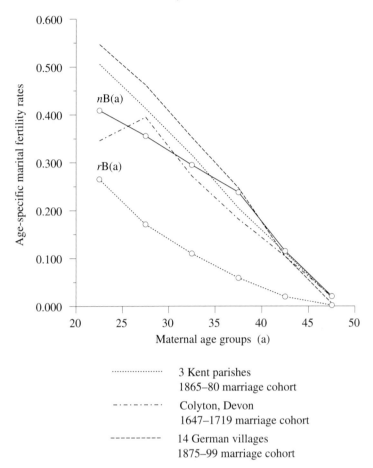

Figure 4.7. British fertility standards (nB(a) and rB(a)) compared with fertility schedules drawn from selected marriage cohorts for three Kent parishes; Colyton, Devon; and 14 German villages

cernible sequence through which schedules pass during a transition to low and controlled fertility? For example, imagine 35 to be the pivotal age: 20–34 is A and 35–49 is B. A and B form a smooth concave curve (i) or a straight line (ii); either way the absence of parity-specific control ensures natural fertility, but in (ii) there may be some effective, even deliberate, birth-spacing and the total fertility produced by (ii) will be less than that produced by (i). Relative decline in B accelerates faster than in A creating a degree of disjuncture in the curve, and in phase (iii) takes on a concave shape. Finally, A increases, but B remains at a very low, almost negligible, level (iv).

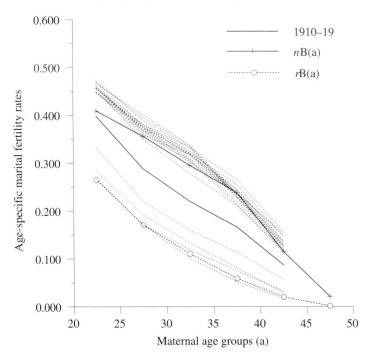

Figure 4.8. Age-specific marital fertility schedules for Sweden, 1750–59
to 1950–59
Note: Schedules for 26 decades are shown and that for 1910–19 is emphasised.

There are very few European countries for which the complete sequence of phases has been recorded from (i) or (ii) to (iii) and then (iv) – although (iii) to (iv) is normally obvious since it occurred after the Second World War. However, Sweden provides an interesting exception which, because it can be documented using reliable registration data, may also help us to judge the value of the evidence summarised in table 4.2 for England and Wales.[51] The experience of Sweden, 1751–60 to 1951–60, is shown in figure 4.8; and in more detail for 1871–80 to 1931–40, in indexed form in figure 4.9. Marital fertility in the eighteenth and nineteenth centuries was clearly of a form consistent with natural fertility, with rates lying close to, but usually in excess of, those in nB(a). By the first decade of the twentieth century fertility had begun to fall especially among women in their early thirties, but the general shape of the curve clearly still indicates natural fertility. During the second, third

[51] The experience of fertility decline in the Republic of Ireland since the 1950s also offers an analogous case of parallel retreat.

and even fourth decades, marital fertility was in sharp decline although once again the general shape of the curve was preserved. Indeed, the geometry of the sequence is reminiscent of what geomorphologists working on slope profiles have termed 'parallel retreat'.[52] However, the indexed numbers in figure 4.9 give a stronger sense of greater decline at higher maternal ages, especially from the 1890s, but still the sharp fall in marital fertility is clear for each age group above and including 20–24. By the 1950s the schedule for Sweden approximated that of rB(a): it was distinctly concave in shape and m exceeded 1.0.

It is now possible to return to table 4.2 and the evidence presented for England and Wales. First, and as figure 4.10 neatly illustrates, the Registrar General's estimates and the pooled family reconstitutions reported by Wrigley *et al.* appear to tell the same story about the pattern of marital fertility in England before the mid-nineteenth century. Although there were some relatively small changes in level, the general structure indicative of natural fertility did not change. In terms of the standard indices, TMFR was at or about 7.44 (6.90 to 7.67); m was close to zero; Ig varied about 0.650; and the proportion of couples permanently sterile is likely to have been greater than the proportion deliberately attempting some form of contraception. Secondly, during the third quarter of the nineteenth century marital fertility rates began to decline in every maternal age group except 20–24. But by 1891 there is clear evidence of widespread family limitation, although the curves in figure 4.6 imply that no more than perhaps 30 or 40 per cent of married women might be said to be active contraceptors at that time. By 1911 the progress of the fertility transition is unmistakable and irreversible. Thirdly, the evidence presented in table 4.2 and figure 4.10 appears to indicate that spacing and stopping behaviour were not alternatives; couples spaced and stopped, but in general it was not until the 1920s and 1930s that couples appear to have attempted to avoid or postpone the first birth, although it must also be remembered that many of those first births would have been conceived before marriage.[53]

How does the experience of Mary Poor relate to these aggregate fertility curves and their associated models? Mary's reproductive behaviour also involved neither spacing nor stopping while she was in her early twenties; but there was spacing in her late twenties and thirties; and stopping in her forties. This would appear to fit rather well the patterns shown for Sweden in figures 4.8 and 4.9. Here again the Poors illustrate

---

[52] Knodel (1977a), figures 1 and 3, shows indexed ASMFRs where the rate for age group 20–24 is set at 100. 'Parallel retreat' is less easy to distinguish when these indexed rates are compared.

[53] See especially Garrett and Reid (1996) and Garrett *et al.* (forthcoming).

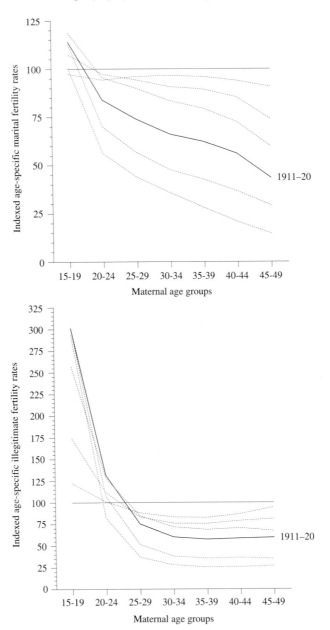

Figure 4.9. Indexed (1871–80 = 100) age-specific marital and
illegitimate fertility rates, Sweden, 1871–80 to 1931–40
Note: The decade 1911–20 is emphasised.
Source: Shorter, Knodel and van de Walle (1971), table 1, p. 384.

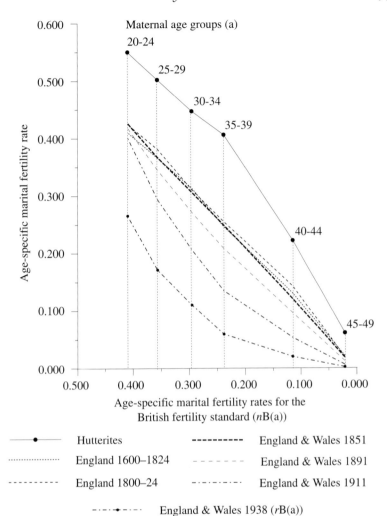

Figure 4.10. The relationship between selected age-specific marital fertility schedules and the British fertility standard
Note: See text for explanation.
Source: See table 4.2.

the point that spacing and stopping were not alternatives, rather they were practised by couples in different age groups and who in consequence were likely to have had different parities. Henry's 'natural fertility', as has often been pointed out, does not distinguish deliberate spacing, *à la* the Poors, from the extension of birth intervals as an unanticipated consequence of other forms of behaviour. This is the very problem faced by Reay and his Kent parishes, for although the adjusted *m* for the 1865–80 marriage cohort was 0.26, by figure 4.6 this might suggest that *Ig* was still close to 0.6 and that perhaps 25 to 30 per cent of married women were practising contraception. If this were so, it would certainly be via spacing rather than stopping. In Reay's argument the gradual increase in *m* between marriage cohorts provides evidence for 'a series of adjustments within the natural fertility regime until family limitation began to dominate', stretching back to the early nineteenth century with no sudden changes in behaviour in the 1870s or 1880s.[54] But it is still not clear whether this was the result of deliberate behaviour or some unintended consequence. Certainly Reay and others are justified in emphasising spacing, in being sceptical about the ability of the Coale–Trussell model to distinguish the outcome of behavioural changes within natural fertility, and in rejecting 'the new stopping behaviour' as *the* key defining characteristic of the Victorian fertility transition.[55]

Illegitimate fertility

A further perspective on the effectiveness of birth control in the Victorian period will be gained if it is assumed that illegitimate births were unwanted and would have been avoided had the means been available or thought appropriate. In the terms adopted above, this would mean 'starting by stopping'. Variations in illegitimate fertility in England and Wales between 1861 and 1911 have already been considered in chapter 3 in terms of the possible influence of nuptiality on illegitimacy, *Im* on *Ih*. This earlier discussion reflects more closely the approach taken by social historians and social anthropologists who see bastardy more as a reflection of a particular set of cultural values. Laslett's famous phrase 'the bastardy prone sub-society' sits alongside

---

[54] Reay (1996), p. 67.
[55] Szreter (1996), pp. 377–89, using the evidence of incomplete fertility among recently married couples in the 1911 Census of Fertility, has also emphasised the importance of spacing in early marriage for many occupations, as has Garrett (1990) in her work on the textile town of Keighley and with the anonymised sample from the 1911 fertility census; see Garrett and Reid (1996), p. 98, Garrett *et al.* (forthcoming).

attempts to understand why in some societies bastardy was almost con-
doned whilst in others unmarried mothers were obliged to abandon
their infants to the care of foundling hospitals.[56] Here we shall take a
rather more demographic line by asking whether the rapid decline in
European illegitimate fertility, a decline which largely coincided with
the decline of marital fertility, implies a substantial increase in the
knowledge of how to control fertility in general and an increase in the
technical ability to apply it. This question reflects the position taken by
Shorter, Knodel and van de Walle in their account of Ih variations in
nineteenth-century Europe. For example, 'one might argue that marital
and non-marital fertility sank at the same time, because both married
and unmarried people resolved to reduce the likelihood that intercourse
would lead to a conception', and 'There is no lack of motivation outside
marriage. What may exist instead is a lack of knowledge and of means
of contraception.'[57]

Figure 4.9 showed the pattern of change in the indexed age-specific
illegitimate fertility rates for Sweden alongside those for marital fertility. In Sweden the illegitimate fertility rate for women in the age groups
25–29 to 45–49 declined substantially and almost equally in each decade
after 1871–80. Only among younger women, especially those in their
teens, did illegitimate fertility increase very dramatically. But the fertility of all Swedish women aged 15–19, whether married or unmarried,
increased in the late nineteenth and early twentieth centuries which
may have more to do with the retreat of tuberculosis and the increase in
fecundity among young women than sexual activity *per se*. Among
older Swedish women, fertility was being controlled more and more
effectively with spacing and stopping for the married, and stopping for
the unmarried. The young sexually active spinsters were probably, as
Shorter *et al.* have suggested, less knowledgeable and certainly more
inexperienced than older women in the arts of contraception.[58]

It is tempting to read too much into figure 4.9, especially when compared with the data available for Victorian England and Wales where
only the illegitimacy ratio and Ih can be calculated.[59] However, some
consideration of variations in Ih among the districts, particularly when
this can be done in conjunction with Ig, may help to develop the various

---

[56] Laslett *et al.* (1980), especially chapters 1 and 8, on the 'Bastardy prone sub-society', by
Laslett.
[57] Shorter *et al.* (1971), quoted from pp. 382 and 385. Schellekens (1995) offers a test of the
Shorter, Knodel and van de Walle hypothesis, but prefers to interpret declining illegitimate fertility principally in terms of rising working-class living standards and the
general decline of agricultural labour.   [58] Shorter *et al.* (1971), p. 385.
[59] Laslett *et al.* (1980), table 1.6, pp. 34–35, reports illegitimacy ratios for English counties
in 1870–72, 1880–82, 1890–92 and 1900–2.

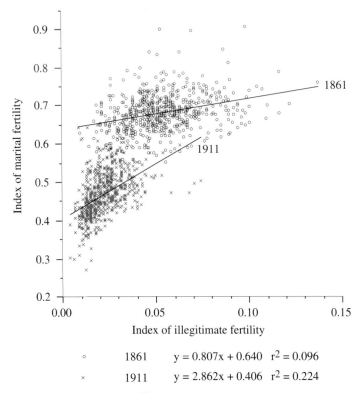

Figure 4.11. The changing relationship between *Ig* and *Ih*, English and Welsh districts, 1861 and 1911

arguments further. Figure 4.11 plots the joint variation of *Ig* and *Ih* among English and Welsh districts in 1861 and 1911, and figure 4.12 (colour section, page *c*) illustrates the changing spatial variation in *Ih*.

Figure 4.11 illustrates several important points. First, the association between marital and illegitimate fertility, *Ig* and *Ih*, was positive but weak in 1861. By 1891 (not shown) and especially by 1911, it was far stronger; both the correlation and *beta* coefficients increased substantially as *Ig* and *Ih* declined together. In terms of the geographical distribution of *Ih*, figure 4.12 shows that illegitimate fertility was relatively high in East Anglia (especially Norfolk), Lincolnshire, east Yorkshire, the northern Pennines and Cumbria, and mid-Wales, but that these regional clusters were hardly discernible by 1911. It seems most likely, as Shorter *et al.* have argued, that those forces responsible for the decline of marital fertility were also involved in the reduction of non-marital fertility. The evidence presented in figures 4.11 and 4.12 is at least consistent with the notion that knowledge about and perhaps also the means of contraception became more widely available towards the end of the nineteenth century.

Demographic balance

The decline of marital fertility during the late nineteenth century may also be viewed as a matter of maintaining demographic balance: as infant and childhood mortality decline, so couples adjust their fertility to keep in step.[60] The evidence on this matter is, once again, unclear. First, as will be shown in chapter 7, there was no secular decline in national infant mortality rates until the turn of the century. Declining infant mortality could not have stimulated a move to lower marital fertility, although its eventual rapid decline would have accelerated or reinforced the desire to restrict fertility in the twentieth century. In the mid-nineteenth century, cross-sectional associations between infant mortality and marital fertility among registration districts were not statistically significant. However, it is also clear that early childhood mortality (ages 1–4 in completed years, but especially ages 2–4) did decline very substantially from the 1860s and that this would have improved the child survival rate and thus the prospect that once a child had reached its second birthday, he or she stood a very good and improving chance of surviving into adulthood.

Secondly, it has already been shown in figures 4.1 and 4.2 that effective average parity (surviving children per couple) varied in different marriage cohorts and occupations in ways that suggest a constant association between effective average parity and average parity (children born per couple) among the 200 occupations reported in the 1911 *Census of Fertility*. The figures in table 4.4 confirm that effective average parity and average parity (B and A) are so related. The relationship between average parity and the child death ratio (children reported to have died as a proportion of live-born children) is shown in the bottom panel of table 4.4 (A and C). Although the associations are highly significant, in all cases they are not very strong. Two additional speculations suggest themselves. First, as fertility declines between marriage durations, the strength of the association tends to increase, as does the effect of the child death ratio on average parity. Secondly, this latter effect also varies with age at marriage; average parity responds more

---

[60] See the contributions to Preston (1977). Francine van de Walle (1986) is inconclusive on the matter of whether a prior decline in infant mortality is a sufficient and necessary precondition for the decline of marital fertility.

quickly to differences in the child death ratio for women who married in their early twenties rather than their late twenties. In short, table 4.4 indicates that the association between fertility and the sum of infant and early childhood mortality (ages 0–4) is significantly positive yet weak, but that the association grew stronger and its slope steeper as fertility declined, or when women married younger. It is certainly inadvisable to make too much of this evidence; not only were the causal links not strong but they were also two-way. It is possible, indeed most likely, that declining marital fertility encouraged the decline of infant mortality, since the initial inefficient use of non-appliance methods of birth control would have tended to lengthen birth intervals and thereby reduce the possibility of infant loss through neglect or the disruption of breast-feeding.[61] Without individual-level data it is unlikely that these partic-ular lines of enquiry can be taken much further.[62]

Preconditions

The final theoretical approach to be considered here is even more broadly based than the others. It sees the decline of marital fertility as a consequence of the transformation of social attitudes, especially as they relate to family limitation. The first element of Ansley J. Coale's tri-partite definition of the preconditions necessary for a sustained decline in marital fertility deals with this point. 'Fertility must be within the cal-culus of conscious choice. Potential parents must consider it an accept-able mode of thought and form of behaviour to balance advantages and disadvantages before deciding to have another child.'[63] Setting aside for the time being both the question of balancing behaviour and the rela-tionship between this and the other two preconditions, let us focus on how the 'calculus of conscious choice' might be changed. There would seem to be at least four possibilities: changes in moral beliefs stemming from secularisation; the effects of mass education; the rise of feminism; and the role of organised propaganda.

Since there was general rejection of birth control and family planning in the teachings of all Christian denominations during the nineteenth century, the notion of secularisation has been used widely in European fertility studies to express the abandonment of those particular prac-tices. The variable is often measured through church attendance or

---

[61] See chapter 7, pp. 295–300.
[62] Knodel (1982) has suggested that the replacement effect post-dates the onset of family limitation (stopping effect), but that 'couples with the most favourable child mortality experience were most likely to adopt family limitation and to reduce their fertility' (p. 200).   [63] Coale (1973), quoted from p. 65.

Table 4.4. *Associations between average and effective parities of women aged 45 and over in 1911 based on 200 occupations in the 1911 Census of Fertility*

	Marriage age 20–24, duration of marriage in years			Marriage age 25–29, duration of marriage in years		
	30–39	25–29	20–24	30–39	25–29	20–24
Average parity (A)						
Mean	6.2	5.5	4.8	4.7	4.1	3.8
Standard deviation	0.82	0.96	0.92	0.54	0.62	0.64
Range	4.1–8.0	3.2–7.6	2.6–6.9	3.3–7.2	2.5–5.6	2.0–5.3
Effective average parity (B)						
Mean	4.7	4.3	3.6	3.6	3.3	3.0
Standard deviation	0.53	0.64	0.64	0.37	0.43	0.45
Range	3.2–6.0	2.7–5.8	2.1–5.2	2.4–4.8	2.1–4.4	1.6–4.1
Child deaths ratio (C)						
Mean	0.24	0.22	0.20	0.24	0.21	0.20
Standard deviation	0.04	0.04	0.04	0.04	0.04	0.04
Range	0.14–0.35	0.10–0.31	0.09–0.32	0.12–0.34	0.11–0.32	0.09–0.31
B with A						
r^2	0.850	0.918	0.935	0.758	0.876	0.905
alpha	0.956	0.761	0.559	0.804	0.583	0.505
beta	0.599	0.639	0.679	0.590	0.644	0.664
A with C						
r^2	0.313	0.412	0.331	0.204	0.293	0.318
alpha	3.358	2.318	2.283	3.351	2.434	2.102
beta	11.533	14.647	12.636	5.655	8.037	8.334

Source: 1911 Census of Fertility, *Fertility of Marriage, Part II* (1923), table XXXV.

anti-clericalism. Whilst the logic of this argument is obvious, there are certain problems associated with its deployment. First, rejection of church membership does not necessarily imply that the entire moral code will be abandoned; nor, conversely, does it imply that the practical implications of the code are always honoured by committed church members. For example, the 1911 *Census of Fertility* shows that the fertility of clergymen's wives in the established Church of England was towards the low side of the distribution, certainly well below the average, and that it declined in step with that of other occupations.[64] Secondly, the point has been made in Banks's discussion of Victorian values that the belief systems of middle-class families were affected by secularism which, coupled with relative economic pressure, encouraged the limitation of family sizes. But '"unconscious" secularism did not result in any obvious change in the family belief system of the working class on any scale comparable to that of the middle class. For them, the flight from parenthood took place much later, after the middle class had developed its own new conception of parenthood.'[65] What influence did the church's teachings have on the sexual and reproductive behaviour of married couples in Britain in 1901 compared with 1851? Very little in either case, but probably even less at the end of the century than at its mid-point. If one turns to the evidence on church attendance – in the traditional manner of assessing secularisation – it is clear that the rate declined during the late nineteenth century while the proportion of marriages not solemnised in a place of religious worship increased from 2 per cent in 1841 to 23 per cent in 1913.[66] There is little reason to think that by the First World War any more than a small minority of married couples made a strong connection between religious observance and reproductive behaviour. English society was secular in deed if not in word throughout the nineteenth century.

   Economic theories of fertility decline tend to emphasise the increasing costs of child rearing, which was exacerbated for the middle class by the expense of private education, and for the working class by compulsory schooling, which delayed their children's entry into the workforce

---

[64] See Szreter (1996), appendix C, p. 608. The average parities for wives of clergymen of the Church of England (aged 45 and over in 1911) were:

		Marriage cohorts			
Age at marriage	1891–95	1886–90	1881–85	1871–80	1861–70
20–24		3.6	4.0	4.9	6.4
25–29	2.8	3.1	3.6	4.1	5.0

Compare with table 4.1 and the experience of doctors' wives in figure 4.3.

[65] Banks (1981), p. 10.

[66] On church attendance, see Curries *et al.* (1977), and on the percentage of civil marriages, see the Registrar General's *Annual Reports*.

and thus reduced their economic value as contributors to the household wage economy. The positive benefits of mass education are considered far less frequently in historical studies, although demographers specialising in African or Asian fertility have repeatedly emphasised the importance of maternal education for both cross-sectional and temporal variations in the level of childbearing and the quality of child care practices.

Figure 4.13 shows one of the more obvious consequences of developing mass education. In 1841 about half the brides who married in England and Wales could sign the marriage register with their name, but by 1901 over 90 per cent could sign. In many families neither husband nor wife could read or write in 1841, but once again in 1901 the proportion had declined substantially. It should not be necessary to emphasise the point that literacy cannot be defined in terms of the ability to sign one's name; there are varying degrees of competence which it is virtually impossible to assess for historical societies. However, the inability to sign one's name at one's own wedding is a sure sign of illiteracy and suggests the absence of any form of basic education, either public or private.[67]

It should be no surprise that literacy rates also varied substantially from district to district in England and Wales. Figure 4.14 (colour section, page *d*) illustrates the pattern in 1861 by showing variations in the percentage of brides who signed the marriage register in that year as well as the residuals from an orthogonal regression of female on male literacy rates. In the latter, those districts with positive residuals have higher literacy rates for females than males.[68] The geography of gender differentials in literacy is especially interesting.

What were the likely consequences of these dramatic changes and variations in literacy? The conventional argument is that improved literacy, especially among women, facilitates the spread and adoption of family planning methods. While this is undoubtedly so, even in the

---

[67] Schofield (1968, 1973).

[68] See Stephens (1987) for a detailed account of the geography of literacy in Victorian England. Vincent (1989), p. 25, also illustrates geographical variations in gender differentials among English counties. The residuals from orthogonal regression are estimated from the following equation:

$$resid_j = f_j - [sf/sm\,(m_j - M)] + F$$

where *resid*$_j$ is the residual for the jth district, f is the percentage of brides signing the marriage register (with F the mean over all districts), m is the percentage of grooms signing the marriage register (with M the mean), sf is the standard deviation of f, and sm the standard deviation of m. For 1861 F was 67.30, sf 13.07, M was 71.36 and sm 10.42. See Humphries (1991) for an application of this approach to gender differentials in mortality.

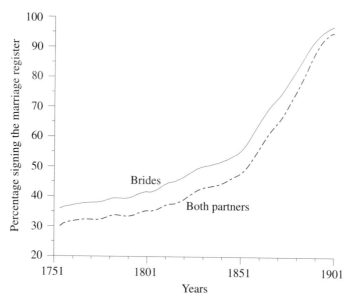

Figure 4.13. Percentage of partners signing the marriage register,
England, 1754–1901
Note: The series for 1754–1844 are based on parish register data kindly made
available by Dr Roger Schofield; the series for 1841–1901 apply to England
and Wales; the two series have been spliced together and smoothed.
Source: Cambridge Group and Registrar General's *Annual Reports.*

historical context, mass education was probably also effective in
implanting certain middle-class values and raising the confidence and
status of literate wives compared with their illiterate mothers. Caldwell
has developed some of these arguments at length, but from the perspective of contemporary fertility transitions. He asserts that 'It seems
improbable – and has yet to be demonstrated – that any society can
sustain stable high fertility beyond two generations of mass schooling',
and that in nearly all of northern Europe effective mass schooling was
achieved in the period 1870–90.[69] Figure 4.13 only serves to add
plausibility to these arguments, even to suggest that in terms of the
movement to full literacy the origins of the substantial changes pre-date
the 1870s by perhaps a generation.

The role feminism should take in an interpretation of the secular
decline of fertility depends very much on the way in which the term is
defined. *Feminism and Family Planning in Victorian England* is particu-

[69] Caldwell (1982), pp. 305 and 310.

larly narrow in its focus on the emancipation movement among middle-class women which, as J. and O. Banks clearly demonstrate, post-dated the fall in middle-class birth rates.[70] If, however, one focuses on the domestic scene and considers marital relationships as a theatre for conflict, allocation and conscious decision-making, then any alteration in the power of the wife to influence her husband would be of fundamental importance. Although this informal domestic feminism cannot be discounted so easily, supporting evidence remains largely anecdotal. The argument, like several others in this approach to the decline of marital fertility, is likely to become circular, since improvements in the domestic bargaining power of women in the interests of themselves and their children will be indexed by the reduction of completed family size.[71]

There is no disputing the fact that contraceptive literature became more widely available in the 1870s and after; what is not so clear is how such propaganda was received and what practical utility it had. There are three issues here. First, who had access to the new or reprinted material? Secondly, was the information contained in *The Fruits of Philosophy*, the *Law of Population* and *The Wife's Handbook* valuable for intending family planners? Thirdly, was not the very discussion of birth control techniques and the idea of limiting family size in itself more important for the development of a 'calculus of conscious choice' than the practical advice offered? None of these questions can be answered directly.[72] It has already been mentioned that most of the new and effective appliance means of birth control were probably beyond the financial reach of working-class couples, while the non-appliance methods were already widely known. It is the third question that is of most significance. The newly reading public was exposed to public debate in the press, as well as advice literature, over the desirability of limiting fertility. Consciousness was raised where before there had been ignorance and doubt, and a new norm for reproductive behaviour was promoted.

---

[70] Banks and Banks (1964). Gittins (1982) and Lewis (1986) provide surveys of what is known on these issues.

[71] There has been a recent upsurge in debate over the role of gender and especially the process of negotiation between women and men over reproduction. What is new in the discussion relates more to the language used than the issues themselves. See the contributions to Greenhalgh (1995) and the symposium on qualitative methods in population studies in *Population and Development Review* 23 (4) (1997), pp. 813–53. There have also been a number of studies demonstrating the importance of female status not only for fertility, but also for childhood mortality. See, for example, Basu (1992).

[72] See Teitelbaum (1984), figure 8.1, p. 209, where the cumulative distribution of these books and pamphlets is illustrated.

From the approaches already considered, it is convenient to draw up a balance sheet of the positive and negative points. On the negative side: the effects of urbanisation, industrialisation or increasing 'strain' do not appear to have been necessary or sufficient to generate the conditions for a general decline of marital fertility. The social diffusion of the ideal of the small family of two or three children, the widespread adoption (at least in the nineteenth century) of new and effective appliance methods of birth control, and the adjustment of fertility to higher child survival rates are all possible, but rather unlikely, as prime movers in their own right. However, they cannot be discounted. On the positive side, relative deprivation among members of the middle classes, mass education, propaganda on birth control issues, and the increasing secularisation of Victorian society are all likely to have encouraged the desire or willingness to restrict family size from the 1860s or 1870s onwards, while declining child and then infant mortality helped to reinforce the downward trend, especially after 1900.

Empirical relationships

If what we surmise is a button, then what we can know of the causes and timing of the secular decline in marital fertility is but a pin head. We have regarded the button and now it is time to consider certain aspects of the pin head: namely surveys, ecological and time-series analyses.

Fabian Tract No. 131 of 1907, *The Decline in the Birth Rate*, contains the results of a postal survey of 316 marriages which its author, Sidney Webb, used as the basis for a number of generalisations.[73] The survey included, among other questions, items on birth histories and steps taken to render the marriage childless or to limit the number of children born. Although the figures quoted by Webb are rendered suspect once it is known that only members of the Fabian Society were surveyed, the observations that accompany his analysis are of considerable interest. Webb asserts that the decline in the birth rate was the result of family limitation – 'deliberate volition in the regulation of the marriage state'; that it was a new phenomenon unconnected with changes in nuptiality or the age composition of the population; that it was not confined to the towns but was most marked 'in places inhabited by the servant-keeping class', among those for whom 'the inconvenience of having children is specially felt' and those who 'give proofs of thrift and foresight'. Many

[73] Webb (1907); see also *The Times* of 11 (p. 10), 16 (p. 7) and 18 (p. 4) October 1906 for first reports of Webb's survey.

of these points are now familiar to us. They were reinforced in the contemporary writings of David Heron, Montague Crackanthorpe, Ethel Elderton, T. H. C. Stevenson and G. U. Yule, but in 1906, when they were first reported in articles in *The Times*, Webb's emphasis on new family limitation behaviour and rejection of 'physical deterioration' as a cause of fertility decline were entirely original.[74]

The 1911 *Census of Fertility* provides, as we have already seen, the most detailed survey of reproductive and child survival patterns, especially among married couples classified by husband's occupation. Yet it lacks the full range of questions to be found in modern fertility surveys. Its results are, as tables 4.1 and 4.4 and figures 4.1 to 4.3 show, of most value when used as a test area for social theories of cross-sectional variations in fertility between occupational or social groups.[75]

The ecological approach to fertility analysis – the approach that underpins the Princeton European Fertility Project – is based on the assumption that analysis of the spatial co-variation of dependent with independent variables will, at best, make it possible to isolate the bundle of variables which is closely related to variations in fertility or, at worst, remove from further consideration those variables that are statistically insignificant and thus causally irrelevant.[76] Once this assumption has been made, other well-known problems ensue: issues of correct scale, problems of measurement and the use of proxy variables, difficulties associated with multi-colinearity between independent variables, of normality and so forth. Despite these problems, few of which are soluble, the ecological approach has proved very attractive not least because it follows most closely the manner in which vital statistics and census population data are reported, annually and in discrete geographical units.

In Britain the application of various forms of the ecological approach has a long history, although many of its early uses had clear epidemiological objectives. In the 1930s D. V. Glass adopted this approach in what is probably the first modern ecological analysis of fertility

---

[74] Heron (1906), Crackanthorpe (1907) – an advocate of family limitation among the working classes in order to avoid the weakening of the population stock – Yule (1906, 1920), Elderton *et al.* (1913), Elderton (1914). These publications may be used to chart the early history of eugenics in Britain, and include the first applications of Karl Pearson's product moment correlation coefficient. Carr-Saunders (1925) offers a brief summary: 'While it is impossible to estimate the prevalence of contraceptive practices and of abstention from intercourse, it is probable that they account for the whole of the decline which the [post-1875 birth rate] figures show.' (p. 42)

[75] See also Szreter (1996).

[76] Something of the history and methodology of the Princeton European Fertility Project was given in chapter 1; the final results are summarised by Coale and Watkins (1986), while Teitelbaum (1984) is the author of the monograph dealing with the British Isles.

variations.[77] He considered variations in the gross reproduction rate (GRR) among the registration counties of England and Wales between 1871 and 1931. With GRR as the dependent variable Glass used four independent variables: the extent of marriage (percentage of women aged 20–44 who were spinsters); women's employment (percentage of women age 20 and over in employment); general occupational type (percentage of men aged 20 and over employed in agriculture and fishing, mining and commerce); and the employment of children (percentage aged 10–14 in employment). His correlation analysis brought to light two distinct problems. First, the use of registration counties obscures a considerable amount of internal variation. Glass intended to tackle this problem by using registration districts. Secondly, while several of the independent variables (marriage, employment of women, occupational type) correlated significantly with GRR on a cross-sectional basis, none was significant when change over time was considered. 'The small coefficient of variation between the falls in fertility experienced by different counties would suggest that the factors at work must be common to all parts of the country and equally powerful on all types of occupational patterns.'[78]

Teitelbaum's more recent analysis makes four distinct advances, and thereby succeeds in overcoming several of the technical problems associated with the use of geographically disaggregated data to examine change over time. Use of the standard Princeton fertility indices makes it possible to distinguish the effects of nuptiality, marital fertility and illegitimate fertility on overall fertility. Multiple regression analysis helps the assessment of combined influences among bundles of independent variables. The precise measurement of fertility decline is assisted by the use of two dependent variables: the date at which the index of marital fertility (Ig) had declined by 10 per cent from a high 'plateau' level, and the date at which Ig fell below 0.6, thereby suggesting that 'a substantial degree of fertility control is being adopted'. Broadening the area of study to include the whole of the British Isles also helped to counter the impression of low variability, while placing Britain in a pan-European context helped to focus attention on Britain's fertility decline as merely part of a far more widespread phenomenon.

Despite these advances the first problem outlined by Glass still remains important. The registration counties of England and Wales obscure much internal demographic variation. Lancashire, for example, contains two large urban centres, a substantial coalfield, a number of textile towns as well as remote rural parishes. Each of these features

---

[77] Glass (1938).   [78] Glass (1938), p. 212.

might be associated with its own distinctive influences on demographic behaviour, and certainly, as we have seen in chapter 3, local circumstances were of special significance for variations in nuptiality.

Figures 4.16 (colour section, page *f*) and 4.17 (colour section, page *g*) show variations in *If* and *Ig*, respectively, among the English and Welsh registration districts in 1861, 1891 and 1911, and are therefore comparable with figures 3.8 (colour section, page *a*) for *Im* and 4.12 (colour section, page *c*) for *Ih*, while figure 4.15 (colour section, page *e*) shows estimates of the total fertility rate (TFR). All three figures illustrate most effectively Glass's reservations, for not only were there intra-county variations, but, in 1861, *Ig* was above 0.6 in virtually every district while in 1911 it was less than 0.5 in the great majority of districts. In fifty years virtually the entire country had passed from natural fertility to substantially lower and almost certainly 'controlled' marital fertility.[79] The position in 1891, when *Ig* for England and Wales was just above 0.6, provides a useful indicator of those areas with 'early' and those with relatively 'late' marital fertility decline. There is no distinctive regional pattern to the districts in which the decline was early; they are neither overwhelmingly urban nor rural, northern nor southern. Marital fertility appears to be lower earlier in districts of the Lancashire–Yorkshire textile belt and the West End of London (see figure 3.12), while it remained higher for longer in the mining districts located throughout the coalfields. These observations also find support in our brief analysis of the 1911 *Census of Fertility* earlier in this chapter. There clearly were occupations with geographically distinct concentrations in which reproductive behaviour was in certain respects conditioned by employment circumstances to the extent that these are also reflected by geographically disaggregated data.

When one considers the changing relationship between the indices of marital fertility and proportion married (*Ig* and *Im*) it is possible to show that in general there was no association among the districts in 1861, but that by 1891 *Ig* had declined most in those districts with relatively low *Im*s and that by 1911 this positive relationship was still in existence, although *Ig* had declined everywhere (figure 4.18). The percentage of the population of England and Wales living in districts with given levels

[79] The shading used in figure 4.17 emphasises *Ig* values above and below 0.5. According to figure 4.6 if *Ig* equals 0.5 then *m* is approximately 0.6, and the percentage of married women practising contraception could be between 40 and 50. It would be safe to suppose that in these circumstances family limitation is being practised by a substantial proportion of a district's population. Bocqet-Appel and Jackobi (1997) attempt to model the spatial diffusion of *Ig* decline among the counties of Great Britain by relating the county measure to the location of the county town. Not surprisingly, the exercise does not prove to be successful.

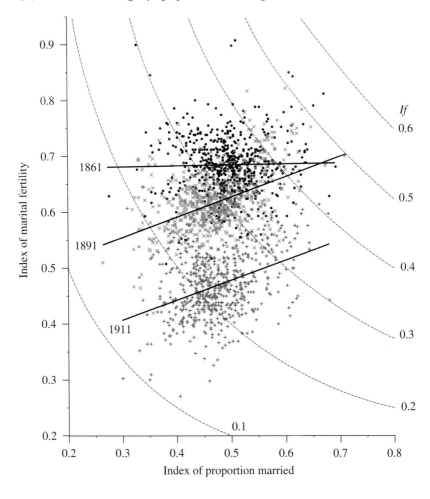

Figure 4.18. Changes in the distribution of *Ig* and *Im*, English and Welsh districts, 1861, 1891 and 1911

of fertility may also be of significance especially in terms of the pattern of change during the fifty-year period and the differences between marital and illegitimate fertility. This is illustrated in figure 4.19. For Ig both the mean and the range of the distribution changed in a highly ordered fashion, but for Ih the range contracted from the upper levels as the mean declined and most of this change occurred between 1861 and 1891; thereafter the distribution is merely accentuated, with an even higher proportion of people living in districts with very low rates of illegitimate fertility.

There are two inferences to be drawn from these figures. First, even when registration districts are used to analyse fertility patterns, as Glass intended, and regardless of which measure is used – TFR, If or Ig – the speed with which decline occurred and the extent to which it was a national phenomenon are the most striking features of the pattern of change. Secondly, it is most likely that any attempt to analyse changes or cross-sectional variations in the level of marital fertility will tend to emphasise the extremes of the distribution, since although the variance of Ig did decrease from 1861 to 1911 it was always substantially less than that for Im.

These problems, together with several others, become apparent when one attempts a multivariate ecological analysis of changes in the level of marital fertility using Ig as the dependent variable and 590 districts as the spatial framework.[80] The first problem to be solved involves the form of the model. Glass employed a simple correlation model to explore the cross-sectional and temporal variations, while Teitelbaum was especially concerned with the latter, his work also benefited substantially from the use of multiple-regression models.[81] Both Glass and Teitelbaum based their work on registration counties, thereby extending the choice of measurable independent variables. The model developed here is especially concerned with the preconditions that were likely to stimulate fertility decline. Most of the variables are drawn from the 1861 census and their associations with Ig for 1861, 1891 and 1911 are explored using stepwise multiple-regression analysis. The use of districts rather than counties makes this expedient necessary because the censuses of 1881, 1891, 1901 and 1911 provide little or no socio-economic data for registration districts.

The independent variables to be used are defined in table 4.5. Their selection requires considerable justification. The proportion of coal miners (C) is a commonly used diagnostic variable which has proved of value on numerous occasions. The farm servants ratio (FS) serves to

[80] London has been counted as one unit for the purposes of this analysis.
[81] Glass (1938), Teitelbaum (1984).

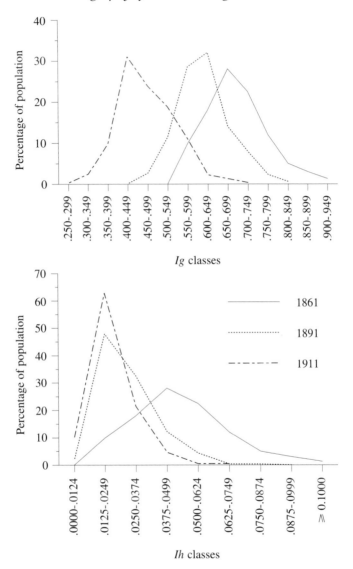

Figure 4.19. Percentage of the population of England and Wales living in districts with different levels of *Ig* and *Ih*, 1861, 1891 and 1911

Table 4.5. *Definitions of variables used in multiple regression analysis of* Ig

Variable	Definition
Ig(date)	The index of marital fertility for various dates
Child survival (CS)	The probability of a child surviving from age 1 to age 10 in 1861
Female servants (S)	Percentage of females aged 20 and over employed as domestic servants in 1861
Textile workers (T)	Log percentage of females aged 20 and over in employment (excluding domestic service) and engaged in the manufacture of woollen cloth, silk, worsted, lace, cotton, hose and stockings in 1861
Farm servants (FS)	Ratio (per thousand) of male and female farm servants to land proprietors, farmers and graziers in 1861
Illiteracy (L)	Percentage of brides signing the marriage register with a mark in 1861
Coal miners (C)	Log percentage of males aged 20 and over employed as coal miners in 1861
Im (date)	Index of proportion married for various dates

distinguish between those rural districts in which labour was organised to serve a largely pastoral economy and those where arable farming was more usual and independent agricultural labourers were in the majority. The percentage of employed adult women who were textile workers (T) is used to reflect a phenomenon the effects of which have already been noted in chapter 3. Both nuptiality and marital fertility are likely to be depressed as a result of greater employment opportunities for women and the possibility of remaining at or returning to work when married with young children. Both figures 4.2 (Social Class VI: for the fertility of wives whose husbands were textile workers) and 4.17 suggest that such specialised employment opportunities may serve to encourage lower fertility, even to hasten the use of family limitation methods. The use of female domestic servants as an independent variable (S) has a dual function: it reflects the distribution of wealth, as Sidney Webb envisaged, and (with FS) it forms a barrier to the early marriage of spinsters. The index of proportion married (*Im*) is used as the measure of nuptiality which may have influenced marital fertility indirectly via the effects of age- and sex-selective migration, social class and occupational specialisation. Child survival (CS) relates to the replacement effect: the higher the level of infant and childhood mortality the higher the level of marital fertility required to compensate. Once child survival improves, fertility may decline.[82] Illiteracy (L) has been included to reflect both the social standing of districts and the effects of mass education which were considerable even by 1861 as far as women's rates were concerned (see figures 4.13 and 4.14 which deal with the rise of literacy rather than the decline of illiteracy).

One would expect these seven independent variables to be associated with marital fertility in the following way:

$$Ig(\text{date}) = f(+C, -FS, -T, -S, -CS, +L).$$

For example, in districts where coal miners abound, where women's literacy is poor, where there are few farm servants and female textile workers or domestic servants, marital fertility is likely to be high. But in the textile districts, or those middle-class areas where many servants are employed, *Ig* will be lower than average.

Once the model has been specified in broad terms it is then possible to move towards implementation. Table 4.6 gives some first results from a simple stepwise multiple-regression model. In terms of the coefficient of multiple determination (R^2), each of the three models proves disappointing, for R^2 never exceeds 0.5 – but since there are 590 observations this might be expected. Some of the relations hypothesised in the functional model described above do hold, but not all. The effects of a strong presence of coal miners and of illiteracy are always positive; those of textile workers and female servants always negative. But farm servants and child survival produce positive rather than negative effects on marital fertility, while *Im* changes from having a slight negative to a strong positive influence. Neither the strength of each individual independent variable's contribution to the models, nor the order of incorporation remains constant. Coal miners (C) and farm servants (FS) are the most important variables, with the other five being of lesser significance and changing order from 1891 and 1911.

Before attempting to draw any conclusions from these observations let us first consider the problem of masked associations created by the combination of districts with disparate characteristics.[83] Tables 4.7 and 4.8 show results comparable with those in table 4.6 which have been derived by partitioning the districts into two broad categories – urban and rural – defined rather crudely in terms of population density. Both the urban and rural models for 1861 yield extremely low values of R^2,

---

[82] The joint effects of early-age mortality are considered at greater length in chapter 7, pp. 295–300.

[83] Lesthaeghe (1977) uses this approach to great effect to distinguish Flanders from Wallonia.

Table 4.6. *Summary of results for stepwise multiple regression analysis on variations in the index of marital fertility (Ig) for 590 districts, England and Wales, 1861, 1891 and 1911*

Variable	b	beta	t	Significance of t	R^2 at each step
Ig1861					
Farm servants (FS)	0.00004	0.19648	5.072	0.0000	0.07118
Coal miners (C)	0.02765	0.22829	5.429	0.0000	0.11476
Textile workers (T)	−0.01733	−0.20579	−5.031	0.0000	0.12777
Female servants (S)	−0.00435	−0.28603	−5.748	0.0000	0.14603
Im1861	−0.20570	−0.24426	−5.075	0.0000	0.18210
Constant	0.81563		31.694	0.0000	
Excluded: CS, L					
Ig1891					
Coal miners (C)	0.05242	0.39847	10.971	0.0000	0.29847
Farm servants (FS)	0.00006	0.23118	7.461	0.0000	0.35714
Im1891	0.23369	0.28053	9.471	0.0000	0.41504
Child survival (CS)	0.23354	0.19454	5.886	0.0000	0.44926
Textile workers (T)	−0.01636	−0.17886	−5.482	0.0000	0.46347
Illiteracy (L)	0.00074	0.18594	5.186	0.0000	0.48713
Constant	0.25857		6.589	0.0000	
Excluded: S					
Ig1911					
Coal miners (C)	0.03395	0.24293	6.083	0.0000	0.18195
Farm servants (FS)	0.00007	0.26756	8.040	0.0000	0.26585
Textile workers (T)	−0.03042	−0.31299	−8.707	0.0000	0.32046
Female servants (S)	−0.00270	−0.15378	−3.472	0.0006	0.38303
Im1911	0.14641	0.16157	3.996	0.0001	0.39323
Illiteracy (L)	0.00068	0.16088	3.691	0.0002	0.40448
Child survival (CS)	0.09742	0.07638	2.117	0.0347	0.40903
Constant	0.29835		5.779	0.0000	

Note:
The variables are defined in table 4.5 and the dependent variables (*Ig*) are shown in figure 4.17. London is one unit.

but among the urban districts R^2 is substantially enhanced in 1911, and especially in 1891. Marital fertility declined first in those urban districts where nuptiality was lower than average, an association that was reinforced where there were also fewer coal miners or farm servants but large numbers of female textile workers. It is unlikely that the influence of *Im* was direct in the causal sense; rather, the late marriage of spinsters, or their not marrying at all, was likely to be influenced by the supply of male partners, social and institutional restrictions on marriage coupled

Table 4.7. *Summary of results for stepwise multiple regression analysis on variations in the index of marital fertility* (Ig) *for 222 urban districts, England and Wales, 1861, 1891 and 1911*

Variable	b	beta	t	Significance of t	R² at each step
Ig1861 (urban)					
Coal miners (C)	0.03582	0.34185	5.358	0.0000	0.16849
Farm servants (FS)	0.00006	0.20699	3.245	0.0014	0.20663
Constant	0.64860		105.299	0.0000	
Excluded: CS, Im, L, S, T					
Ig1891 (urban)					
Im1891	0.46400	0.47588	7.848	0.0000	0.45677
Coal miners (C)	0.03734	0.29008	5.110	0.0000	0.57887
Farm servants (FS)	0.00007	0.20418	4.974	0.0000	0.63044
Textile workers (T)	−0.01931	−0.20974	−4.366	0.0000	0.66398
Child survival (CS)	0.21325	0.14344	3.488	0.0006	0.67467
Illiteracy (L)	0.00109	0.24387	3.257	0.0013	0.68385
Female servants (S)	0.00239	0.15629	2.080	0.0387	0.69011
Constant	0.12638		1.742	0.0830	
Ig1911 (urban)					
Coal miners (C)	0.04578	0.35683	6.113	0.0000	0.34697
Textile workers (T)	−0.02436	−0.26544	−5.650	0.0000	0.43216
Im1911	0.27660	0.27711	4.849	0.0000	0.49582
Farm servants (FS)	0.00007	0.19581	3.980	0.0001	0.52779
Child survival (CS)	−0.17507	−0.11815	−2.482	0.0138	0.54089
Constant	0.44873		6.551	0.0000	
Excluded: L, S					

Notes:
Urban districts are those with a population density greater than 100 persons per km² in 1861. The variables are defined in table 4.5, the dependent variables (*Ig*) are shown in figure 4.17 and the residuals are plotted in figure 4.20.

with class or employment, or alternative employment opportunities. In the rural districts in 1911 (when R² was largest) low values of *Ig* were associated with higher literacy, concentrations of domestic servants, but the absence of coal miners or farm servants.

Figure 4.20 (colour section, page *h*) shows the standardised regression residuals for *Ig*1891 (urban) and *Ig*1911 (rural). The former is over-predicted in many of those districts in which there are also substantial numbers of female textile workers, or which are resorts or ports in the south of England. It is under-predicted in a collection of districts which range from Penzance, Exeter, Oxford, Norwich and Carlisle to the dis-

Table 4.8. *Summary of results for stepwise multiple regression analysis on variations in the index of marital fertility (Ig) for 368 rural districts, England and Wales, 1861, 1891 and 1911*

Variable	b	*beta*	t	Significance of t	R^2 at each step
*Ig*1861 (rural)					
*Im*1861	−0.25076	−0.29076	−5.057	0.0000	0.06930
Coal miners (C)	0.02706	0.15593	3.149	0.0019	0.10272
Female servants (S)	−0.00299	−0.14863	−2.727	0.0067	0.11622
Farm servants (FS)	0.00003	0.13840	2.632	0.0089	0.13277
Constant	0.83166		26.764	0.0000	
Excluded: CS, L, T					
*Ig*1891 (rural)					
Coal miners (C)	0.06585	0.39825	8.723	0.0000	0.19164
Illiteracy (L)	0.00058	0.16120	3.320	0.0010	0.22957
Farm servants (FS)	0.00005	0.22148	4.648	0.0000	0.24996
Female servants (S)	−0.00271	−0.14114	−2.687	0.0075	0.27666
Child survival (CS)	0.17797	0.12362	2.668	0.0080	0.28735
*Im*1891	0.08489	0.11709	2.313	0.0213	0.29775
Constant	0.41300		6.135	0.0000	
Excluded: T					
*Ig*1911 (rural)					
Coal miners (C)	0.04706	0.24747	5.510	0.0000	0.10538
Farm servants (FS)	0.00008	0.33895	7.432	0.0000	0.18208
Female servants (S)	−0.00521	−0.23564	−4.601	0.0000	0.26769
Illiteracy (L)	0.00089	0.21643	4.597	0.0000	0.28895
Child survival (CS)	0.29190	0.17631	3.917	0.0001	0.31544
Textile workers (T)	−0.01701	−0.14663	−3.344	0.0009	0.33744
*Im*1911	0.10057	0.11669	3.374	0.0181	0.34766
Constant	0.16476		2.168	0.0308	

Notes:
Rural districts are those with a population density less than 100 persons per km² in 1861. The variables are defined in table 4.5, the dependent variables (*Ig*) are shown in figure 4.17 and the residuals are plotted in figure 4.20.

tricts of mid-Lancashire. The pattern of residuals shown in figure 4.20 for *Ig*1911 (rural) is likewise difficult to interpret; there is little consistent regional clustering of similar residuals in adjacent districts. It seems likely that the R^2 value for both *Ig*1891 (urban) and *Ig*1911 (rural) would not be greatly improved by the inclusion of additional independent variables, except that certain negative residuals in the *Ig* 1891 (urban) model could be reduced by inserting a variable specific to the Lancashire–Yorkshire textile belt into the equation.

The conclusions, many of them negative, to be drawn from this multi-variate ecological analysis may be summarised as follows. First, the models outlined in tables 4.5 to 4.7 provide a means of identifying those background variables that appear to be linked with conditions for retarding or accelerating the decline of marital fertility. In urban districts, Ig was lower in 1891 where nuptiality was also low in 1891, where there were no coal miners and few farm servants, and where textile workers were prominent in 1861. The models do not capture changes in the independent variables, and they only capture change in marital fertility indirectly by comparing models for particular points in time. Secondly, apart from Ig1891 (urban), the values of R^2 are relatively low; overall statistical explanation is not encouraging, yet none of the independent variables makes a consistently non-significant contribution. Thirdly, the choice and measurement of independent variables is limited, by the data available, to those that are surrogates for more directly relevant indices. None of the proximate determinants of marital fertility – such as coital frequency, fecundity, natural sterility, abortion or even the practice of breastfeeding – can be captured by this approach. Fourthly, when Teitelbaum's results are compared with those reported above, several positive points do emerge.[84] Teitelbaum's most successful Model V for England and Wales gives R^2 as 0.82144 when the date at which Ig reaches 0.6 is taken as the dependent variable. The six independent variables measure the distribution of coal miners, women's non-domestic employment, men's illiteracy, those born in France, Roman Catholics and Conservative voters in the 45 registration counties. The inclusion of Im1891 as an independent variable in Model V for England and Wales did not prove significant. The coal miners and illiteracy variables were, with Im1891, common to both analyses. In those counties where women's employment was important and/or there were higher proportions of French-born, Ig was likely to fall below 0.6 relatively early (before 1893); but where one or more of Teitelbaum's other independent variables had a high value, the decline of marital fertility was unlikely to be retarded. Some of the differences between Teitelbaum's findings and those reported above are a direct consequence of data availability, but others are related to the use of different scales of analysis. Female textile workers would not appear an important variable in its own right where counties are used, since the boundary of the textile belt coincides far less well with county borders than those of, for example, the coalfields. The importance given to Im1891 in the Ig1891 (urban) model and Teitelbaum's Model V provides an addi-

---

[84] Teitelbaum (1984), pp. 161–75.

tional example of how the ability to partition the data set can radically affect the results.

Although the multivariate ecological analysis takes us closer to the issues of fertility decline – since it is based on far more homogeneous areas – both analyses are severely limited by the variance problem, the problem of variable measurement, and the inherent technical difficulties associated with the use of multivariate parametric statistics with socio-economic data. The most that can be hoped for is that some of the background social, economic and demographic variables which are associated with extreme levels of marital fertility, as it declines rapidly, will be distinguished. The approach is, after all, essentially concerned with variation rather than change.

Let us turn now to consider this particular issue directly by looking at the chronologies of social, economic and demographic change in the late nineteenth century especially as they relate to the decline of fertility. Crafts has used a time-series analysis of marital fertility as the basis for the following conclusion: 'child costs are seen as the main impetus to fertility decline taking the period 1877 to 1938 as a whole. Changes in contraceptive knowledge, child mortality and incomes played more minor supporting roles. Whilst the simple SKW [Shorter, Knodel and van de Walle] hypothesis that only better contraceptive knowledge mattered is refuted, the economic theory of fertility is not.'[85] Child costs are assessed in terms of women's opportunity costs since 'It is generally assumed that the wife's time is intensively used in child care and that the effect of a rise in the female wage rate will tend to lower the demand for children (the substitution effect dominating) whereas a rising male wage rate is generally expected to raise the demand for children.'[86] The rate of illegitimate fertility is used as a proxy for reduced contraceptive costs, but illiteracy would have produced similar results. Crafts claims that his results 'suggest the improved [contraceptive] knowledge could account ceteris paribus for about one half of the pre-1895 [i.e. 1877–95] decline in fertility and about 15 per cent of the post-1895 [1895–1938] decline.'[87] Child mortality and income are measured in conventional fashion.

There are very good reasons not to accept Crafts's conclusions at their face value; partly because of his particular formulation of the problem, and partly because of other difficulties associated with the more general use of multivariate analysis with time-series data. Crafts makes clear that it is particularly difficult to construct a series for women's wage

[85] Crafts (1984a), quoted from p. 588. It should be noted that the 'SKW hypothesis' is rather more subtle than Crafts implies.   [86] Crafts (1984a), p. 579.

[87] Crafts (1984a), p. 584.

rates. The series he uses gives values of 82 to 83 in the late 1870s, rising to 100 in 1900 and 114 in 1913, but in the 1920s and 1930s the values range between 240 and 260. Between 1877 and 1938 marital fertility is clearly lower when indexed women's wage rates doubled after the First World War. If women's opportunity costs measure child costs, the latter certainly did rise before the First World War, but not dramatically. The use of illegitimacy as a proxy for effective contraception has been considered earlier, but in Crafts's formulation it takes on a new and more precise meaning. It seems beyond doubt that contraceptive knowledge, efficiency and practice all improved during the 1920s and 1930s. Illegitimate fertility declined in step with marital fertility between 1870 and the First World War so that it is tempting to argue, from reduced illegitimacy, that contraceptive knowledge was growing and/or costs were being reduced, and thus that marital fertility was also affected. But the direct evidence on costs of contraception tells a different story before 1914. Childhood mortality did decline between 1877 and 1938; the link between enhanced survival in childhood and marital fertility cannot be inferred from the simple statistical association between trends.

Several of these difficulties stem from Crafts's choice of time period. Since marital fertility declined during the 1870s and after, Crafts's use of 1877 as a starting date fails to capture the pre-decline levels of marital fertility and thus diverts attention from the causes and timing of the onset of secular decline. This criticism could also be made of his use of cross-sectional ecological analysis with urban districts in 1911 and with 87 urban registration districts in 1871, 1881 and 1891.[88] The results from these studies have been used to confirm the conclusions drawn from the time-series work, but also to emphasise that marital fertility decline 'did not come first in districts with many servants' and that 'illiteracy "accounted for" about half the pre-1895 fertility decline but relatively little thereafter'.[89] The former appears not to be the case while the latter may be true, but for reasons not explained in detail by Crafts.

Econometricians have demonstrated the value of time-series analysis for the exploration of economic–demographic relationships. However, it must be recognised that their most successful models have been applied either to long series with strong cyclical features or to short-run series with violent fluctuations. In the case of marital fertility decline there is a clear secular trend which has a distinct plateau and cliff-like form and is a relatively short-lived phenomenon. In these circumstances the wavelength and periodicity of cycles in long series cannot be com-

---

[88] Crafts (1984b), pp. 89–107.   [89] Crafts (1984b), pp. 105 and 104.

pared and one is left to rely on chronology: if the decline in *A* precedes a decline in *B*, then *A* may have influenced *B*. Figure 4.21 illustrates the point. The secular decline of marital fertility together with the fall in illiteracy among women, the rise in real wages and the manifest secularisation of Victorian society, indicated on this occasion by the increase in the proportion of civil marriages, all show substantial change between 1830 and 1910. Real wages improved, especially in the 1870s and 1880s, the obvious influence of the established church waned, literacy improved apace and marital fertility declined. Simultaneous changes; but how are they connected?

Why there are still no firm conclusions

Each of the approaches considered in this chapter provides clues to help solve the mystery of what caused the secular decline of marital fertility in nineteenth-century Europe. In order to focus the discussion, let us begin by formally stating a number of propositions which appear consistent with the analyses considered above. These propositions will be divided into those taking negative (N) and positive (P) forms.

N The secular decline of marital fertility in England and Wales was *not* directly related to the following:

N1 the development of an urban-industrial society;

N2 the social diffusion of the small family size ideal from the middle classes (who were experiencing the effects of 'the relative income compression phenomenon') to the working classes via domestic servants;

N3 the innovation, diffusion, adoption and use by a majority of fecund couples of appliance methods of birth control.

P The causes of the timing and extent of the secular decline of marital fertility in England and Wales were as follows:

P1 The immediate cause was related to the substantial and very rapid change in public opinion towards family limitation, making it both legitimate and personally acceptable, a change which was encouraged by a flood of family planning propaganda during the 1870s, 1880s and 1890s.

P2 This change in attitude was facilitated by the revolution in mass education which gathered pace from the 1840s. The effect of this was to create a largely literate society (at least among young adults) by the 1870s and to narrow the gender divide in terms of educational standards, compared with earlier generations. The confidence and

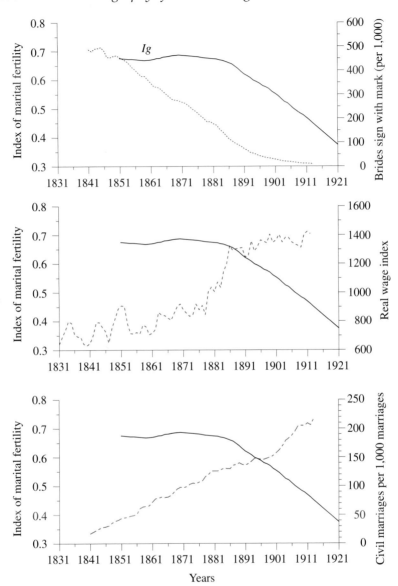

Figure 4.21. Time-series for marital fertility, literacy, real wage and secularisation indices, England and Wales

bargaining power of wives increased with the advance of domesti-cally oriented 'informal feminism'.

P3 The secular decline of early childhood mortality (ages 1–4) which began in the 1860s, and of infant mortality which did not commence until the late 1890s, together helped to confirm the downward trend in marital fertility.

P4 The increasing secularisation of late Victorian society and the rise in real wages helped to foster the planning and implementation of a small family size ideal by weakening the religious connotations of reproduction and encouraging the formation of a consumer-oriented, fashion-conscious society in which to have two or three children was thought respectable and to have more than five was not.

We may now confront these propositions with a number of conflicting points.

First, it has often been suggested that the timing of the decline of marital fertility was late in Britain.[90] However, to expect it to be early reflects an over-reliance on classical transition theory in which the industrial and urban revolutions are regarded as paramount, and ignores the fact that overall fertility (TFR, GRR or *If*) declined almost continuously throughout the nineteenth century. The increase in fertility during the late eighteenth century is more likely to have been assisted by rapid economic growth than is the decline of marital fertility in the late nineteenth century.

Secondly, how do these propositions relate to the continuing debate over the nature of fertility decline as a process of adjustment or innovation?[91] The arguments outlined above stress the importance of innovation, of changed attitudes towards reproduction (the new calculus of conscious choice) and, though to a lesser extent, of non-appliance techniques for fertility control. The decline of marital fertility is in general

---

[90] See, for example, Teitelbaum (1984), pp. 220–22. Teitelbaum also concludes his analysis by considering some propositions. He speculates that 'the conditions were ripe for a substantial and irreversible decline in marital fertility in Britain in the middle of the nineteenth century. The majority of the population in England and Wales was urban and at least minimally literate, there was substantial female employment in non-domestic, nonagricultural occupations, and knowledge of effective contraception was available' (p. 225). Fluctuating economic conditions for the middle classes, the Bradlaugh–Besant trial, and 'the spread of fertility control practices to the working classes [which] may have been facilitated by the rapid communications possible in an urban industrial population, and by the widespread employment of young working-class women as domestic servants in middle-class homes' (pp. 225–26) are all stressed as factors of importance. Finally, Teitelbaum argues that 'for the British case, a sub-stantially modified and qualified version of transition theory is the most adequate available explanation of the timing and nature of marital fertility decline' (p. 227).

[91] This debate was initiated by Carlsson (1966).

not an adjustment to 'strain', urbanism, increased child costs, even perceived increases in the costs of rearing children or falling childhood
mortality. In terms of Coale's preconditions for fertility decline, it is the
conscious choice that is new, while the ability to control fertility remains
unused and the economic and social necessity relatively constant for a
majority of the population.[92] The argument favoured by Shorter, Knodel
and van de Walle emphasises attitudes and techniques in apparently
equal measure, yet it still seems most likely that in late nineteenth-
century England appliance methods were already widely known.[93]
Although the publication of family planning material after the
Bradlaugh–Besant trial of 1877 would have improved knowledge, its
most important function was to raise consciousness, to break those
unquestioned assumptions that automatically lead to patterns of
natural fertility.

Thirdly, the propositions have significant implications for the use of
social theory in demography. They point to the need for a highly flexible mode of theory construction for the explanation of demographic
behaviour, one in which the criteria of 'sufficient and necessary' are
inappropriate. For example, and as was argued in the preceding section,
the decline of illiteracy in England and Wales during the early stage of
mass education was neither a sufficient nor a necessary cause of the
decline of marital fertility, but would have served to encourage subsequent demographic change in the particular context of late Victorian
Britain. The search for universal demographic variables will be a vain
one. Whereas Kingsley Davis's 'multiphasic demographic response
theory' focuses on cause and consequences, what is required is a theory
that deals with interchangeable and mutually supporting causes with
only one consequence. The problems associated with the verification of
demographic theory are also troublesome, since several of the propositions are not susceptible to formal testing. The results of multivariate
ecological and time-series analyses reported here clearly illustrate the
vulnerability of such approaches to problems of measurement and
scale, which are capable of generating important differences in the patterns of association between dependent and independent variables.
Further, the crucial question of 'how' fertility was brought under effective control is likely to defy empirical investigation, while theoretical
and empirical approaches to the question of 'why' and 'why then' are
not likely to move beyond hypothesis. Verification must, therefore, rest
on the disconcerting criterion of 'plausibility prior to rejection'.

Fourthly, do the propositions have any general utility beyond the par-

---

[92] Coale (1973).   [93] Shorter *et al.* (1971).

ticular case of England and Wales? There are good reasons for being wary of attempts to extend their range. There were in England no strong cultural barriers to retard the communication of ideas; there was one integrated economy and a society focused on London, which was divided by class rather than regional, ethnic, religious or linguistic affinities. This cannot, of course, be said of Scotland and Wales and certainly not of the Ireland. The role of the Bradlaugh–Besant trial must have been peculiar to Britain, yet the extent of simultaneity in the timing of fertility decline among the populations of north-western Europe was perhaps the most remarkable feature of the entire process of demographic change. The importance of family limitation propaganda remains, along with the actual means of fertility control, very much an under-explored area.

Despite these limitations, the propositions outlined above contain at least two general points. Neither transition theory nor those theories developed by economists to explain fertility variations give sufficient weight to changes in attitudes to family limitation and the notion of an ideal family size. The very question, 'How many children should we have?' was new to most Victorians. The process of fertility control initiated in the last half of the nineteenth century was an innovatory process, not just a matter of changed motivations. New norms for personal behaviour were developed, traditional methods of birth control were deployed and, ultimately, new and more effective techniques became accessible.[94]

[94] See Garrett and Reid (1996), pp. 97–99, and Szreter (1996), pp. 432–39, but also Tilly (1996) for interpretations that offer somewhat different emphases, as well as Anderson (1998b) who also focuses on the 'growing legitimacy of certain forms of behaviour' (p. 197). Caldwell (1999) asks why marital fertility did not decline earlier in the nineteenth century but ignores the influence of high levels of childhood mortality.

5

The laws of vitality

the laws of vitality are the central points of the science of medicine, and . . . it is only through observations on collective vitality that any precise or numerical knowledge can be obtained representing the laws of individual vitality. The only sure index of the practical success of the science of medicine is in the increase of collective vitality, or in the diminution of collective mortality, without reference to particular diseases.[1]

Like many of his statistician and actuary colleagues – especially Benjamin Gompertz and T. R. Edmonds – William Farr believed not only that certain 'laws of vitality' existed, but that they could be described precisely. What Farr called 'laws' we would now refer to as persistent and general regularities in the structure of mortality. For example, what has come to be known as 'Farr's law' is concerned with the relationship between death rates and population density, while Gompertz and Edmonds are associated with the link between mortality and age, and to some extent sickness and age. Both Gompertz's 'one uniform law of mortality from birth to extreme old age' and Farr's law provide useful pegs on which to hang a general discussion of the structure and varia- tions in mortality in Victorian England and Wales, especially in terms of the ways they were influenced by age and environment. This will also require us to take some account of other rather less law-like regularities in mortality patterns, such as the role of gender. The question of occupa- tional and social variations in mortality will be left to chapter 6 and the 'laws of disease' will reappear in chapter 8.

Age

In the years before the passing of the 1836 Registration Act and the sub- sequent development of civil registration, actuaries employed by the

---

[1] Edmonds (1834–35), quoted from p. 5.

life assurance companies were especially concerned to establish the true relationship between the risk of mortality and age. By 1815 they had Richard Price's life table for Northampton and Joshua Milne's for Carlisle, 1778–87.[2] Neither was entirely satisfactory, as Farr subsequently demonstrated, but the latter was at least based on careful surveys not only of age at death but also population at risk distributed by age.[3] It is highly likely that the Northampton table seriously overestimated the level of mortality and that the Carlisle table may even have under-estimated it, but little could be done to remedy the problem in practical terms until the development of full and accurate national systems of both vital registration and census enumeration. In the 1820s and 1830s several of the most able actuaries turned their attention to the 'laws of mortality' by which they hoped to be able to specify the exact mathematical relationship between the progressive increase in the probability of dying with increasing age and age itself. Once such a law had been specified it could be used to predict mortality given age and to smooth out irregularities in any empirically derived mortality tables.

Benjamin Gompertz is now remembered as the first to provide a formal mathematical description of the law in a paper read before the Royal Society on 16 June 1825.[4] He argued that 'It is possible that death may be the consequence of two generally co-existing causes; the one, chance, without previous disposition to death or deterioration; the other, a deterioration, or an increased inability to withstand destruction', and that mankind was 'continually gaining seeds of indisposition, or in other words, an increasing liability to death'.[5] From this biological base, Gompertz deduced that a form of the following equation could be used to capture the force of mortality:

$$q_x = B \bullet C^x \tag{5.1}$$

---

[2] Price (1771) and Milne (1815). See O'Donnell (1936), especially pp. 317–79, for an account of the early work on mortality tables. Alborn (1994) considers the actuaries as statisticians.

[3] William Farr, 'The Northampton table of mortality', in Registrar General's *Eighth Annual Report for 1845* (BPP 1847–48/XXV), pp. 290–325. The fourth edition of Price's *Observations* (1783) also contains life tables for Sweden and Stockholm which use data for the number dying at each age and the number alive at those same ages. Milne believed that these were the first life tables to be based on the 'data that are required to determine the law of mortality'. See Milne (1842).

[4] Benjamin Gompertz (1779–1865) was actuary to the Alliance Assurance Company from 1824. For his principal contributions, see Gompertz (1820, 1825, 1862, 1872). The last (Gompertz, 1872) is the transcript of a paper presented at the Fourth International Statistical Congress held in London in 1860. However, Gompertz was not the first to talk about the laws of mortality nor, perhaps, the first to attempt some mathematical formulation. See Dupâquier (1996).

[5] Gompertz (1825), p. 517.

where q_x is the probability of dying at exact age x, and B and C are constants.[6] Of course this would not apply over the full range of x, but from ages 15 or 20 to 50 or 60 Gompertz had certainly succeeded in identifying both a theoretical and practical law of mortality. In 1867 William Matthew Makeham suggested an important modification:

$$q_x = A + B \bullet C^x \qquad (5.2)$$

in which the third constant, A, is used to represent the influence of causes of death not dependent on age.

> I do not profess to be able to separate the whole category of diseases into the two classes specified – viz., the diseases depending for their intensity solely upon the gradual diminution of the vital power [B], and those which depend on other causes, the nature of which we do not at present understand [A]. I apprehend that medical science is not sufficiently advanced to render such a desideratum possible of attainment at present. I propose only at present to show that there are certain diseases – and those too of a well-defined and strictly homogeneous character – which follow Mr. Gompertz's law far more closely than the aggregate mortality from all diseases taken together.[7]

Makeham was able to offer empirical justification for his modification by using material for the 1850s on age and cause of death reported in the *Supplement* to the Registrar General's *Twenty-fifth Annual Report* (for diseases of the lung, heart, kidneys, brain, stomach and liver) and the *Twenty-sixth Annual Report* (for bronchitis), to show that B did vary with age in a regular fashion and as predicted by Gompertz, but only for certain causes of death. He found it rather more difficult to demonstrate that A was constant with age 'varying only with the peculiar characteristics which distinguish different sets of observations from each other'.[8] Once again, it must be emphasised that the Gompertz–Makeham hypothesis only applies to ages 15 and over.

Apparently independently of Gompertz's elegant but rather abstract

---

[6] This is the modern equivalent of Gompertz's original notation from his 1825 paper. See Brownlee (1919), Greenwood (1928), Dublin *et al.* (1949), especially chapter 5, 'Biological aspects of the life table', for a more detailed discussion. In June 1927 Raymond Pearl gave a series of lectures at University College London entitled 'Experimental vital statistics'. These became *The Rate of Living, Being an Account of Some Experimental Studies on the Biology of Life Duration* (Pearl, 1928), a work concerned almost exclusively with the fruit fly, but which seems to have stimulated interest among epidemiologists like Major Greenwood who sought to develop parallel models for human populations. But see also Fisher (1930), chapter II, 'The fundamental theorem of natural selection', which uses life table and table of reproduction concepts to discuss evolutionary theory. There has recently been a revival of interest in these issues associated with the problems of ageing; see Olshansky and Carnes (1997) on Gompertz, Makeham, Brownlee, Pearl, etc. on senescence and the 'force of mortality' in old age.

[7] Makeham (1867), quoted from p. 335; see also Makeham (1872). Brownlee (1919), p. 43, refers to this as the 'Gompertz–Makeham hypothesis'.

[8] Makeham (1867), p. 337.

formulations, the young political economist T. R. Edmonds also began to work on the laws of vitality in the early 1830s. Edmonds has not had a law or even a hypothesis named after him, and his work as a political economist has been almost completely ignored, but it is Edmonds who is now credited with having had a particular influence on Farr at just that time when he was acquiring his self-taught statistical knowledge.[9] For example, Eyler argues that 'It was Edmonds's law of mortality which seems to have been Farr's paradigm. In his own statistical studies he hoped ultimately to discover laws analogous to the one Edmonds found in life tables.'[10] Because of their influence on the future work of the Statistical Superintendent as well as their range and substantive content, Edmonds's publications, especially those in *The Lancet* of 1835 and 1836, deserve special attention.[11] As table 5.1 makes clear, merely to list the titles of these works gives an indication of Edmonds's pre-occupations and his practical influence.

In *Life Tables* (pp. v–vi), Edmonds outlined his approach to defining the law of mortality.

During the succession of years and moments, measured from the birth of any individual, the continuous change in the force of mortality is subject to a very simple law, being that of geometric proportion. But the same geometric progression is not observed from birth to the end of life. Instead of one there are *three* distinct orders of progression, corresponding to three remarkable periods of animal life. The force of mortality at all ages is expressible, – by the terms of three consecutive geometric series, so connected that the last term of the one series is the first of the succeeding series, – or by the ordinates of three contiguous segments of three log arithmetic curves. The common ratios of the three geometric series (or the constants of the curves) appear to be fixed and immutable, for all human life in all ages of the world. These three constants, now first

---

[9] Thomas Rowe Edmonds (1803–89) is largely unknown today although his early work as a political economist offers an interesting contrast with that of his contemporary, T. R. Malthus. For example, his *Practical Moral and Political Economy; or, the Government, Religion, and Institutions, most conducive to Individual Happiness and to National Power* (Edmonds, 1828) has chapters on 'Population' and 'On the size of towns'. Edmonds's second book, which like Malthus's first was published anonymously, deals with the same problem: *An Enquiry into the Principles of Population, exhibiting a System of Regulations for the Poor; designed immediately to lessen, and finally remove, the evils which have hitherto pressed upon the Labouring Classes of Society* (Edmonds, 1832). Burrow (1966) describes the former as 'quite original, being an attempt to introduce into social thinking the Lamarckian and (Erasmus) Darwinian idea of adaptation' (p. 78).

[10] Eyler (1979), p. 76. The extent of Edmonds's influence on Farr can also be judged from the latter's chapter entitled 'Vital statistics; or the statistics of health, sickness, diseases, and death' (Farr, 1837).

[11] Edmonds graduated from Trinity College, Cambridge, in 1824 and was appointed actuary to the Legal and General Life Assurance Society in 1832, a post he held for 34 years. In March and May 1835 Edmonds gave his address as Grafton Street, Fitzroy Square, London. Farr lived at 8 Grafton Street between 1833 and 1841 where he is known to have taken in lodgers. See Greenwood (1936), p. 95.

Table 5.1. *The principal publications of T. R. Edmonds on the subject of health and mortality*

Life Tables, Founded upon the discovery of a Numerical Law regulating the existence of every human being: illustrated by a New Theory of the cause producing Health and Longevity (London: James Duncan, 1832)

'On the laws of collective vitality', *The Lancet* 2 (605) (1834–35), pp. 5–8 (28 March 1835)

'On the mortality of the people of England', *The Lancet* 2 (614) (1834–35), pp. 310–16 (30 May 1835), 'Errata', 2 (615) (1834–35), p. 368

'On the law of mortality in each county of England', *The Lancet* 1 (640) (1835–36), pp. 364–71 (7 November 1835) and (641) (1835–36), pp. 408–16 (December 1835)

'On the mortality of infants in England', *The Lancet* 1 (648) (1835–36), pp. 690–94 (18 January 1836)

'On the laws of sickness, according to age, exhibiting a double coincidence between the laws of sickness and the laws of mortality', *The Lancet* 1 (651) (1835–36), pp. 855–58 (13 February 1836)

'On the mortality of Glasgow and the increasing mortality of England', *The Lancet* 2 (667) (1835–36), pp. 353–59 (4 June 1836)

'Statistics of the London Hospital with remarks on the law of sickness', *The Lancet* 2 (679) (1835–36), pp. 778–83 (27 August 1836)

'Corrections of errors in statistics at the British Association', *The Lancet* 2 (680) (1835–36), pp. 837–38 (5 September 1836)

'On the influence of age and selection on the mortality of members of the Equitable Life Assurance Society during a period of sixty-seven years ending in 1829', *The Lancet* 1 (739) (1837–38), pp. 154–62 (21 October 1837)

'On the duration of life in the English peerage', *The Lancet* 1 (754) (1837–38), pp. 705–9 (13 January 1838)

'On the mortality and sickness of soldiers engaged in War', *The Lancet* 2 (765) (1837–38), pp. 143–48 (21 April 1838)

'On the mortality and diseases of Europeans and natives in the East Indies', *The Lancet* 2 (773) (1837–38), pp. 433–40 (2 June 1838)

'The lineage of English peers of ancient titles exhibited by means of diagrams', *The Lancet* 1 (810) (1838–39), pp. 867–73 (February 1839)

'On the mortality and sickness of artisans in London', *The Lancet* 2 (817) (1838–39), pp. 185–93 (April 1839)

'On the mortality of the members of the Amicable and Equitable Assurance Societies', *The Lancet* 2 (994) (1841–42), pp. 839–49 (September 1842)

'On the law of human mortality; and on Mr. Gompertz's new exposition of his law of mortality', *Journal of the Institute of Actuaries* 9 (1861), pp. 327–40

---

discovered, correspond to the three grand divisions of life, – Infancy, Manhood (or Florescence), and Old Age. For regulating the continuous change in the force of mortality, Nature uses one constant for Infancy, another for Mankind, and a third for Old Age. The constant for *Infancy* confirms life, or indicates a continued diminution of the force of mortality; the constants for *Mankind* and *Old Age* indicate decay of life, or a continued increase in the force of mortality; but the decay of life is much more rapid in the period of Old Age than the period of Manhood.

Edmonds also recognised a fourth period (represented here by p_2) 'between Infancy and Manhood where the force of mortality is stationary and at its minimum' (p. vi). Table 5.2 summarises Edmonds constants – p_1, p_2, p_3 and p_4 – together with the range of ages to which they apply, as well as some of his examples of the level of mortality in various life table populations.[12] In his first *Lancet* paper Edmonds remarked that Dr Richard Price, the author of the Northampton life table, was probably the first to identify the three principal age-components of mortality but that Price did not express the numerical values of the constants.[13] Edmonds also acknowledged in *Life Tables* the prior claim of Gompertz to have first discovered that 'some connexion existed between Tables of Mortality and the algebraic expression (a^{bx})', but he continued to assert that his discoveries had been made independently, that his four constants scheme was more appropriate and that 'The new Theory is *universally* true'.[14] The only exception he allowed was for death in early infancy.

It is only below the age of six weeks that the theory appears to fail, especially for the male sex. The apparent error may be attributable, either to the effects of the act of birth, or to the greater mortality of infants born between the seventh and ninth month from conception. It does not however appear improbable, that the date of conception, and not the date of birth, is the proper commencement of the "infancy period".[15]

---

[12] Edmonds's *Life Tables* also contains some interesting observations on the maximum human birth rate, gender mortality differentials, urban–rural mortality differentials (the combined result of excessive poverty and excessive impurity of air), the poor quality of the recent population returns, and the relation between sickness and death. It concludes with a review of material for the calculation of annuities.

[13] 'According to Dr. Price [in 1769], human life, from birth upwards, grows *gradually stronger* until the age of 10 years, then *slowly loses* strength until the age of 50, then *more rapidly loses* strength, until, at 70 or 75, it is brought back to all the weakness of the first month.' Edmonds (1861), quoted from p. 327.

[14] Edmonds, *Life Tables* (1832), p. xvii. In the early 1860s Edmonds fell into a rather acrimonious dispute with Gompertz's supporters over who had first stated the law of mortality. See Glass (1973), p. 104. In the 1870s other actuaries began to work on the whole mortality curve apparently without reference to Edmonds. For example, Thiele (1872). The publication of this paper led Makeham to have Gompertz (1872) reprinted in the same journal.

[15] Edmonds, 'Laws of collective vitality', *The Lancet* (March 1835), p. 6. It is not clear how Edmonds came to this conclusion, but it will be taken up again in chapter 7, pp. 255–61.

Table 5.2. *T. R. Edmonds's rate of mortality constants for specified age ranges and minimum mortality rates for various life table populations*

Constants	Value of p	$\log p$	Age range
p_1	0.6760830	−0.1700	0–8
p_2	1.0	+0.0	8–12
p_3	1.0299117	+0.0128	12–55
p_4	1.0796923	+0.0333	55–end of life
Life table	Minimum mortality	Mortality at birth	Life expectancy at birth in years
Village (Carlisle)	0.005	0.1612228	39.46
Mean	0.00636431	0.1457979	38.69
City	0.00795539	0.1822474	33.01
Northampton	0.009	0.3049598	24.16
Stockholm	0.0127286	0.4313017	15.78

Note:
Edmonds believed that the true age ranges for the Village table (for which he used Carlisle) were 0–9, 9–10, 10–55 and 55–end of life; while for the high mortality corrected Northampton and Stockholm tables they were 0–9, 9–12, 12–62 and 62–end of life. 'City' refers to the largest English towns and cities. Mortality is measured by deaths per year of life.
Source: Edmonds, *Life Tables* (1832), pp. vi and ix.

Edmonds described his law of mortality in the following way:

$$\log y_x = \frac{k^2 \bullet M_0}{\log p}(1 - p^x), \tag{5.3}$$

where y_x represents the proportion surviving at any age x ($y_0 = 1$); k is the modulus of the common logs. system (0.43429); M_0 is the annual rate of mortality when x is 0; $\log p$ is the log of the annual constant rate of increase of mortality and can take on four values depending on x ($p_1, \ldots, p_4$ in table 5.2). Once the lengths of the segments are known and the minimum mortality rate defined, then equation 5.3 may be used to estimate y_x and thereafter l_x given a number born (l_0), and '[f]rom the general formula may easily be deduced an expression for the probability of living one year, at any age; by means of which, Tables of Mortality may be constructed with great rapidity and secure from error'.[16]

Figure 5.1 shows how Edmonds's law of mortality would work using his example of the Mean mortality experience for England and Wales, the constants for which are given in table 5.2.

[16] Edmonds, *Life Tables* (1832), p. xvii. Equation 5.3 is a modified version of the one presented in his *Lancet* paper of April 1839 (p. 191).

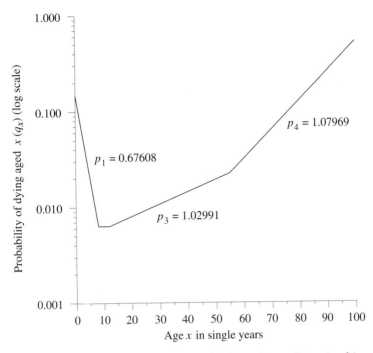

Figure 5.1. Illustration of T. R. Edmonds's law of mortality using his
Mean mortality for England and Wales
Note: See table 5.2.

The three- or four-segment curve is an extremely interesting device and, if mortality were to operate in the way Edmonds envisaged, many of the problems faced in representing patterns and constructing life tables would be solved.[17] For actuaries in the 1820s and 1830s it was an especially attractive theory because it allowed the entire mortality curve to be constructed once the minimum rate of mortality had been specified since this value summarised the level of mortality while the constant ps determined the actual age-specific rates. Unfortunately, as we

[17] In the 1890s Karl Pearson, apparently independently of the earlier work by the actuaries, identified five distinct age components in the mortality curve: infancy, childhood, youth, middle age and old age. See Pearson (1897). Anson's (1993) work on the shape of mortality curves has placed nineteenth-century England and Wales in the 'troughed' category, as opposed to the 'rectangular'. Had England and Wales been more rectangular than troughed, Edmonds would have found it far more difficult to justify a simple three or four component model. The geographical patterning of age-specific mortality structures has been explored via factor analysis using the registration districts for England and Wales in 1861 by Woods (1982b).

shall see, matters were not quite so simple, but it required the development of a full national system of civil registration and the work of
William Farr to show exactly and in detail how mortality did vary with
age.

Farr's first attempt to do this, with due acknowledgement to both
Gompertz and Edmonds, appeared in an appendix to the Registrar
General's *Fifth Annual Report for 1841*. The first English Life Table (ELT
1) was constructed using the 1841 census together with the deaths registered in the same year and the births registered in 1840 and 1841.[18]
Prior to the calculation of age-specific death rates Farr made a number
of small corrections to the data. The census had been taken on the night
of 6–7 June, and in order to estimate the age and sex structure of the
population at mid-year (1 July) the totals within each age group were
multiplied by $r^{0.07}$ where $r = 1.01334$ (the average annual rate of population increase between 1831 and 1841) and 0.07 was determined for the
24 days between 6–7 June and 1 July by $(24/365 = 0.0658 = 0.07)$. The age
structure of the small number of persons enumerated or registered
without ages was assumed to be identical to the rest of the population.
Finally, deaths were considered to have taken place at equal intervals
throughout the year which allowed q_xs to be calculated using the
formula $q_x = (M_x)/(1 + M_x)$ where M_x is the age-specific death rate. Once
these adjustments had been made, Farr calculated mortality rates for
ages 0–4 and then for five-year age groups. He noted:

Upon a slight inspection it will be seen (1) that the mortality of both sexes
decreases until a minimum is attained at the age 10–15; (2), that the mortality
increases from 15 to 55 at a slow rate; and (3), that after 55 the mortality is more
than doubling every 10 years.[19]

Farr was convinced of the truth of Edmonds's law and consequently he
adopted a method of decomposing the mortality rates for five-year age
groups into single years by superimposing the law of mortality onto the
data, thus ironing out any irregularities. The series of M_xs had shown
that the mortality of females aged 25–29 was greater than that of females
aged 30–34 and Farr explained this difference in terms of age misreporting caused by the tendency of some to give their ages in decennial
increments (i.e. reporting age 30 even though their actual age was
between 30 and 39).[20] Farr corrected for this problem by smoothing the

---

[18] *Fifth Annual Report*, pp. 161–65. 'The following pages contain an account of the methods
which were employed in constructing the English Life Table . . . the language employed
consists of a very few words the interpretation of which can be easily recovered or
acquired' (p. 161).   [19] *Fifth Annual Report*, p. 163.

[20] *Fifth Annual Report*, p. 162: 'In practice it was found that neither the ages of the living
nor of the dead were stated with sufficient exactness to form the basis of calculations;

two five-year age group series 15–54 and 55–94. Because of the age-heaping, the series 15–54 was treated as two separate geometrical series (15–19, 25–29, 35–39, 45–49 and 20–24, 30–34, 40–44, 50–54) and the ratio between each term was calculated. The geometric mean of these six ratios was then calculated and this formed the common ratio of the corrected series. The first and subsequent terms of the corrected series could then be calculated by assuming that the sums of both the uncorrected and corrected series were equal.[21] Farr now had the necessary raw material to reconstruct his data. Mortality rates for the first five years were based on the actual annual mortality rates in ages 1–4 together with the infant mortality rate, derived from the mean numbers born in 1840 and 1841. For ages 5–9, the M_x for the group was taken to be representative for the ages 7–8 with the other ages being calculated by interpolation, assuming Edmonds's law. It is not clear how Farr treated the age group 10–14, although the shape of the q_x curve suggests that the pattern for the age group 5–9 was simply extended. For the higher age groups it was relatively straightforward to interpolate for the individual years once the overall pattern had been established.[22]

Much of Farr's explanation concerns the practicalities of performing the various necessary calculations required to smooth the data. This involved tedious calculations involving logarithms, with Farr using the difference method to simplify them. Indeed, he realised that many of the calculations could 'I suppose, be calculated by Mr. Babbage's machine'.[23] Farr's method provides the first attempt to construct a national life table for England and Wales. Yet because of the perceived shortcomings of the data, it actually represents a marriage of both the theoretical and practical considerations and in many ways it is a triumph of the application of simple mathematics to the study of populations. However, the pattern of mortality revealed by the first English Life Table is essentially one that owes a great deal to Edmonds's law of mortality.

The *Fifth Annual Report* also contains abridged life tables for three localities: London, non-metropolitan Surrey and Liverpool.[24] An

---

and if the age had been correctly stated in single years, it would have been necessary to add the numbers together in quinquennial or decennial periods to obtain uniform results.' Figure 2.18 shows that these problems were still present even in 1911.

[21] This can be done using the formula $S_n = a (r^n - 1)/(r - 1)$ where S_n = sum to n terms, n = number of terms, a = first term and r = common ratio. In practice, Farr used logarithms to perform these calculations which reduced most of them to a series of additions. I am particularly grateful to Dr Chris Galley for his mathematical advice on this point.

[22] There is a small anomaly in Farr's method since the central series for males was taken from 15 to 55, while that for females from 15 to 54 presumably to provide a better fit with the final series.   [23] *Fifth Annual Report*, p. 167.

[24] See chapter 2, pp. 60–61.

appendix to the *Seventh Annual Report* gives an equivalent table for Manchester. The problem with all of these tables is that they are based on material that was probably defective in at least three ways: (a) deaths were under-registered, (b) the population was under-enumerated and (c) ages were often misreported or not reported at all. Of the three, it seems that (b) and (c) were probably the most damaging but that age misreporting in (c) could probably be corrected for by using Edmonds's theory. Farr's early life tables were in any event a significant advance on the Northampton and Carlisle tables upon which actuarial calculations had been based prior to the 1840s.[25] However, it was not until 1864 and the separate publication of the third English Life Table (ELT 3) that Farr felt sufficiently confident about having captured the true character of England's mortality level and structure that he provided his own actuarial calculations.[26] ELT 3 was based on age structure data for two censuses, 1841 and 1851, and age at death data for the 17 years 1838–54. Its construction provides the most reliable cornerstone we can have for a discussion of Victorian mortality.[27]

Figure 5.2 shows the probability of dying at age x (q_x) for females from ELTs 1, 3 and 7 (for 1901–10), as well as the equivalent curve from Edmonds's theory which was used by Farr as a guide to the overall shape of the mortality curve. There are certainly two critical turning points; one in the teens and a second in the fifties, but the minimum rate of mortality in ELT 3 is 0.0049 at ages 12 and 13, and mortality between ages 10 and 20 is in any case rather different in form to that envisaged in the theory. What is interesting about figure 5.2 for the theory, apart from the fit, is that the mortality curve derived by Edmonds appears even closer to the one realised in England and Wales by the 1890s with two clear turning points, one at age 11 (minimum q_x is 0.0022) and another later in life at age 55.

Figure 5.2 clearly illustrates just how focused the decline of mortality in Victorian England and Wales was on that particular age range between 1 and 50 years. This is shown in an even more striking way in figure 5.3. Neither infant mortality nor mortality in old age declined in

[25] The Northampton table, as Farr showed in an appendix to the Registrar General's *Eighth Annual Report*, almost certainly over-estimated the level of mortality ($e_0 = 25.18$) while the Carlisle table under-estimated it ($e_0 = 39.46$).
[26] ELT 2 had been calculated using the age structure from the 1841 census, but also deaths for the seven years 1838–44. These tables shared many of the weaknesses of ELT 1 which stemmed from problem (a) outlined above. Farr (1864) is the most important of his many works on life tables and annuities.
[27] Wrigley and Schofield (1981), appendix 14, 'The derivation of two families of "English" life tables', pp. 708–14, discuss the quality of ELT 3 as the basis for back projection especially in relation to the effects of age misreporting over age 50 in the 1841 and 1851 censuses, but in terms of early age mortality ELT 3 appears to be trustworthy (see p. 59, figure 2.11).

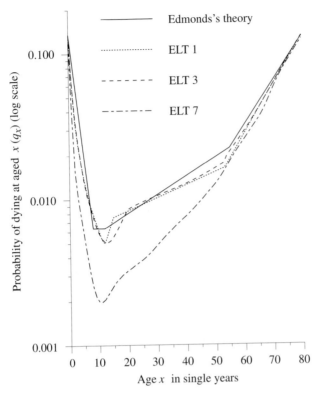

Figure 5.2. The probability of dying by single years of age (q_x) from English Life Tables 1 (1841), 3 (1838–54) and 7 (1901–10) for females compared with Edmonds's theory

the nineteenth century; indeed mortality was reduced at those very ages in which it was already relatively low.

Alongside his actuarial efforts, Farr was also convinced that the new-found ability to construct life tables for a variety of populations also offered a means to measure and thus monitor the health of the nation, its constituent groups and areas. The life table was the 'biometer' for mortality and health. In the late 1850s this line of argument had encouraged Farr to construct a special life table precisely for what he called the 'healthy districts' of England and Wales.[28] These registration districts all had mean crude death rates less than 17.5 in the decade 1841–50. There

---

[28] Farr (1859). These healthy districts had real significance for Farr. Eyler (1979), p. 159, refers to a letter from Farr to Florence Nightingale dated 2 August 1858 in which he advises her to take periods of rest in one of his healthy districts. In 1860 Farr took his own advice by moving from St John's Wood in north London to Bromley, Kent, one of the nearest healthy districts to the metropolis. He lived there until his death in 1883. Charles Darwin had made a similar move to nearby Downe in 1842.

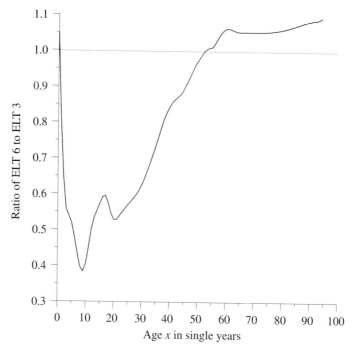

Figure 5.3. The age pattern of mortality decline shown by the ratio of q_xs (ELT 6/ELT 3), males and females combined
Note: For those ages where the curve falls below the horizontal line, mortality was lower in 1891–1900 than in 1838–54.

were 64 of these, but one (Haltwhistle, Northumberland) was not included by Farr. (Figure 5.4, shows the location of the 63 registration districts.) For these 63 districts in combination Farr constructed full life tables for males and females using the 1851 census and reported deaths in the five years from 1849 to 1853.[29] Once again he discussed the various methods at his disposal, including the hypothetical work of Messrs Gompertz and Edmonds, but he chose to rely on empirically based estimates with some interpolation.

But Farr's Healthy Districts Life Table of 1849–53 (HDLT 1) represents an important development in the measurement of Victorian mortality more for the purposes to which it was put than in its method of construction. For Farr and many other sanitarians it became the yard-stick against which to assess the progress of public health, and a crude

[29] Lewis-Faning (1930) traces the progress of the 63 up to 1911 and, with some difficulty, even beyond. Using standardised death rates he estimates that the 63 healthy districts experienced a level of mortality 76.19 per cent of that in England and Wales in 1851–60 (e_0 for the 63 was 49.12) and 76.43 per cent of that in 1901–10 (e_0 57.14).

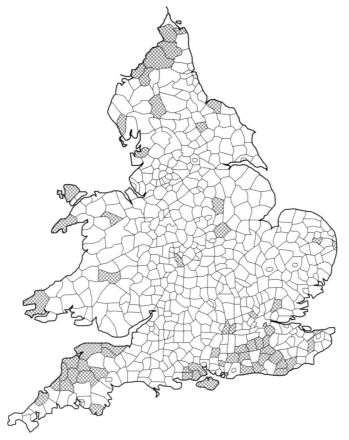

Figure 5.4. Location of the 63 districts selected for Farr's Healthy Districts Life Table 1, 1849–53

death rate of 17 was repeatedly used as an attainable target to which all districts, and especially the urban ones, could aspire. In terms of the curve of mortality, HDLT 1 can also be used to identify excess mortality in certain age groups. Figure 5.5 shows ELT 3 in comparison with HDLT 1 for males and females separately. As one would expect, mortality at every age is higher in the national table than in the one based on specially selected areas, but the shapes of the curves are maintained and the two turning points are repeated. Figure 5.6 shows the ratios of q_xs from ELT 3 and HDLT 1, as well as those for ELT 6 and the third Healthy Districts Life Table for 1891–1900 (HDLT 3).[30] It is apparent that

[30] HDLT 2 was constructed for 1881–90. Although HDLTs 2 and 3 were developed on similar principles to HDLT 1, and certainly for the same reason, far larger numbers of registration districts were selected. In consequence it is probably unreasonable to make comparisons between HDLTs for the middle and end of the century.

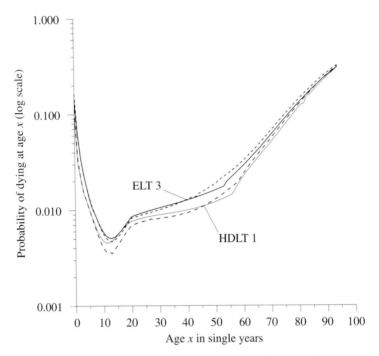

Figure 5.5. The probability of dying by single years of age,
comparison of English Life Table 3 (1838–54) and Healthy Districts Life Table 1
(1849–53)
Note: Females are shown by solid lines and males by dashed lines.

mortality during the early and middle years of life was largely responsible for excess mortality outside the healthy districts.

Comparison of life table functions provides a rather simple way of identifying changes in the structure of age-specific mortality patterns. Another method involves the selection of certain indicative age groups and plotting annual variations in their particular mortality rates. This approach is illustrated in figure 5.7 using the following age groups: 0–4, 15–19, 25–34 and 55–64. It shows that mortality in childhood did begin to decline from the early 1860s but that decline accelerated substantially from the turn of the century, and that in the age groups 15–19 and 25–34 mortality also appears to have begun a continuous decline from some point in the 1860s. At older ages (55–64 for example) the picture is far less clear with increase coming before decrease especially for the mortality of males. As well as capturing differential trends, figure 5.7 is interesting in terms of the opportunity it offers to pin-point short-run fluctuations. For example, mortality in the adult age groups was espe-

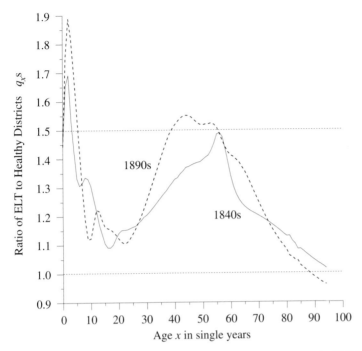

Figure 5.6. Ratio of national to healthy districts q_xs for ELT 3 and HDLT 1 for the 1840s, and ELT 6 and HDLT 2 for the 1890s

Note: For those ages where the curves rise above the 1.5 horizontal line there is especially high excess mortality.

cially heightened in the late 1840s at the time of the Irish famine, and among young children the year 1911 is associated with substantially higher mortality.[31]

Age-specific gender differentials in mortality rates are also apparent in figure 5.7. These can be seen in detail in figure 5.8 which gives the ratio of male to female q_xs from ELT 3 and HDLT 1. It is clear that at least in the 1840s females were likely to experience excess mortality in the age range 8–40 or 45, but it is also obvious that the excess was greater in those 63 'healthy districts' used to construct HDLT 1 and in which, as we have already seen, mortality was lower at every age than in the

---

[31] These period effects will be obscured when decennial averages are used in comparative analyses. For example, it seems likely that ELT 3, which spanned the late 1840s, would have given lower life expectancy at birth than the background level of mortality warranted. The average annual CDR for 1838–54 was 22.44, for 1846–49 it was 24.01 and for 1838–45 it was 21.76. This may explain why the e_0s for ELT 1 (1841) were 40.19 and 42.18 (males and females); for ELT 2 (1838–44) they were 40.36 and 42.04; but for ELT 3 (1838–54) they were lower at 39.91 and 41.85.

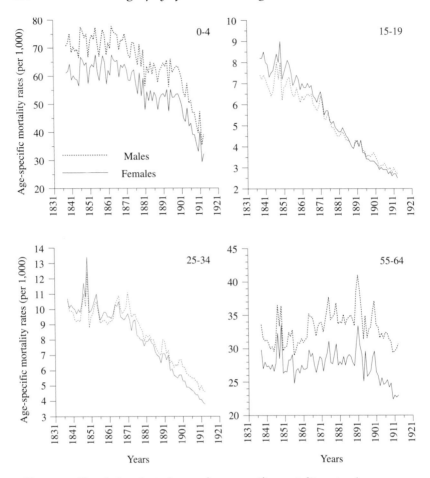

Figure 5.7. Trends in selected annual age-specific mortality rates (0–4, 15–19, 25–34, 55–64), England and Wales, 1838–1913

English and Welsh population as a whole (see figures 5.5 and 5.6). Figure 5.9 gives a different perspective on the same issue. It shows smoothed time-series for the same four age-specific mortality rates selected in figure 5.7 and charts their change between 1838 and 1913. It would probably be unwise to read too much into the trends for 15–19 and 25–34, but it would seem that the period of excess female mortality in the latter age group ended in the early 1860s while for the former it was the late 1880s. By 1891 there was male excess mortality at all ages, although not necessarily in all places and all marital statuses, as there still is today in England and Wales. The series for 25–34 appears to

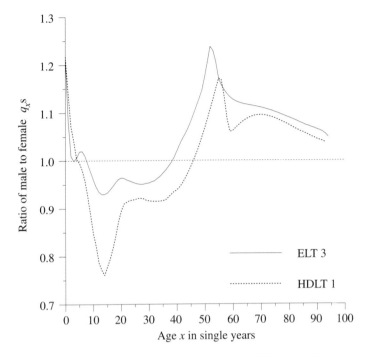

Figure 5.8. Ratio of male to female q_xs from ELT 3 and HDLT 1
Note: For those ages where the curve falls below the horizontal line,
mortality was higher for females than males.

suggest that female excess mortality may have been a phenomenon
restricted to the middle decades of the nineteenth century, but we have
no way of establishing this for certain.[32]

In the paper Edmonds completed for the *The Lancet* in February 1836,
he pointed out what he called the double coincidence between the law
of mortality and the law of sickness. 'In both observations, the quantity
of sickness suffered by a given number living, increases with the age
according to the same rate. *The rate of increase is identical with the rate of
increase in mortality according to age;* and is expressible by the number or
"constant" which I have used in the construction of all my theoretical
tables of mortality, between the ages of 15 and 55 years.'[33] As the empirical basis for his argument Edmonds used material prepared by the
editor, William Farr, and published in the *British Medical Almanack* for
1836. In subsequent papers, especially that of September 1842, he was

[32] Henry (1989) attempts an international historical comparison, but reaches few firm
conclusions, although he does stress the importance of tuberculosis and the role of
maternal mortality.   [33] Edmonds, 'Laws of sickness' (1835–36), p. 856.

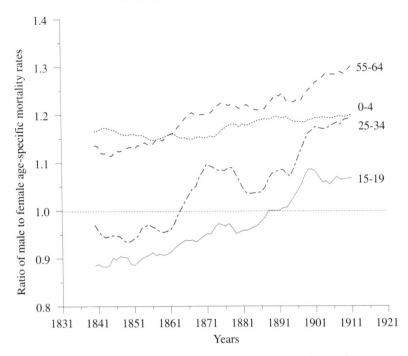

Figure 5.9. Trends in the ratio of male to female annual mortality rates
for selected ages (0–4, 15–19, 25–34, 55–64), England and Wales, 1838–1913
Note: 5-point moving means have been applied to the ratios. For those years in
which the curve falls below the horizontal line, there was excess female
mortality.

able to show that his theoretical Mean mortality table matched rather
closely the experiences of the Equitable and Amicable Life Assurance
Societies, but the definition and reliable measurement of sickness posed
a considerable problem for actuaries of his and subsequent generations.[34] The matter was made somewhat simpler by the 1890s when
several of the larger friendly societies had accumulated sufficient
members as well as mortality and sickness experience to make surveys

---

[34] Whereas death has only an incidence, sickness has both an incidence (new cases of
illness) and a prevalence (how many people are sick at any one time and what is the
average duration of their sickness). The self-reporting and medical certification of sickness also must be distinguished. For the life assurance companies and the friendly
societies, sickness came to be measured as the average duration of certified work-preventing ill-health. There was also a selection effect in terms of the characteristics of
those holding and withdrawing from cover, a problem which Edmonds tried to quantify in several of his papers. Farr's work on this problem is summarised in 'Sickness
and health insurance', in Farr, *Vital Statistics* (1885), pp. 498–517. See also Riley (1997),
especially pp. 239–40.

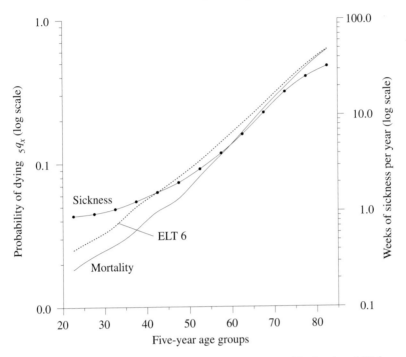

Figure 5.10. Age-related mortality and sickness curves, England and Wales
Note: $_5q_x$s for males from ELT 6 (1891–1900) are shown alongside $_5q_x$s and
average number of weeks of work-preventing sickness per year from the
1893–97 survey of members of the Independent Order of Oddfellows.
Source: Watson (1903), table 1.

based on their records reasonably reliable. Figure 5.10 uses data from
perhaps the best known of these surveys, the one conducted by Alfred
W. Watson for the Manchester Unity of the Independent Order of
Oddfellows (IOOF) in the years 1893–97.[35] It compares three age-related
curves: the probability of dying and the average number of weeks of
work-preventing sickness per year from the IOOF survey, and male
adult mortality from ELT 6 for 1891–1900. While the two mortality
curves have the same shape, the slope of the sickness curve flattens out
below age 50. Figure 5.10 also illustrates what would appear to be lower
mortality among the friendly society members than in the male population as a whole.

The laws of mortality and sickness by age are not now accepted in the
way that their discoverers hoped. Edmonds was clearly too ambitious

---

[35] Watson (1903). See also Watson (1931) and on the problems of using these data for pre-
dictive purposes, Woods (1997).

in his claims to have found a universal truth, and even the more restricted law advanced by Gompertz has gained currency as a method of smoothing rather than as an invariant structural regularity. None of this is surprising. Only Farr's successors could begin to see the ways in which mortality patterns might change over time. Before the 1880s far more effort was needed to establish some of the fundamental regularities, to check the quality of data, to develop new methods of estimation and, for those working before the 1840s, to attempt to say anything of a reliable nature about even the level of mortality let alone its age structure certainly required an act of faith. Farr himself was an enthusiastic advocate of the effort to identify laws of vitality. This is especially clear from his work on cholera and elevation, and the 'laws of disease'.[36] The latter, which are concerned with an individual's chances of recovery, the course of an epidemic over time, and the effects of environmental differences on disease patterns, have proved the most resilient. Brownlee, for example, has claimed that 'the first attempt to describe epidemics quantitatively is due to Dr Farr'.[37] But Farr's own particular, distinctive and lasting contribution to the search for laws of mortality is principally associated with his description of the relationship between mortality and population density. It is this which has come to be known as 'Farr's law'.

Farr's law

From the *Fifth* to the *Fortieth Annual Report*, Farr returned repeatedly to the observation that the populous and densely crowded towns not only experienced higher mortality than the rural areas of England and Wales, but that the relationship between mortality and population density could be expressed in a mathematical fashion and that it too was one of the laws of mortality. Farr's first formal assertion of his law came in the *Supplement* to the *Thirty-fifth Annual Report* for the 1860s where he showed that the crude death rate (CDR) in the registration districts of England and Wales, excluding London, varied with the 12th root of

---

[36] Farr (1852). This was not one of Farr's most successful attempts at quantification, but even so its approach still highlights his concerns and the variables he thought significant: 'In the county of Hereford only one death from cholera was registered in 1849. This county lies high up the River Wye; the population is scattered, and engaged in agriculture: it is out of the line of railways. The common drink of the people is cider.' (p. 155)

[37] Brownlee (1915), quoted from p. 250. Brownlee was thinking especially of Farr's efforts to model the rise and fall of the number of new cases in an epidemic over time. He attempted this exercise on cattle plague, smallpox and cholera with some success. See also the discussion of measles and scarlet fever in chapter 8 (p. 319).

their population density and the 6th root of their average proximity.[38] But even in the early 1840s, in an appendix to the *Fifth Annual Report*, Farr had demonstrated that among the 30 registration districts of London the death rate varied with the 6th root of population density.[39] Figure 5.11 illustrates the method he adopted in the 1870s. Farr first grouped the 593 districts in terms of the death rate – groups I to V with CDRs 15–17 to 27–30 – plus two separate categories for Manchester and Liverpool, making seven in all. The density of population per square mile, the average proximity in yards and the observed CDR were then calculated for these seven groups of districts. Figure 5.11 shows the association between the observed CDR and density as well as the fitted curve for the 8th root. The 53 group I districts with CDRs less than 17.5, the healthy districts of the 1860s, proved to be somewhat exceptional, however, with lower death rates than the law would predict on the basis of population density. Farr explained this anomaly in the following terms.

It will be noticed that there is not much difference in the density of groups I and II, and yet the mortality in group I is much lower than the mortality in group II. It may therefore be inferred that there are many more small towns in group II than in group I, and in those small towns the effects of a higher density are felt, whereas in group I the population is more evenly distributed over the area. Were the population aggregated to the same extent as it is in group II, it is probable that the mortality would approximate to 18.90 [the predicted value of CDR for group I].[40]

Although convincing, this explanation also highlights the problem of using arbitrarily defined districts – in some areas, small towns and scattered settlements were combined within the same district whereas in other places towns were made separate districts in their own right. Farr was aware, of course, of the problems associated with the use of death rates (what demographers now term crude death rates), but at the time these were the simplest measures to use if all registration districts were to be included in the analysis.[41]

[38] In fact the 8th root ($x^{0.125}$) is closer. See also Farr, *Vital Statistics* (1885), p. 175. Brownlee (1920) substitutes life table death rates for crude death rates and compares the 1860s, 1880s, 1890s and 1900s, while Bowley (1923) considers the influence of housing density, measured by persons per room, using data for 1911–13.

[39] William Farr, 'Causes of high mortality in town districts', in *Appendix* to Registrar General's *Fifth Annual Report*, pp. 200–15.

[40] Farr, *Vital Statistics* (1885), p. 175. The observed CDR for group I was 16.75. Farr used this same grouped mean method to consider the effects of density on male and female mortality separately, as well as its differential effects on age-specific mortality.

[41] The Statistical Society of London regularly debated the problem of how to measure the quality of life and relate it to prevailing sanitary conditions. See, for example, Chadwick (1844), Neison (1844) and Humphreys (1874). Farr contributed to the discussion of Humphreys's paper. The debate continues: for example, Crafts (1997) and Sen (1998).

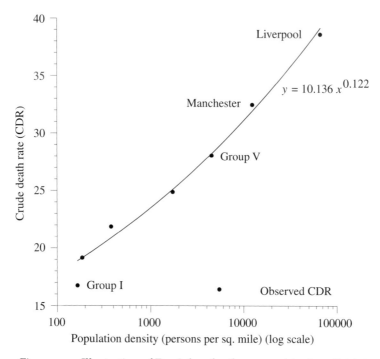

Figure 5.11. Illustration of Farr's law for the 593 registration districts
of England and Wales (excluding London), 1861–70
Note: See text for definitions of the groups.

We are now able to cast Farr's law in terms of the relationship
between life expectancy at birth in years (e_0) for decades and population
density, to consider each district rather than groups, and to compare
the associations during the last five decades of the nineteenth century,
again using the districts of England and Wales (614 including 25 for
London).[42] These relationships are summarised in figure 5.12, and table
5.3 gives the regression coefficients.

Considering the number of districts, there was certainly a close and
statistically significant relationship between life expectancy at birth and
population density. It is also clear from the positions and slopes of the
regression lines that in terms of average mortality the whole system
improved during the half century. However, the slight reduction in the
beta coefficients (*b*) indicates that, if anything, the more densely popu-

---

[42] The Registrar General's *Decennial Supplements* for 1851–60, 1861–70, 1871–80, 1881–90
and 1891–1900 provide age at death as well as cause of death data for the registration
districts of England and Wales. The 614 comparable districts are shown in figure 2.1.
See also Woods and Shelton (1997).

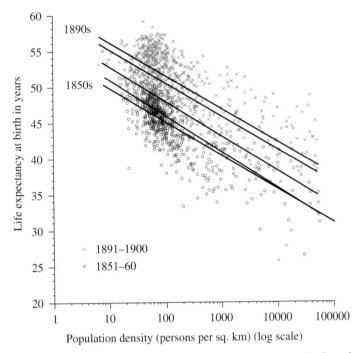

Figure 5.12. The association between life expectancy at birth and
population density among English and Welsh districts for the five decades
1851–60 to 1891–1900
Note: For simplicity only observations for the 1850s and 1890s are shown, but
each of the five regression lines is illustrated. The regression coefficients are
given in table 5.3.

lated districts were experiencing higher rates of decline. It is also clear
that improvements between decades were not equal; mortality decline
faltered between the 1880s and 1890s. On the evidence of figure 5.12 it
is certainly reasonable to accept the existence of a strong and persistent
association between mortality and population density. The principle of
Farr's law is just as appropriate as the Gompertz–Makeham hypothesis
or Edmonds's multi-component law of mortality. None has the status of
a physical law, but each summarises important characteristics of
mortality patterns and structures.

However, the association that Farr's law attempts to summarise is, if
anything, substantially more diffuse than the influence of age on
mortality. It is also less easy to justify in theoretical terms and, under
certain circumstances, may not even apply when either particular measures of mortality are selected or sets of specific localities are chosen. For

Table 5.3. *The changing association between life expectancy in years (y) and population density measured by persons per sq. km. or population size (x) among 614 English and Welsh districts using the equation $y = a - b\log x$*

Decade	Life expectancy at birth with population density			Partial life expectancy ages 25–65 with population density			Life expectancy at birth with population size		
	a	*b*	r^2	*a*	*b*	r^2	*a*	*b*	r^2
1851–60	54.457	−4.698	0.581	29.529	−1.237	0.340	85.035	−9.304	0.526
1861–70	55.778	−4.979	0.603	29.696	−1.332	0.333	85.085	−7.784	0.496
1871–80	57.532	−4.805	0.554	30.498	−1.472	0.357	85.744	−8.168	0.544
1881–90	59.645	−4.608	0.567	31.195	−1.405	0.339	87.468	−9.152	0.552
1891–1900	60.591	−4.592	0.528	32.195	−1.522	0.359	88.005	−9.786	0.584

Note:
The simpler log function is fitted here rather than the power function ($y = ax^b$) adopted by Farr. The goodness of fit is not substantially reduced. See figures 5.12, 5.15 and 9.2.

example, one problem with the approach adopted in the construction of figure 5.12 is that each district is given equal weight in the analysis despite their containing very different proportions of the total English and Welsh population.[43] For example, of the 614 districts just 103 contained half the national population in the 1860s, with 55 per cent in those same districts by the 1890s. The positions of these 103 districts are shown in figure 5.13, which also reproduces the five regression lines for the decades and the full set of districts from figure 5.12. Now the association between life expectancy at birth and population density appears not only less close, but also less sensitive to variations in density. Taking this line of argument one step further, one-third of the population of England and Wales lived in 50 districts in the 1860s and in only 39 in the 1890s. The positions of these 50 and 39 districts are illustrated by figure 5.14. In the 1890s the 39 most populous districts, which together contained a third of the total population of England and Wales, did not conform to Farr's law; increasing density did not, on average, adversely affect the level of mortality. Farr's law could be broken, indeed it was his intention that this should happen as a consequence of the public health movement and sanitary reform. It was by no means inevitable that places with high population densities should be obliged to suffer high mortality. In this respect Farr's law is better thought of as a general rule, another yardstick for comparison, just as his Healthy Districts Life Table was used to set the low mortality standard, so the death-rate density law could be used to establish normal expectations.[44]

Farr himself recognised that the relationship he had discovered was created by the combination of all ages and causes of death; that individual age groups may not conform to the law. This point can be illustrated by using the case of adult mortality as measured by the partial

---

[43] Farr's own method of grouping districts with similar death rates does not give each district equal weight, rather it averages away substantial intra-group variation. Farr used the same method here that he had adopted in his work on the influence of elevation on cholera mortality in 1849, and the problem had been commented on at the time by Dr W. H. Duncan (Medical Officer of Health of Liverpool, 1847–63):

> Taking the districts [of Liverpool] singly where the difference of elevation is only 2 or 3 feet, I find the law is not carried out, but apparently overpowered by disturbing elements which come into operation. But when the districts of approximating elevations are grouped together, and the groups so formed contrasted, the results distinctly point to a relation between the elevation of the soil, and mortality from cholera. (From a letter by Duncan to Farr dated 15 May 1852 published in Farr (1852), p. 183.)

[44] The case of Liverpool, repeatedly (and some would claim unfairly) singled out by Farr and others as the unhealthy urban standard, illustrates this point. Dr Duncan, the Liverpool Medical Officer of Health, frequently protested the unfairness of this treatment. See Frazer (1947), especially pp. 99–102 and 116–19.

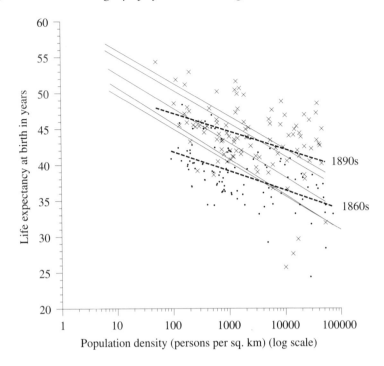

$$1861\text{–}70 \quad y = -2.684\text{LOG}(x) + 47.225 \quad r^2 = 0.291$$

$$1891\text{–}1900 \quad y = -2.510\text{LOG}(x) + 52.213 \quad r^2 = 0.168$$

Figure 5.13. The association between life expectancy at birth and population density among the 103 most populous districts of England and Wales

Note: 103 districts in the 1860s contain half of the population; the same districts contain 55 per cent in the 1890s.

life expectancy between ages 25 and 65 ($e_{25\text{–}65}$, maximum 40 years). Figure 5.15 adopts the same method used in figure 5.12. For partial life expectancy between 25 and 65 the gradients are even shallower and the fits less good even than those for e_0 (table 5.3).

Although Farr's law does summarise a persistent statistical relationship between mortality and density it is clearly sensitive to the way in which mortality is measured. Mortality among adults, especially those of working age, is not influenced to any considerable extent by variations in population density. The inference to be drawn must therefore be that mortality in infancy and childhood is highly sensitive to variations in density, and that it is therefore mortality at early ages in general that

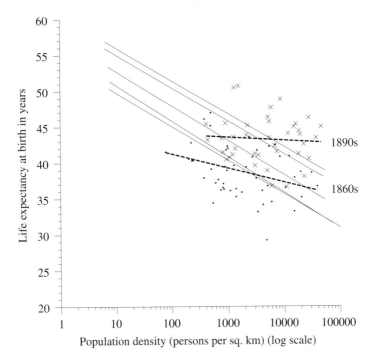

$$1861–70 \quad y = -1.984\text{LOG}(x) + 45.201 \quad r^2 = 0.123$$

$$1891–1900 \quad y = -0.441\text{LOG}(x) + 44.868 \quad r^2 = 0.006$$

Figure 5.14. The association between life expectancy at birth and population density among the most populous districts of England and Wales
Note: 50 districts shown for the 1860s and 39 for the 1890s contain a third of the population.

makes Farr's law appear to operate. Further, some causes of death must be far more responsive to population density differences, especially those like measles which require a pool of susceptibles where infection can spread rapidly in densely crowded conditions, and the water-borne diseases like diarrhoea, dysentery and cholera which thrive in poor sanitary environments, particularly when they coincide with high population density. We shall return to these matters and consider them at greater length in chapter 8, which deals with geographical variations in cause of death, and chapter 7, which considers variations in infant and childhood mortality in detail.[45]

[45] See also Woods and Shelton (1997).

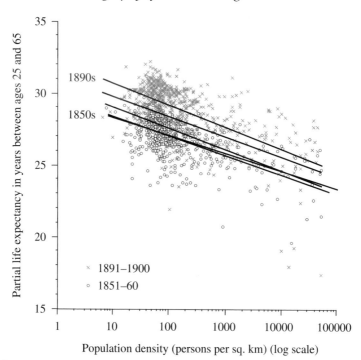

Figure 5.15. The association between partial life expectancy ages 25–65 and population density among English and Welsh districts for the five decades 1851–60 to 1891–1900
Note: For simplicity only observations for the 1850s and 1890s are shown, but each of the five regression lines is illustrated. The regression coefficients are given in table 5.3.

Finally, it may be worth pausing to consider the extent to which Farr's law could also have applied to change over time in the level of mortality: was the extent of relative change also associated with population density in the way that the general mortality rate was? If we measure relative change in mortality via life expectancy at birth and in partial terms between ages 25 and 65, then the answer seems to be that for adult mortality population density did not predict the rate of change between the 1860s and the 1890s while for life expectancy at birth the higher density districts did indeed tend to be those which experienced some of the higher rates of mortality decline. In most of the populous, high density districts life expectancy at birth improved by about 10 to 20 per cent during the 40-year period while in a substantial number of the low density rural districts life expectancy improved to only a modest extent. Part of the reason for the lack of association illustrated in figure 5.16

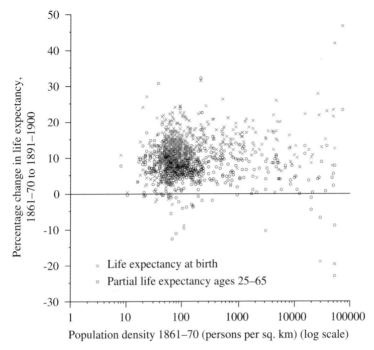

Figure 5.16. Relationship between percentage change between the 1860s and the 1890s in life expectancy at birth and partial life expectancy 25–65 and population density among English and Welsh districts

relates to the initial level of mortality at mid-century. Where mortality was high and life expectancy low there was also considerable scope for relatively rapid change, but in many of those rural districts where the environmental penalty was at a minimum, life expectancy could not improve much further in the nineteenth century.

While Farr and his successors were fully aware that there were distinct geographical variations in mortality patterns which could be summarised to some extent by the population density law, the calculation of e_xs for all the registration districts was beyond the computational capacity of the Victorian General Register Office. We are now in a position to complete the process of description which the statistical superintendents began. Figures 5.17 and 5.18 (colour section, pages *i* and *j*) show life expectancy at birth and the partial life expectancy between ages 25 and 65 for the 614 districts and the five decades 1851–60 to 1891–1900.

Table 5.4 charts the changing mean and variance measures of life expectancy for decades alongside e_0 and e_{25-65} for England and Wales as a whole. It shows, first, that while the life expectancies for England and Wales were followed by those for the district means and medians, the latter were always higher because of the skewed size distribution of districts. A small number of populous districts had high mortality, as table 5.3 and figures 5.13 and 5.14 also confirm. Secondly, the coefficient of variation indicates that overall mortality was substantially more variable than adult mortality alone, that mortality among males was more variable than among females, and that, in general, variability among the districts increased somewhat during the nineteenth century although this was more marked in the age group 25–65 than it was for life expectancy at birth.

Finally, we are also able to chart geographical variations in the pattern of mortality differentials between males and females, again using e_0 and e_{25-65}, and to establish their stability by comparing the 1860s and the 1890s. Figure 5.19 (colour section, page *k*) shows the orthogonal residuals for the two life expectancy measures for the two decades.[46] In general the districts in the south of England show the highest positive residuals although there are important local variations. In those districts females fared better than males in terms of their life chances.

The Gompertz–Makeham hypothesis, Edmonds's theory and Farr's law each plays their part in the history of actuarial and demographic science in the nineteenth century. Each one symbolises the vigour with which laws were sought and the tenacity with which they were defended once discovered. Edmonds's work never received the recognition it deserved from the scientific establishment; Gompertz was always preferred and he it is who is still remembered today. But Edmonds had a substantial influence both in his own right and via Farr. It was Edmonds and Farr who were the pioneers of practical medical statistics through their work on the measurement of mortality, the identification of regularities, the specification of achievable standards and the direct communication of their findings to medical practitioners through the pages of *The Lancet*, the *British Medical Almanack* and the Registrar General's *Annual Reports*.[47] Their empirical work on the laws of vitality helped contemporaries to appreciate more clearly how mortality varied especially with age and among different environments,

[46] See Humphries (1991) for an exercise using orthogonal regression on the registration counties. Orthogonal regression was also used to illustrate gender differences in literacy; see figure 4.14 and footnote 4.68 (p. 147). See also Woods and Shelton (1997), pp. 134–41.

[47] This is the approach taken by Newsholme (1923). Newsholme's own contribution to medical statistics is considered in chapter 7 with respect to infant mortality and in chapter 8 on tuberculosis.

Table 5.4. *Variations in the level of mortality among the 614 districts of England and Wales, 1851–60 to 1891–1900*

Decade	Life expectancy at birth in years					Partial life expectancy ages 25–65				
	England & Wales	Mean	Median	Variance	Coefficient of variation	England & Wales	Mean	Median	Variance	Coefficient of variation
1838–54 (ELT 3)	40.88					25.42				
1851–60	41.11	44.49	45.09	16.95	9.25	25.97	26.90	27.15	2.01	5.27
1861–70	41.19	45.06	46.09	19.42	9.78	25.67	26.83	27.23	2.52	5.92
Males	39.86	44.17	45.22	22.83	10.82	25.19	26.71	27.15	4.40	7.85
Females	42.56	46.10	46.88	16.66	8.85	26.16	27.01	27.15	1.79	4.95
1871–80	42.97	46.06	48.23	20.71	9.88	25.96	27.29	27.64	3.02	6.37
1881–90	45.34	49.50	50.60	19.58	8.94	26.71	28.10	28.59	3.04	6.20
1891–1900	46.14	50.39	51.35	22.26	9.36	27.33	28.81	29.28	3.60	6.59
Males	44.38	49.18	50.34	25.67	10.30	26.62	28.36	28.74	4.89	7.80
Females	47.92	52.12	53.30	20.71	8.73	28.05	29.26	29.62	2.84	5.76
1901–10	50.92					29.05				

Source: Derived from the Registrar General's *Decennial Supplements* for 1851–60 to 1901–10 using the districts shown in figure 2.1. The coefficient of variation is the ratio of the standard deviation to the mean expressed here as percentages; see also table 6.5.

and how life chances might be improved by public health interventions. Although the laws of vitality were crucial for the identification of problems and the monitoring of change, they were never able to capture all of the regularities to which Victorian mortality patterns were subject. Chapter 6 considers perhaps the third most important dimension – occupation. It focuses especially on the 25–65 age group.

6

Mortality by occupation and social group

Independently of the influence of the material and of the work itself on health, the place in which men work exercises so great an influence that it has to be taken into account in judging of the salubrity of their occupations.[1]

Mortality may be said to depend upon two factors, the man himself and his circumstances or environment, including his occupation.[2]

Even now there exists a discernible mortality gradient between social groups defined by combinations of occupations in terms of some preconceived status hierarchy. It is a commonplace that income, education and housing quality are linked in a self-reinforcing fashion; and that poor diet and heavy smoking and drinking are in broad terms also connected. There exists today a 'trailing class' – one made up from the most vulnerable, the least healthy, the most prone to long-term unemployment and the one whose members have the lowest life chances. Among the other social classes there are some signs that, in the late twentieth century, convergence accompanied the steady rise in life expectancy. Occupation, and thus social class, is but a mirror to wealth and habit; work itself is likely to be more or less dangerous, but the labour market acts as both a sieve and a social labelling device.

Prompted by the Black Report of 1980 many recent studies have attempted to chart changing trends in the level of mortality and the extent of ill-health between sub-populations defined in terms of adult

---

[1] William Farr, 'Health of men engaged in various occupations', in *Supplement* to the Registrar General's *Thirty-fifth Annual Report* (BPP 1875/XVIII, Part II), p. lvii.

[2] T. H. C. Stevenson in his introduction to 'On the mortality of men engaged in certain occupations during the three years 1910, 1911 and 1912', in *Supplement* to the Registrar General's *Seventy-fifth Annual Report*, Part IV.

male occupations.[3] They have encountered at least four problems. First, and in practical terms, the classification of occupations into social classes may change from census to census, but social scientists are now far more conscious of 'class' as a debased concept in relation to gender, race and ethnicity. Yet the social grading of occupations is still practised and its influence on the way society has been represented in the twentieth century remains profound. Secondly, measurement of class mortality patterns may prove difficult, especially if numerator–denominator biases are encountered in terms of the numbers dying and those at risk, and their representation will not be straightforward. Thirdly, strong selection effects may be present with poor health causing or accompanying downward social mobility. Fourthly, if the object is to explore mortality and health differentials then it will be important to distinguish the effects that are truly occupation- or class-related from those that have an environmental bearing, such as poor quality housing. When social classes are spatially segregated it may prove difficult to separate the social from the environmental.[4]

Even when the mortality differentials can be charted with some degree of confidence there are still problems of interpretation. For example, studies of the health and mortality of British civil servants have been used to emphasise the importance of relative deprivation and not just material well-being. Marmot has proposed the 'general susceptibility hypothesis' by which he argues that certain groups will be at higher risk of death whatever the causes, although the operation of specific causes is not denied.[5] 'People's life courses vary, to a great extent, by social location. And negative effects on health may accumulate throughout a person's life. That influences on health cluster in such a way as to produce among social groups differing degrees of disadvantage with respect to susceptibility to most diseases is undeniable.'[6] Marmot also suggests other possibilities. A process of indirect selection may create a link between the conditions of early life and the health risks in adulthood. A particular form of this effect has come to be known as the 'Barker hypothesis'. Here the link is between foetal

---

[3] Townsend and Davidson (1982). The Acheson Report, *Independent Inquiry into Inequalities in Health: Report* (London: The Stationery Office, 1998), has now succeeded the Black Report. Both of these reports adopt a 'socio-economic model of health and its inequalities' which while appropriate for the late twentieth century cannot be said to apply with equal force to the nineteenth century.

[4] Some of these problems have been discussed by Fox *et al.* (1985), Goldblatt (1989), Sloggett and Joshi (1994), and Drever and Whitehead (1997).

[5] Marmot (1994). Even when age and smoking are standardised, for the gradient of relative risk of heart disease persists with administrative grades less vulnerable than clerical.   [6] Marmot (1994), p. 206.

development measured by birthweight and the risks of heart disease in later life.[7]

Most of these recent studies are especially concerned with mortality differentials, how they are structured in terms of gender, social group, place of residence, and whether they are widening. Life expectancy is generally high and slowly rising, and most lengthy periods of ill-health are concentrated in old age. It is assumed that high quality medical care exists although it is acknowledged that access to it may be restricted in ways that are socially and geographically constrained. Further, the importance of individual behaviour and personal health is emphasised especially in terms of diet, smoking, alcohol consumption and exercise. The medical establishment in Victorian England was also concerned with mortality and morbidity differentials and especially as they manifested themselves in geographical and social terms. But medical care was generally ineffective and far more emphasis was given to material conditions in the home, at the workplace and in the local environment generally. Solutions were sought first in terms of public health measures – sewerage and water supply – and subsequently in terms of individual responsibility – personal hygiene, spitting and maternal care. We have already seen in chapter 5 that geographical inequalities in mortality persisted throughout the Victorian era. If Farr's law can be said to have operated in the 1850s, then it was still working in the 1890s; life expectancy was associated with population density. But were there also strong differences between occupations and social groups in terms of mortality? Was there a Victorian social mortality gradient? In the absence of effective medical therapy, were material conditions principally responsible for whatever differentials existed or, then as now, did relative deprivation have an important bearing on health and mortality risks?

Since modern studies of social class mortality levels and differentials have encountered important methodological problems, several of which are mentioned above, it will come as no surprise that nineteenth- and early twentieth-century studies were also bedevilled by difficulties. The Registrar General first defined 'Social Classes' for use with the 1911 *Fertility of Marriage Census* and these have been used in chapter 4 to illustrate one of the characteristics of fertility patterns in the late Victorian and Edwardian period. The eight groups, five social classes and three occupational groups, are defined in table 4.1. For 1921–23, and in subsequent attempts to record social class mortality patterns, the Registrar

---

[7] Barker (1994). See also Barker and Osmond (1987) who suggest that 'past variations in prenatal and early postnatal influences determined the current geographical distribution of ischaemic heart disease and stroke in England and Wales' (p. 752).

General merged the three groups – textile workers, miners and agricultural labourers – with the five classes. The classes are supposed to reflect the social status that accompanies skill, but for 1910–12 there is a tendency to rely on industrial sectors which conceal differences in skill levels between workers and which are, in any case, self or relative reported either on a census enumeration or a death certificate.[8] The occupations combined into classes are for adult males but, as for fertility so with mortality, married women can be classified according to their husband's occupation. It may also be significant whether a man is occupied or retired since it is often impossible to separate the two other than by considering only selected age groups and assuming that there are few retired members at those ages. The device used to measure mortality may also introduce distortions. The standardised mortality ratio (SMR) applied to occupied and retired men of all ages has proved perhaps the most popular measure, but it is often indexed so that 'all classes' is set at 100. Alternative approaches calculate SMRs for particular age groups – 25–64 for example – or estimate life table functions such as life expectancy at age 20 (e_{20}) or partial life expectancies (e_{25-65}).[9]

Some of these problems of measurement and representation are illustrated in figure 6.1 which also helps to identify the social class mortality patterns that prevailed in the first half of the twentieth century. The mortality gradient for 1930–32 for males in the age group 25–64 (figure 6.1a) is unambiguous. The SMR increases in an almost linear fashion from class I to class V and is closely followed, with the exceptions of classes I and II, by the curve for married women.[10] For 1921–23 classes II, III and IV have SMRs similar to those for 1930–32, but the professional group (I) experienced lower mortality and the unskilled manual workers (V) higher mortality than in 1930–32. Figure 6.1b for 1910–12 and using the indexed SMR for all occupied and retired men does not show such a clear mortality gradient. Here classes I, II, III and IV appear rather similar in level, but class V has much higher mortality. Of course, some of the differences between 1910–12 and 1921–23 result from the way in which three substantial occupational groups (VI, VII and VIII)

[8] Stevenson was especially sensitive to the problem of using industrial categories rather than occupation, but he regarded the new classification of 1921 as much improved in this respect. See Stevenson (1923), especially pp. 382–83, and Stevenson (1928).

[9] The following provide discussions of some of these classification and measurement problems: Collis and Greenwood (1921), Greenwood (1922, 1939), Yule (1934), Vernon (1939), Logan (1954), Pamuk (1985).

[10] Dr Percy Stocks, who took over from T. H. C. Stevenson as Chief Medical Statistician at the General Register Office in 1933, used the differences between the relative social mortality gradients for men and married women in 1930–32 to illustrate the true influence of occupation and social class on mortality. See Stocks (1938).

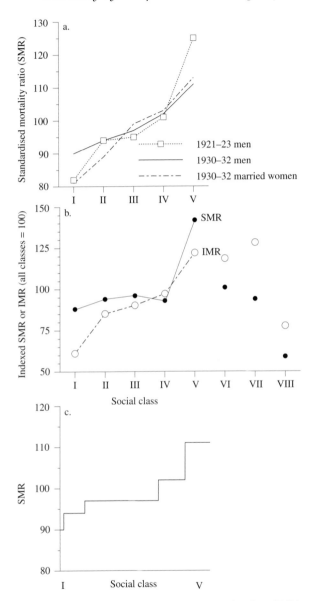

Figure 6.1. The social class mortality gradient in England and Wales: (a) SMRs for age group 25–64, 1921–23 and 1930–32; (b) indexed SMRs for occupied and retired men, 1910–12, and legitimate infant mortality rates (IMRs), 1911; (c) SMRs for occupied and retired men, 1930–32, where length of line represents relative size of group

Source: Vernon (1939), p. 186; Logan (1954), tables III and VIII.

have been removed from the general classification in 1910–12 and given separate status, but were incorporated in I to V in subsequent classifications. The agricultural labourers (VIII) have very much lower mortality even than members of class I; place of residence is probably more important in this case than occupation. Figure 6.1b also shows indexed estimates of the class-specific legitimate infant mortality rate (IMR) for 1911.[11] The IMRs help to define an additional dimension of the social mortality gradient and one that for several interesting reasons does not conform exactly to the pattern that can be established via SMRs for adult males.[12] Finally, figure 6.1c illustrates the effect that large differences in group size may have. In 1930–32, 49.2 per cent of all occupied and retired men were placed in class III (skilled manual workers), and only 2.5 per cent in class I.

The examples provided in figure 6.1 help to set the context for our examination of occupational-specific and social-group specific mortality in the preceding sixty years. Unfortunately, the picture they paint is far from clear. For example, they could be used to argue that before the First World War only on the bottom rungs of society were life chances sufficiently differentiated from the experience of the middling sort for any form of gradient to be identified. Such a view would be consistent with the idea that although there may have been occupation-specific mortality differentials in the nineteenth century they were confounded by even stronger environmental differences and that these, in conjunction with a rather more simple class structure, created very different patterns to those evident in the 1930s.

Before attempting a detailed reconstruction of the Victorian pattern of occupational mortality based on the Registrar General's statistics it may prove helpful to review briefly the results of some of the other studies of social differences conducted in the period.[13] Unfortunately, there are few such reliable studies and these focus either on the aristocracy or the upper middle classes, and deal not just with adult males but with family members in general. In other words, they are studies of mortality among families of the peerage and the upper and professional classes rather than occupational mortality as such. Two of the most interesting of these are provided by Bailey and Day on the families of British peers, and Charles Ansell on the families of members of the upper and profes-

---

[11] Registrar General's *Seventy-fourth Annual Report for 1911*, table 28b, p. 88. The total legitimate IMR in 1911 was 124.9.

[12] The relationship between infant and adult mortality poses some interesting and complicated problems which will be considered later in the chapter and at greater length in chapter 7.   [13] Woods and Williams (1995) offer a longer-term perspective.

Table 6.1. *Comparison of social differences in mortality levels in nineteenth-century England and Wales*

	e_{20}		e_{25-65}	
	Males	Females	Males	Females
Peers' families	41.46	43.48	27.26	26.42
Upper and professional class families	42.11	46.02	27.10	27.74
HDLT 1 (1849–53)	43.40	43.50	27.93	27.59
ELT 3 (1838–54)	39.48	40.29	25.30	25.53
ELT 4 (1871–80)	39.40	41.66	25.13	26.56

Sources: Peers – Bailey and Day (1861), tables I and II; upper and professional classes – Ansell (1874), table III.

sional classes.[14] Bailey and Day's population comprised those peers, sons and daughters of peers, and sons and daughters of the eldest sons of peers who lived between 1800 and 1855, while Ansell's was a retrospective survey conducted in 1871 of the life events of nearly 50,000 children whose fathers were clergymen, lawyers or doctors. Their findings are summarised in table 6.1 using life expectancy at age 20 in years (e_{20}) and the partial life expectancy between ages 25 and 65 (e_{25-65}). The mortality experiences of male and female family members are compared, as are those summarised by the third and fourth English Life Tables (ELTs 3 and 4) and the first healthy districts life table (HDLT 1).

Table 6.1 illustrates three points. First, there is little clear sign of a mortality gradient. Certainly there were differences in terms of mortality experience between the top of the social status hierarchy and the average. For example, among males, while the peers and professionals enjoyed 70 per cent of the maximum possible 40 years of life between ages 25 and 65, in England and Wales as a whole the figure was about 63 per cent at mid-century, but in the healthy districts it was also 70 per cent. Secondly, females usually experience superior life expectancies to males, but the differences between groups are in line with those for males. Thirdly, the measures selected in table 6.1 show rather different

[14] Bailey and Day (1861) and Ansell (1874). These are both extremely interesting studies in terms of their methodologies and the comparisons they adopt. Both make a point of saying that they intend to rely on the facts, rather than hypotheses (Ansell, p. 15) or graduation (Bailey and Day, p. 310), in order to make their calculations. Bailey and Day are also highly critical of other peerage studies, including those of T. R. Edmonds (see p. 174 above). Other interesting studies, at least in terms of the methods they adopted if not their results, include: Guy (1843b, 1843c, 1844, 1845), Humphreys (1887) and Dunlop (1909).

aspects of the mortality pattern and it may be that social differentials are especially vulnerable to misinterpretation because of the index chosen. The most important point that table 6.1 illustrates is that it is not a simple matter to identify a Victorian social mortality gradient from studies based only on individually selected groups. However, this may still be possible using the Registrar General's material.

The official reporting of occupational mortality in Victorian England

The Registrar General's *Fourteenth Annual Report for 1851* contained the results of the first efforts by William Farr to record the mortality of occupations, that is deaths among adult men aged 15 and over. There followed six further attempts to repeat the exercise before the First World War: for 1860–61, 1871, 1880–82, 1890–92, 1900–02 and 1910–12. These were recorded three times by Farr himself, once by William Ogle (1880–82), twice by John Tatham and once by T. H. C. Stevenson. They appeared in *Supplements* to the *Twenty-fifth, Thirty-fifth, Forty-fifth, Fifty-fifth, Sixty-fifth* and *Seventy-fifth Annual Reports*. Every one of these seven reports, with accompanying tables, represents an impressive statistical achievement. In each case the Statistical Superintendent used individual death certificates as his basic source, thus permitting combination into occupations, age groups, causes of death and occasionally geographical areas according to the stated information. However, Tatham and Stevenson tended to focus on cause of death and occupation, and as we have already seen, the latter also defined social classes, while Farr did not use causes of death and avoided reporting geographical variations disaggregated by age at death. Ogle provided comparatively rudimentary material on age, cause and geography for 1880–82.[15] Table 6.2 offers a summary of the data available in the seven *Supplements*.

Something of the spirit of the undertaking, and the extent of its rapid development once initiated, can be gained from Farr's first, rather brief report on the 'Mortality of Persons in Different Occupations'.

There is considerable difficulty in determining the mortality and duration of life among men of all the professions, owing to the uncertainty in the naming of trades. But some occupations are well defined; and of those the mortality is shown in the annexed Tables . . .

As in the case of towns, so it may be said of men of unhealthy occupations;

---

[15] The discussion of Dr Stocks's paper to the Royal Statistical Society contains some interesting observations by Major Greenwood and others on the reasons the statistical superintendents probably had for shifting their emphasis in the *Supplements* from geographical variations to causes. Greenwood, for example, remarks that Ogle profoundly distrusted the occupational mortality data. See *Journal of the Royal Statistical Society* 101 (1938), p. 697.

the mortality is susceptible of reduction by the investigation and removal of its causes.

Thus the miner may be protected from explosions; and to a large extent from underground injuries by greater care on his own part, and on the part of the managers and proprietors. He may be saved from the excessive fatigue of ladder climbing; and if the mines were well ventilated, he would not break down by so early and premature an old age.

The publican has only to abstain from excesses in spirits and other strong drinks to live as long as other people.[16]

How may the material in these *Supplements* be used to answer the questions posed at the beginning of the chapter? Ideally, one would wish to have data for a large and consistently defined set of occupations reported by five-year age groups and with some consistent indication of cause and place of death. This would provide the numerator of any ratio while the population censuses, to which these reports were at least notionally anchored, would provide the denominator, the 'at risk' element. It is also highly desirable to trace changes over time, rather than simply consider variations at a point, and to deal consistently with occupied *or* occupied and retired men.[17]

Let us begin the tortuous process of consolidation and comparison with the implications of this last point. Farr's work uses material from occupied and retired men, while Ogle's and Tatham's uses that for occupied only but also reports occupied and retired for 1900–02 along with Stevenson's for 1910–12. Because Ogle's data for 1880–82 are further limited by their reporting of five age groups, and then only two between 25 and 64, it would seem reasonable to exclude 1880–82 from further consideration in a comparative analysis, although it should be remembered that Ogle did pioneer the tabulation of cause of death for some occupations and that he also began the important process of refining the number of occupations considered, a task continued by his successors. The exclusion of 1880–82 and 1890–92 from further consideration would make for an extremely narrow window of observation if it also proved impossible to employ Farr's compilations. Here the problem is that Farr only used one year of mortality data in 1871 and it would therefore seem unwise to let that year stand on its own as the single representative for the mid-century. Farr himself solved the problem by combining mortality data for the three years 1860, 1861 and 1871 which he related to 'at

---

16 William Farr in his letter to the Registrar General as part of the *Supplement* to the *Twenty-fifth Annual Report of the Registrar General* (BPP 1865/XIII), pp. xxxv–xxxvi. The text of Farr's entire report on occupational mortality is quoted.

17 Haines (1991), especially table 10.1, gives death rates for males in the age group 25–65 in 1860–61 with 1871, 1880–82 and 1890–92 without reference to the 'occupied' or 'occupied and retired' problem.

Table 6.2. *Data on occupational mortality in the* Supplements *to the Annual Reports of the Registrar General*

Number	1	2	3	4	5	6	7
Period	1851	1860–61	1871	1880–82	1890–92	1900–02	1910–12
Supplement to Report	*14th*	*25th*	*35th*	*45th*	*55th*	*65th*	*75th*
Statistical Superintendent	William Farr	William Farr	William Farr	William Ogle	John Tatham	John Tatham	T. H. C. Stevenson
Occupations	For E & W: for occupied and retired men reports 17 classes, 88 sub-classes, 360 occupations	For E & W: for occupied and retired men reports 6 classes, 18 orders, 83 sub-orders, 360 occupations	For E & W: for occupied and retired men *Supplement* **Table 63** has 72 occupations for 1860–61 & 1871	For E & W: for occupied men *Supplement* Table J has 100 occupations mostly comparable with 3 (Table 63), also reported in Table 6	For E & W: for occupied men *Supplement* Part II, Table I equivalent to Table 6 in 4	For E & W: for occupied, and occupied and retired men *Supplement* Part II, Table II as for Table I in 5 but gives death rates	For E & W: for occupied and retired men *Supplement* Part IV, Table III reports occupation-specific age-standardised mortality measures
Age groups	For E & W: 20–24, 25–34, 35–44, 45–54, 55–64, 65–74, 75–84, 85+	For E & W: 5–9, 10–14, 15–19, 20–24, 25–34, 35–44, 45–54, 55–64, 85+	For E & W: **Table 63** has 15–19, 20–24, 25–34, 35–44, 45–54, 55–64, 65–74, 75+	For E & W: Table J has 25–44, 45–64; Table 6 has 15–19, 20–24, 25–44, 45–64, 65+	For E & W: Table I has age groups as for Table 63 in 3, but for 65+	For E & W: age groups as for 5	For E & W: age groups as for 3
Causes of death	None	None	None	Fo r E & W: Table K has 13 causes for 43 occupations for ages 25–64;	For E & W: Table III has 24 causes of death for age group 25–64;	For E & W: Table III as for Table III and **Abstracts Table** in 5	For E & W: **Abstracts Table** gives 27 causes for occupations and social classes

	Places	Notes
	For ages 20+: divisions	Brief report with 2 tables of rates
	For E & W ages and occupations: divisions, 80 town districts, town districts in divisions	Longer report with special table on mortality among butchers and publicans
Table L has comparative rates	None	Detailed report with many special tables
Abstracts Table has 24 causes and age groups as Table I	None	Very detailed and extensive report with many special tables
	Deaths classified as occurring in London, industrial registration districts, agricultural districts, other districts, but not systematically tabulated	Again, very detailed report
None		Explanatory notes rather than full report

Note:
The principal sources used in this chapter are highlighted in bold.

risk' estimates drawn from the 1861 and 1871 censuses in order to calculate mortality rates for 62 occupations. This procedure will also be followed here. The 1851 material will also be excluded since it too relates to only one year and the information on occupational categories in 1851 was probably less safe than in subsequent censuses.

Thus far the following common elements have been identified: deaths among men who were occupied in or retired from certain occupations and who died aged between 25 and 64 (broken down into four equal ten-year age groups) in the years 1860–61 with 1871, 1900–02 and 1910–12. Other age groups could have been used, but including 65 and over would introduce unnecessary distortions in terms of those who were not currently occupied at their deaths while the younger age groups, 15–19 and 20–24, were not only likely to have been occupationally volatile in terms of employment turnover, but at such ages mortality rates were at their lowest in adulthood.

How should those 'certain occupations' be defined? For 1880–82 and 1890–92 Ogle and Tatham, respectively, used 100 occupations which Tatham extended to 105 in 1900–02 and Stevenson to 132 in 1910–12. After an exhaustive process of shifting and matching, 71 distinctive occupations were finally chosen for comparison. Each selected occupation appeared in a consistent form in the 1860–61, 1871, 1900–02 and 1910–12 *Supplements* and in the 1861, 1871, 1901 and 1911 censuses. These 71 occupations provide the building blocks for the discussion of occupation-specific and social-group specific mortality in the remainder of this chapter.[18]

Mortality among occupations

It might be objected at the outset that 71 occupations will not be sufficient to capture the true level or diversity of adult male mortality, but table 6.3 indicates that these objections should be set aside in the case of level and probably also in terms of variation. The 71 occupations contributed 46 to 48 per cent of all deaths in England and Wales among men aged 25–64, and 46 to 53 per cent of that male population was to be found in those occupations. When it comes to an assessment of mortality levels, there are certain obvious problems.[19] The standardised

---

[18] Williams (1990) provides a detailed description of the occupations used to report mortality in the *Supplements* and the censuses.

[19] Farr, of course, understood these difficulties only too well. 'The mean age at death of people in different businesses often furnishes very erroneous indications, as it is affected as much by the ages at which people enter and leave, and by the increase or decrease of employment, as by the salubrity or insalubrity of any particular profession. The only way in which the mortality, and the duration of life, of miners, tailors, farmers,

Table 6.3. *Standardised mortality ratios (SMRs) for men, England and Wales*

	1860–61 & 1871	1900–02	1910–12
SMR for all men aged 25–64	374	339	268
SMR for men in the 71 occupations	372	314	248
Percentage of deaths among men aged 25–64 contributed by the 71 occupations	46	46	48
Percentage of male population aged 25–64 in the 71 occupations	46	51	53

Note:
The standardised mortality ratio (SMR) uses the male population of England and Wales in 1911 as its standard.

mortality ratios (SMRs) for the 71 occupations are close to, but up to 7 per cent lower than those for all men. Table 6.4 shows that, with one exception, the age-specific probabilities of dying ($_{10}q_x$s) are lower for the 71 occupations in combination. The simplest explanation is that some of the least well-defined or repeatedly redefined occupations also tended to have higher than average mortality. They are more likely either to be among the 30 or so occupations which appear in the 1900–02 list, but are not among the 71, or they were not even selected by Tatham or Stevenson in the first place. In general, there is every reason to think that these 71 occupations will be capable of representing the wide variety of mortality experiences among all occupations and that they will adequately capture trends as well as differentials – although, once again, it should be remembered that there are many industrial groups among the 71.

What measures should be used to capture the mortality experience? Tables 6.3 and 6.4 adopt different approaches: SMR and $_nq_x$. The standardised mortality ratio has the advantage that it is a single number indicator and is certainly appropriate for comparative work between the 71 occupations, but it cannot readily be used to make comparisons with other groups or periods unless the standard population is the same. Life table measures are superior in this respect. The four

labourers, or any other class of men can be accurately determined is to determine the ratio of deaths at each age to the living during a certain time – in fact to apply the same method to each class as is applied to determine the mortality and the mean life-time of all classes in a town, in a district, or in the whole kingdom.' Quoted from William Farr's report on occupational mortality in the *Supplement* to the Registrar General's *Thirty-fifth Annual Report* (BPP 1875/XVIII, Part II), p. liii.

Table 6.4. *Probabilities of dying in ten-year age groups among all men aged 25–64 in England and Wales and men in 71 occupations*

Age groups	1860–61 & 1871		1900–02		1910–12	
	All men	71 occup.	All men	71 occup.	All men	71 occup.
25–34	0.094	0.092	0.062	0.055	0.047	0.042
35–44	0.123	0.120	0.104	0.093	0.077	0.069
45–54	0.170	0.169	0.171	0.158	0.137	0.126
55–64	0.277	0.281	0.296	0.289	0.259	0.249

age-specific probabilities of dying – $_{10}q_{25}$, $_{10}q_{35}$, $_{10}q_{45}$ and $_{10}q_{55}$ – have been used where appropriate, in table 6.4 for example, but it will also be of benefit to select single number indices to reflect the entire experience of occupation-specific mortality among adult men. In this case the same measures as those used in table 6.1 will be adopted – life expectancy at age 20 in years and the partial life expectancy between ages 25 and 65 where the maximum is 40 years – to assist comparison with other mortality estimates for Victorian England and Wales. Life expectancy at age 20 has been estimated by finding $_{40}q_{25}$ (the probability of dying between ages 25 and 65) from the four $_{10}q_x$s and using Coale and Demeny's West models to derive e_{20} (by using e_{20}(males) = 62.720 − 42.848$_{40}q_{25}$).[20] This procedure has the disadvantage that it makes assumptions about the relationships between mortality in the 25–64 age group and that in the 20–24 and over-65 age groups. The former is probably more justifiable than the latter. An equivalent procedure has been used to derive e_{25-65}. It is important to appreciate that any single number mortality measure that is used to summarise the entire experience of adult mortality will be synthetic in the sense that it will reflect the experience of the hypothetical person who remains in the same occupation from age 20 or 25 until his death. For example, according to the West models, if e_{20} is 40 years then only 43 per cent of 20-year-olds will reach their sixtieth birthday.

Figure 6.2 shows the life expectancy at age 20 for all men and those in the 71 occupations for 1860–61 with 1871, 1900–02 and 1910–12, and for comparative purposes the equivalent e_{20}s for the English Life Tables and Healthy Districts Life Tables. ELTs 3 to 5 show e_{20} for men to be about 40 years from the 1840s to the 1890s, rising to 41 in the 1890s (ELT 6), 44 by 1910–12 (ELT 8) and 46 by 1920–22 (ELT 9). In the healthy districts, e_{20}

[20] Coale and Demeny, with Vaughan (1983).

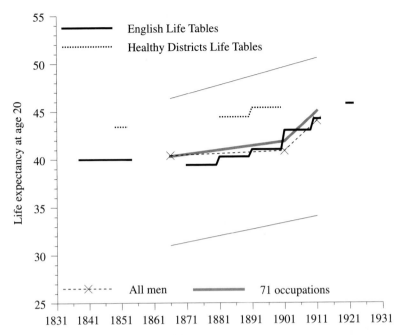

Figure 6.2. Variations in life expectancy at age 20 among men,
England and Wales, 1831–1931
Note: The two upward sloping diagonal lines indicate the general range of
mortality experienced by the 71 occupations. They are also shown on figures
6.7 to 6.13.

for men was approximately four years longer. The slightly divergent
diagonal lines mark out the range of experience among the 71 occupations.

To summarise, we have estimates of $_{10}q_x$s for four age groups and e_{20}s
for 71 occupations for the periods 1860–61 with 1871, 1900–02 and
1910–12. The estimates for the 71 occupations in combination are sufficiently close to those for all men aged 25–64 and these in their turn
capture a fifty-year slice of the longer-run slow improvement in adult
mortality which began to accelerate in the last decades of the nineteenth
and on into the early twentieth century.[21]

There are several ways in which this material can be manipulated
and its essential points extracted. Here we shall consider in turn,
first, changes in the age structure of mortality levels among the 71
occupations; secondly, the possibility that as mortality began to fall

[21] See table 5.4 and figure 5.18 for variations in e_{25-65} among the districts.

occupation-specific mortality differentials actually widened in the late nineteenth century; thirdly, variations and changes among the occupations in terms of life expectancies; fourthly, broader social group mortality patterns using some of the 71 occupations; and, fifthly, certain individual, often notoriously unhealthy, occupations from the perspective of their place in the history of occupational health. Finally, an attempt will be made to identify some aspects of the direct effect of occupation on mortality as opposed to the other social, economic and environmental conditions consequent upon being engaged in a particular occupation.

It is a rather complicated matter to disentangle regularities in the age components of mortality change among so many groups and during two time periods. To simplify, only change between 1860–61 with 1871 and 1910–12 will be considered in detail, although it should be remembered that a disproportionate amount of the decline in adult mortality observed occurred in the last decade compared with the first two. Figure 6.3 provides a framework for the examination of changes in $_{10}q_x$ among occupations. It plots the four $_{10}q_x$s for 1910–12 against those for 1860–61 with 1871 and links the points so that the level of overall mortality between ages 25 and 64 can be assessed. The three lines linking $_{10}q_{25}$ to $_{10}q_{35}$, $_{10}q_{35}$ to $_{10}q_{45}$, $_{10}q_{45}$ to $_{10}q_{55}$ would be expected to increase in length as the chances of dying normally increase with age, while the total length of the three lines reflects $_{40}q_{25}$ and thus the general level of adult male mortality. The central diagonal in figure 6.3 would be followed if there had been no change in the mortality components, while the three spaces – A, B and C – contain those components that have declined by up to 25 per cent, 25 to 50 per cent and by more than 50 per cent, respectively. In the case of the 71 occupations in combination: $_{10}q_{25}$ falls in C, $_{10}q_{35}$ in B and $_{10}q_{55}$ in A, while $_{10}q_{45}$ falls on the 25 per cent reduction line.

As far as the 71 occupations are concerned, mortality appears to have declined in a systematic fashion and this is neatly illustrated by figure 6.3. However, among the occupations there is the appearance of greater diversity with increasing age, suggested by the lengths and angles of the regression lines in figure 6.4. For example, the regression line through the $_{10}q_{55}$s appears to break the trend of increasing steepness shown by the other three regression lines. In some occupations mortality in the 55–64 age group declined by as much as 25 per cent, but in others it increased and in the 25–34 age group mortality declined by more than 50 per cent in nearly all occupations. Figure 6.4 encourages the observation that occupation-specific mortality declined between the 1860s and 1910–12 mainly because mortality under age 45 declined substantially in all occupations, and the further speculation that these changes

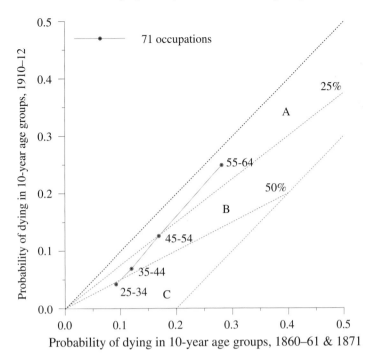

Figure 6.3. A framework for describing the age composition of
mortality change among 71 occupations
Note: See text for explanation.

affected most occupations in a near uniform fashion. What caused
mortality to fall in most occupational groups was not to do with the
occupations themselves, but was far more universal in its consequences.
Differentials in mortality levels persisted because rates of decline were,
on the whole, not occupationally differentiated.

Figure 6.5 picks out four individual occupations to illustrate some of
the more interesting untypical variations. Mortality among clergymen
was particularly low compared with the other 70 occupations and especially compared with members of the medical profession whose mortality levels remained at least as high as the average for the 35–54 age
group, but among many young doctors mortality did not decline very
substantially at all. Physicians and surgeons shared the mortality level
of butchers in the 1860s and rose to a position slightly above that of carpenters by 1910–12. Of the occupations shown in figure 6.5 the notori-
ous 'dangerous trades' of file maker and potter exemplify the worst
levels of mortality. In both cases the lines are far longer than the ones for

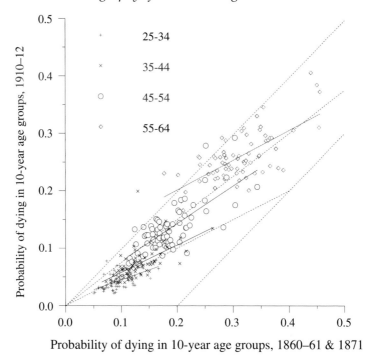

Figure 6.4. Age composition of mortality change among 71 occupations
Note: Regression lines have been plotted through the distributions for each of
the four 10-year age groups.

all 71 occupations in combination, but in each age component there has been reduction of mortality although this was relatively slight among young potters and elderly file makers. We shall return again to these and other examples of the experiences of members of particular occupations later in the chapter. At this stage, figure 6.5 merely suggests some points that may be taken up later.

As we have already seen, there has been a long and at times acrimonious debate in the recent medical literature about the extent and causes of persistent mortality differentials in the twentieth century and especially since 1931. Much of this debate has focused on occupational groups or, more often, on social classes, although geographical areas have become increasingly popular as units for comparison. There has been discussion about the most reliable statistical means by which to monitor changes in differentials. For example, Illsley and le Grand have argued that measures which summarise the entire level of mortality – such as standardised mortality ratios and life expectancies at birth, or at

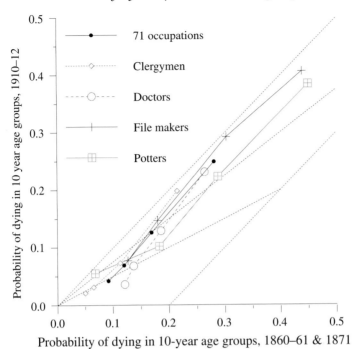

Figure 6.5. Age composition of mortality change among four occupations: clergymen, doctors, file makers and potters

age 20 in this case – may disguise distinctive and important age differentials.[22] Figure 6.4 also encourages this view. The substantive point at issue is summarised by the contention that as rapid change occurs – decline in mortality, for instance – differentials are bound to increase as leading and lagging occupations or areas move into the phase of transition at different speeds. Towards the end of the period of overall change, differentials will narrow. Today the arguments are rather different; now they focus on the way that, despite low mortality and continuing slow further decline, differentials still persist. During the second half of the nineteenth century when mortality began a steady secular decline from a high level, one would probably expect differentials to be accentuated, but to what extent and in which ways?

Table 6.5 reports the log variance (the variance of the logged values) of the $_{10}q_x$s for the 71 occupations. These are also captured in figure 6.6. As anticipated, the level of inequality in adult mortality (ages 25–64)

[22] Illsley and le Grand (1993).

Table 6.5. *Inequalities in age-specific mortality among 71 occupations measured by log variance and the coefficient of variation for the partial life expectancy between ages 25 and 65*

Age groups	1860–61 & 1871	1900–02	1910–12
25–34	0.0109	0.0155	0.0190
35–44	0.0124	0.0203	0.0204
45–54	0.0102	0.0127	0.0144
55–64	0.0068	0.0050	0.0050
25–64	0.0038	0.0050	0.0054
Coefficient of variation for e_{25-65}	8.88	8.29	7.49

Note:
The log variance is the variance of the logged values; the coefficient of variation is the ratio of the standard deviation to the mean expressed here as percentages. See also table 5.4.

increased during the 50-year period, but it did so because mortality differentials within the age groups 25–34, 35–44 and 45–54 increased (although these were to some extent offset by a reduction among 55–64 year olds). Relative inequalities were consistently at their highest in the 35–44 age group and rather less pronounced in the 25–34 and 45–54 age groups, in that order. The patterns and processes revealed in figure 6.6 while not entirely clear-cut are generally in keeping with the notion of increasing inequalities in mortality experiences between occupations in the last half of the nineteenth century, a process that probably only began to be reversed among adult men after 1931. Figure 6.6 also encourages speculation that mortality inequalities among occupations may have been even lower in the first half of the nineteenth century and that, with the exception of the 55–64-year-olds, they were very similar.

Despite the obvious advantages of considering the age components of mortality separately, there is still considerable value in representing an occupation's mortality level by a single measure. The one favoured here is life expectancy in years at age 20 (e_{20}), although the partial life expectancy (e_{25-65}) will also be used on occasions. Table 6.6 gives estimated e_{20}s for each of the 71 occupations in 1860–61 & 1871, 1900–02 and 1910–12. It is arranged in descending rank order of the e_{20} for 1860–61 & 1871. The percentage change between 1860–61 & 1871 and 1910–12 is also given. A cursory inspection of table 6.6 will reveal that there is no single, clear picture. There are occupations which would have been dangerous and poorly paid, others that were only poorly paid; some

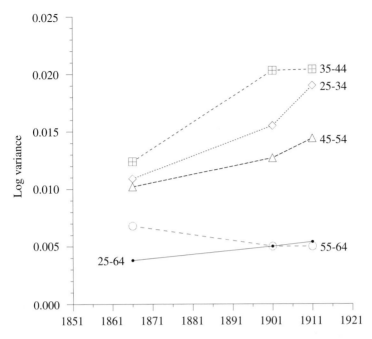

Figure 6.6. Trends in age-specific mortality differentials (log variance) among 71 occupations

that were dangerous yet relatively well remunerated, and some that were poorly rewarded but conducted in relatively healthy environments. Once again, it is the extreme positions in the list that catch the eye: clergymen, gardeners and farmers compared with potters, file makers, sweeps, inn servants and tin miners.

However, it may prove more interesting to consider bundles of occupations which, on the basis of common status, employment or career experience, one would assume would have encountered similar life chances. Six groups have been selected for closer examination: the professions, shopkeepers, clerks and officials, miners, those engaged in the production or sale of alcohol, and skilled tradesmen.

Although generally above the average for the 71 occupations, clergymen, lawyers, schoolmasters and doctors showed substantial differences in their mortality experiences (figure 6.7). Life expectancy at age 20 rose rapidly for schoolmasters, but, as we have already seen, among doctors it began from a below average position in the 1860s. The practice of medicine was at that time a hazardous profession in both financial and health terms; lawyers had practices that were overwhelmingly

Table 6.6. *Estimates of male life expectancy at age 20, in years, for 71 occupations, England and Wales*

	e_{20} 1860–61 & 1871	e_{20} 1900–02	e_{20} 1910–12	Percentage change 1860–61 & 1871 to 1910–12
Clergyman, priest, minister	46.35	48.99	50.08	8.04
Gardener, nurseryman, seedsman	45.90	49.49	50.55	10.12
Farmer, grazier, farmer's son	45.67	48.37	49.65	8.72
Grocer	44.58	45.49	46.78	4.93
Fisherman	44.43	42.80	43.88	−1.23
Wheelwright	42.98	44.56	46.39	7.93
Silk, satin, crape manufacturer	42.82	43.02	44.74	4.49
Maltster	42.76	45.20	47.10	10.15
Paper manufacturer	42.51	44.87	45.42	6.85
Sawyer	42.45	46.09	48.56	14.40
Coal merchant, coal burner	42.34	45.66	47.29	11.69
Carpenter, joiner	42.20	44.16	45.46	7.73
Stationery manufacturer	41.81	43.83	46.66	11.61
Domestic coachman, groom	41.75	44.28	46.51	11.41
Barrister, solicitor	41.71	45.26	46.66	11.88
Shoemaker	41.48	42.13	43.65	5.25
Wool, worsted manufacturer	41.44	41.78	43.27	4.43
Ironmonger	41.03	46.16	47.36	15.42
Schoolmaster, teacher	40.78	47.15	48.93	19.97
Tin, tinplate manufacturer	40.45	41.12	42.33	4.65
Carpet, rug, felt manufacturer	40.31	41.89	46.01	14.13
Artist, engraver	40.27	44.76	45.88	13.93
Fruiterer, greengrocer	39.94	42.84	45.02	12.71
Cabinet maker, French polisher	39.86	43.09	45.13	13.20
Currier	39.75	42.67	44.10	10.95

Occupation				
Tobacconist	39.70	42.88	44.92	13.15
Engine, machine, boiler maker, millwright	39.68	43.14	44.49	12.12
Miller, cereal food manufacturer	39.62	42.96	45.83	15.67
Watch, clock maker	39.58	44.32	45.58	15.15
Baker, confectioner	39.35	43.60	45.95	16.78
Saddler, harness maker	39.35	42.43	44.54	13.20
Physician, surgeon, general practitioner	39.34	43.16	45.66	16.06
Tanner, fellmonger	39.30	45.24	46.64	18.67
Gunsmith	39.30	40.30	41.13	4.66
Paperhanger, plasterer, whitewasher	39.29	41.99	44.52	13.33
Civil service messenger, workman	39.26	44.81	47.15	20.09
Tailor	39.26	41.63	43.68	11.28
Shipbuilder, shipwright	39.15	45.16	46.90	19.82
Textile dyer, bleacher, finisher	39.13	40.45	42.51	8.63
Chemist, druggist	38.89	42.16	44.69	14.91
Rope, twine, card maker	38.85	43.53	45.76	17.79
Railway official, clerk	38.66	45.45	47.21	22.14
Tallow, soap manufacturer	38.36	44.35	47.75	24.48
Cotton, flax manufacturer	38.28	40.29	42.72	11.60
Coal miner	38.27	43.73	44.83	17.12
Coach, carriage, railway coach maker	38.09	45.71	48.89	28.35
Chemical manufacturer	37.80	42.09	45.86	21.33
Slater, tiler	37.79	39.45	40.83	8.07
Draper, linen draper	37.76	44.34	46.61	23.42
Butcher	37.67	39.68	41.87	11.16
Ironstone miner	37.47	45.32	46.32	23.61
Commercial traveller	37.37	41.66	44.39	18.80
Commercial clerk	37.11	42.56	43.78	17.98
Printer	36.95	42.30	44.38	20.12
Hatter	36.71	41.97	44.56	21.39
Fishmonger, poulterer	36.57	42.14	44.58	21.90

Table 6.6. (cont.)

	e_{20} 1860–61 & 1871	e_{20} 1900–02	e_{20} 1910–12	Percentage change 1860–61 & 1871 to 1910–12
Glass manufacturer	36.57	39.07	41.50	13.48
Bargeman, lighterman	36.16	37.42	39.26	8.59
Bookbinder	36.07	43.64	44.42	23.14
Hairdresser	36.00	39.68	41.61	15.58
Carman, carrier	35.56	39.93	42.07	18.30
Coal heaver	35.33	39.26	41.38	17.12
Innkeeper, publican	34.49	34.10	37.40	8.44
Tin miner	33.96	32.01	34.20	0.71
Musician, music master	33.50	39.70	41.73	24.60
Law clerk	33.02	43.23	44.57	34.99
Brewer	32.71	37.78	40.44	23.62
Potter, earthenware manufacturer	32.65	35.36	37.25	14.10
File maker	31.87	33.35	34.05	6.83
Chimney sweep, soot merchant	31.30	37.75	40.38	29.01
Inn, hotel servant	31.00	33.90	39.18	26.38
Men in 71 occupations	40.31	41.85	44.98	11.59
All men	40.40	40.94	44.00	8.91

Note:
Male life expectancies at age 20 in years (e_{20}) have been estimated using $_{40}q_{25}$ and Model West from Coale and Demeny, Regional Model Life Tables and Stable Populations (1966).
Source: See table 6.2.

urban in location and especially metropolitan; compulsory education fostered the expansion and professionalisation of school teaching; most clergymen were well connected, well educated and comfortably housed in their rural parishes.[23] The four occupations referred to loosely as shopkeepers also show interesting differences (figure 6.8), especially between the grocers and the butchers. It is among the clerks and officials that some of the most spectacular improvements in mortality are to be found (figure 6.19), and among the miners some of the biggest surprises (figure 6.10). Mortality among coal miners, in particular, appears far lower than might be expected of a notoriously accident-prone occupation. The 'demon drink' was popularly believed to be the ruin of publicans, inn and hotel servants, but not it appears of maltsters (figure 6.11). We have already seen in figure 6.5 that potters and file makers suffered particularly high levels of adult mortality and this is generally confirmed by the e_{20}s in figure 6.12. These were skilled trades, but because of the working conditions or the use of dangerous chemicals, they were also far more hazardous to health and life than the working conditions endured by carpenters, tailors, gunsmiths or printers.[24]

The life expectancies reported in table 6.6 and shown in figures 6.7 to 6.12 would not appear to encourage efforts to combine occupations into broader social groups on the assumption that similar kinds of occupations might be expected to experience generally similar mortality levels. Social classes defined in terms of skill or status may, it seems, contain occupations which experienced substantially different levels of mortality. However, the exercise is still worth pursuing since it may help to shed more light on the problem of which units – occupations, classes, geographical areas, for example – are more or less appropriate for describing mortality differentials. In this case 'social groups' have been defined by selecting 28 illustrative occupations rather than forcing each of the 71 occupations into a class. While groups A to D are probably not exceptionable, group 'E' is based on the experience of only three occupations and yet unskilled workers represent a substantial section of the male adult workforce. Table 6.7 reports male life expectancy at age 20 as well as the partial life expectancy from ages 25 to 65 for five social groups constructed in this rather *ad hoc* and entirely subjective fashion, and figure 6.13 sketches out the trends. Again, the slightly divergent diagonal lines give the range for the 71 occupations.

[23] 'The clergy lead a comfortable, temperate, domestic, moral life, in healthy parsonages, and their lives are good in the insurance sense. The young curate compared with the young doctor has less cares.' Quoted from Farr's report on occupational mortality in the *Supplement* to the Registrar General's *Thirty-fifth Annual Report* (BPP 1875/XVIII, Part II), p. lv.   [24] On the potters, see Holdsworth (1995, 1997, 1998).

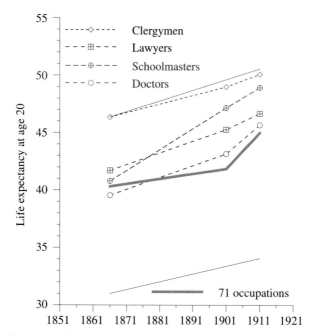

Figure 6.7. Variations in life expectancy at age 20 among male
members of selected professional occupations

Two points are immediately obvious and rather striking. First, social
groups A and 'E', and C and D tend to run parallel to one another while
maintaining the social mortality gradient. But, secondly, adult male life
chances in B, the white collar workers, dominated by clerks and lesser
officials but also now including schoolmasters, rise above those in D
and converge with C. This pattern can be seen even more clearly in
figure 6.14 which represents the social mortality gradient in the conventional way shown in figure 6.1. It also includes Ansell's estimate of e_{20}
for male members of the upper and professional classes, reported in
table 6.1 as 42.11 years, with which the figure for group A at 42.59 years
corresponds rather well.

In combination, table 6.7 and figures 6.13 and 6.14 illustrate three
important points. First, it is possible to gain some idea of the dimensions
of the Victorian social mortality gradient by combining example
occupations. Secondly, the gradients so produced for 1900–02, 1910–12
and 1921–23 all show that the intermediate white collar workers (B or
II) and the skilled manual workers (C or III) experienced similar life
expectancies, and that these were lower than those of the professions
but higher than those of the less skilled groups. Thirdly, the position of

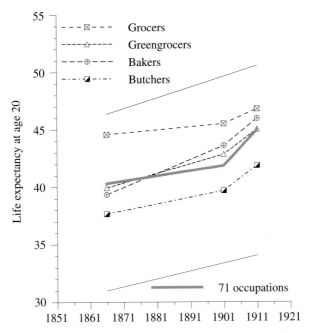

Figure 6.8. Variations in life expectancy at age 20 among male members of selected shopkeeping occupations

social group B improved dramatically in the second half of the nine-teenth century in both absolute and relative terms. Figure 6.9 helps to show how this came about in terms of some of the individual occupa-tions involved. The improvement in the life chances of this group of lower middle-class occupations is perhaps the most significant finding to emerge from this exercise. Finally, although group B is the most inter-esting case, it seems that adult mortality among all the groups declined between the 1860s and 1910–12 although the reduction was sub-stantially greater in the first decade of the twentieth century than earlier decades.

Having considered the form of the Victorian social mortality gradient and the ways in which male mortality in particular occupations varied, it now remains for us to focus on notoriously unhealthy occupations as a way of revealing the contribution of material conditions to adult health. In so doing it will also be possible for us to explore some related aspects of the Victorian effort to improve occupational health, and to advance a little further the discussion of the relative importance of the nature of the job itself or the environment in which employment was located for the rate of mortality experienced.

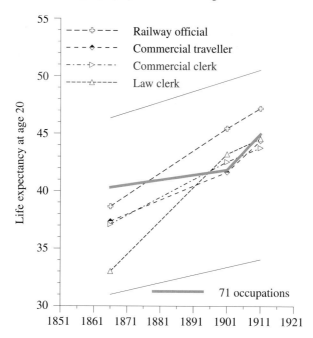

Figure 6.9. Variations in life expectancy at age 20 among male
members of selected clerical occupations

Two dangerous trades: medicine and mining

The health and mortality of members of the Victorian medical profession is of interest for several reasons. First, because one would expect doctors to have had the most medical knowledge which they could apply to themselves, to their families as well as to their patients, the mortality experience of members of the medical profession should act as a yardstick against which others can be compared. Secondly, unlike members of most other occupations, medical men were doctors for life and there was far less distinction between occupied and retired. In terms of the material listed in table 6.2, all *Supplements* can therefore be used to trace the changing level of mortality experienced. Thirdly, there were important differences of skill, status and specialisation within the medical profession which may be used to explore some aspects of the problem of within, as opposed to between, occupation variation in mortality. Finally, whilst not a subject for public or state concern the health experiences of doctors were of interest to the professionals themselves and this led to the publication of a number of important contem-

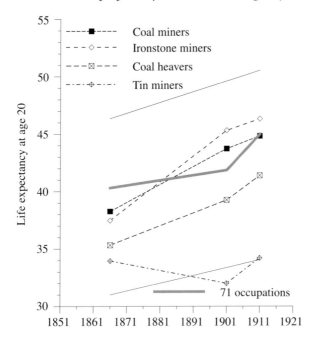

Figure 6.10. Variations in life expectancy at age 20 among male members of selected mining occupations

porary studies. Some of these points can also be made in relation to the miners. In particular, mining was differentiated in terms of health risk, in terms of type – coal, tin, slate, etc. – as well as location. It was a notoriously dangerous occupation because of the risk of accidents, but it could be relatively well paid especially for men in their twenties. Mining was also the subject of a Royal Commission in the 1860s to which William Farr, among others, gave specialist evidence.[25]

We have already seen something of the mortality pattern of Victorian doctors in figures 6.5 and 6.7 and table 6.6, but in this case other estimates of life expectancy can be made using the data in other

[25] Other occupations could have been selected for special attention, such as pottery workers, who were especially vulnerable to lead poisoning, and the file makers and grinders, who suffered from a range of respiratory diseases especially 'grinders' lung', but these have been relatively well documented elsewhere. See, for example, Arlidge (1892), Oliver (1902), Collis and Greenwood (1921) and Legge (1934). This chapter will not focus on the history of factory legislation, the attempt to control industrial diseases and the work of Sir John Simon (as Medical Officer of Health to the Privy Council) and Dr Edward Greenhow; for these see Wohl (1983), pp. 257–84, and Collis and Greenwood (1921), chapter 2, pp. 19–44.

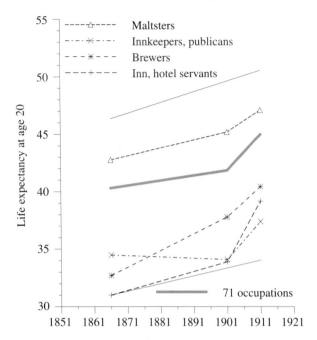

Figure 6.11. Variations in life expectancy at age 20 among male members of selected occupations engaged in the production or sale of alcohol

Supplements. It is also possible to use the short biographies for fellows of the Royal Colleges of Physicians and Surgeons published as *Munk's Rolls* and *Plarr's Lives* to derive mortality estimates.[26] These are shown in table 6.8 which also gives e_{25-65} for fellows of the Royal Medical and Chirurgical Society during the period 1805–49.[27] What is especially interesting about the medical profession is its generally high level of mortality compared with the other professional groups and even compared with the total adult male population, the way life expectancy improved in the nineteenth century so that doctors had similar experiences to men in general by about 1900, and the internal differences within the profession in terms of life chances.

The most vulnerable sub-section of the profession seems to have been

[26] These and other sources are considered at greater length in Woods (1996). See also William Farr, 'Medical profession. Draft report, as an example of the proposed mode of describing the professions (Class I.) in connection with the statistics of the census, 1861', in *Census of England and Wales for 1861, Volume III, General Report* (BPP 1863/LIII, part I), pp. 243–48. This even contains estimates of the 'numbers constantly sick to one medical man' for 1851–60 in the 11 registration divisions (table 4).

[27] Neison (1852), data from p. 216.

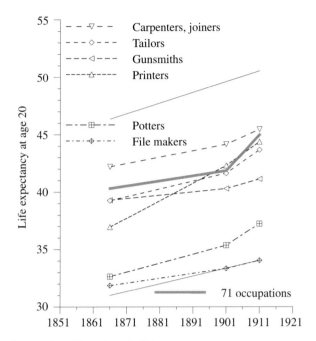

Figure 6.12. Variations in life expectancy at age 20 among male members of selected skilled trades

the younger doctors, those in their twenties and thirties who found it difficult to get started in practice.

Physicians and surgeons from youth up to the age of 45 experience a mortality much above the average; after that age they do not approach the priesthood in health, but differ little from the average. Many young practitioners have hard struggles to encounter. They are in contact with the sick; are exposed to zymotic disease, and their rest is disturbed. In states of depression deadly poisons are at hand. There is an excess of practitioners in cities. Country practitioners have to visit their patients in all weathers, at all hours. The causes from which medical men suffer deserve careful study.[28]

The élite of the profession, those who became fellows of the Royal Colleges, experienced lower levels of mortality, although not as low as that of the clergy. What is surprising is that, among the élite, the surgeons and the physicians – the FRCSs and the FRCPs – had similar

---

[28] Farr in *Supplement* to the *Thirty-fifth Annual Report for 1872* (BPP 1875/XVIII, part 2), p. lv. One of the reasons Farr turned to medical statistics and journalism was the problem he encountered establishing a practice in London in the 1830s without social connections or a university degree. See Digby (1994).

Table 6.7. *Measures of mortality for five social groups and their constituent male occupations, England and Wales*

Social groups and occupations	1860–61 & 1871		1900–02		1910–12	
	e_{20}	e_{25-65}	e_{20}	e_{25-65}	e_{20}	e_{25-65}
All men aged 25–64	40.40	26.20	40.94	26.56	44.00	28.59
Men aged 25–64 in 71 occupations	40.31	26.15	41.85	27.17	44.98	29.23
A. Professional	42.59	27.67	45.49	29.59	47.47	30.90
Clergyman, priest, minister	46.35	30.14	48.99	31.88	50.08	32.60
Barrister, solicitor	41.71	27.07	45.26	29.42	46.66	30.34
Physician, surgeon, GP	39.34	25.50	43.16	28.03	45.66	29.68
B. White collar	37.66	24.41	42.76	27.78	45.09	29.32
Law clerk	33.02	21.33	43.23	28.08	44.57	28.96
Schoolmaster, teacher	40.78	26.46	47.15	30.67	48.93	31.84
Commercial traveller	37.37	24.20	41.66	27.04	44.39	28.84
Commercial clerk	37.11	24.03	42.56	27.63	43.78	28.44
Railway official, clerk	38.66	25.05	45.45	29.55	47.21	30.71
C. Skilled manual	40.70	26.42	42.50	27.61	45.05	29.30
File maker	31.87	20.57	33.35	21.55	34.05	22.01
Carpenter, joiner	42.20	27.39	44.16	28.69	45.46	29.55
Gunsmith	39.30	25.48	40.30	26.14	41.13	26.69
Wheelwright	42.98	27.91	44.56	28.95	46.39	30.16
Watch, clock maker	39.58	25.67	44.32	28.79	45.58	29.63
Slater, tiler	37.79	24.48	39.45	25.58	40.83	26.49
Saddler, harness maker	39.35	25.51	42.43	27.55	44.54	28.94
Printer	36.95	23.93	42.30	27.46	44.38	28.84
Bookbinder	36.07	23.35	43.64	28.34	44.42	28.86
Cabinet maker, French polisher	39.96	25.85	43.09	27.99	45.13	29.33
D. Semi-skilled	38.78	25.15	39.73	25.78	43.55	28.31
Domestic coachman, groom	41.75	27.10	44.28	28.77	46.51	30.24
Carman, carrier	35.56	23.01	39.93	25.89	42.07	27.31
Bargeman, lighterman, waterman	36.16	23.40	37.42	24.23	39.26	25.45
Fisherman	44.43	28.87	42.80	27.79	43.88	28.51
Sawyer	42.45	27.56	46.09	29.96	48.56	31.60
Chemical manufacturer	37.80	24.49	42.09	27.32	45.86	29.81
Textile dyer, bleacher, finisher	40.31	25.37	40.45	26.24	46.01	27.60
'E'. Unskilled	35.31	22.86	37.70	24.04	41.62	27.03
Civil service messenger, workman	39.26	25.46	44.81	29.12	47.15	30.67
Inn, hotel servant	31.00	20.00	33.90	21.91	39.18	25.40
Coal heaver	35.33	22.86	39.26	25.45	41.38	26.85

Source: See tables 6.2 and 6.6.

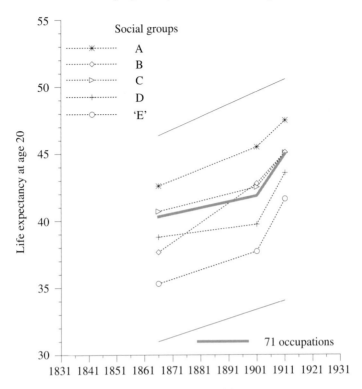

Figure 6.13. Social group-specific variations in life expectancy at age 20 among men, England and Wales

experiences. It might be expected that the surgeons would have had higher mortality since they were more regularly exposed to the risks of infection and accidents in the operating theatre which, in the years before Lister's anti-sepsis revolution took hold in hospitals, would have been extremely dangerous places for all concerned.[29] These differences between the élite and the rest of the profession had diminished by the first decade of the twentieth century and, as figure 6.15 illustrates, this was also the time when life expectancy for doctors first began to exceed that for all adult males.

It is not a simple matter to explain in detail why the life chances of doctors improved and just why some of the status and skill differences were so substantial at mid-century. Farr's opinion must carry some

[29] Joseph Lister (1827–1912) pioneered his antiseptic treatment in 1865 and published his findings in 1867 and his proposals for hospital procedures in 1870. It took 20 or 30 years for his ideas to be accepted and practised in Britain.

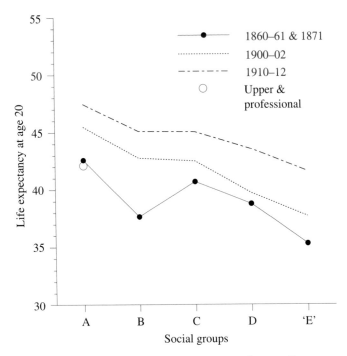

Figure 6.14. The Victorian social mortality gradient
Source: See table 6.7.

weight here. Young doctors were especially vulnerable in financial terms
as well as being exposed to a wide variety of diseases. But during the
second half of the nineteenth century, as the status of the medical profession began to rise slowly and knowledge about the causes of diseases
and the means of their prevention were advanced, doctors were able to
take at least some elementary measures to protect themselves. It is probably also significant that the medical profession represented one of those
groups for which the mortality experienced by the doctors themselves
was in relative terms at a higher level than the infant mortality experienced by their children. This would tend to suggest the importance of
the occupational hazards of medicine compared with the high quality of
the home environment and the child care provided in doctors' families.[30]

---

[30] In 1911 when the legitimate infant mortality rate for children whose fathers were
members of the medical profession was only 39, the total legitimate IMR was 125. Table
6.10 also shows the position of doctors in terms of estimated adult male excess mortality. The medical profession is also one of the groups contributing to the mismatch
between the position of adult males and infants in social class I as illustrated by figures
6.1b and 6.17.

Table 6.8. *Estimates of partial life expectancy between ages 25 and 65 in years among members of the medical profession, England and Wales*

	Partial life expectancy between ages 25 and 65 in years
Fellows of the Royal Medical and Chirurgical Society	
1805–49 (D = 96)	26.71
Fellows of the Royal College of Surgeons	
1851–60 (D = 147)	28.56
1861–70 (D = 270)	26.26
1871–80 (D = 338)	28.46
1881–90 (D = 331)	28.76
1891–1900 (D = 311)	30.91
1901–10 (D = 224)	31.02
1861–1910 (D = 1474)	29.60
Fellows of the Royal College of Physicians	
1861–1910 (D = 401)	29.34
Medical profession	
1851 (D = 235)	24.79
1860–61 & 1871 (D = 689)	24.12
1880–82 (D = 661)	24.63
1890–92 (D = 740)	25.59
1900–02 (D = 804)	27.22
1910–12 (D = 731)	29.64
1921–23 (D = 822)	30.82
1930–32 (D = 806)	30.94
1949–53 (D = 1002)	33.71
Mean for 1860–61 & 1871 to 1910–12	25.89

Note:
D is the number of deaths in the period. The 50 years 1861–1910 provide a convenient period for comparison, but the 1850s may also be considered for the FRCSs although not the FRCPs (D = 19). The e_{25-65}s in table 6.7 differ slightly from those above because they were estimated from model life tables using $_{40}q_{25}$.
Source: Woods (1996), tables 1 and 8.

Among miners, as figure 6.1b also shows for class VII, the opposite applied. The infant mortality among miners' children was higher, relatively speaking, than the mortality of the miners themselves. What is interesting about the miners from the point of view of occupational mortality is that they too were divided into important sub-groups in terms of the kind of mining that was being undertaken, but they were also geographically segregated. Did the miners in the South Wales

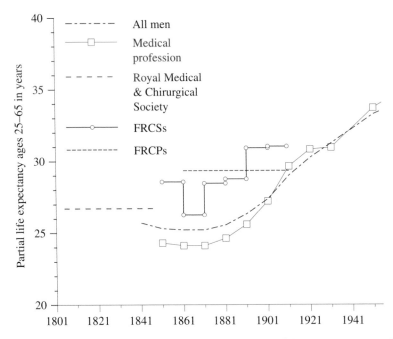

Figure 6.15. Partial life expectancy between ages 25 and 65 in years among all men and members of the medical profession, England and Wales

coalfield experience the same mortality risks as those in Staffordshire or County Durham? Figure 6.10 has already shown the differences between coal miners, ironstone miners, tin miners and coal heavers in terms of life expectancy at age 20 and in comparison with the 71 occupations. Coal and ironstone miners change places in the relative rankings, but for both groups there is improvement during the second part of the nineteenth century which places them just above the 71 by 1900–02. Coal miners appear to be more favourably placed than coal heavers who in their turn are better placed than tin miners. The position of coal heavers raises again the old problems of selection and the description of occupations. Only the strongest and healthiest men would have been able to work at the coal face; those who became unfit, the victims of the industry's diseases or of accidents might find jobs as surface workers or in other less demanding specialist roles. In the coalfields, coal heavers may have tended to be drawn largely from ex-face workers although elsewhere they are more likely to have been general labourers with no particular skills. For tin miners the conclusion seems inescapable: their life chances were not only especially poor, but conditions did not improve.

While there is little that can be done to remove the selection effect on mortality estimates, by using the results from one of Farr's special studies it is possible to consider in a little more detail not only the differences between the experiences of miners in certain districts, but also the life expectancies of non-miners in those same districts. As part of his evidence to the Royal Commission on Mines Farr provided some special mortality tabulations for 19 English and Welsh registration districts in the years 1849–53 and 1860–62. These are summarised for the earlier period in table 6.9 by using the partial life expectancy between ages 25 and 65. As one would expect, non-miners did fare better than miners in the combined 19 districts, but less well than the male inhabitants of the 63 healthy districts. But what is especially interesting about table 6.9 is the differences between and within the various mining areas. The miners of Merthyr Tydfil had partial life expectancies only a little over half the possible 40 years, while the figure for those in Durham and Northumberland was 69 per cent which was even better than for the non-miners. In the six Cornish districts the differential between miners and non-miners was at its greatest; indeed it seems most likely that had it not been for tin, lead and copper mining even more Cornish districts would have joined the ranks of the healthy districts (see figure 5.4). Conditions in Merthyr Tydfil were universally poor, even worse it seems than in highly urbanised Staffordshire. In short, even the mortality experience of coal miners was not the same in each field, nor for that matter was the occupational effect constant, that is, the difference between the background level of mortality and that additional danger associated with being a miner.[31]

The figures presented in tables 6.8 and 6.9 should not be used to oversimplify the story of occupational mortality in the nineteenth century. They suggest that, at the extremes, the type of work in which an adult was engaged could injure his or her health through crowding together in an insanitary environment, through contact with poisonous substances, through exposure to situations with a high accident risk, or through contact with the already ill. However, the figures also suggest that within a large occupational group there might be significant differences in experience and that the wider environment certainly did have an important bearing. Table 6.9 in particular helps to reinforce the point that the mortality experienced by adult men grouped in terms of occupation reflects far more than just the risks that are particular to that

---

[31] Stocks (1938), table II, p. 674, shows the relative mortality of coal miners in different coalfields, 1880–1932. In terms of highest to lowest mortality among miners the list is: Lancashire and South Wales, Staffordshire, Yorkshire, Durham and Northumberland, and Nottinghamshire and Derbyshire.

Table 6.9. *Estimates of partial life expectancy between ages 25 and 65 in years among miners and non-miners in 19 registration districts of England and Wales, 1849–53*

	Partial life expectancy ages 25–65	
	Miners	Non-miners
All 19 districts	23.60	26.58
Cornish districts	23.56	27.77
Staffordshire districts	22.23	25.64
Durham and Northumberland districts	27.49	26.01
Merthyr Tydfil, South Wales	20.40	21.91

Note:
6 Cornish districts – Liskeard, St Austell, Truro, Helston, Redruth, Penzance;
6 Staffordshire districts – Wolstanton, Stoke-on-Trent, Wolverhampton, Walsall, West Bromwich, Dudley;
6 Durham and Northumberland districts – Auckland, Durham, Easington, Houghton-le-Spring, Chester-le-Street, Tynemouth.
For England and Wales, e_{25-65} for all men is given as 25.13 and for the 63 healthy districts as 27.96 years.
Source: Derived from William Farr, 'Statistics and evidence', in *Appendix B* to *Report of the Commissioners Appointed to Inquire into the Condition of All Mines in Great Britain . . . Health and Safety of Persons Employed in such Mines* (BPP 1864/XXIV, part 2), pp. 154–78.

occupation, 'That mortality is influenced more by the conditions of life implied by various occupations than by the direct occupational risks entailed.'[32] By way of conclusion let us consider this problem in a little more detail for the nineteenth century.

The social class gradient of male mortality – the interplay of occupational, economic, environmental and selective factors

This is the question Stocks attempted to answer using data for 1930–32 and a comparison of the mortality gradients for men and married women.[33] He concluded as follows.

---

[32] Quoted by Stocks (1938), p. 686, from the Registrar General's *Occupational Mortality Report* for 1921–23.
[33] The question is asked by Stocks (1938), p. 688, but see also Collis and Greenwood (1921), pp. 72–74, for an earlier attempt to tackle the same problem, and a review of the approaches made by Francis Neison and Alfred Watson using material from Friendly Societies (pp. 66–71).

Remembering that the social class mortality of men is influenced by the direct effects of the occupations composing the social classes added to the indirect effects which influence also their wives, it is evident that the contributions made by the actual work done to the man's social mortality gradient from all causes [of death] must be very small compared with the contribution made by the accompanying environmental, economic or selective factors.[34]

The form of analysis undertaken by Stocks cannot be repeated using nineteenth-century data, nor is it possible to substitute infant mortality by father's occupation for the mortality of married women by husband's occupation in the years before 1911. Instead, the question can only be tackled indirectly and in a rather tentative fashion although, as is clear from the statements by Farr and Stevenson which opened this chapter, the problem was one of long standing.

Farr himself came closest to answering the question in his special study for the Royal Commission on Mines. The partial life expectancies reported in table 6.9 can be used to demonstrate the direct importance of occupational risks in the case of Cornish miners, but also the advantages of being a miner in the case of Durham and Northumberland. The estimates of life expectancy at age 20 given in table 6.6 provide several examples of occupations and industrial sectors that are by their very nature tied to specific locations or certain sorts of environments. The gardeners and farmers groups obviously enjoyed low mortality not only because they were not particularly dangerous occupations, but because they were undertaken in low-mortality rural environments, while the file makers and potters were vulnerable to the higher risks to health of urban living as well as the special dangers of their trades. But the material summarised in table 6.6 also helps us to consider changes in the mortality of occupations. Given that the level of occupational mortality is the sum of direct and indirect effects, to what combination of effects may changes in mortality be ascribed? In general, there seems little reason to think that the direct effects were primarily responsible for the 11.59 per cent improvement in e_{20} among the 71 occupations in combination. The effect of improvements in background conditions and the accompanying environment were probably far more important for most occupational groups. The medical and legal professions offer some interesting counter examples. In both cases it seems as though life chances for the most lowly sections of the profession improved in the late nineteenth century. We have already considered this point for the medical profession, but in the legal profession the experiences of barristers and solicitors may also be compared with those of law clerks. If the life expectancy of barristers and solicitors is set at 100 then that for the law clerks will be

[34] Stocks (1938), p. 690.

79, 98 and 96 in the three periods covered by table 6.6. In the case of the law clerks and perhaps also the other clerical jobs, it is likely that their economic circumstances improved sufficiently for them to take advantage of new suburban environments especially round the metropolis. Since the barristers, solicitors and law clerks shared the same location for their employment and, in terms of health risk, also undertook similar tasks, it seems improbable that it was the clerks' working conditions that improved substantially. It is reasonable to extend this argument from law clerks to other occupations that might be thought of as lower middle class, white collar workers, etc. – that is, the sorts of occupations combined in table 6.7 to form social group B and whose relative position in relation to other social groups was illustrated in figures 6.13 and 6.14. For teachers, clerks and minor officials as a broad group, life chances appear to have improved substantially without reference to working conditions. This is the point illustrated by figure 6.4 and discussed earlier.[35]

Although it is not possible to use the Victorian *Decennial Supplements* to make comparisons between the mortality experiences of adult males, their wives and their children distinguished by occupation, it is possible to compare adult male mortality in 1910–12 with infant mortality in 1911.[36] Let us assume that the legitimate infant mortality rate is a reliable and sensitive indicator of the health effects of domestic living conditions, including to some extent maternal health. On this basis it would be possible to use the residuals from regression analysis to explore the difference between the actual level of mortality experienced by father's occupation and the expected level predicted by the infant mortality of their children. This is attempted in figure 6.16 which shows the relationship between e_{25-65} in 1910–12 for the 71 occupations reported in table 6.6 as well as the five social groups in table 6.7 and the legitimate IMR in 1911 for the same occupations and social groups. There is in general a statistically significant inverse association: as the infant mortality rate increases so the partial life expectancy declines with rising mortality. The negative residuals should therefore give some indication of the level of excess mortality experienced by adult males in an occupation over and above what would be expected on the basis of the occupation's average domestic health conditions as measured by infant mortality.[37]

[35] See p. 218.

[36] Stocks (1938), p. 706, makes some interesting and largely positive observations about the desirability of substituting IMR for the mortality rate of married women as a means of distinguishing the true occupational effect on the mortality of fathers-husbands.

[37] Here we are focusing on those occupations in which the expected e_{25-65} is greater than the observed and thus the occupation may be thought to experience excess mortality. Figure 6.16 also shows that there were other extreme occupations in which infant mortality was for some reason 'too high' compared with adult male mortality. This is a separate story which will be left to chapter 7.

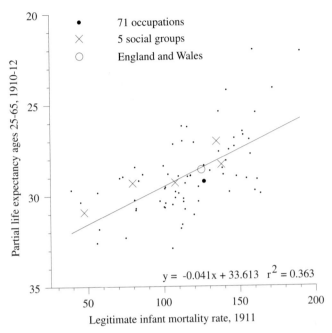

Figure 6.16. The relationship between partial life expectancy between ages 25 and 65 for males and the legitimate infant mortality rate among 71 occupations, England and Wales

Note: The axis showing partial life expectancy has been reversed giving a positive slope to the plotted regression line.

Table 6.10 illustrates the result of this exercise. In many respects, it is largely as expected. Of the 71 occupations 19 are reported in table 6.10 in terms of years of life lost between ages 25 and 65 which might be regarded as the direct result of the work involved or the special work environment. Some of the notoriously dangerous trades are included – file makers, tin miners, potters, those involved in the sale and production of alcohol – but there are other occupations which we have come to regard as particularly vulnerable – the medics, butchers, tailors, lawyers and clerks. The listed occupations lose from 12.7 to 2.5 per cent of their possible 40-year life span, although most are towards the bottom end of the range. While these are not negligible proportions it would seem that Stocks's assessment of the relative contributions of direct and indirect effects of occupation, at least as far as the 71 are concerned, is also appropriate for the early twentieth century.[38] The balance of evidence

---

[38] The positions of the five social groups are also shown in figure 6.16. For these the regression equation is $y = -0.034x + 32.405$ with $r^2 = 0.824$. This would give slight excess mortality in B and 'E'.

Table 6.10. *Estimated excess mortality experienced by certain occupations, England and Wales, c. 1911*

Occupation	Excess mortality in terms of years of partial life expectancy lost between ages 25 and 65
File maker	5.08
Tin miner	3.70
Innkeeper, publican	3.58
Chimney sweep, soot merchant	2.83
Brewer	2.64
Inn, hotel servant	2.63
Potter, earthenware manufacturer	2.43
Physician, surgeon, GP	2.34
Butcher	2.08
Hairdresser	2.00
Commercial clerk	1.85
Chemist, druggist	1.66
Law clerk	1.65
Musician, music master	1.61
Bargeman, lighterman	1.58
Artist, engraver	1.47
Barrister, solicitor	1.42
Commercial traveller	1.23
Tailor	1.14

Note:
The excess mortality is the difference between the observed e_{25-65} and the expected based on the relationship between e_{25-65} for 71 occupations in 1910–12 and IMR for 1911 shown in figure 6.16. Only those occupations with an excess of more than one year are reported.

presented here would suggest that 'the contribution made by the accompanying environmental, economic and selective factors' to the life chances of adult males was substantially greater than 'the actual work done' in the nineteenth century.

Finally, let us return to the matter of the general social mortality gradient by comparing the picture as drawn by the level of adult male mortality with that described by infant mortality, again using our five social groups. Figure 6.1b illustrated these patterns for 1910–12 using the Registrar General's eight social classes and the indexed standardised mortality ratio and infant mortality rate, while figure 6.14 used life expectancy at age 20 for males for the social groups. We are now in a position to consider an alternative approach, one that uses the five social groups and compares implied levels of life expectancy at birth in years

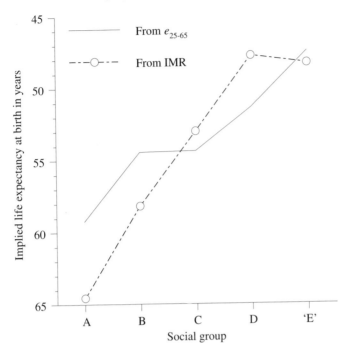

Figure 6.17. The social mortality gradient in England and Wales *c.* 1911
Note: Life expectancy at birth has been estimated using Model West and
partial life expectancy ages 25–65 or infant mortality rate for social groups.

(e_0).[39] The result is shown in figure 6.17. In the case of both adult male
mortality and infant mortality there is a clear social mortality gradient,
although there are interesting differences between the two. For adult
men there is the characteristic step with groups B and C at equivalent
levels by 1911, but the infant mortality gradient shows clear differences
between social groups A to D in an almost linear association. Group 'E'
is somewhat anomalous, but then it is based on a very small number of
occupations considering the actual size of the unskilled working
population. Figure 6.17 helps to reinforce the point that the domestic
conditions that so influenced infant mortality were far more differentiated in social terms in early twentieth-century England and Wales even
than the circumstances that influenced the life chances of adult males –

[39] Since the infant mortality rate and measures of life expectancy are given in different
units there will always be a problem where comparisons are required. Here we have
used IMR and e_{25-65} with the Model West life tables for males in order to identify
implied e_0s. ELT 8 for 1910–12 gives e_0 for males as 51.50 and for females as 55.35.

the combined direct and indirect effects of occupation and social class. It is certainly appropriate, therefore, that for this and other good reasons we should devote an entire chapter to the subject of infant and childhood mortality. It is to this important topic that we now turn having reconfirmed the importance of domestic circumstances and the local environment even for the life chances of adult males when compared with working conditions.[40]

[40] See Reid (1997).

7

The origins of the secular decline of childhood mortality

By childhood mortality we mean the deaths of live-born infants who have not yet reached their first birthday together with children who have not reached their fifth birthday. Thus childhood mortality is the combination of infant mortality and early childhood mortality. While the infant mortality rate (IMR) did not decline substantially in England and Wales in the nineteenth century, it did enter a precipitous and sustained decline after 1899 which has continued throughout the twentieth century, but is now faltering. The early childhood mortality rate (ECMR for ages 1–4 years), on the other hand, began to decline in the middle of the nineteenth century, and certainly ECMR had parted company from IMR in the 1860s. In these circumstances the origins of the secular decline of childhood mortality become much more complicated. We shall see that the reported causes of death among infants and young children were quite dissimilar. Infants were especially vulnerable at birth and weaning, while infectious diseases such as measles, scarlet fever, whooping cough were prominent causes of death among the young children. In epidemiological terms it should not be surprising that IMR and ECMR did not follow exactly similar paths. There is also some reason to suspect that, unlike infant mortality, early childhood mortality passed through a cyclical upswing in the mid-nineteenth century and declined thereafter, and thus that some of the diseases of childhood may have been less prominent in the early years of the nineteenth century. If this does prove to be the case, then the true origins of the secular decline of childhood mortality (ages 0 and up to 5 years) would lie with infant mortality at the end of the century rather than early childhood mortality (ages 1 and up to 5 years) in the 1850s and 1860s.

Most discussions on infant mortality, apart from those by a small number of distinguished Edwardians, to whom we shall return later, have fallen into two distinct groups. The social historians consider the

decline of infant mortality in terms of the politics of motherhood, contemporaries' views of the nation's need for a healthy population of
potential soldiers, or improvements in the environment into which
babies were born. The second group is composed of demographers or
epidemiologists whose concern to analyse long-term movements in
mortality has obliged them to focus on the contributions made by infant
and child mortality. Of the two, the first has tended to see relationships
in simple monocausal terms while the second has failed to capture the
enormous significance of the dramatic secular decline of infant mortality for the late nineteenth- and early twentieth-century rise in life
expectancy at birth. One reason for these failures has been the dearth of
detailed empirical studies which focus explicitly on the long-term
contribution of childhood mortality, and especially infant mortality, to
the improvement in life chances between the nineteenth and twentieth
centuries.

This point is well illustrated by the still highly influential work of
Thomas McKeown and his associates. They have estimated that 33.6 per
cent of the decline in age-standardised mortality rates in England and
Wales between 1901 and 1971 relates to infant mortality and a further
15.7 per cent to early childhood mortality, that is, nearly half to childhood mortality in general. Despite this significant finding, they do not
give the point special prominence and proceed to their interpretation
via an examination of cause of death data, which is their hallmark. By
setting the total fall of age-specific infant and early childhood mortality
between 1901 and 1971 equal to 100, they show the relative contributions of major causes of death. Of the decline for infants, under the
heading 'conditions not attributable to micro-organisms', prematurity,
immaturity and other diseases of infancy contributed 26.5 per cent for
males and 26.2 for females; under 'conditions attributable to micro-
organisms', bronchitis, pneumonia and influenza contributed 15.3 and
14.6 per cent; diarrhoea and dysentery, 22.6 and 23.4 per cent; and
convulsions and teething, 14.1 and 13.6 per cent.[1] In sum, just four broad
cause of death categories were responsible for approximately 78 per
cent of the decline in infant mortality between 1901 and 1971, and one-
third of the reduction in total mortality during that period was due to
infant mortality.

McKeown, Record and Turner make more specific points about diarrhoea and dysentery, most of the decline from which occurred between
1911 and the 1930s, when effective therapy was introduced. Their main
explanation for this decline is improvement in hygienic measures intro-

---

[1] McKeown *et al.* (1975), table 1, p. 395. The McKeown interpretation is considered again
in chapter 8, pp. 344–59.

duced during the late nineteenth century and extended in the twentieth century. 'Under the term hygienic measure we include a wide range of influences – purification of water, improved disposal of sewage, removal of refuse, sterilisation and pasteurisation of milk, supervision of food handling etc. – which had in common that they limited exposure to micro-organisms spread in food and water.'[2] Not surprisingly they found it difficult to assess the importance of individual hygienic measures, but among young children the most important seemed to be: 'a progressive improvement in milk supplies, particularly the introduction of dried foods for infant feeding and, later, the use of pasteurisation; education of mothers on the feeding and care of infants; and more efficient disposal of sewage . . . In older age groups the diarrhoeal diseases must also have been influenced by continued improvement in water supplies and food handling.'[3] Children's general state of health, determined mainly by their nutritional state, greatly influenced the mortality outcome of diarrhoeal infections. The final statement of their contribution, whilst in some ways ambiguous, returns us to the particular point of debate: 'the decline in mortality owed a good deal to specific measures but was also influenced considerably by improvements in standards of living, particularly in respect of infant feeding and care'.[4]

When McKeown and Record considered infant mortality in the nineteenth century they were clear about the absence of improvement between the 1840s and the 1890s, although they did note mortality decline between the ages of 3 and 34 from before 1880. Therefore, they concluded quite properly that infant mortality could have had little bearing on the slow rise in life expectancy at birth, but that the joint effects of decline in whooping cough, measles, diphtheria and especially scarlet fever on mortality among those aged 1–4 would have been significant, even before 1901.[5] In *The Modern Rise of Population*, McKeown also stressed the importance of infected milk supplies in prolonging the high level of infant mortality: 'The protection of milk was particularly important, for milk provides an excellent medium for the growth of micro-organisms and was largely responsible for the high level of infant mortality which continued until 1900.'[6]

The McKeown interpretation, as it has come to be known, contains three distinct methodological flaws, which his approach to childhood mortality only serves to highlight and which it will be useful to recap

---

[2] McKeown *et al.* (1975), p. 416.
[3] McKeown *et al.* (1975), p. 417.
[4] McKeown *et al.* (1975), p. 422.
[5] McKeown and Record (1962), especially p. 100.
[6] McKeown (1976), p. 162.

here. First, his analysis is almost completely based on the use of cause of death data; it largely ignores age-specific variations, and entirely ignores place-specific variations. Secondly, the periodisation adopted by McKeown – 1841–50 to 1891–1900 and 1901 to 1971 – is especially unfortunate in its coincidence with the major turning point in the secular decline of infant mortality. Thirdly, the particular emphasis on tuberculosis and nutrition, for which McKeown's work is well known, gives too much attention to adult mortality and diverts interest from the potentially even more critical issue of how infants and young children were cared for. However, it must also be said that the McKeown interpretation is still highly influential among members of the medical profession and that it does provide a simple model which demands attention and criticism.[7] It is for these reasons that McKeown's work has been singled out to provide both an illustration of how childhood mortality might be approached and an introduction to the chapter. It raises valuable points which should be borne in mind while considering the more descriptive accounts in the following sections.

Chapter 7 has been arranged in three sections. The first is demographic, epidemiological and descriptive. It focuses on the characteristic patterns and trends in childhood mortality during the Victorian era. The second section considers the various approaches that have been proposed for the analysis of infant and childhood mortality both historically and for the Third World today. It compares the work of such notable contemporaries as Sir George Newman and Sir Arthur Newsholme with the especially influential Mosley–Chen framework, as well as the McKeown interpretation in as far as it has a bearing on childhood mortality studies. The final section of the chapter considers some potentially interesting explanations of the origins of childhood mortality decline, but particularly the role of fertility control, the importance of poverty and the influence of female education and status.

The characteristics of childhood mortality in Victorian England and Wales

A considerable amount of effort has already been expended by both contemporary medical statisticians and modern historical demographers in the task of charting the changing patterns of infant and childhood mortality trends and variations.[8] If we focus exclusively on the

---

[7] See Johansson (1994) for a recent critical reappraisal of the McKeown interpretation; also chapter 8, pp. 344–59.
[8] Woods *et al.* (1988, 1989) provide the most comprehensive review to date. See also Morris and Heady *et al.* (1955), and Preston and Haines (1991). Also, on the problems of measurement, Royal Statistical Society (1912).

Victorian era we can say that infant mortality did not decline but that early childhood mortality did, along with mortality in late childhood and early adulthood (see figure 5.7); that the risks of dying in childhood varied in a distinct fashion with age; that those risks were far greater if the child's mother was not married, if the father was unskilled, poorly paid, unemployed; that the risks were especially high if the baby was born in an urban environment or in winter, was born premature with a low birthweight, was not breastfed or was weaned early. The risks were also high if the mother was in her teens, late thirties or forties or if the child was the first born (parity 1) or above parity 5 to 6. Thanks to the Victorian system of civil registration we are able to document some of these variations in risks, and from the 1890s this can be complemented by a number of special reports and studies of infant mortality. However, there are particular problems in dealing with infant mortality statistics, some of which have already been discussed in chapter 2. First, the infant mortality rate, the ratio of deaths under one year of age to live births in a given time period, is derived purely from vital registration. The measure therefore has the advantage that it does not rely on census data for the estimation of the population at risk of dying, but it may suffer from the difficulty of defining a live birth. If, for some reason, the registration of the birth is delayed then death may occur first, in which case neither the birth nor the death will be recorded. The accurate estimation of IMR and ECMR is not without its problems, therefore, some of which may prove to be substantial for the early phase of civil registration in the 1840s and for particularly vulnerable sub-groups, such as the children of unmarried mothers.

Let us begin by attempting a reconstruction of the long-term trend in childhood mortality so that the Victorian period can be placed in context. Figure 7.1 shows a rough approximation of the long-term trend in the child mortality rate (CMR, $_5q_0 \times 1{,}000$) for decades from the 1580s to the 1940s. It also shows the ratio of IMR to ECMR ($_1q_0/_4q_1$). Before the twentieth century the chances of a newly born baby surviving to its fifth birthday were normally less than 75 per cent and, on occasions, closer to 70 per cent or even lower. However, the childhood mortality rate was far from constant. There were cyclical upswings in the late seventeenth and early eighteenth centuries and, it appears, a rather more short-lived increase in the mid-nineteenth century. The IMR/ECMR ratio in figure 7.1 also indicates that the balance of components within childhood mortality, the first 12 months compared with the next 48, also fluctuated. However, apart from several anomalous decades in the middle and late seventeenth century there was generally a downward trend between the late sixteenth and mid-nineteenth centuries. But what is

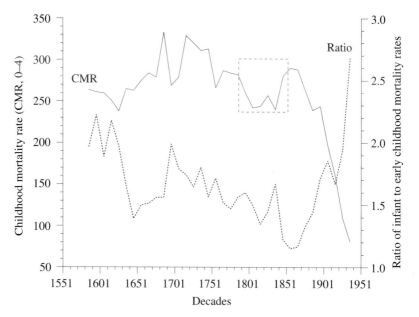

Figure 7.1. Approximate trends in the childhood mortality rate and the ratio of infant to early childhood mortality, England and Wales, 1580s to 1940s

most interesting about figure 7.1 is its illustration of the dramatic and secular decline of CMR in the twentieth century and the accompanying reversal and upward trend in the IMR/ECMR ratio as an ever increasing proportion of childhood deaths occurred in the first few months after birth.

Figure 7.1 should be treated with some caution, however, for it combines and simplifies estimates based on data from different sources and for different periods. The least safe period is the one shown in the box – the 70 years before civil registration began. This critical phase in England's demographic and economic history at the end of the eighteenth and beginning of the nineteenth century is also the most difficult to reconstruct via the failing system of registering baptisms and burials.[9] We are on far safer ground once civil registration data are available although, as has already been shown, the recording of live births and infant deaths may not be completely reliable until perhaps the fourth quarter of the century. Figure 7.2 shows the annual infant and childhood mortality series from 1841 onwards. It distinguishes IMR, ECMR and

[9] The unreliability of Anglican parish registers at this time is well known. See Wrigley *et al.* (1997), especially pp. 73–118.

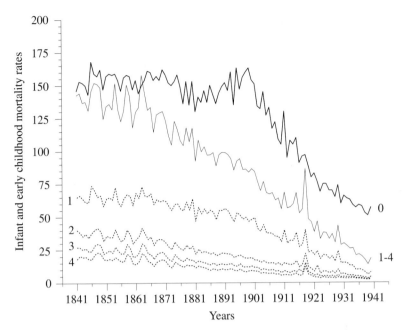

Figure 7.2. Annual infant mortality rate (IMR, 0) and early childhood
mortality rate (ECMR, 1–4) series, England and Wales, 1841–1940
Note: q_1, q_2, q_3 and q_4 (all $\times$ 1,000) are also shown.

the single-year components of ECMR. It is clear from figure 7.2 that
ECMR did decline before IMR; that the former was especially volatile
during the middle decades of the nineteenth century before secular
decline set in; that for IMR the secular decline did not occur until the
turn of the century; and that on average IMR was about 150 during
the six decades, although it was obviously higher in the 1890s than the
1880s. The trends illustrated by figure 7.2 appear to be clear and may be
regarded as reliable.

But what of the boxed period in figure 7.1? What happened to infant
and childhood mortality in the decades before 1841 and did CMR pass
through a cyclical upswing in the middle of the nineteenth century
because mortality in the age group 1–4 increased then? Figure 7.3
summarises currently available estimates of IMR and ECMR, those that
in simplified form were used to construct figure 7.1. The pre-civil
registration IMR series have been derived in two ways. First, by using
Wrigley and Schofield's estimates of life expectancy at birth (e_0) created
by the aggregate back projection method which was anchored to the
third English Life Table (ELT 3), it is possible to derive the implied

IMR.[10] This series of IMRs is bound to correspond well with the series based on civil registration data at the point of overlap. The other series of IMRs has been derived by pooling selected family reconstitution studies, and it too links in rather well with the civil registration series as well as following closely the implied IMR series, apart, that is, from the boxed period defined in figure 7.1.[11] Figure 7.3 also shows legitimate ECMR for the pre-civil registration period derived from family reconstitutions in the same way as IMR, except that the latter has been corrected to allow for all births. The mismatch between the family reconstitution-based ECMR series and the one derived directly from civil registration data obviously poses important problems and, once again, especially during the boxed period.[12] Whatever the explanation for this mismatch it seems reasonable to conclude that there was a cyclical upturn in ECMR during the middle decades of the nineteenth century, and although this was not accompanied by a similar increase in IMR, the effect on the overall childhood mortality rate was to make it rise to a peak in the 1850s before falling in the 1870s.[13]

It has often been pointed out that the division of childhood mortality into the periods up to and after 12 months of life is somewhat arbitrary, being more an administrative device than one with clear demographic or epidemiological significance. The distinction between neonatal and post-neonatal mortality, which focuses on the first month of life compared with the following 11, or perinatal mortality, which combines stillbirths with deaths during the first week, may be of greater significance for the age pattern of mortality in childhood. Unfortunately, the number of stillbirths was never reported in the Victorian civil registration system, and even age at death in months or groups of months was not reported on a regular basis until the 1890s. We are therefore left to draw what inferences we can from the sketchy

---

[10] Wrigley and Schofield (1981), table 7.15, p. 230, report the estimated e_0 series by quinquennia. These were used with their 'English' model life table (appendix 14) in which the relationship between IMR and e_0 is summarised by:

$$IMR = 1184.5 - 626.87(\log e_0).$$

Wrigley *et al.* (1997), table A9.1, pp. 614–15, give revised estimates for e_0. Woods (1993, 1994) discusses the various problems of converting e_0 to IMR via model life tables.
[11] Wrigley *et al.* (1997), pp. 214–17.   [12] See Wrigley *et al.* (1997), p. 259.
[13] Huck (1994, 1995) has attempted to fill the gap with IMR estimates for nine parishes in northern England. They are as follows (Huck, 1994, table 2, p. 519; 1995, table 1, p. 534):

Of 9 parishes:	1813–18	1819–24	1825–30	1831–36
Average	151	163	167	172
Aggregate	160	173	169	180

They are broadly in line with the IMRs shown in figure 7.3, but do not necessarily help to support the argument for worsening economic circumstances as Huck suggests.

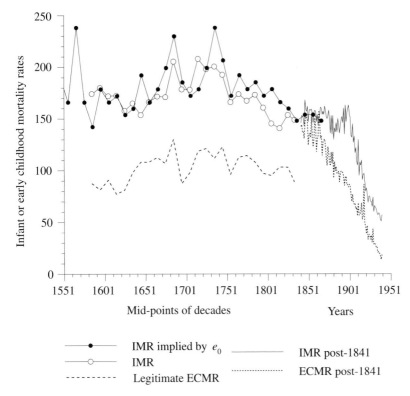

Figure 7.3. Estimates of infant and early childhood mortality rates based on parish register data compared with those based on civil registration data post-1841

Note: IMR and legitimate ECMR are from Wrigley *et al.* (1997), tables 6.1 and 6.2; implied IMR has been estimated from e_0 in Wrigley and Schofield (1981), table 7.15. See text for explanation.

material that is available and to estimate often by using twentieth-century data.[14]

One of the rare glimpses we do have of the age and cause of death pattern of early age mortality is provided in a special tabulation prepared by William Ogle and published in the Registrar General's *Fifty-fourth Annual Report for 1891*. The tabulation covers the three years

---

[14] Chapter 2 contains some discussion of the problems encountered in using biometric methods to check the quality of baptism and birth registration. Stillbirths probably represented between 40 and perhaps up to 60 (in some places and circumstances) per 1,000 live births in the nineteenth century. See Galley and Woods (1998), Wrigley (1998) and Hart (1998).

1889–91 and applies to the three low mortality rural counties of Dorset, Hertfordshire and Wiltshire, together with the three high mortality towns of Blackburn and Preston (Lancashire) and Leicester (Leicestershire). What is unusual about this material is that it provides the opportunity to explore in considerable detail the age profile of mortality under one year, to distinguish 'rural' and 'urban' conditions and to identify the reported causes of death. It also allows for the possibility of estimating the average mortality curve for England and Wales and of extending that curve backwards to include stillbirths as well as infant deaths.

Ogle's data are shown in table 7.1 and the estimated life table l_x functions in table 7.2. Let us begin by focusing on the age pattern of mortality. Table 7.2 takes the 'urban' and 'rural' cumulative infant mortality rates, averages them and then readjusts the rates so that total IMR is set at 150 per 1,000 live births, the mean rate for England and Wales in the Victorian period. Column 1 gives the resulting estimate of the English and Welsh infant life table. This is set alongside equivalent tables for 'urban' and 'rural' derived directly from Ogle's data in columns 2 and 3. The remaining columns of table 7.2 report three parallel infant life tables, but now stillbirths are included and age 0 is set at 28 weeks after conception. The numbers of stillbirths for 'urban' and 'rural' have been estimated using the 'under one week' mortality rates and the association between the number of stillbirths per 1,000 live births and the 'under one week' mortality rate for England and Wales in the twentieth century.[15] The England and Wales average in column 4 has again been set so that IMR is 150.

[15] This procedure is explained in more detail in Galley and Woods (1998). The association between the under one week mortality rate (x) and the number of stillbirths per 1,000 live births (y) for years (England and Wales, 1927 onwards) is given by $y = 0.048x^2 + 0.810x + 0.211$ ($r^2 = 0.993$). This equation has been used to estimate the numbers of stillbirths which were then disaggregated using the following proportions: 0.16, 0.17, 0.25 and 0.42 for the four foetal ages in table 7.2. See Bongaarts and Potter (1983), p. 39. Far more research needs to be done in this broad area of foetal–infant mortality, based for example on the work of Bakketeig *et al.* (1978) who are able to construct a full foetal-infant life table for Norway between 1967 and 1973. What has been accomplished so far remains at the tentative stage. For example, Hart (1998) has attempted to estimate long-run series for stillbirths mortality by multiplying estimates of mortality in the first week by the constant 1.8 derived from the ratio of stillbirth mortality to under one week mortality in England and Wales in 1930. She takes her under one week mortality estimates from Wrigley *et al.* (1997), table 6.6 (mortality to legitimate births in 0–6 days). As well as mis-specifying or failing to specify periods precisely, Hart's table 2 (p. 226) is of dubious value for periods before the 1840s. A constant conversion factor cannot be assumed nor, for that matter, would it be appropriate to apply the above equation (to do so would massively inflate stillbirths over and above even the high levels estimated by Hart). Wrigley's (1998) approach is to use endogenous mortality to approximate stillbirths, at least as far as trend is concerned. In terms of level this would suggest that

The mortality patterns summarised in table 7.2 can be represented most clearly in graphical form and this is done in figure 7.4 following the pattern of figure 2.11. Age in days has now been transformed in the fashion proposed by Jean Bourgeois-Pichat and for mortality above one week this provides an effective method of adjusting the cumulative mortality curves. The 'urban' and 'rural' patterns for 1889–91, summarised by tables 2.1 and 2.2, can now be compared with curves for urban and rural counties in 1905, which were also used in chapter 2 as a guide to the quality of age at death reporting. The curve labelled E&W has been derived from column 4 in table 7.2. Figure 7.4 illustrates a number of important points. First, despite the log^3 transformation the age profile of foetal and very early age mortality appears highly curvilinear. Of those foetuses that survived 28 weeks from conception but did not survive to reach their first birthday, 36 per cent died either in utero or within seven days of parturition. In these circumstances it is quite clear that any system of birth registration will suffer if it is not tied closely to the birth event itself and instead allows a variable amount of time to elapse before registration is required. Secondly, not only are there marked differences between 'urban' and 'rural' in terms of final IMR, but the mortality curves in figure 7.4 show that whilst for 'rural' the transformation is successful in straightening the line, for 'urban' the mortality curve turns upwards in the post-neonatal period above one month.[16] While neonatal mortality is 1.4 times higher in 'urban' than 'rural', post-neonatal mortality is 2.7 times higher, which largely accounts for IMR being 2.2 times higher.[17]

Before we consider in detail the way in which distinctive cause of death patterns combined to make the disease environment in Victorian cities especially dangerous for young children, a process which can be begun using table 7.1, let us consider two further aspects of the infant mortality pattern: gender and legitimacy. The infant mortality rate among male babies was 1.21 to 1.23 times higher than

while stillbirth mortality in England and Wales in the nineteenth and early twentieth century was about 40 per 1,000 live births, in the seventeenth and first half of the eighteenth century it was much higher (over 100). Despite Wrigley's (1998), footnote 51, p. 453, implied criticism of Hart's approach, similar results are achieved by using 1.8 and under one week mortality and, say, 1.5 and endogenous mortality.

[16] Since the mortality rates are logged in figure 7.4, R1 appears straighter than U2. Knodel and Kintner (1977) show how the duration of breastfeeding can affect the biometric curve. The curve will kick-up from the age at weaning. In this case we have no additional information to suggest that weaning took place earlier in the 'urban' than the 'rural' places (see p. 285).

[17] Unfortunately, it is not possible to compare the 1889–91 (U1, R1) curves with those for 1905 (U2, R2) in figure 7.4, but it does seem that U1 is even more urban than U2, and R1 even more rural than R2. Given the selection of towns and counties this is only to be expected.

Table 7.1. *Causes of death in infancy in three towns ('Urban', U) – Blackburn, Leicester and Preston – and three rural counties ('Rural', R) – Dorset, Hertfordshire and Wiltshire – 1889–91*

| | Cumulative infant mortality rate from 100,000 live births up to the following ages: | | | | | | | | | | | |
| | 1 week | | 1 month | | 3 months | | 6 months | | 9 months | | 12 months | |
Cause of death	U	R	U	R	U	R	U	R	U	R	U	R
Premature birth	1508	1020	2054	1267	2237	1340	2270	1369	2276	1375	2279	1381
Atelectasis	105	39	141	45	149	49	149	53	149	55	149	55
Congenital malformations	78	107	175	157	209	194	228	206	234	220	234	228
Whooping cough			12	17	94	100	263	204	490	304	694	416
Measles					20		69	13	263	81	626	176
Scarlet fever							3		14	4	31	6
Diarrhoeal diseases	3	4	189	39	1191	155	2606	322	3490	407	3961	481
Enteritis			22	21	152	43	296	75	428	103	497	122
Erysipelas			23	9	26	21	37	27	43	29	43	31
Syphilis	3	2	23	10	106	26	161	45	181	49	190	53
Liver disease	11	17	52	63	74	69	86	75	89	79	89	79
Dentition						2	86	24	228	100	424	187
Other diseases of the digestive organs	17	13	56	48	111	93	211	149	258	169	284	189
Convulsions and other diseases of the nervous system	435	233	901	444	1672	748	2673	1036	3348	1220	3776	1381
Tubercular meningitis	3		6	6	40	12	151	39	268	79	379	138
Tabes mesenterica	3		6	4	94	45	281	115	425	163	577	216
Other tubercular diseases			3	8	53	16	142	40	200	89	261	118
Atrophy	360	579	862	968	1607	1329	2276	1564	2561	1675	2734	1738

Diseases of the respiratory organs	25	22	189	168	839	585	1754	1103	2723	1604	3701	2105
Injury at birth	3	7	3	9	3	9	3	9	3	9	3	9
Navel haemorrhage		11	13	14	13	14	13	13	14	13	14	13
Suffocation	17	14	42	34	134	73	217	101	226	111	232	113
Other violence	8	33	11	38	19	38	26	43	34	48	51	54
All other causes	67	67	166	122	282	220	424	305	499	366	574	428
All cases	2646	2163	4947	3488	9126	5180	14426	6932	18444	8352	21803	9717

Note:

Atelectasis – an imperfect expansion of the lung at birth; erysipelas – an infectious inflammation of the skin; atrophy – wasting. The original tables were prepared by Dr William Ogle using death certificates.
Source: Registrar General's *Fifty-fourth Annual Report for 1891*, Tables D and E, pp. xiv–xv.

Table 7.2. *Infant life tables for Victorian England and Wales, 'rural' and 'urban' places*

Days	England and Wales 1	'Rural' 2	'Urban' 3	England and Wales 4	'Rural' 5	'Urban' 6
28 weeks gestation				100000	100000	100000
32 weeks gestation				99286	99382	99162
36 weeks gestation				98527	98725	98272
40 weeks gestation				97411	97759	96963
Birth	100000	100000	100000	95537	96137	94764
1	98912	98998	98802	94499	95174	93629
2	98534	98702	98317	94138	94889	93169
3	98225	98421	97973	93843	94619	92843
4	97991	98189	97737	93620	94396	92620
5	97843	98037	97593	93478	94250	92483
6	97719	97917	97463	93359	94135	92360
7	97626	97837	97354	93271	94058	92257
14	97022	97364	96581	92694	93603	91524
21	96394	96902	95740	92096	93159	90727
30	95896	96512	95103	91621	92784	90124
61	94389	95527	92923	90185	91837	88058
91	93095	94820	90874	88954	91157	86116
122	91857	94147	88907	87775	90510	84252
152	90744	93528	87158	86715	89915	82595
183	89792	93068	85574	85810	89473	81094
213	88876	92585	84099	84938	89009	79696
243	88068	92102	82873	84169	88544	78534
274	87237	91648	81556	83377	88108	77286
304	86435	91172	80336	82614	87650	76130
335	85694	90717	79226	81908	87213	75078
365	85000	90284	78197	81247	86796	74103

Note:
The IMR for England and Wales has been set at 150. IMR for 'rural' is 97 and for 'urban' it is 218. For England and Wales there are 46.71 stillbirths per 1,000 live births; the endogenous mortality rate is 22.13; the perinatal mortality rate is 70.43; and the neonatal mortality rate is 41.04. The 'rural' places are the counties of Dorset, Hertfordshire and Wiltshire and the 'urban' places are the three towns of Blackburn, Leicester and Preston.
Source: See table 7.1 and Galley and Woods (1998).

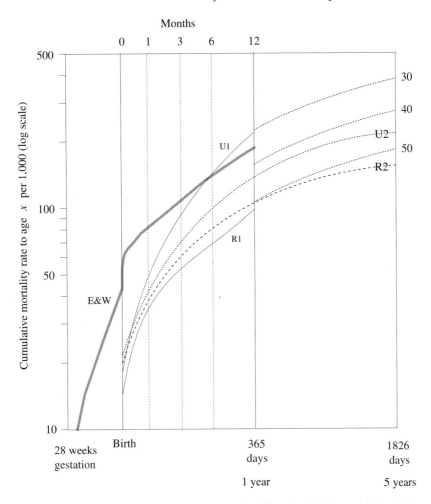

Figure 7.4. Cumulative mortality rate from 28 weeks gestation to five years generalised for Victorian England and Wales comparing urban and rural places

Note: U1 and R1 relate to urban and rural places in 1889–91 defined in table 7.1; U2 and R2 relate to urban and rural counties in 1905; and E&W illustrates an estimated mortality curve for England and Wales assuming IMR is 150. See text for explanation.

Source: See tables 7.1 and 7.2, and figure 2.11.

that among females. This ratio remained roughly constant throughout the Victorian period, although the sex ratio of birth of about 1040 (males per 1,000 females) did vary somewhat.[18] Probably of greater significance for the risks to infant life was the matter of legitimacy. The ratio of illegitimate to legitimate IMR was 1.98 in England and Wales in the period 1906–10, but varied from 2.07 in London in 1902 to 1.59 in a selection of rural counties. Illegitimate births represented 6.7 per cent of all births in 1846–50, but with the decline of illegitimate fertility this had reduced to 4.0 per cent by 1906–10 and this would have had some bearing on the total national IMR as well as the rate in those areas where illegitimate fertility was especially high (see figure 4.12 for *Ih*).[19]

We have already seen in chapter 5 and the discussion of 'Farr's law' that mortality levels were highly variable between localities in nineteenth-century England and Wales, but especially between urban and rural places. It may be readily imagined how infant and early childhood mortality played especially important parts in this variation and, with the aid of table 7.1, how the child populations of urban and rural places are likely to have experienced rather different combinations of causes of death. It has also been shown in figures 6.16 and 6.17 that legitimate IMR varied with father's occupation and by social groups in 1911. The remainder of this section will focus on the following issues: first, geographical, occupational and social class variations in IMR and ECMR; secondly, cause of death patterns in early age; thirdly, the changing influence of certain particular causes of death, such as prematurity and diarrhoea and dysentery; fourthly, the effects of fertility variations and decline; and, finally, the extent to which infant and childhood mortality decline in England and Wales coincided with similar changes in other parts of Europe.

Figures 7.5 and 7.6 (colour section, pages *l* and *m*) illustrate the geographical variations in infant and early childhood mortality rates by decades among the 614 districts of England and Wales. The observable variations have been commented on at some length elsewhere and will not be repeated here save to say that the pattern of high and low IMR variations is obviously one with a strong, although – especially in the middle decades of the century – not exclusively, urban–rural component and that there was a substantial element of continuity from decade to decade. In the case of early childhood mortality there were not only

[18] The decline in the SRB from 1052 in 1841–45 to 1039 in 1906–10 was considered in chapter 2 as a means of detecting biased birth registration. See figure 2.10 and table 2.2.

[19] Legitimate IMR was 28 per cent higher in London than rural England while illegitimate IMR was 75 per cent higher in 1902. See Woods *et al.* (1988), table 2, p. 353.

clear urban–rural differences, but the rate declined from decade to decade as is also obvious from figure 7.2.[20]

The case of high infant mortality in certain rural districts is a particularly interesting one, however. In several districts of Norfolk, Cambridgeshire, Lincolnshire and the East Riding of Yorkshire, infant mortality was especially high in the 1850s and 1860s, but declined thereafter for reasons that are still obscure.[21]

The geographical variations in IMR and ECMR shown in figures 7.5 and 7.6 appear rather clear-cut: they existed and persisted in the case of the former, but for early childhood mortality there was definite change. Environment had an obvious impact on the level of childhood mortality especially beyond the first week. Father's occupation and social class also had a bearing, but the extent of their influence is rather more difficult to assess partly because of the data that are available and partly because, as we saw with the experience of adult males, the influence of occupation will be confounded by what may prove to be the more direct effect of the local environment on a young child's life chances. Despite the first problem and possibly as a result of the second, the influence of father's occupation on childhood mortality has proved an intriguing area for researchers. The Registrar General's *Seventy-fourth Annual Report for 1911* provides not only extensive commentary by T. H. C. Stevenson on the legitimate infant mortality rates experienced by some 373 male occupations, but also extensive special tabulations of births and infant deaths for the year 1911. Alongside this material the results of the 1911 *Census of Fertility* may also be used to estimate the level of legitimate IMR for certain larger occupations as well as the eight 'Social Classes' defined by the Registrar General.[22] The results of this reconstruction exercise are summarised in table 7.3 and illustrated by figure 7.7.

What is especially interesting about these estimates is not so much the impression of difference in level that they give, but the clear regularity

---

[20] Newman (1906) shows maps of IMR by English and Welsh counties for 1845–54, 1871–80, 1881–90, 1891–1900 and 1901–05 (pp. 21–29) and for Scotland in 1899–1904 (pp. 30–31). These appear to be the first maps of infant mortality rates. See Woods *et al.* (1988), pp. 353–63; Williams and Mooney (1994); Williams and Galley (1995); Woods and Shelton (1997).

[21] Henry Julian Hunter, 'Report of Dr Henry Julian Hunter on the Excessive mortality of Infants in some rural districts of England', *Sixth Report of the Medical Officer of the Privy Council for 1863* (BPP 1864/XXVIII), appendix 14, pp. 454–62; see also Dobson (1997), especially pp. 167–83, on infant mortality in the marshland districts of south-east England.

[22] These 'Social Classes' were first introduced in chapter 4 along with the *Census of Fertility*, see table 4.1 and pp. 115–22. Watterson (1986, 1987, 1988) outlines the indirect methods used to estimate IMR. This procedure has been replicated by Haines (1995).

Table 7.3. *Estimates of legitimate infant mortality rates for 'Social Classes',*
England and Wales

'Social Class'	1895–97	1898–1900	1901–03	1905	1907	1910	1911
I	114.5	99.4	89.6	82.1	63.7	56.2	76.4
II	130.7	128.5	122.0	113.4	97.2	87.5	106.4
III	139.3	137.2	130.7	122.0	104.8	91.8	112.7
IV	141.5	139.3	132.8	125.3	111.2	99.4	121.5
V	157.7	157.7	156.6	149.0	135.0	119.9	152.5
VI	155.5	152.3	146.9	142.6	127.4	116.6	148.1
VII	159.8	155.5	155.5	150.1	140.4	125.3	160.1
VIII	103.7	99.4	98.3	97.2	86.4	82.1	96.9

Note:
Legitimate IMRs have been estimated for 1895–97 to 1910 and then adjusted
so that the weighted mean approximates the national rate (i.e. inflated by
1.08). For 1911 the reported rates are given. In 1907 legitimate IMR was 113, it
was 102 in 1910, but it increased to 125 in 1911.
In 1911 'Social Classes' based on father's occupation were defined in the
following way:
I. Upper and middle class
II. Intermediate class (excluding scholars)
III. Skilled workmen
IV. Intermediate class
V. Unskilled workmen
VI. Textile workers
VII. Miners
VIII. Agricultural labourers
Source: Woods *et al.* (1988), table 5, p. 364; Registrar General's *Seventy-fourth*
Annual Report for 1911, table 28B.

in the pattern of change that is evident. Certainly there is an indication
that class I was fastest off the mark between 1895–97 and 1898–1900, but
thereafter IMR in classes II, III and IV declined in step, and only class V
lagged behind until 1905. Mortality among the children of textile
workers and miners also followed the pattern of V as did that for the
agricultural labourers, but here there was very little change between
1895–97 and 1910.[23] What is also interesting about these estimates is the
way they may be compared with the full record for 1911, an abnormal

[23] Spree (1988), table 4, p. 194, provides IMRs for specific occupation groups in Prussia,
1877–1913, which should be comparable with those shown in figure 7.7, but he combines legitimate IMR for father's occupation with illegitimate IMR for mother's
occupation. Even so there are important similarities, with total IMR declining from 201
to 148, and all groups contributing to the decline, but with decline rather faster and
from a lower initial rate among the professional groups (see figure 1, p. 65). Another
example is provided by Ewbank and Preston (1990).

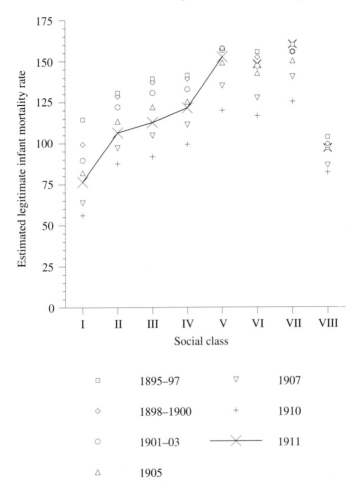

Figure 7.7. Changes in class-specific legitimate infant mortality rates, England and Wales
Source: Table 7.3.

year by all accounts.[24] In classes I to IV the legitimate infant mortality rate was pushed back towards the level for 1905, but in classes V, VI and especially VII regression was even more extreme. Among the mining families the conditions of 1911 produced levels of infant mortality as unfavourable as those experienced in the mid-1890s. Watterson's

[24] Figure 7.7 also brings into question the wisdom of drawing wider conclusions about socio-economic inequalities from a comparison of occupation-based IMRs in just two years: 1900 in the United States and 1911 in England and Wales. See Haines (1985).

detailed analysis of these estimates, together with the impression given by figure 7.7, confirms that during the 15 years prior to 1910 infant mortality declined in all classes although it did not do so at quite the same rate in each.[25]

Before we return to the question of urban–rural mortality differentials and the ways they were created by particular proximate determinants it may be worth pausing to reflect on the extent of diversity within the Registrar General's 'Social Classes' and to establish, at least for 1911, the various combinations of causes that created the pattern of differences so evident in figure 7.7.

Table 7.4 shows the extent to which the 'Social Classes' contained occupations with variable levels of IMR. Analysis of variance confirms that the differences in mean IMRs between the classes are indeed significant. Although there are obvious problems in using the Registrar General's 'Social Classes' in terms of the internal cohesion within each class, their mere existence and the enthusiasm with which their promoters – especially T. H. C. Stevenson – used them in official publications and statistical tables makes them difficult to ignore.[26] This certainly proves to be the case when one wishes to explore not only social variations in the level and trend of infant mortality, but also what the reported causes of death in early age were. Once again the Registrar General's *Annual Report for 1911* provides important insights, although it must be remembered what an exceptional year 1911 was for infant mortality. Figure 7.8 illustrates the benefits of considering causes of death in infancy in terms of the eight 'Social Classes'. Only four broad groups of causes are used here, plus the residual 'other causes', but even these are sufficient to show how the differentials were built up in an additive fashion, especially by the combination of 'developmental and wasting diseases' and 'diarrhoea and enteritis'. Both categories display a social gradient although it is the latter in particular which appears to highlight the social distinctions.[27] Comparison of I, V and VIII is most revealing. I and V are closest in terms of shared urban environment, if

---

[25] Watterson (1986, 1988) stresses the importance of environmental change, over and above the influence of income or fertility. Clearly there was some common experience which all classes shared to nearly the same degree. She stresses the importance of interaction effects: 'Infant mortality decline in this period was facilitated by the housing and residential environment irrespective of income but was enhanced and advanced by high or regular income or regular employment' (1988, p. 300). We shall return to these effects later in the chapter.

[26] The classes were revised for use in 1921–23 and the new classes I–V have proved popular devices for monitoring health differentials. See, for example, Antonovsky and Bernstein (1977) and Pamuk (1988).

[27] Using Bourgeois-Pichat's technique it is possible to estimate the level of endogenous mortality (deaths associated with congenital defects and the trauma of birth) for the

Table 7.4. *Variations in legitimate infant mortality rates within the 1911 'Social Classes'*

'Social Class'	N	Mean	Median	Max.	Min.	Variance	Coefficient of variation	IMR
I	33	65.1	62.5	122.2	26.9	525.8	35.22	75.7
II	64	99.5	98.1	161.3	48.4	798.1	28.39	104.5
III	85	114.0	112.3	161.5	66.2	471.8	19.05	112.6
IV	88	125.9	128.4	191.8	47.1	927.8	24.19	121.5
V	43	144.1	140.3	198.7	75.7	699.1	18.35	152.5
VI	9	146.5	141.0	184.0	110.6	520.3		147.9
VII	6	126.3	99.9	190.3	84.5	1723.1		160.1
VIII	1							96.9

Note:
Of the 373 occupations listed in table 28A the following have been excluded: 'Others', those with fewer than 100 births in 1911 and 'Finance agents, clerks' (115 births, but only 2 infant deaths). There remain 329 occupations. IMR is the legitimate IMR for the 'Social Class' as constituted from the stated number of occupations. It may differ from the figure reported in table 7.3. The 'Social Classes' are defined in table 7.3. The mean IMR for the 329 occupations was 114.4. The coefficient of variation is the ratio of the standard deviation to the mean expressed as a percentage. Despite some overlap in the distributions, analysis of variance on I–VII shows that at the 1 per cent level there were statistically significant differences between the 'Social Classes' in terms of IMRs.
Source: Registrar General's *Seventy-fourth Annual Report for 1911*, table 28A.

not particular neighbourhoods, while V and VIII are closer in terms of status and income. Although it is not possible to reconstruct the cause-specific and class-specific patterns for earlier years, it seems most probable that legitimate IMR in 1911 was pushed upwards by increased mortality from causes in the 'diarrhoea and enteritis' category and that this had an especially important influence on mortality in classes V, VI and VII. In other words, the differences between I, V and VIII were exacerbated in a 'bad year'. The children of the agricultural labourers (VIII) were even more protected by their less dangerous rural environment than those of the professionals (I) while those of the least skilled urban working classes (represented in V to VII) faced the highest risks from poverty and the environment.

'Social Classes' of 1911. They are: I 20.09 (22.8), II 22.69 (26.3), III 23.21 (27.6), IV 24.61 (28.6), V 26.19 (31.4), VI 25.29 (32.4), VII 29.31 (34.4) and VIII 24.20 (28.3) using cumulative mortality to 1, 3, 6, 9 and 12 months (under 1 month mortality from developmental and wasting diseases is given in brackets).

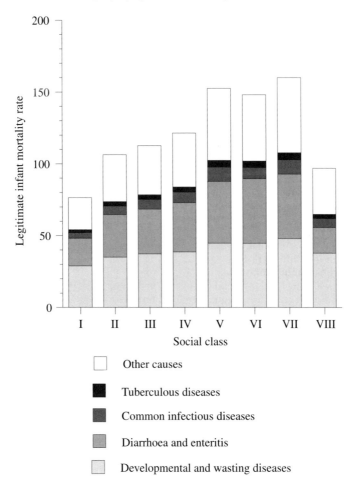

Figure 7.8. Social class differentials in legitimate infant mortality rate distinguished by broad cause of death categories, England and Wales, 1911
Source: Registrar General's *Seventy-fourth Annual Report for 1911*, table 28B.

But 1911 was a most particular year; the 'Social Classes' are ambiguous amalgamations; and the cause of death categories are far from detailed. By what causes did children die in Victorian England and Wales? We have already seen in table 7.1 perhaps the most detailed classification of causes of death attempted in the Victorian period.[28]

---

[28] For the years 1860, 1861 and 1862, Farr (1865), tables VIII and IX, gives causes of death for infants and children aged 0–4, respectively, in England and Wales using 93 categories, but deaths are not broken down by age groups within the first year.

While it provides important insights into the pattern of very early age mortality and allows us to identify the combinations of causes that created such striking differences between urban and rural environments it does not help us to describe the patterns within childhood nor to establish which causes did or did not change. This can only be done, as far as it may be accomplished at all, by using the Registrar General's *Annual Reports* or the *Decennial Supplements* to the *Annual Reports*. The principal drawback of these materials is that they employ statistical nosologies that were not designed especially for the reporting of deaths in childhood, as was William Ogle's nosology in table 7.1. Their other drawbacks, as we shall see at greater length in chapter 8, relate to the failure to report age with cause for registration districts in the *Annual Reports*, the breadth of certain categories in the statistical nosologies applied, changes in those nosologies especially in the early 1900s and 1880s, and the more general and fundamental problems associated with the medical identification of cause of death together with its accurate, consistent and simple recording on a death certificate.[29]

The cause of death data for infants and even older children can only provide a very broad indication of the kinds of diseases that were prevalent; the differences between age groups, places and classes; and the circumstances in which substantial changes occurred. Figure 7.8 provides one example for the 'Social Classes', others are to be found in figures 7.9 and 7.10 which use the nosologies adopted by the Registrar General for the reporting of cause of death by age groups for the registration districts of England and Wales in the 1860s and the 1900s.[30] The age groups 0 (infancy), 1–4 years (early childhood), 5–9 (late childhood) and 10–14 are illustrated for males in England and Wales as a whole. There are obvious differences in the two nosologies which thwart simple comparison. For example, typhus and typhoid were combined in the 1860s but separated by the 1900s; broad 'Diseases of' categories were used in the 1860s but replaced by more specific disease descriptions in

---

[29] Some of these matters were introduced in chapter 2 (p. 56); they are discussed at greater length in chapter 8 (pp. 312–16), in Woods and Shelton (1997), and in Hardy (1993). It must be acknowledged that the regular reporting of cause of death in infancy by the Registrar General in the Victorian period is fraught with problems simply because it was often difficult to distinguish exactly what the cause of death was. Hence 'Convulsions and other diseases of the nervous system' and 'Atrophy' in table 7.1 together contribute at least 30 per cent of IMR. We are probably on safer ground with early childhood mortality where the common and more readily identifiable diseases of childhood (e.g. measles, whooping cough, scarlet fever, etc.) were prominent.

[30] See Woods and Shelton (1997), table 2, p. 23, and table 8.1 below. For the sake of completeness, figures 7.9 and 7.10 use the full nosologies reported in the *Decennial Supplements* for 1861–70 and 1901–10 regardless of whether a particular cause is strictly appropriate for children.

the 1900s; and the various forms of tuberculosis were far more prominent in the 1900s than the 1860s when only 'Phthisis' was mentioned.
Nonetheless, the evidence summarised in the two figures can be used
to make some comparisons between the decades and to show how
reported causes varied between the age groups.

In the 1860s, and ignoring 'Other causes', the principal causes of death
among infants were: 'Diseases of the Brain' (this included convulsions),
'Diseases of the Lung' and 'Diarrhoea & Dysentery'. The first two were
also important in early childhood, but they were accompanied by 'Scarlet
fever', 'Measles', 'Whooping cough' and then 'Diarrhoea & Dysentery'
again. In later childhood, not only was mortality substantially lower but
the pattern of causes was far less distinct, with 'Scarlet fever', 'Other
violent deaths' (mainly accidental deaths) and 'Typhus' to the fore. In the
age group 10–14, accidents were prominent, but 'Phthisis' began to
emerge as a principal cause. Turning to the 1900s, 'Diarrhoea & Dysentery'
were the most important causes in infancy, followed by 'Pneumonia' and
'Bronchitis' (both diseases of the lung), 'Whooping cough', 'Measles' and
'Violence'. In early childhood the common infectious diseases as well as
the respiratory diseases were once again prominent although 'Diarrhoea
& Dysentery' and 'Violence' were important. 'Diphtheria' was more
prominent and 'Scarlet fever' far less so. In later childhood, mortality was
even lower and again there were no dominant causes. Assuming that the
pattern shown in figure 7.9 for the 1860s was broadly typical of the middle
decades of the nineteenth century, what additional information does table
7.1 provide about the particular pattern of causes in infancy and the differences between urban and rural environments? 'Premature birth' followed
by 'Convulsions' and 'Atrophy' dominated the first week, but by the ninth
to twelfth months 'Diarrhoeal diseases' and 'Diseases of the respiratory
organs' had come to dominate. In general, the ratio of 'Urban' to 'Rural'
infant mortality was 2.24, but for 'Premature birth' it was 1.22, for
'Convulsions' 2.73, 'Atrophy' 1.57, 'Diseases of the respiratory organs'
1.76, and for 'Diarrhoeal diseases' 8.23.[31]

The uses to which the Registrar General's cause of death data have
been, can be and should be put will be considered at greater length in the
next chapter. Although it is especially unwise to base too firm conclusions
on this material, a number of tentative points are in order. First, there were
clear differences between urban and rural places in terms of mortality at
early ages and these differences were largely the result of the water- and
food-borne diseases (especially diarrhoea and dysentery) in infancy, the
common infectious diseases (especially measles, whooping cough and

[31] The equivalent ratios of 'Social Classes' V to I in 1911 (figure 7.8) were: 'Premature birth'
1.38, 'Convulsions' 1.93, 'Bronchitis' 3.00, 'Pneumonia' 2.91, and 'Diarrhoea and enteritis' 2.24. The overall ratio was 2.00.

scarlet fever) in early childhood, and the respiratory diseases among children in general. Secondly, there were also significant differences between the infant mortality rates experienced by children in the official 'Social Classes' which reflect differences between fathers' occupations. It is far less easy to see how these differences were created by combinations of different causes of death. It is probably unwise to take the analysis of cause of death in infancy much further given the nature of registration and changes in the nosologies adopted, apart, that is, for some brief reference to deaths recorded as premature and those associated with diarrhoea and dysentery – the former because changes in the extent of prematurity may provide some additional evidence of the level of perinatal mortality and the latter because such diseases were highly sensitive to variations and changes in the quality of the public health environment.

Figure 7.11 shows the annual infant mortality rate due to premature birth together with the percentage of all infant deaths that were reported as due to premature birth for the period 1860–1913. Although the increases are obvious, there is no simple explanation for the trend. It may just be that the series reflect reporting fashion.[32]

Deaths reported as due to diarrhoea are rather more straightforward to deal with. Annual series for England and Wales, London and Birmingham are illustrated in figure 7.12. It is obvious, especially in the cases of England and Wales as a whole and of Birmingham, just how important the diarrhoeal diseases were for infant mortality in the 1890s and how, once the effects of these causes have been removed, infant mortality appears to be in steady decline from at least the late 1880s. The unusually high mortality in 1911 is also shown very clearly. There was a highly significant relationship between the infant mortality rate from diarrhoea and annual climatic fluctuations denoted by the number of rainy days in the third quarter of the year (negative relationship) and the mean earth temperature again during the third quarter of the year (positive relationship).[33] It seems that infant mortality in the late 1890s,

---

[32] Ward (1993) reconstructs time-series for average birthweight, but he is obliged to rely on hospital records. In the case of the Edinburgh Royal Infirmary Maternity Hospital mean birthweight appears to have declined during the second half of the nineteenth century (p. 40). Although this evidence cannot be used to generalise about the experience of mothers in England and Wales at the time, it may be that the proportion of miscarriages and even stillbirths was declining and that this led to an increase in prematurity. See also Dupâquier (1997).

[33] See Woods *et al.* (1988), table 4, p. 362. The R^2 from the two independent multiple regressions on the 42 years 1870–1911 is 0.6086, significant at the 1 per cent level. The fit is not perfect, therefore, and there would certainly be differences between towns. Compare London and Birmingham in figure 7.12. Attempts to link meteorology and disease patterns were common in the nineteenth century; see, as an example of one of the first, Guy (1843a). Newman (1906), pp. 153–70, on the relation of meteorology to diarrhoea, quoted with approval the finding that the summer rise in diarrhoea did not commence until the mean temperature at the four-foot earth thermometer had risen to 56°F.

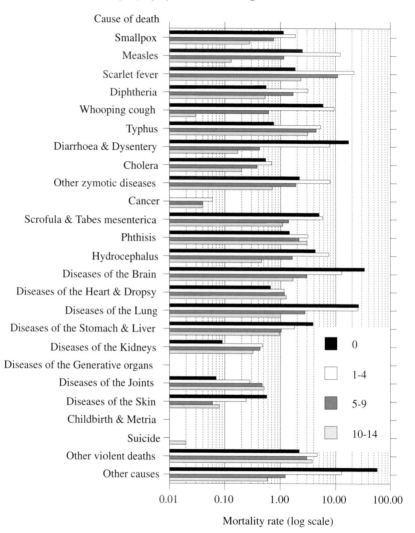

Figure 7.9. Cause- and age-specific mortality rates for males, England
and Wales, 1861–70
Note: The 'all causes' mortality rates for males were: IMR (0) 168.1; ECMR
(1–4) 137.3; (5–9) 39.9; (10–14) 22.1.

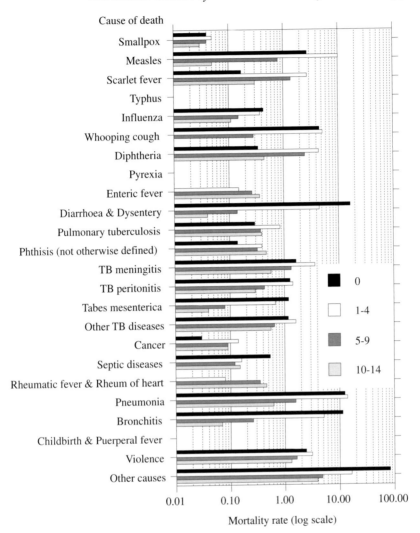

Figure 7.10. Cause- and age-specific mortality rates for males, England and Wales, 1901–10

Note: The 'all causes' mortality rates for males were: IMR (0) 140.3; ECMR (1–4) 72.8; (5–9) 17.4; (10–14) 10.2.

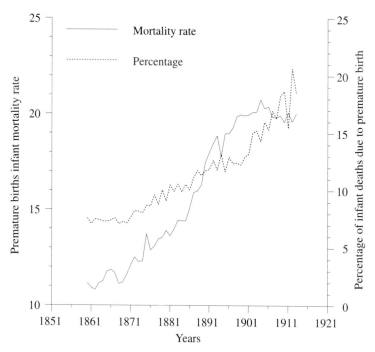

Figure 7.11. Annual premature birth infant mortality rates, England
and Wales, 1860–1913
Note: The rate is defined as the number of deaths per year reported as due to
'premature birth' per 1,000 live births.
Source: Registrar General, *Annual Reports* and for 1860–62, Farr (1865), table
VIII, pp. 125–49.

in 1904, 1906 and 1911, and particularly in such cities as Birmingham,
was exacerbated by especially high levels of diarrhoea mortality associated with the hot, dry summers.[34] The 1899 turning point in the IMR
series is accentuated by the particular climatic conditions of the late
1890s; the appearance of sudden decline from that point onwards may
be misleading, therefore.

Figure 7.12 also shows the neonatal mortality rate for England and
Wales from 1888 onwards to emphasise the point that decline in IMR
was principally the result of changes in post-neonatal mortality.
However, it should be remembered that there were probably substantial
variations in neonatal mortality rates among the registration counties

---

[34] The French termed this dramatic increase in summer infant mortality the 'Eiffel Tower
effect'. See Budin (1900, 1903); also Huck (1997) and Woods and Shelton (1997), p. 59.

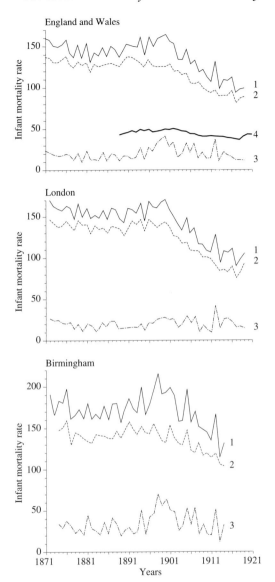

Figure 7.12. Time-series for selected annual infant mortality rates,
England and Wales, London and Birmingham compared
Note: 1. infant mortality rate, 2. non-diarrhoeal infant mortality rate,
3. diarrhoeal rate, 4. neonatal mortality rate. Rates are × 1,000.
Sources: For England and Wales, and London: Registrar General's *Annual
Reports*; for Birmingham: John Robertson, *Report of the Medical Officer of Health
on Child Welfare in 1913* (Birmingham: Hudson and Son, 1914), p. 6.

throughout the Victorian period although these can only be illustrated for the 1840s.[35]

Of all the dimensions of Victorian childhood mortality, the most difficult to assess are those of age of mother and parity, but the high level of fertility and the interval between births may have had an important bearing on the level and trend of infant mortality in particular. While low childhood mortality made low fertility possible, lower fertility will also have helped to reduce the risks to life at early ages as overall family size declined and birth intervals lengthened, and the average age of a mother at first and last birth became older and younger, respectively. Infant mortality has been found to bear a 'tick-like' relationship with both age of mother and parity. Of course this cannot be illustrated for Victorian England, but it can for Sweden. For example, figure 7.13 shows the relationship between IMR and parity among 20,626 infants born in Sundsvall, northern Sweden, during the nineteenth century.[36] It also gives an indication of the contribution of each parity to the total infant mortality rate. Thus, supposing that each parity-specific IMR remained unchanged but that stopping behaviour was so effective that 3 became the maximum parity then total IMR would decline by more than a third from 145 to 94. The mortality experienced by parity 1 children would obviously have to decline for very low IMRs to be achieved, but family limitation could still have had an important bearing on the decline of infant mortality.

The picture from Sweden can be complemented by that established by Robert Morse Woodbury in his influential study of the experiences of 22,967 children born in eight American cities during the period 1916–18. Figure 7.14 illustrates the effects of both the parity and the age of mother. The lowest risks were faced by parities 2 and 3 born to mothers in their late twenties. But Woodbury's data also show that IMR would only have been reduced from 111.2 to between 95 and 100 if no high parity births had occurred and no women under 20 or over 30 had given birth. Thus, while the process of fertility reduction (especially if this combines later marriage and parity-specific control and spacing) could have an important bearing on infant mortality, particularly if fertility started from a high level, only a certain amount of progress

---

[35] Table 2.2, column G, gives the neonatal mortality rate for England and Wales in 1839–44 as 46.4, which is consistent with line 4 in figure 7.12, but table 2.2 and figure 2.13 also show that the rate varied from 30.4 (Cornwall) to 62.1 (Bedfordshire).

[36] Lynch and Greenhouse (1994). This paper is especially important for its emphasis on the intra-familial dimension of infant mortality. Recent work by members of the Cambridge Group has been able to shed a little more light on the effects of parity. See Reid, 'Infant and child mortality from the 1911 census', chapter 3 of Garrett *et al.* (forthcoming).

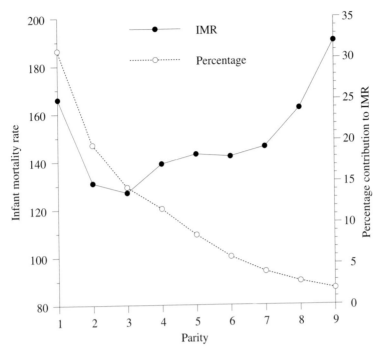

Figure 7.13. Relationship between infant mortality and parity,
Sundsvall, Sweden, nineteenth century
Note: IMR was 144.8 and mean parity 3.1.
Source: Lynch and Greenhouse (1994), table 2, p. 121.

could be generated by this direct means alone. For very low rates of
infant mortality to be achieved, both curves would need to move substantially further to the right; for them merely to flatten out would mean
much less in terms of mortality decline.[37]

Woodbury's various statistical studies of infant mortality were of
special importance in the United States not only because of the data

[37] Woodbury (1926). In Britain the 1949–50 birth cohort studies demonstrate the important independent effects of mother's age and parity on infant mortality, see Daly *et al.*
(1955). Pearl (1939), p. 89, and Sutherland (1949), p. 26, have also illustrated the effects
of maternal age on the stillbirth rate. Using data for England and Wales, July 1938 to
December 1940 (legitimate births only) and the USA in 1932 they show that while the
total stillbirth rates were, respectively, 36 and 38 per 1,000 total births (live and still) the
following rates applied to particular maternal age groups:

	15–19	20–24	25–29	30–34	35–39	40–44	45–49
E&W, 1938–40	26	26	30	38	50	68	94
USA, 1932	41	32	32	37	49	64	87

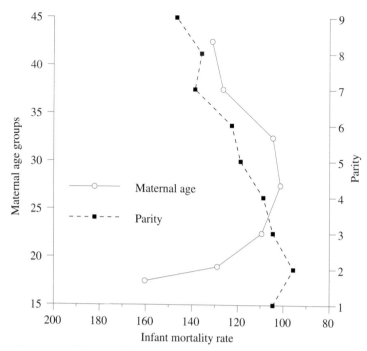

Figure 7.14. Relationship between infant mortality and maternal age
and parity, eight United States cities, 1916–18
Note: For 22,967 live births the total IMR was 111.2.
Source: Woodbury (1926), tables 7 and 8.

used but also the methodology adopted.[38] In attempting to summarise
the characteristics of infant and childhood mortality patterns in
Victorian England and Wales it may prove helpful, therefore, to refer to
his checklist of factors.

A preliminary survey showed a number of factors each of which might apparently have a close connection with infant mortality. These include age of the
infant; seasonal conditions; sex; factors related to the health and physical conditions of the mother during pregnancy and at confinement; factors related to frequency of births – age of mother, order of birth, interval since preceding birth, and
interval before succeeding pregnancy; factors associated with birth or confinement, – including prematurity, single or plural birth, and type of delivery; types
of feeding; racial or nationality factors; and social and economic factors including, earnings of the father, per capita income of the family, and employment of
the mother during pregnancy or during the infant's first year of life.[39]

---

[38] Woodbury (1922) develops and applies Harald Westergaard's method (first reported in
1882) of standardisation and partialling out the effects of different factors: age, parity.
income, etc.   [39] Woodbury (1926), pp. 40–41.

Woodbury was principally concerned to distinguish the factors that led to different levels of infant mortality rather than the causes of secular decline, but the information he assembled on nearly 23,000 births was exceptional for the early twentieth century, and closer in many respects to the 1949 birth cohort study in Britain. Despite this, there were areas in which even his data were less adequate. For example, for the single city of Baltimore, Woodbury reported that 'Infants whose mothers were known to have had tuberculosis had a mortality (271) two and one-half times as high as that (102) among other infants.'[40] We know very little about the general health of mothers and the way it affected the life chances of the newly born beyond what may be inferred from mortality rates among young women or directly associated with maternal mortality. As far as maternal mortality is concerned, there is little sign of significant decline until the 1930s in England and Wales with rates at or about 4.7 to 5.0 maternal deaths per 1,000 live births although there were important geographical variations.[41] Clearly, this is a problematical area especially if, as was the case with pulmonary tuberculosis, mortality at least declined substantially in the nineteenth and early twentieth centuries and did so particularly among young women. But in general we can know little of the morbidity experienced by pregnant women or mothers just as we can have little idea of the extent of sickness among their children.

England and Wales was not alone among European countries in experiencing rapid secular decline in infant mortality from the beginning of the twentieth century preceded by the decline of early childhood mortality.[42] In Scotland IMR was approximately 20 parts per thousand lower than in England and Wales, decline set in at about the same time, but was not as rapid. In France the decline of IMR began from a higher plateau than in England and Wales and became evident only after 1895. There, too, early childhood mortality was in obvious decline from the 1860s, some 30 years before the decline in the infant mortality rate, and the background level of mortality in late childhood (5–14) was probably also in decline from an even earlier date.[43] In Norway and Austria there is also some evidence of a turning point in the 1890s, but Italy and

---

[40] Woodbury (1926), p. 43. Some of the early studies in eugenics attempted to look at the extent to which parity and the chances of contracting tuberculosis might be linked, but their conclusions do not bear close statistical scrutiny. See Greenwood and Yule (1914).

[41] Loudon (1992), especially pp. 11–19 and 158–65, and Woods and Shelton (1997), pp. 115–18.

[42] Vallin (1991), especially figure 3.4, p. 50, charts the European experience by individual countries.

[43] Meslé and Vallin (1991), especially figure 9, p. 50, and Perrenoud and Bourdelais (1998), especially p. 76.

Sweden provide some interesting exceptions. In Italy the national IMR began to decline from the 1860s (270 in 1861) while for Sweden there was decline throughout the nineteenth century (143 in 1861).[44] Most if not all European countries have experienced continuous decline throughout the twentieth century, although it would prove more difficult to generalise about the causes of international variations in levels and the timing of change. Some of the problems for generalisation relate to the very recording of live births and thus infant mortality – there was a greater likelihood in certain regions that some stillbirths would be recorded as live born; others relate to the extent and duration of breast-feeding, and yet others to the balance within childhood mortality as a whole of deaths in infancy and in early childhood.[45]

The childhood mortality problem: contemporary and recent approaches

There is always the possibility that we shall discover, apparently for the first time, that which was well understood by Victorians themselves. In the study of childhood mortality this possibility appears very real, for a substantial number of medical men, statisticians and social reformers concerned themselves with the infant and childhood mortality problem. During the 1850s and 1860s informed opinion, reflected here by Sir John Simon, considered that infant mortality variations were

> due to the varying prevalence of two local causes: first, to differences of degree in common sanitary defects of residence; some places abounding more than others in the foul air and foul water of undrained, unpaved, unscavenged, unlighted, unventilated, localities and houses; and secondly, to occupational differences among the inhabitants; there being certain large towns where women are greatly engaged in branches of industry away from home; where, consequently, the home is ill kept; where the children are little looked after; and where infants who should be at the breast are improperly fed or starved, or have their cries of hunger and distress quieted by the various fatal opiates which are in such request at the centres of our manufacturing industry.[46]

During the 1890s and 1900s one of the most influential, and certainly the most perceptive, of the observers who took up these themes was Sir

---

[44] For Italy, see Del Panta *et al.* (1996), especially Marco Breschi's estimate of IMR for Tuscany post-1640 using back projection (p. 153) as well as the national series from 1861 (pp. 180–81). Without the long-run series it would not be evident that IMR began to decline from the time of unification.

[45] These comparative problems have been discussed and illustrated in Corsini and Viazzo (1997) and Bideau *et al.* (1997). Farr (1866a) also attempted to make some comparisons in a highly polemical paper and with the aid of his network of European statistical correspondents. There is also an early reference to 'Darwin's law' (p. 12).

[46] Sir John Simon, then the Medical Officer of the Privy Council, made these observations in both his first and sixth reports; see *Sixth Report of the Medical Officer of the Privy Council, 1863* (BPP 1864/XXVIII), p. 34.

Arthur Newsholme (1857–1943).[47] Newsholme served as Medical Officer of Health for Brighton (1888–1908) and Medical Officer of the Local Government Board (1909–19). While at the Local Government Board he prepared a series of five detailed reports which were wholly or in large part concerned with the infant mortality problem.[48] These appeared in 1910, 1913, 1914, 1915 and 1916, but it is the first report for 1910 that provides Newsholme's most comprehensive summary of his analysis and recommendations.[49] It will be used here both as the basis for a discussion of the reasons for variations especially in the infant mortality rate which were popular with contemporaries, and also as a device for comparison with more recent frameworks.

Newsholme's approach is summarised in table 7.5. It ran as follows. The influence of certain factors on the infant mortality rate could be established without dispute. The quality of care provided during delivery was important and could be improved by effective implementation of the 1902 Midwives Act. Poverty and poor sanitation were obvious factors. The latter could be divided into the effects of insufficient scavenging of domestic refuse, problems with the disposal of excreta and the absence of paving in streets or yards. Each of these defects could be remedied by local sanitary authorities, especially by the adoption of the water-carriage system of sewerage and the associated water closet. 'Thus local sanitary authorities are largely responsible for the continuance of excessive infant mortality, and until they fulfil satisfactorily their elementary tasks, efforts in the direction of domestic hygiene can only be partially successful.'[50] Newsholme's emphasis on sanitation stemmed from his experience as a local Medical Officer of Health and his belief that this factor, at least, could be ameliorated by local government action. His presidential address in 1899 to the Incorporated Society of Medical Officers of Health dealt with the subject of epidemic diarrhoea in the great towns and was quoted again in his 1910 report. The 1899 address also recognised the effects of rainfall and temperature which, other things being equal, were likely to exacerbate the influence of epidemic diarrhoea especially in hot, dry summers.[51] The point was well made and is clearly confirmed by the analysis presented earlier in this chapter.

---

[47] Eyler (1997) provides an illuminating account of Newsholme's work in Brighton and at the LGB.

[48] Eyler's (1997), pp. 295–316, account of Newsholme's several reports echoes Woods *et al.* (1989).

[49] *Thirty-ninth Annual Report of the Local Government Board, 1909–10. Supplement to the Report of the Board Medical Officer Containing a Report by the Board Medical Officer on Infant and Child Mortality* (BPP 1910/XXIX, Cd. 5263, p. 973), referred to here as Newsholme's *First Report* of 1910.   [50] Newsholme's *First Report* (1910), p. 76.

[51] Newsholme (1899).

Table 7.5. *A summary of the factors influencing infant mortality proposed by Sir Arthur Newsholme*

A Mother	B Care of mother	C Care of child	D Poverty	E Housing	F Sanitary environment	G Personal factors
Age	Ante-natal	Delivery (midwifery)	Housing	Type	Pure water	
Work	Post-natal	Visiting (care, advice)	Unemployment	Crowding	Excreta disposal	
Family size	Maternal	Feeding	Wife's work		Scavenging	
Illigitimacy	mortality	Breast	Other children's		Paving	
		Artificial	work			
		form				
		preparation				

The importance of population density and crowding was also more or less obvious. Infant mortality was higher in urban than in rural areas, partly as a consequence of defective sanitation in a crowded environment, but also because the worst industrial conditions and the lowest industrial classes were found in such environments. Newsholme, through his work on London's Peabody Buildings, was also aware that, as he put it, 'Infant mortality is always highest in crowded centres of population: but a high infant mortality can be avoided under conditions of dense aggregation of population.'[52]

Newsholme's approach to poverty was more equivocal. Its influence on childhood mortality, though of importance, was usually dealt with in indirect terms as it affected infant feeding, the employment of women, housing and sanitation. The direct financial implications of poverty were not singled out, probably because they lay outside the public health sphere and the remit of the Local Government Board.[53]

The care of infants by their mothers, their feeding habits and the employment of mothers outside the home occupied particularly important positions in Newsholme's list of factors. During the first decade of the twentieth century the most controversial of these social issues was women's employment. Here Newsholme refused to go with the crowd:

under circumstances of extreme poverty the money earned by the mother, who has to leave her infant for this purpose, may have greater influence in reducing infant mortality than the same mother would be able to exercise under the circumstances of still deeper poverty which her stay at home would have meant. It will be agreed by all, however, that the industrial employment of mothers under such circumstances is a serious evil.[54]

Newsholme's difficulties stemmed from his inability to isolate a highly significant statistical association between infant mortality rates and the employment of women outside their homes despite the determination of most of his male contemporaries, both medical and lay, to believe the worst. He was clearly doubtful in 1899, but his views on the complexity of the relationship were confirmed by his work for the reports of 1914 and 1915. Infant mortality could be high where women's employment was common, but cases where high proportions of women employed outside the home coincided with high infant mortality were becoming

---

[52] Newsholme's *First Report* (1910), p. 75, also Newsholme (1891).
[53] *Forty-second Annual Report of the Local Government Board, 1912–13. Supplement in Continuation of the Report of the Medical Officer of the Board for 1912–1913 Containing a Second Report on Infant and Child Mortality by the Medical Officer to the Board* (BPP 1913/XXXII, Cd. 6909, p. 1), Newsholme's *Second Report* of 1913; see especially p. 89 on poverty.   [54] Newsholme's *First Report* (1910), p. 57.

less common, whereas high proportions in employment and low infant mortality rates continued to be found together.[55]

If there was doubt about the contribution of mothers' wage employment to high infant mortality, there could be none about the importance of infant feeding practices and the general problems of maternal ignorance and fecklessness. As table 7.5 suggests, the problem could be divided into a number of sub-issues, to each of which Newsholme made his own significant contribution. First, mothers needed to be educated and professionally advised on infant and child care, and domestic hygiene. Secondly, a safe and accessible supply of milk had to be made available. Thirdly, mothers needed to be encouraged to breastfeed whenever possible, since this was the natural and most effective form of nutrition for infants. The first objective was being achieved by instruction in schools, by the system of early birth notification and by the health visitor schemes, each of which was becoming increasingly widespread and effective during the 1900s.[56] On the second, Newsholme re-emphasised the importance of poor sanitation and lack of domestic hygiene in bringing about the contamination of pasteurised or evaporated milk, even when it had been pure on arrival in the home.[57] However, it is on the third issue that Newsholme made some of his most telling points. For example:

probably 80 per cent of the mothers of infants in wage-earning populations suckle their infants partially or entirely and the proportion of mothers in the well-to-do classes who are able or willing to continue to give their infants this immensely important start in life is believed, I think rightly, to be much smaller. There must be reasons of great potency, enabling the infants of the well-to-do to survive in much higher proportions to the end of the first year of life, notwithstanding this heavy handicap against them.[58]

And, it is the ability to obtain skilled guidance in the preparation of infants' food, to spend sufficient money in purchasing it, and to prepare such food under the safest conditions that explains in large measure the lower infant mortality among the non-industrial classes.[59]

---

[55] Some of these points are considered at greater length by Dyhouse (1978) as well as Holdsworth (1997) and Garrett (1998), but see also the original reports: *Forty-third Annual Report of the Local Government Board, 1913–14. Supplement in Continuation of the Report of the Medical Officer of the Board for 1913–14 containing a Third Report on Infant Mortality dealing with Infant Mortality in Lancashire by the Medical Officer of the Board, and Drs. Copeman, Manby, Farrar, and Lane-Claypon* (BPP 1914/XXXIX, Cd. 751, p. 371), Newsholme's *Third Report* (1914) and *Forty-fourth Annual Report of the Local Government Board, 1914–15. Supplement in Continuation of the Report of the Medical Officer of the Board for 1914–15 Containing a Report on Maternal Mortality in Connection with Childbearing and its relation to Infant Mortality* (BPP 1914–16/XXV, Cd. 8085, p. 157), Newsholme's *Fourth Report* (1915).

[56] Dwork (1987) provides an interesting review of the various infant feeding and health visitor schemes.   [57] Newsholme (1902, 1902–03).

[58] Newsholme's *First Report* (1910), p. 54.   [59] Newsholme's *First Report* (1910), p. 71.

If Newsholme's claims regarding the prevalence of breastfeeding are correct, they provide an explanation for the relatively low levels of infant mortality in England compared with several other European countries. They also suggest a reason why the mortality differential between social classes was less than that between localities. And they encourage the belief that if the extent and/or the duration of breast-feeding could have been increased then infant mortality would have been reduced. Unfortunately, very little is known about breastfeeding practices in England during the late nineteenth and early twentieth centuries, and what is known is restricted almost entirely to working-class mothers. Newsholme drew the 80 per cent figure from his studies in Brighton where 84.4 per cent of infants aged less than two months were breastfed, but among all infants of working-class parents aged 0 to 11 months in Brighton and Derby only 62.7 and 63.2 per cent, respectively, were breastfed.[60]

Tables 7.6 to 7.8 summarise efforts to supplement these data, but they must be treated with caution. They have been compiled from surveys carried out with different definitions and methods. The main difficulties relate to the form of the surveys, the ages of children surveyed, and the definition of feeding practices. For example, Newsholme's own Brighton data come from a house-to-house inspection in which the ages of infants were also recorded, while the data for Salford emphasise the early period of infancy because they were obtained from a scheme for post-natal care based on health visitors. The matter is further complicated because, apart from infants who were only fed on breast milk, the form of supplementation used – cow's milk, condensed milk, farinaceous or solid food – was not always specified and, in any case, needs to be matched with the infant's age.[61]

Despite these obvious limitations, the picture seems reasonably clear. First, while not universal, the practice of breastfeeding infants, especially young babies, appears to have been general in urban England. There were variations between towns, and perhaps also in the accepted normal duration of breastfeeding, but there is good reason to agree with Newsholme's view that the breastfeeding norm among working class mothers must have helped to reduce infant mortality where poverty, environment and sanitation would otherwise have resulted in higher rates. Secondly, local and national medical officers made strenuous efforts to emphasise the point illustrated in part by the tables. Hand- or

---

[60] On Brighton, see Newsholme (1906a), and on Derby, Howarth (1905).
[61] Unfortunately Knodel (1977b), especially table 2, p. 1113, uses English breastfeeding data for this period without noting these difficulties. Some of these problems are taken up in Winikoff (1981).

bottle-fed infants were more likely to die from epidemic diarrhoea, especially in years with hot, dry summers. Brighton's breastfeeding percentages were certainly high, but not exceptional: those for Liverpool were based on data for 500 consecutive admissions to the city's Infirmary for Children, and those for Birmingham were based on very substantial surveys. In all cases they provided useful warning about the dangers of bottle feeding, despite defective sampling procedures. Thirdly, it seems likely that many mothers were unable to breastfeed for seven, eight or nine months, rather than that they were unwilling to do so, regardless of postpartum mortality. The figures in table 7.6 show that in Salford 7.4 per cent of all babies were never breastfed, but the equivalent figure was 20.2 per cent for those infants who died during the first six months of their lives. Further, table 7.8 clearly illustrates the slow fall-off in breastfeeding between the first and sixth months which suggests that mothers were more likely to be unable to start breastfeeding than prepared to abandon it prematurely once started. In Finsbury, London, George Newman's survey of 357 dead infants showed that 48.7 per cent of their mothers were unable to suckle their infants through 'want of milk'.[62] Fourthly, on the evidence of table 7.6 there is little reason to suppose that either the incidence or duration of breastfeeding increased during the first decade of the twentieth century in the towns for which there are data, but infant mortality rates declined everywhere, especially the post-neonatal rates and rates from diarrhoea.

The material in tables 7.6 to 7.8 offers a tantalising picture of the form and duration of infant feeding patterns, but it obscures much that modern surveys would have clarified. The current round of Demographic and Health Surveys includes rather more penetrating questions on the form of infant feeding being used. For instance, the Zambian DHS identifies whether infants are being fed only on breast milk or breast milk and water or breast milk with other supplements. After the third month more than 50 per cent of infants are fed on breast milk and water, thereby making the quality of the water supply of vital importance for infant survival even before weaning. Were this also to have applied in England, the absence of safe, clean water would certainly have distorted the prophylactic effect of breastfeeding, and its increasing availability when combined with breast milk should have assisted the decline of childhood mortality.

[62] Newman (1906), p. 88. The recommended time to wean was during dentition, between the ages of seven and nine months and certainly not before seven months; see Kanthack (1907). The point also relates clearly to Fogel's (1986), pp. 439–55, arguments about the significance of nutritional status among pregnant women for both the health of the foetus and the subsequent life chances of the child after birth, especially in terms of the mother's ability to care for the infant.

Table 7.6. *Methods of infant feeding in selected English towns in the 1900s*

Town	Year	Breast milk	Breast milk and other food	Other food only	Number surveyed	Number of births
Salford	1902	75.7	13.2	11.1	494	1285
(Greengates	1903	81.7	8.1	10.2	1069	1262
district)	1904	81.1	8.1	10.8	1044	1065
	1905	83.5	6.1	10.4	1112	1124
	1906	87.8	5.8	6.5	956	967
	1907	83.7	6.1	10.2	957	968
Salford	1907	85.2	5.4	9.7	2262	6956
	1908	82.6	10.6	6.7	3485	7264
	1909	79.5	12.5	8.1	3628	6778
	1910	76.2	16.5	7.4	4017	6594
Stockport	1903	68.6	6.1	25.3	1010	2800
	1904	68.8	5.6	25.6	1420	2566
	1905	74.6	6.9	18.5	1211	2668
	1906	71.1	7.7	21.2	919	2686
	1907	71.0	10.2	18.8	1714	2730
	1908	86.4	4.9	8.7	2158	2860
	1909	84.2	5.8	10.0	2731	2731
	1910	57.4	13.8	28.8	2334	2691
	1911	67.6	15.0	17.4	900	2545
Derby	1900–04	65.4	15.9	18.7	11034	12579
	1904–05	70.6	13.8	15.5	2240	3096
	1905–06	72.9	11.6	15.6	2543	2926
	1906–07	69.0	12.5	18.5	2560	3528
Brighton	1903–05	62.7	15.3	22.0	1253	–
Birmingham	1908	56.9	20.1	23.0	1043	1503
(St George's and	1909	54.5	23.5	22.0	1285	1514
St Stephen's wards)						

Sources: Salford (Greengates district), 1902–7, Medical Officer of Health's *Annual Report*, 1907, table 1, p. 55 and table B, p. 59; Salford, 1907–10, Medical Officer of Health's *Annual Reports*, 1908–11; Stockport, Medical Officer of Health's *Annual Reports*, 1903–11; Derby, Medical Officer of Health's *Annual Reports*, 1905, table IIIa, p. 16; 1906, table IV, p. 17; 1907, table IV, p.15 (figures are for November to November); Brighton, Arthur Newsholme, 'Domestic infection in relation to epidemic diarrhoea', *Journal of Hygiene* 6 (1906a), pp. 139–48; Birmingham, 1908, John Robertson, *Report on Industrial Employment of Married Women and Infantile Mortality*, City of Birmingham Health Department (Birmingham, 1910); 1909, Jessie G. Duncan, *Report on Infant Mortality in St George's and St Stephen's Wards*, City of Birmingham Health Department (Birmingham, 1911).

Table 7.7. *Method of infant feeding by age groups in selected English towns*

	Percentage of infants fed on:		
	Breast milk	Breast milk and other food	Other food only
Brighton, 1903–05 (N = 1253)			
0–2 months	84.4	6.9	8.7
3–5 months	66.8	11.6	21.6
6–11 months	48.2	22.4	29.4
Liverpool (N = 364)			
0–2 months	48.7 (50)	20.7	30.6
3–5 months	37.3 (20)	24.5	38.2
6–11 months	35.8	24.5	39.7
Finsbury, London, 1905 (N = 1822)			
0–2 months	82.5	9.7	7.8
Birmingham, 1903			
0–5 months			
Healthy (N = 1200)	56.8	28.8	14.4
Deceased (N = 236)	10.0	10.0	80.0

Sources: Brighton, Arthur Newsholme, 'Domestic infection in relation to epidemic diarrhoea', *Journal of Hygiene* 6 (1906), p. 141; Liverpool, H. R. Jones, 'The perils and protection of infant life', *Journal of the Royal Statistical Society* 57 (1894), p. 82 (the figures in parentheses are opinions from E. W. Hope, 'Observations on autumnal diarrhoea in cities', *Public Health* 11 (July 1899), p. 661); Finsbury, George Newman, *Infant Mortality: A Social Problem* (London: Methuen, 1906), p. 242; Birmingham, John Robertson, *Special Report of the Medical Officer of Health on Infant Mortality in the City of Birmingham* (Birmingham, 1904).

In general, although breastfeeding practices helped to depress mortality, they do not appear to have changed substantially and cannot be credited with making a major contribution to the decline of infant mortality. However, it is possible that the proportion of mothers who could breastfeed increased slowly in the late nineteenth century and that infant mortality was reduced thereby, but as yet there is no evidence to support such a speculation.[63]

Apart from one influence, about which Newsholme was equivocal, the list is now complete. Sanitation, poverty, poor feeding, maternal

[63] Fildes (1980) considers evidence for the timing of the start of breastfeeding after birth and its link with the decline of neonatal mortality in the eighteenth century. Similar arguments cannot be made for the late nineteenth and early twentieth centuries, but see Fildes (1992, 1998).

Table 7.8. *Duration of breastfeeding in Salford, 1908–10*

Duration of breastfeeding	Total births cumulative per cent	Survived to 6 months cumulative per cent	Died before 6 months cumulative per cent
At least:			
1 month	85.1	87.6	68.8
2 months	83.3	86.1	65.4
3 months	82.2	85.1	63.4
4 months	81.1	84.0	61.7
5 months	80.2	83.2	60.4
6 months	79.6	82.6	59.3
N	11078	9655	1424

Source: Medical Officer of Health's *Annual Reports*, 1908–10, section V, Work of the Health Visitors, and Supervision of Midwives (Salford, 1909–11). Of those who died before 6 months, 20.2 per cent were fed on other food from birth.

ignorance and fecklessness, and complications during delivery were the main factors at work. 'The chief means for a lower infant mortality are efficient domestic and municipal sanitation, good housing and intelligent and painstaking "mothering".'[64] Although the lists of factors responsible for high childhood mortality compiled by other contemporaries overlapped substantially with Newsholme's, they did not necessarily agree either on matters of interpretation or in their recommendations for the solution of the infant mortality problem. Several of the recommendations also passed through phases of popularity when their sponsors could see no other solutions: sanitation, housing, milk depots, 'motherhood' and health visitors among them. For example, Dr John Robertson's *Special Report of the Medical Officer of Health on Infant Mortality in the City of Birmingham* (1904) contained eight recommendations. Three dealt with housing, two with cleanliness, and one each with poverty, day nurseries and last, but of most importance, the need to provide a clean milk supply.

Apart from Newsholme, the most important contemporary commentator on the infant mortality problem was Sir George Newman (1870–1948). He acted as Medical Officer of Health for Finsbury (1900–07) and Medical Officer of the Board of Education (1907–35) and the newly established Ministry of Health (1919–35). Newman's approach and emphasis differed from Newsholme's in a number of

[64] Newsholme's *First Report* (1910), p. 75.

ways.[65] Newman focuses particularly on motherhood: 'Wherever we turn, and to whatever issue, in the question of infant mortality, we are faced with one all-pervading primary need – the need of a high standard of physical motherhood.'[66] The problem of maternal ignorance could be tackled by the instruction of mothers, the appointment of women health visitors and the education of girls in domestic hygiene, while the 'necessary evil' of women's employment outside the home and its 'injury to infancy' could be lessened by revision of the Factory Acts, improvement of factory sanitation and the provision of crèches. The health of the infant could also be protected by early birth registration coupled with a visiting scheme, and the provision of a clean milk supply at special milk depots. The environment would benefit from improved sanitation and urban cleanliness, but Newman's stance is best summarised by the following passage from *Infant Mortality: A Social Problem* (1906):

A mother suckling her infant requires nourishment, and it is lack of nourished mothers among the poor – many of whom are half-starved – that leads to the inability to provide milk for their offspring. This, in turn, leads to early weaning, which involves artificial feeding, which is one of the most difficult undertakings in the tenement homes of the poor.[67]

Both Newsholme and Newman were careful analysts: their combined list of factors is comprehensive and their recommendations are entirely sensible. There were certainly differences of emphasis in terms of cause and solution, but both overlapped to a considerable degree. However, it must be emphasised that even in the years just before the First World War neither observer recognised that the infant mortality rate had peaked in 1898–99 and, apart from particular individual years like 1911, was to decline continuously thereafter despite the War and the economic depression of the 1930s. Nor did they place much emphasis on the decline of early childhood mortality from the 1860s. Newman in 1906 and Newsholme during a longer period from the 1890s were looking for factors that were influencing variations in infant mortality rates rather than the causes of secular decline, which was far from

---

[65] The two men's careers paralleled one another in certain respects. Newsholme retired from public service to concentrate on writing and lecturing when Newman was appointed to the Ministry of Health in 1919. See Eyler (1997), pp. 316–37 on the initial co-operation and then rivalry between the two men and their departments especially for the health of children remit.

[66] Newman, *Infant Mortality* (1906), p. 257. This book was Newman's most important contribution to the debate.

[67] Newman (1906), p. 260. Newman was obviously writing from his own direct experience in Finsbury, but in general the early weaning claim is difficult to substantiate.

apparent even to Newsholme in writing his later reports, although the matter seemed to be clearer by the time the final edition of *The Elements of Vital Statistics* was published in 1923. Returning to table 7.5, it is likely that many of the factors listed would have improved during the 1890s and the first decade of the twentieth century in ways that should have contributed to lower mortality rates. But it has already been shown that infant mortality declined dramatically, especially in some of the largest urban places with the highest rates, and that all areas and all social classes were affected to some degree. A number of universal factors, operating alone or in a synergistic fashion, seem to have been at work and to have had a significant and immediate effect. While the short run of hot, dry summers in the 1890s was certainly responsible for demonstrating the vulnerability of urban sanitary environments to epidemic diarrhoea, improvements in housing quality, the standard of living, the care of infant and mother through midwifery and post-natal health visiting schemes were at best gradual, often differing in their effects between localities and social groups, and occasionally entirely inconsequential.[68]

For example, it has been argued that 'the onset of this improvement [the rapid decline of infant mortality] coincided with the beginning of the movement towards a safe milk supply and the continuation of the improvement has, in large part, been the result of the fulfilment of this development'.[69] Beaver's point seems plausible, indeed it has often been quoted with approval, but the improved quality of cow's milk could not on its own have generated such a substantial and dramatic change in infant life chances compared with the quality of drinking water and when set against the extent of breastfeeding. It also ignores the point made by Newsholme in his invective about house flies; even if the milk was pure when it first reached the shops and street, in the home it would quickly become contaminated.[70] This is not to say that pasteurisation and the bottling of milk did not represent substantial advances, but merely to remain sceptical about their direct and immediate impact on infant mortality at the turn of the century.

Newsholme's checklist of the factors influencing infant and child mortality, summarised here in table 7.5, helps us to see quite clearly how early twentieth-century specialists approached the issue and indeed

---

[68] On midwifery, see the evidence compiled for Rotherham by Robinson (1908, 1909), and on infant feeding in Huddersfield, Marland (1993).

[69] Beaver (1973), p. 247. Beaver's argument was referred to with approval by McKeown *et al.* (1975), p. 417, and McKeown (1976), p. 162.

[70] Newsholme (1906a) and Dwork (1987) give sharp insights on the 'milk debate'.

how they turned the health of children into a problem for public concern and state intervention.[71] It can also help us to see how the problem was compartmentalised and dichotomised: the environment *or* mothering, sanitation *or* housing, employment *or* education, water *or* milk. How is the same problem conceptualised today with respect to the still high levels of childhood mortality in Third World countries? And do the research frameworks developed in recent years help in our understanding of Europe's past experience?

Of the frameworks now available the one developed in 1983 by Mosley and Chen has proved the most influential and the most durable.[72] The Mosley–Chen framework attempts the integration of the social and medical science approaches via the specification of a set of five proximate determinants, intermediate variables that directly influence the risk of morbidity or mortality.[73] These are: (1) maternal factors: age, parity, birth interval; (2) environmental contamination: air, water/food/fingers, skin/soil/inanimate objects, insect vectors; (3) nutrient deficiency: calories, protein, micro-nutrients (vitamins and minerals); (4) injury: accidental, intentional; (5) personal illness control: personal preventive measures, medical treatment.[74] The socio-economic determinants which work through these five proximate determinants are also divisible into groups: (1) individual-level variables: individual productivity (fathers, mothers), traditions/norms/attitudes; (2) household-level variables: income/wealth; (3) community-level variables: ecological setting, political economy, health system.[75] Finally, the outcome variable is also redefined to include not only childhood mortality itself, but also 'growth faltering' as a consequence of sickness. Mosley and Chen also develop a diagrammatic representation of the 'operation of the five groups of proximate determinants on the health

---

[71] How infant mortality came to be problematised is a long and complicated story which involves concern about physical deterioration and the eugenicists' challenge. See Titmuss (1943), especially on class inequalities, and Armstrong (1986) on the origins of the problematic. In demographic terms, it is linked with the fact that the birth rate declined before IMR. See Eyler (1997) and chapter 4, pp. 143–44, and below, pp. 295–300.

[72] Mosley and Chen (1984). The Supplement to *Population and Development Review*, which contains the most important interdisciplinary review of the subject conducted for several decades, offers no historical perspective on how childhood mortality came to decline in the West.

[73] In its use of the notion of 'proximate determinants' the Mosley–Chen framework parallels the proximate determinants of fertility model pioneered by Davis and Blake and operationalised by Bongaarts, but as Mosley and Chen (1984), pp. 28–29, point out: 'The problems posed by mortality analysis, however, are far more complex [than fertility analysis] because a child's death is the ultimate consequence of a cumulative series of biological insults rather than the outcome of a single biological event.'

[74] Mosley and Chen (1984), p. 27.   [75] Mosley and Chen (1984), p. 34.

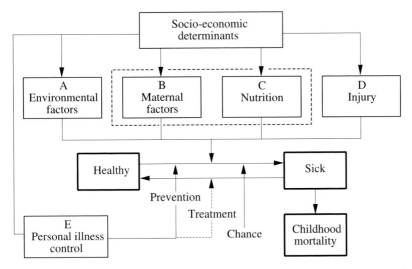

Figure 7.15. Revised version of the Mosley–Chen framework for studying the factors affecting childhood mortality
Source: Revised and redrawn from Mosley and Chen (1984), figure 2, p. 29.

dynamics of a population' which is reproduced here in modified form as figure 7.15.[76]

Figure 7.15 shows how the Mosley–Chen framework might be applied in the context of Victorian England. The role of 'Treatment' has been reduced to a dashed line to symbolise the limited effect this could have had on recovery prospects and 'Chance' has been inserted to represent the random and often arbitrary nature of the occurrence of some childhood diseases in the nineteenth century. Table 7.5 and figure 7.15 do not, of course, correspond exactly, but there is sufficient overlap for us to be mindful of the limited extent to which opinion on the key factors influencing childhood mortality has changed. Newsholme's list of variables and the Mosley–Chen framework each lay particular stress on the role of the mother, nutrition and the environment. These can alter the balance between a mother or child being healthy or sick, as can prevention and treatment. Some recent research has also stressed the importance of death clustering, where a significant proportion of childhood deaths occur to a small minority of women. For example, Das Gupta has argued that 'this death clustering can be explained to a very large extent by the basic abilities and personal characteristics of the

---

[76] The modification involves the insertion of 'Chance' and the removal of a 'Growth faltering' box.

mother, independently of education, occupation, income, and wealth'.[77] Table 7.5 does take some note of personal characteristics, although the Mosley–Chen framework does not. Neither of the frameworks is arranged with the explicit objective of helping us to understand the causes of decline in childhood mortality as opposed to its variation, although both are correct in emphasising the complexity of the relationships involved, their multivariate nature and the need to integrate the medical and social science approaches.[78]

For nineteenth- and early twentieth-century England and Wales, what caused infant and childhood mortality to begin to decline and that decline to be maintained? In broad terms, there are eight possibilities:

1. the health of the mother improved;
2. the nutrition of infants and young children improved;
3. fertility was reduced;
4. the public health, but especially the sanitary environment, improved;
5. the material circumstances of parents improved, especially in terms of real incomes and housing quality;
6. knowledge about best child care practices, including personal hygiene, improved and was communicated to parents;
7. the disease environment normally experienced by children changed for the better;
8. obstetric and paediatric medical care improved.

Each of these eight would have had a beneficial influence on the rate of childhood mortality. However, it is clear from what we have already seen that some could have been of only minor importance before the 1930s and 1940s, and that others were insufficient in themselves to sustain substantial decline, although they could have assisted its initiation, while the effects of some would have acted synergistically with others once the decline had gathered momentum. There was no one fixed route for mortality decline; no simple list of necessary and sufficient causes. However, it is clear that very low levels of childhood mortality ($_5q_0$ less than 0.03) could not be reached and sustained without positive contributions from all eight influences.[79]

---

[77] Das Gupta (1990), quoted from p. 490. This must also have been an important factor in historical populations, but it is not possible to establish the extent of death clustering in the nineteenth century.

[78] Williams and Galley (1995), pp. 417–18, provide a more recent approach to the problems of representing the factors that influenced infant mortality.

[79] This is the level proposed by Mosley and Chen (1984), p. 27, for an 'optimal setting'; it implies a life expectancy at birth of at least 70 years. The series of annual reports prepared by UNICEF entitled *The State of the World's Children* (Oxford: Oxford University Press) provide the most up-to-date review of policies directed to improve childhood

The problem remains: What was the sequence of influence and which factors were of most importance at what times? Of the items in the above list the role of fertility control may prove to have been of particular importance to the initiation of mortality decline in childhood. We shall consider this problem first before incorporating poverty alleviation and education.

Fertility and infant mortality

Both Newsholme and Newman considered the contribution of fertility decline to the reduction of infant mortality, but the former initially rejected its significance on the entirely proper grounds that he could find no statistical evidence which would strongly support it, whilst the latter was at one time convinced that the causal link involved was in the opposite direction. One may further speculate that their reasons for eliminating perhaps the most simple answer to their problem was as much ideological as scientific.

Newman believed that the relationship between the birth rate and infant mortality was of importance for three reasons. If a country's birth rate were to fall while infant mortality remained high, then the continued existence of such a nation would be placed in jeopardy. Illegitimacy and infant mortality were obviously related. Lastly, 'the same practices which lower the birth rate tend to raise the infant death rate'.[80] Newman drew his evidence for this last point from a report of the Royal Commission on the Decline of the Birth Rate in New South Wales (1904), for 'the reader . . . will not be slow to understand what the New South Wales Commission calls "preventing conception by artificial means" and the marked increase of "induced miscarriage" may be operations having pernicious effects upon the life of infancy', and presumably he wished to illustrate an analogy between Britain and New South Wales.[81]

In the third edition of Newsholme's important text *The Elements of Vital Statistics* (1899) he expressed his argument in the following way:

The association ['the infantile death rate should be increased by a higher birth rate'] is by no means regular, nor do we consider it inevitable. There is nothing

---

mortality. For example, the 1994 report stresses the importance of synergisms: the interaction between health and nutrition, the education especially of girls and family planning in countering poverty, population growth and environmental stress (PPE) in developing countries. Basu (1992) provides an interesting exploration of the interaction between these variables and especially the key role of female status. Some of these issues are taken up in chapter 10.   [80] Newman (1906), p. 216.

[81] Newman (1906), p. 216. Since establishment reaction to the declining British birth rate was highly censorious, there was bound to be resistance to any suggestion that it could have positive benefits for childhood mortality (see chapter 4).

surprising in the frequent association of a high birth rate and a high rate of infantile mortality. The highest birth rates usually occur in crowded industrial towns, in which the evil effects of industrial occupation of married women are commonly associated with those of intemperance, ignorance, and neglect with all that these factors imply.[82]

The point is also made in Newsholme's first report to the Local Government Board: 'There is no essential causal relation between a high birth rate and a high rate of infant mortality'.[83] In the 1923 edition of *Elements of Vital Statistics* extracts from the 1910 report are also quoted.

The connection commonly observed between a high birth rate and a high rate of infant mortality probably is due in great part to the fact that large families are common among the poorest classes, and these classes are specially exposed to the degrading influences producing excessive infant mortality.[84]

But Newsholme went further:

it may be argued that in the last 14 years [since 1909] a much higher proportion of the total births than in the previous 23 years occur under the assumed more favourable circumstances of smaller families, rendering the effect visible in the reduced infant mortality in England; but this leaves it still open to doubt whether nationally the reduced birth rate has influenced greatly or only to a minor degree the course of the infant death rate. Further facts must be adduced on this problem.[85]

Between 1876 and 1899 the national infant mortality rate either failed to decline or actually increased while fertility declined. How could these 'facts' be reconciled if, indeed, there was a positive causal link? Figure 7.16 suggests one line of enquiry. If the diarrhoeal component of infant mortality is ignored, because it was critically influenced by short-run meteorological variations, then the underlying long-run trend of infant mortality began to move downward from 1891, if not earlier, in a manner that is similar to the decline of q_2 (also shown in figure 7.16) and early childhood mortality in general (figure 7.2). It is therefore possible that a positive link might be established, but until demonstrated con-clusively it is best expressed in hypothetical form: the decline of fertil-ity – both within and outside marriage – could have exerted a powerful influence on the subsequent decline of infant and even early childhood mortality by relieving the mother of caring for large numbers of off-spring, but also because longer birth intervals would tend to improve the chances of an older child receiving adequate care while the mother

[82] Newsholme (1889), quoted from the third edition (1899), pp. 133–34.
[83] Newsholme's *First Report* (1910), p. 75.
[84] Newsholme (1923), p. 117, and *First Report* (1910), p. 49.
[85] Newsholme (1923), p. 116.

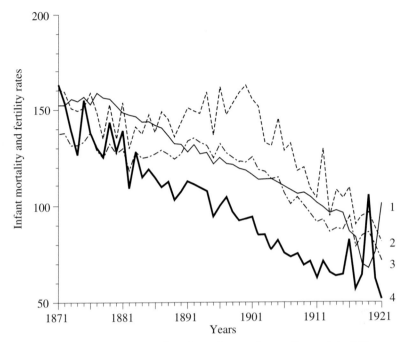

Figure 7.16. Time-series for selected annual mortality and fertility
rates, England and Wales

Note: 1. general fertility rate (live births per 1,000 women aged 15–44), 2. infant
mortality rate, 3. non-diarrhoeal infant mortality rate, 4. $q_2 \times 5{,}000$. All rates,
apart from 4, are $\times 1{,}000$.

*Source: OPCS Birth Statistics, Historical Series, 1837–1938, England and Wales,
Series FM1, No. 13* (London: HMSO, 1987), table 1.4, pp. 26–28; 2 and 3, figure
7.12; 4, figure 7.2.

was nursing a newly born baby. These are known as the high parity and
short birth interval effects.[86]

Attempts to study the relationship between fertility and infant
mortality have a long and complicated history. It is usually supposed
that the decline of childhood mortality in particular acts as a spur to the
control of marital fertility; indeed, the mechanism is a critical part of
classical demographic transition theory in which mortality decline precedes and is a prior condition for that of fertility.[87] However, efforts to
provide conclusive empirical evidence for this dynamic, as distinct from

[86] It is interesting to note that the 1923 edition of *The Elements of Vital Statistics* contains
diagrams showing both the marital fertility and infant mortality rates (figure 12, p. 115)
and one of the infant mortality and non-diarrhoeal infant mortality rates (figure 67, p.
425), but makes no connection between the two. For his final views on the relationship
between fertility and infant mortality, see Newsholme (1935).   [87] See Szreter (1993).

cross-sectional relationship, have rarely proved successful. Francine van de Walle's conclusion to a survey of European data reads like a cry of despair: 'At the end of this quest we cannot report that the historical evidence confirms that the declines of infant mortality led to the decline of fertility.'[88] Here, too, there is obvious reluctance to reverse the direction of the causal link, yet when infant mortality is taken as the dependent variable the chronology of demographic change in late nineteenth- and early twentieth-century Europe appears more straightforward, although by no means simple. There are three principal difficulties. First, the link between fertility and infant mortality is confused by the effect of breastfeeding on both variables. Secondly, the replacement effect may operate when fertility is controlled, thereby allowing it to adjust to infant and child mortality, but while marital fertility is being reduced the effects of both short birth intervals and high parity births on infant mortality will be reduced. In these circumstances the nature of dependence is blurred. Thirdly, the form of the historical data available not only places severe constraints on the analysis of these relationships, but also raises new problems when findings derived from ecological and family-based studies conflict.

The widespread use of breastfeeding usually helps to reduce infant mortality, but it may also, especially if prolonged, reduce the level of fertility by extending the post-partum non-susceptible period, thereby increasing the length of birth intervals. High rates of child survival should encourage family limitation. Knodel's ecological analysis using data for southern Germany provides some evidence for the negative link between breastfeeding and infant mortality and the positive link from infant mortality on to fertility. Further analysis of individual level data for German villages gives additional support to the negative link between breastfeeding and infant mortality, a link which is all too obvious in the English material.[89]

The principal difficulty in conceptualising these relationships relates to the nature of infant care and feeding in general, but especially the form of breastfeeding pattern widely practised. In those populations in which breastfeeding is unusual, it is most likely that both fertility and infant mortality will be high. Where breastfeeding was universal but of short duration – to dentition at about seven or eight months, but no longer – fertility may have remained relatively unaffected, although infant mortality would have been lower than in the first example.

[88] Francine van de Walle (1986).
[89] These relationships are sketched in Knodel and van de Walle (1967). See also Knodel (1968, 1978, 1979, 1982, 1988), Knodel and Wilson (1981), and especially Knodel and Hermalin (1984).

Where breastfeeding was prolonged beyond 12 or even 18 months then dampening effects on both fertility and infant mortality would be expected.[90]

The argument advanced here is that the practice of breastfeeding reduced infant mortality and that it had some reducing effect on fertility, that early childhood mortality and marital fertility operated in a mutually reinforcing and, from the mid-nineteenth century, downward progression while the decline of fertility also exerted a positive effect on infant mortality. The downward spiral of fertility and childhood mortality once begun was sustained by other helpful positive factors. During the early twentieth century when both fertility and infant mortality were in decline, the fall in infant mortality also contributed to the fall in fertility, and the influence of breastfeeding on fertility was disturbed by the deliberate control of marital fertility. It would also be reasonable to hypothesise that the decline of early childhood mortality throughout the second half of the nineteenth century encouraged family limitation in the last decades of the century. However, the ability to provide direct empirical support for these arguments is still limited by the restricted access to birth and death data for individuals, beyond that available in parish registers or a handful of birth and death certificates from the civil registration system.[91]

[90] There is a rapidly growing literature on these relationships based largely on data drawn from the world fertility and demographic and health surveys. Hobcraft *et al.* (1983, 1985), Cleland and Sathar (1984), Palloni and Tienda (1986), Lantz *et al.* (1992) and, on the theoretical relationships, Trussell and Pebley (1984).

[91] Wilson's (1984, 1986) work on natural fertility and sterility tends to support the notion that breastfeeding patterns were generally fairly stable in the long run in England. Although there may have been certain groups who regularly used wet nurses, there was a tradition of breastfeeding infants where possible. Fildes (1986) has provided a rather different account using contemporary material which largely reflects the habits of the social élite or the recommendations contained in manuals. The March 1946 birth cohort study contains information on breastfeeding in different social classes which suggests that there were by then at least relatively few differences between classes; nearly 80 per cent of babies were breastfed at the end of their first month and about 25 per cent at the end of their eighth month. See figure 1 and pp. 51–52 of Douglas (1951), and especially Douglas (1950). These figures for 1946 are generally in line with what little may be discovered of patterns at the turn of the century, although the data for Salford shown in table 7.8 suggest higher levels of breastfeeding at six months (80 per cent compared with 40 per cent). Douglas has also used the 1946 data to argue that when a woman does not succeed in breastfeeding her baby, the birthweight of her next baby is likely to be low, and that as the duration of breastfeeding increases so too does the birthweight of the succeeding child: see Douglas (1954). These points are of obvious importance because they draw attention to the difficult problem of birth weight and, by implication, prematurity. See Millman and Cooksey (1987). Kintner (1985) has also raised the possibility that the proportion of infants breastfed could increase while the average duration of breastfeeding declined. The micro-level associations which cannot be explored using English data have been considered for Sweden; see Lithell (1981, 1985).

Two earlier attempts to link these variables proved largely inconclusive, partly for the same reason. Brass and Kabir, who based their study of the association between child mortality (under age 5) and fertility in nine English regions plus Wales, argued that economic and social development was the driving force that influenced the virtually simultaneous movement of both variables. 'Perhaps the weightiest argument is the difficulty in formulating a quantitative description of how the relatively small changes in fertility in an interval could have such strong impacts on child deaths.'[92] Winter, using registration county data, failed to find significant correlations between changes in marital fertility and the infant mortality rate in three periods: 1901–11, 1911–21 and 1921–31.[93]

Although the results of the empirical analysis reported earlier do represent some advance, they are far from conclusive. On balance they suggest that the decline in fertility beginning in the 1870s, but according to m and Ig (table 4.2 and figure 4.6) only confirmed as significant in the 1890s, would have had a positive influence on the succeeding downward trend of infant mortality once the effects of epidemic diarrhoea are removed, and that childhood mortality (1–4 years) may have influenced fertility and been affected in like fashion. There remains the possibility that, as Brass and Kabir suggest, some other variable or variables directly influenced both fertility and infant mortality in sequence. The demographic significance of mutual decline in fertility and childhood mortality remains inescapable.[94]

Poverty, female education, fertility and childhood mortality

Earlier chapters on variations in nuptiality and the decline of fertility have suggested that both real wages and the level of female education

[92] Brass and Kabir (1980), quoted from p. 86.
[93] Winter (1982), especially p. 723. Judging by figure 7.2 it seems most unlikely that the First World War was anything other than irrelevant for long-term trends in infant mortality, especially when the low level of fertility and the excess mortality among children (e.g. q_2) associated with the 1918–19 influenza pandemic are taken into account.
[94] Both Hope (1917) and especially Burns (1942) provide some support for the argument on the link between fertility and child mortality. More recently Reves (1985) has presented the hypothesis that 'the decline of fertility rate in England and Wales in the late 1800s was a major cause of the decline of infant mortality that began in 1900. The decline in fertility altered the family size and age distribution, leading to an increase in the median age at infection for most infectious diseases, thereby lowering the case fatality rate' (p. 114). While I would largely support the point expressed in the first sentence (apart from the emphasis on 1900), the mechanism suggested in the second sentence remains unconvincing in the absence of direct evidence on parities, birth intervals, morbidity and mortality. Reves's use of data relating to mortality from measles (a disease which was in any case far more important for 1–4-year-olds) bears interesting comparison with work on Sunderland reported by Aaby *et al.* (1986).

Table 7.9. *Definitions of variables used in infant mortality path analysis model (figure 7.17)*

Variable	Definition
Infant mortality (IMR) (X_0)	Non-diarrhoeal infant mortality rate for the decade 1901–10
Fertility (FERT) (X_1)	*If* 1891
Female education (ED) (X_2) (measured in a negative fashion)	Percentage of brides signing the marriage register with a mark in 1881
Poverty (POV) (X_3)	Percentage of females aged 20 and over employed as domestic servants in 1861
Population density (PD) (X_4)	Log persons per square kilometre in 1861

improved, the latter dramatically, during the second half of the nineteenth century.[95] Their importance has also been confirmed by demographic studies in Third World countries.[96] However, efforts to relate changes in infant mortality to occupation-specific income levels have merely tended to demonstrate that infant mortality rates after 1895 were capable of declining independently of income level. But it is possible that the long-term rise in real wages did have an influence on the slow decline of infant mortality from causes other than diarrhoea.

Once again, it has proved impossible to explore any of these relationships directly and in ways that would prove conclusive. Only registration district data enable the associations between infant mortality, fertility, female education and poverty to be explored in any detail. These variables are defined in table 7.9.[97] Four path models are shown in figure 7.17.[98] By convention, circles represent the dependent variables (X_0); rectangles, the independent variables (X_1, . . .,X_4); the paths between variables show direction and sign of association with the *beta*-coefficient providing the weight; the arrows to X_1, . . .,X_4 originating outside the model show the unexplained variance, $\sqrt{(1-R^2)}$. The first two models relate to the variables described above and defined in table 7.9

[95] See figures 4.13 and 4.14 (colour section, page *d*).
[96] See especially the international analysis by Hobcraft *et al.* (1984) on the key role of women's education. Caldwell (1979, 1982), pp. 301–30, has presented the case for the importance of educational advances in the decline both of fertility and of mortality.
[97] Clearly, there are bound to be measurement problems associated with such variables as female education and poverty. The former, expressed by an illiteracy measure for 1881, is reasonably well served by a negative index (i.e. absence of education), but the latter is far more difficult to measure in a consistent way, and the use of domestic servants for this purpose leaves a lot to be desired.
[98] Path analysis provides an extension of multiple regression analysis. For an introduction and examples, see Duncan (1966) and Lesthaeghe (1977), pp. 203–19.

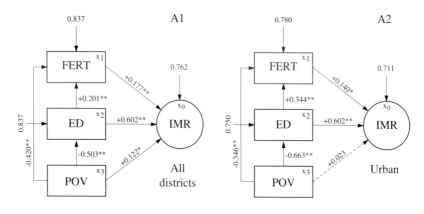

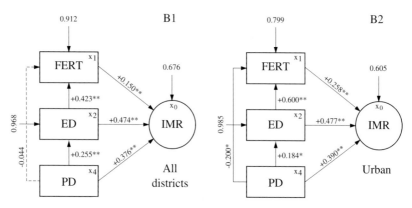

Figure 7.17. Path models of the effects of fertility, female education, poverty and population density on variations in infant mortality (non-diarrhoeal infant mortality rate, 1901–10), among the districts of England and Wales

Note: *denotes significant at $P \leq 0.005$, ** $P \leq 0.00005$, and dashed lines indicate non-significant associations. Variables are defined in table 7.9. See text for explanation.

using data for all the districts in England and Wales with London counted as a single unit (A1, B1), and the urban districts (A2, B2). In model A1, $R^2 = 0.4197$ and in model A2 $R^2 = 0.4950$ when, for illustrative purposes, the infant mortality rate from causes other than diarrhoea between 1901 and 1910 was used as the dependent variable. Although the direct contribution of the poverty variable to infant mortality was either only weakly significant in the case of model A1, or non-significant in the case of A2, it did influence both variations in female education and fertility and thus, indirectly, infant mortality. Fertility also made a significant contribution, but the strength of the association was exceeded by that of female education which proved consistently to be the most important independent variable, especially when its indirect influence by way of fertility was also considered. Models B1 and B2 have population density, used as an index of urbanisation, substituted for the poverty variable which is especially difficult to measure, and which, in its present form, did not prove to be particularly successful. The resulting R^2s were increased to 0.5429 for all districts (B1) and 0.6345 for the 270 urban districts (B2).[99]

The four models shown in figure 7.17 suggest several interesting points which bear on the analysis of both cross-sectional variations in infant mortality and the causes of its rapid decline, but they also leave many questions unanswered. First, there is good supporting evidence for the argument that advances in the education of women (the decline in illiteracy among women) would have had both direct and indirect influences on the decline of infant mortality; that the decline of fertility would also have served to depress infant mortality; and that the effects of urban–rural differences remained important influences even when the epidemic diarrhoea component had been removed. Secondly, the direct influence of poverty is ambiguous in the models, but its indirect effects via fertility and female education are clear. If the incidence of poverty had declined during the late nineteenth century, there would have been a positive effect on infant mortality, but infant mortality seems to have declined irrespective of changes in living standards. Thirdly, the special importance of a minority of urban districts in dictating national trends has been re-emphasised once again. Models A1, A2 and B2 show that it is possible to account for rather more of the variations in infant mortality rates among urban districts than in the total national set but that, in general, similar forms of association hold.[100]

The four models are also limited because they are all cross-sectional in nature, relying on principles of ecological association to highlight the

[99] There are 590 units in the all districts models and 270 in the urban districts ones. The latter are defined as those districts with a population density greater than 100 persons per square kilometre in 1891. See table 4.7 for the results of a parallel model using *Ig* as the dependent variable.

[100] The distribution of standardised residuals from model B2 suggests that predicted infant mortality is too high especially in the south of England, in and around London, but also in several large towns in the Midlands and north. Predictions are consistently too low in the coalfield districts throughout England and Wales. Possible reasons for this distinctive distribution of positive residuals include those suggested by Buchanan (1985). Removal of these residuals would require the incorporation of particular locality-specific variables.

most plausible relationships and thereby relegating the improbable to the sidelines. Their further development and application is limited in practical terms by the absence of independent variables that trace change over time, and more generally by the problems set by conceptualisation → operationalisation → interpretation. Their strength lies in their ability to sift away the unlikely, not in their capacity to provide even a limited form of causal explanation.

Some preliminary conclusions

This chapter has had two objectives: to present a detailed demographic analysis of the changing pattern of infant and childhood mortality in England and Wales at the end of the nineteenth century and during the first decades of the twentieth century, and to provide, as far as possible, an interpretation of those regularities, but especially the circumstances under which the secular decline was initiated. With respect to the first objective, the dimensions of childhood mortality have been documented in terms of their time-series components, variations among registration districts and between social classes. It is clear that nationally the rates changed at the end of the 1890s and that as a direct consequence the upward trajectory of life expectancy at birth was accelerated rapidly into and through the first decades of the twentieth century. Despite some serious problems in terms of the quality and variability of registration, this chapter has added to what Dyhouse suggested was necessary for a fuller understanding of the causes of change: description based on detailed quantitative research.[101]

The second objective proved more difficult to achieve, but demographic analysis and the work of contemporaries provided five clues. First, the timing of infant mortality decline, with very few although rather interesting exceptions, was remarkably consistent throughout the country between districts and social classes. Secondly, in urban places where childhood mortality was particularly high and where childhood mortality contributed the majority of deaths, the decline of infant mortality from the turn of the century appeared even more precipitous. Thirdly, although neonatal mortality rates remained relatively unchanged, suggesting among other things that the effectiveness of obstetric practice did not improve radically between the mid-nineteenth century and the 1930s, post-neonatal mortality fluctuated from year to year and was largely responsible for at least the first stage of the secular decline of total infant mortality rates. Fourthly, the increase in infant

---

[101] Dyhouse (1978), p. 250.

mortality during the 1890s was largely due to the contribution of hot, dry summers creating favourable conditions for epidemic diarrhoea especially in urban areas in which the effectiveness of sanitary provision was still in doubt. Once the contribution of diarrhoeal diseases was removed, infant mortality appears to have declined continuously from 1891 or the late 1880s. Fifthly, the widespread practice of breastfeeding probably gave England a lower level of infant mortality than several other western European countries. In Sweden, for example, the increased adoption of breastfeeding is known to have contributed to infant mortality decline, and the same pattern must also have been followed in parts of southern Germany.[102] The establishment of milk depots and the pasteurisation of milk would have helped to reduce the high mortality among those infants who were not breastfed, but neither could have made a dramatic impact on such a large scale in the early 1900s.

How then should the origins of the secular decline in infant mortality and, more broadly, childhood mortality be interpreted? Returning to Sir Arthur Newsholme's scheme of the various factors affecting infant mortality, it is unlikely that there were advances under every heading during the decades preceding the 1930s, but what were the principal factors responsible for initiating that decline from the 1880s or 1890s, and for early childhood mortality from the 1850s or 1860s? The account proposed here is based on the following points.

1. The decline of fertility, both marital and illegitimate, from the 1870s and certainly from the 1890s served to reduce the level of infant mortality both by affecting the number of pregnancies a woman might experience and by increasing the intervals between successive births. Efforts to control marital fertility either in a parity-specific way using unreliable methods of contraception or by sexual temperance would tend to reduce the number of pregnancies and lengthen birth intervals. The direct control of fertility should have had an important influence on the downward trend of infant and perhaps even early childhood mortality through both the parity and spacing effects.

2. Long-term improvements in levels of female education helped not only to increase the likelihood that family limitation would be attempted, but also to improve the status of women, their access to written information, the way in which they cared for their children and the way in which they were themselves cared for. They may even have encouraged more women to breastfeed.

[102] Kintner (1987).

3. The 'health of towns' movement did make significant advances possible, most of which bore fruit during the late nineteenth century or early twentieth century when the availability of uncontaminated water was transformed by schemes for water carriage and purification. But as the evidence for 1911 reminds us, epidemic diarrhoea could still prove a potent short-term influence on infant mortality rates when the climatic circumstances were unpropitious.

4. The improvement in milk supply and food quality, the availability of more highly qualified midwives, the institution of ante-natal care and the extension of the post-natal health visitor service were all of special significance, particularly the last mentioned, but usually they served to reinforce an existing trend by focusing medical and health service attention on those mothers and children most at risk in areas with the highest childhood mortality rates.[103]

Although each of these four points is entirely consistent with the findings presented in this chapter, it must be emphasised again that the analysis has been restricted by the availability and quality of data. It has proved reasonably straightforward to consider the cross-sectional variation in infant mortality patterns, but far more difficult to look at change and the factors that influenced change. It was not possible to examine relationships at the micro-level within individual families and it has therefore been necessary to present plausible hypotheses supported by the results of ecological analyses. Apart from this major drawback, there are four additional problems which have a bearing on the generality of the conclusions it is possible to draw. How did the decline in childhood mortality in England and Wales compare with that in other western European countries? Any distinctive English and Welsh trends probably resulted from high levels of both urbanisation and breastfeeding. The coincidental timing of the European fertility transition should have generated strong similarities in the timing of infant mortality decline, save that independent changes in the practice of breastfeeding, as well as the proportion of the population living in poor sanitary environments, would have blurred the lagged association between fertility decline and infant mortality. With these provisos in mind it may prove useful to speculate on the general effects of family limitation on the course of European demographic change which may provide a counter to the long-established wisdom associated with transition theory, in

---

[103] This approach differs from the one adopted by Teitelbaum (1984). At least initially, fertility decline influenced the decline of infant mortality; infant nutrition may have improved, it certainly did not deteriorate; and the urban sanitary environment did deteriorate temporarily during the 1890s. See also Smith (1979), p. 122, on sanitation, milk supply, health visitors and the importance of family limitation.

which infant mortality decline in particular acts as a spur to fertility control.[104]

The second problem relates to the association between infant and early childhood mortality. Figure 7.16 shows that q_2 and the general fertility rate declined at roughly the same time and at the same rate, but that infant mortality from causes other than diarrhoea only began its secular decline 10 to 15 years later. Were the factors influencing infant and childhood mortality similar; if so, why was there a lag between the decline of the national time-series? If the factors were not common, what were they, and how were their differential effects manifested? While both infant and early childhood mortality would be affected by positive advances in female education, lower family size and longer birth intervals, with general improvements in nutrition and the sanitary environment, infants and young children were not subjected to the same disease patterns. It is, therefore, conceivable that a disease like scarlet fever which, according to McKeown and Record, contributed 20 per cent to the general decline of mortality during the second half of the nineteenth century and which appears to have become markedly less virulent irrespective of human intervention or any environmental change, would have acted to reduce childhood mortality independently of the factors listed above.[105] It is not that the factors influencing infant mortality were irrelevant, rather that autonomous changes in the childhood disease pattern served to bring forward the origin of secular mortality decline for that particular group.[106]

Thirdly, the arguments relating to the positive association between parity and infant mortality may appear reminiscent of the debate between McKeown and Schofield on the influence of rising fertility on infant mortality in England during the late eighteenth and early

---

[104] Chapter 4 considers the problems of identifying the causes of family limitation in the nineteenth century. The methods of birth control employed will probably never be known for certain in a way that would enable them to be quantified; yet birth spacing and ineffective stopping behaviour would both have had their impact on infant mortality. See Knodel (1987) on stopping as innovative behaviour, and David and Sanderson (1986) on the Mosher Survey and the importance of sexual abstinence. The most recent empirical findings, mainly for Third World countries, are summarised in Montgomery and Cohen (1998).

[105] McKeown and Record (1962), p. 117. Scott and Duncan (1998) take an alternative perspective by analysing the time-series regularities in annual deaths data (pp. 303–20).

[106] It is also possible that the cohort effect identified by Preston and van de Walle (1978) would have produced a lag between the decline in childhood mortality and the decline in infant mortality as healthier children grew up to become healthier adults and healthier mothers whose babies might not only have been heavier at birth, but also better fed. The point is consistent with the one made by Douglas (1954) regarding the link between the duration of breastfeeding and the weight of successive babies born.

nineteenth centuries.[107] Indeed, it seems that in the decades after 1750 the ratio of infant to total deaths increased as fertility increased and mortality declined. There is, however, a fundamental difference between an increase in overall fertility induced largely by changes in nuptiality and a decline in fertility determined mainly by the control of reproduction within marriage as happened during the late nineteenth century. In the first case, when marital fertility remained relatively unchanged while more women married and bore children, one would not expect to find a parity effect on infant mortality. More infants may have died while infant mortality rates remained stable, or even declined, and adult mortality changed little. It is regrettable that McKeown did not explore the implications of his argument for a positive link between parity and infant mortality in the context of the late nineteenth and early twentieth century when both were in decline.[108]

Fourthly, it has not been possible to dwell at any length on the arguments relating to the nutritional status of pregnant women, intrauterine malnutrition and their effects on low birth weight, and thus infant mortality. While it may be presumed that the doping of infants and young children with opiates became less important after the 1860s, little is known about the excessive consumption of alcohol or salt by pregnant women. Even the physiological effects of overwork remain poorly understood or documented for the Victorian period. The stability of neonatal and maternal mortality rates between the 1860s and the 1930s suggests that neither conditions *in utero* nor obstetric practices improved radically. Variations in post-neonatal mortality indicate that the nutrition of infants at the time of weaning could have had an important bearing on subsequent survival chances, but even here firm evidence on changes in breastfeeding practice remains elusive before 1900. Fogel's emphasis on the nutritional status of pregnant women seems important, yet its effects on infant mortality are untested and may prove untestable. On the basis of the evidence assembled in this chapter, it is doubtful whether improvements in this particular form of nutritional status could have had a profound bearing on the initial stages of the secular decline of infant mortality; yet it would be rash to ignore the possibility that the nutritional status of those in late infancy or early childhood might not have been less harmful.[109]

---

[107] For the origins of the debate, see Schofield (1977, 1984) and McKeown (1978).

[108] Since some of McKeown's early work was concerned with the relationship between fertility and infant mortality, this omission is particularly surprising. See Gibson and McKeown (1950, 1951, 1952), but especially part VII, and also Reves (1985).

[109] See Fogel (1986) and, on infant doping, Berridge and Edwards (1981), especially pp. 97–105. Wrigley's (1998), pp. 459–62, argument linking the decline of the stillbirth rate, increased marital fertility and 'a rise in maternal net nutrition' in the eighteenth

In conclusion, this chapter has presented an argument for giving special attention to infant and child mortality in the general demographic transition; it has, once again, illustrated the significance of the 'urban effect' in England and Wales; it has insisted that the origins and causes of childhood mortality decline are to be found by examining long-term changes during the nineteenth century rather than by seeking evidence for dramatic advances during the early twentieth century; and it has suggested that the arguments used by demographers in their work on contemporary populations in Africa and Asia, especially those relating to fertility and the education of females, are also relevant for Europe in the nineteenth century.

century should also be noted, although the late nineteenth-century experience appears to have been different: little change in the stillbirth rate, decline in marital fertility, improvement in the nutritional status of females perhaps, yet an increase in prematurity (figure 7.11).

8

Places and causes

In Victorian England and Wales, where one lived had an especially important bearing not only on when one died, but also on how one died. We have already seen many examples of this, from Farr's law, considered in chapter 5, to the geographical variations in infant and childhood mortality illustrated in chapter 7. But the distinctive morbidity and mortality environments created by industrialisation, occupational specialisation, urban growth and residential segregation and proximity in conjunction with the effects of climate, relief and aspect are of fundamental importance for our understanding of the ways in which life expectancy began to improve during the Victorian era.[1] Until the decline of infant mortality after 1900, the range of mortality levels experienced in different geographical areas was not only roughly constant, but also greater than the difference between the national levels for England and Wales in the 1840s and the 1890s. To make the same point in a different way: suppose a pregnant woman living in the area with the worst mortality in the 1840s or 1850s was to be given a choice of moving either in time or in space. While her own life chances would undoubtedly also be enhanced, for the sake of her soon to be born child she should certainly opt to move in space – from Lancashire to Devon, perhaps – unless, that is, she was able to travel forward in time to the middle of the twentieth century. In statistical terms this means that among mortality rates for geographically disaggregated areas, the maximum and the minimum (and thus the range) remained largely unchanged during the nineteenth century, but the national mortality rate was affected, first, by the number of areas experiencing given levels of mortality shifting within the range and, secondly, by population growth and migration between areas. In the twentieth century, by contrast, the mortality rates

---

[1] Woods and Shelton (1997) and Mercer (1990) provide useful background material for this chapter in terms of geographical and temporal variations in causes of death.

experienced by the best and worst areas declined and the range narrowed substantially.[2]

Chapter 9 takes up the theme of population redistribution and the effect of urbanisation on the national experience of mortality. In this chapter we shall focus explicitly on the differences between places in terms of their population's mortality by considering how certain causes of death became associated with particular environmental conditions. The most obvious example is provided by the water- and food-borne diseases – cholera, diarrhoea, dysentery, typhoid, enteric fever, etc. – which were the principal targets of the Victorian sanitary movement and its drive for effective sewerage, pure water and food inspection. But there are other, perhaps more interesting, examples of the ways in which local circumstances conditioned local disease and mortality environments. The infectious diseases of childhood – measles and scarlet fever, for example – were especially sensitive to the effects of crowding where infection could spread easily among a large and regularly replenished population of susceptibles. Similarly, the respiratory diseases – bronchitis and pneumonia in particular – were important killers among the young and the old, but their influence went largely untouched by the Victorian public health movement, a testament to industrial success and the domestic consumption of coal. Finally, pulmonary tuberculosis, that most destructive of nineteenth-century diseases, provides an interesting counter-example of ambiguous environmental associations in terms of both its concentration in certain localities and the way in which tuberculosis mortality declined.

Before we can consider these four sets of examples in any detail it will be necessary to introduce the various nosologies with which we shall be obliged to deal.[3] The final section of the chapter reconsiders the implications for the McKeown interpretation which relies so heavily for support on reported cause of death.[4]

---

[2] Something of this effect may be seen in figure 5.12 and table 5.3 which were used to illustrate Farr's law. The lengths of the regression lines, which show the range, remained unchanged while the slopes become less steep and life expectancy at birth slowly improved.

[3] Cliff *et al.* (1998) have used six marker diseases (measles, scarlet fever, whooping cough, diphtheria, enteric fever and tuberculosis) in their analysis of weekly deaths for 100 cities. Unfortunately, they are not able to measure age-specific cause of death rates, a matter which is of special importance for the childhood diseases, although they are able to illustrate the remarkable complexity of the international disease environment at this time and the value of selecting certain examples as markers.

[4] McKeown (1976). The McKeown interpretation was introduced in chapter 1. It was also considered briefly in chapter 7 in relation to childhood mortality (pp. 248–50).

Causes of death

Chapter 2 has already described the development of civil registration in England and Wales and the part death certification played. We have also seen how successive Registrars General and, more importantly, their Statistical Superintendents developed and refined the reporting of deaths for occupational groups (table 6.2). The six *Decennial Supplements* for 1851–60 to 1901–10 report cause of death by age for the registration districts. These data were used to construct *An Atlas of Victorian Mortality* to which the reader is referred for an account of the broader picture of the geography of causes of death together with the various qualities of the material. Here it will be sufficient to outline the nosologies adopted by Farr and his successors, to justify the selection of particular illustrative causes and to describe their distinctive age profiles. However, it may prove useful to reflect for a moment on the origin of these cause of death data. Figure 8.1 shows a copy of a partially completed specimen Medical Certificate of Cause of Death.[5] These proformas were first circulated to Registrars and thence to members of the medical profession in 1845. The accompanying instructions required doctors certifying death to give primary and secondary causes, but in the early years of civil registration many deaths were not medically certified and Registrars were obliged to obtain information as best they could or to make a 'Cause of Death: Unknown, Not Certified' return to the General Register Office. In cases where the cause of death certificate was completed, only the first cause – scarlet fever in figure 8.1 – was further classified and reported in published returns.[6]

Table 8.1 lists the six nosologies used in conjunction with registration districts. Although there was a substantial amount of consistency from decade to decade, the nosology for 1901–10 was based on a new and fundamentally different classification of diseases and, whilst most of the childhood diseases were comparable, those related to tuberculosis and the respiratory system were not. The nosology for 1851–60 combined Cholera with Diarrhoea & Dysentery thus limiting comparison with

---

[5] This particular specimen is taken from p. 138 of Angus (1854). Angus was a member of the staff of the General Register Office.

[6] The Registrar General's *Seventh Annual Report for 1843 and 1844* (BPP 1846/XIX), pp. 249–328, contains Farr's second *Statistical Nosology* with accompanying instructions to Registrars and members of the medical profession from the Registrar General. The development of cause of death registration was not only technically complicated, but also politically sensitive. For example, Farr fell into a dispute with Edwin Chadwick over the use of 'starvation' as a cause of death. See Glass (1973), pp. 146–67, and Hamlin (1995).

CERTIFICATE OF CAUSE OF DEATH.

I hereby certify that I attended _____ *aged*

_____ *last Birthday; that I last saw h___ on* _____

that___ he died on _____ *at* _____

and that the cause of h___ death was

	Cause of Death.	Duration of Diseases.
(a) First	Scarlatina...............	8 days
(b) Second	Meningitis	48 hours

Signed _____ John Brown,

Prof¹. Title _____ M.R.C.S.,

Address ____ 52, Guilford Street,

Russell Square.

Figure 8.1. Copy of a medical cause of death certificate used in the 1850s

other decades.[7] Finally, the broad groups of causes of death labelled 'Diseases of:' were changed for the 1870s *Supplement*, but in the particular case of Diseases of the Lung and Diseases of the Respiratory system there appears to be such a close fit that comparison is not seriously affected. We shall concentrate, therefore, on the decades 1861–70 to 1891–1900 in terms of district comparisons and on the following reported causes of death: Measles, Scarlet fever, Diarrhoea & Dysentery, Phthisis (pulmonary tuberculosis) and Diseases of the Lung or Respiratory system (mainly bronchitis and pneumonia).[8]

The selected causes of death had rather different age profiles and in the case of two there was substantial mortality decline between the 1860s and the 1890s which had an important bearing on the general

[7] Specific causes of death for which statistics were reported in the *Decennial Supplements* will be referred to as, for example, Cholera, Diarrhoea & Dysentery, etc. to distinguish them from the more general references to diseases given as cholera, diarrhoea, dysentery, and so forth.

[8] These are, of course, problematic data for a variety of reasons. The reporting of cause of death is a notoriously variable matter, as figure 8.1 suggests, which may be as much the victim of fashion as advances in epidemiology. It is certainly possible to establish that, as far as the nosologies in table 8.1 are concerned, the very young and the very old were most likely to have their deaths classified as due to Other causes. In the case of infants it is clear from a comparison with table 7.1 that some of the major causes of death specific to early life, such as prematurity, were merely excluded from simplified general classifications intended to cover all ages. Many of these problems may be suspected, but cannot be corrected for. See Woods and Shelton (1997), especially pp. 21–46, and Hardy (1994).

Table 8.1. *Nosologies used in Registrars General Decennial Supplements to report cause of death for registration districts, England and Wales, 1851–60 to 1901–10*

1851–60	1861–70	1871–80	1881–90	1891–1900	1901–10
Smallpox	Smallpox	Smallpox	Smallpox	Smallpox	Smallpox
Measles	**Measles**	**Measles**	**Measles**	**Measles**	**Measles**
Scarlet fever	**Scarlet fever**	**Scarlet fever**	**Scarlet fever**	**Scarlet fever**	**Scarlet fever**
Diphtheria	Diphtheria	Diphtheria	Diphtheria	Diphtheria	Diphtheria
Whooping cough	Whooping cough	Whooping cough	Whooping cough	Whooping cough	Whooping cough
					Influenza
Typhus, Typhoid Cholera, Diarrhoea & Dysentery	Typhus	Typhus	Typhus	Typhus	Typhus
	Cholera **Diarrhoea & Dysentery**	Cholera **Diarrhoea & Dysentery**	Cholera **Diarrhoea & Dysentery**	Cholera **Diarrhoea & Dysentery**	Cholera **Diarrhoea & Dysentery**
		Enteric fever	Enteric fever	Enteric fever	Enteric fever
		Simple continued fever	Simple continued fever	Simple continued fever	Simple continued fever
					Pyrexia
Other zymotic diseases	Other zymotic diseases				
Cancer	Cancer	Cancer	Cancer	Cancer	Cancer
Scrofula & Tabes mesenterica	Scrofula & Tabes mesenterica	Scrofula Tabes mesenterica	Tabes mesenterica	Tabes mesenterica	Tabes mesenterica
Phthisis	**Phthisis**	**Phthisis**	**Phthisis**	**Phthisis**	
			Other tuberculous & Scrofulous diseases	Other tuberculous & Scrofulous diseases	

Hydrocephalus	Hydrocephalus	Hydrocephalus			*
Diseases of:	*Diseases of:*	*Diseases of:*	*Diseases of:*	*Diseases of:*	*Diseases of:*
Brain	Brain	Nervous system	Nervous system	Nervous system	Nervous system
Heart & Dropsy	Heart & Dropsy	Circulatory system	Circulatory system	Circulatory system	Circulatory system
Lung	**Lung**	**Respiratory system**	**Respiratory system**	**Respiratory system**	**Respiratory system**
Stomach & Liver	Stomach & Liver	Digestive system	Digestive system	Digestive system	Digestive system
Kidneys	Kidneys	Urinary system	Urinary system	Urinary system	Urinary system
Generative organs	Generative organs	Generative organs	Generative organs	Generative organs	Generative organs
Joints	Joints				
Skin	Skin				
		Puerperal fever	Puerperal fever	Puerperal fever	Puerperal fever & Childbirth
Childbirth & Metria	Childbirth & Metria	Childbirth	Childbirth	Childbirth	
	Suicide	Suicide			
Violent deaths	Other violent deaths	Other violent deaths	Violence	Violence	Violence
Other causes	Other causes	Other causes	Other causes	Other causes	Other causes

Note:
* The 1901–10 classification also contains the following causes of death: Pulmonary tuberculosis, Phthisis (not otherwise defined), Tuberculous meningitis, Tuberculous peritonitis, Other tuberculous diseases, Septic diseases, Rheumatic fever and Rheumatism of heart, Pneumonia, Bronchitis.
The causes of death explored in this chapter are shown in bold type.

increase in life expectancy at birth that occurred during that period.[9] Figure 8.2 illustrates these patterns for five causes plus total mortality in the 1860s, while figure 8.3 focuses on Scarlet fever, Phthisis, Diarrhoea & Dysentery, causes of death that changed. As we have already seen in figures 7.9 and 7.10, Measles and Scarlet fever were especially prominent causes of death in childhood, although not so important in infancy. For both diseases it would be appropriate to select the age group 1–4 and to measure their impact and distribution via cause-specific $_4q_1$ (ECMR, ages 1–4). Figure 8.3 further reminds us that the mortality rate due to Scarlet fever declined substantially so that by the turn of the century the disease was not only far less influential, but also even more of a disease of childhood than it had previously been. The curves for Diarrhoea & Dysentery and Diseases of the Lung or Respiratory system display the classic 'tick' shape in common with the general mortality distribution, and of course in accordance with Edmonds's theory, to which in combination they make a very important contribution. The latter are far more significant than the former since Diarrhoea & Dysentery has a negligible impact between ages 10 and 55. In both cases the cause-specific rates may be captured using infancy and old age (q_0 and $_{10}q_{65}$), and in neither was there significant decline during the nineteenth century, although there was some reduction among the water- and food-borne diseases at ages above 1 year and where mortality rates were already at a low level. The fifth cause, Phthisis (pulmonary tuberculosis), has perhaps the most distinctive age profile in its concentration on early adulthood as well as its significant reduction. Phthisis mortality will be measured using the age group 20–34 ($_5q_{20}$ and $_{10}q_{25}$).

These five sets of causes of death each reflect a particular aspect of the mortality environment experienced by the population of England and Wales. Measles and Scarlet fever could be taken to reflect the effects of crowding; Diarrhoea & Dysentery, the quality of the sanitary environment; Diseases of the Lung or the Respiratory system might be used to suggest the impact of non-sanitary aspects of the environment, especially air quality and general pollution; and, finally, Phthisis could be considered partly as a corrective to the other four because, although it displayed important local variations, like Scarlet fever its decline was not strongly differentiated in geographical terms.

---

[9] Woods (1993) discusses the relationship between the components of mortality curves including cause of death as estimated by Preston *et al.* (1972).

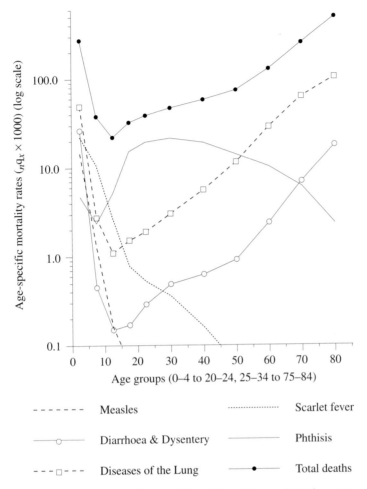

Age-specific mortality rates ($_nq_x \times 1000$) (log scale)

Age groups (0–4 to 20–24, 25–34 to 75–84)

– – – – – – Measles ⋯⋯⋯⋯⋯ Scarlet fever

⎯o⎯ Diarrhoea & Dysentery ⎯⎯⎯ Phthisis

– – –□– – – Diseases of the Lung ⎯●⎯ Total deaths

Figure 8.2. Age-specific mortality patterns from selected causes among females, England and Wales, 1861–70
Source: See table 8.1.

Crowding

Measles is commonly an acute viral infection among children. It is highly communicable and spreads through droplet infection from the nose or throat. The need for a continuous chain of susceptibles, together with the lifelong immunity that an attack of the disease confers, means that in populous areas measles is likely to be endemic with epidemics

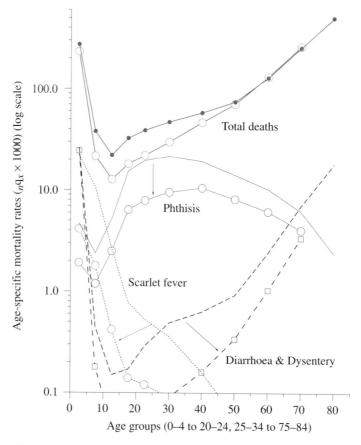

Figure 8.3. Change in age-specific mortality patterns from selected causes among females, England and Wales, 1861–70 to 1891–1900
Source: See table 8.1.

every two to five years, while in sparsely populated areas the virus will need to be introduced and the periodicity of epidemics may consequently be less frequent. The aetiology of the disease was not properly understood until the twentieth century, but Victorian doctors were fully conversant with the symptoms, the course they would take, that isolation was preferable and that 'in its ordinary course measles is a disease unaccompanied with danger', but that there could be serious complications which would take the form of disorders of the respiratory system, especially bronchitis and pneumonia. As for treatment, a warm room and a sparse diet would be sufficient for the mild cases, together with attentive nursing.[10]

Contemporary statistical studies took three forms. Some, like Charles Creighton's *A History of Epidemics in Britain* (1894), attempted to chart the incidence of particular diseases from earliest times, focusing especially on the eighteenth-century Bills of Mortality and concluding with a review of the statistical period since 1837.[11] Others were concerned with the form of the epidemic wave and the periodicity of such diseases as measles. For example, Arthur Ransome's 1882 account begins in the following manner.

> The course of an epidemic disease through a country may aptly be compared to a wave gradually rising and then falling, with more or less regularity, again to rise after a period which varies indeed, but which, in the same disease, is sufficiently regular to entitle it to comparison with 'a wave upon the enridged sea'.[12]

Ransome continues with various illustrative references to the epidemiological experiences of Sweden and Manchester before making the following observation in an attempt to account for the general form of the epidemic wave:

> If we assume that all the susceptible individuals in a district are attacked, and that the disease spreads from one to another in a series of concentric circles, like a spark spreading in tinder; it would not be difficult to calculate the curve that would be assumed by an epidemic wave in any district of which the boundaries were known. This would be a simple mathematical problem; and even if several district centres of infection were established, although this circumstance would complicate the problem, a solution would probably be attainable with a fair degree of accuracy.[13]

Ransome also made extensive reference to the work of William Farr on the form of epidemics and especially his predictions on the course of the 1865–66 outbreak of cattle plague, but he did not himself add significantly to our statistical understanding.[14] Subsequent contributions to the *Transactions of the Epidemiological Society* by A. Campbell Munro and B. Arthur Whitelegge dealt explicitly with measles and its incidence in

---

[10] West (1884), lecture XLV illustrates the classic Victorian account of both measles and scarlet fever for members of the medical profession. For an example of an influential home-care manual, see Bull (1861), especially pp. 342–50.

[11] Creighton (1894), especially pp. 632–65 on measles and pp. 678–736 on scarlet fever.

[12] Ransome (1881–82), quoted from p. 96.

[13] Ransome (1881–82), p. 105. Ransome was, of course, rather over-optimistic about the simplicity of mathematical models of the epidemic wave; see Anderson and May (1992) and Cliff *et al.* (1993).

[14] Farr (1866b). Ransome does not refer to Farr's earlier statistical work on smallpox epidemics which appeared in the *Second Annual Report of the Registrar General*, among other places, and which probably best reflects his work on the form of the epidemic wave. See Farr, *Vital Statistics* (1885), p. 317, 'Laws of epidemics'; also above, p. 190.

Britain. Dr Munro dealt particularly with the case of Jarrow-on-Tyne in the 1880s. For him the chief factor in the spread of measles was 'the greatly increased aggregation of susceptible material in our elementary schools', and 'the most usual source of infection is probably the attendance at school of children in the pre-eruptive but infective stage of the disease'.[15] Whitelegge argued, again using the highly evocative language that seems to have characterised the Victorians' wonderment at and certainly fear of epidemics, that 'In large towns, measles epidemics, especially those of low intensity, often wander about in a somewhat flickering fashion, according to the balance between many conflicting influences.'[16] These influences were thought to be three in number: 'we have in an ordinary town measles always present and ready to spread, susceptible children always accumulating and getting nearer and nearer to the degree of density requisite for epidemic extension', but, thirdly, certain climatic conditions also provided 'maximum facilities for the outbreak'.[17] Like all other observers Whitelegge was struck by the exceptional regularity in the periodicity of measles epidemics, but he also believed he could detect the presence of minor and major epidemics and the special role that pneumonia could be playing in the latter. 'I cannot help thinking that the keynote to the epidemiology of measles is stability of type, amid violent fluctuations in quantity.'[18]

These were still matters for debate when, in the early twentieth century, John Brownlee reconsidered the issues of periodicity and virulence using his new statistical device, the periodogram.[19] Brownlee found that in the case of London, 1840–1912, the periodicity of measles was 97 weeks with a secondary periodicity at 87 weeks, but that on closer investigation the latter was only evident in south London, while north of the Thames the 97-week periodicity dominated. The periodicity in other British cities varied somewhat although it was usually 97 to 101 weeks. In Manchester–Salford it was 90–92 and in Sheffield, 95. From this evidence Brownlee concluded that, apart from the recognised theory of susceptibles, the measles virus must have different strains which affect the organism's life cycle: 'an epidemic ceases because the organism varies in its potency to cause infection. A cycle of epidemics now coinciding and now differing in their maxima can thus be explained.'[20]

[15] Munro (1890–91), quoted from p. 107.
[16] Whitelegge (1892–93), quoted from p. 40.
[17] Whitelegge (1892–93), p. 41. The influence of climate has proved of negligible significance.
[18] Whitelegge (1892–93), p. 53. The case of Sunderland in the 1880s, and especially the major epidemic of 1885, was used to support this conclusion.
[19] Brownlee (1918–19), pp. 77–120.   [20] Brownlee (1918–19), p. 97.

None of these early measles or epidemic wave studies was able to tackle the case fatality rate problem since all relied on registered deaths alone rather than notified cases linked to subsequent recovery or death. This difficulty could only be overcome if cases of such infectious diseases as measles were routinely and accurately notified and if the system for registering causes of death was also accurate. The work attempted by Farr, Edmonds and others on recovery rates using hospital records might give some impression of the effectiveness of hospitalisation, but it provided an insecure basis for the estimation of the general recovery rate and case fatality.[21] Without this evidence the question of measles's variable virulence could not be resolved. One of the first studies to at least partially overcome this problem was undertaken by George N. Wilson using data for Aberdeen, 1883–1902.[22] Of course a run of 20 years is not sufficient to detect anything other than rapid changes in virulence, but it is sufficient to permit the estimation of age-specific attack and case fatality rates. These are summarised in table 8.2 using life table procedures assuming 100,000 births and the removal from susceptibility after a single infection. By their tenth birthday, 42 per cent of children would have been infected of whom 3 per cent would have died of measles. Table 8.2 also suggests that a concentrated population of about 214,000 would be required to generate an average of 100 measles deaths per year, and any population less than 2,140 would be unlikely to average one a year.[23]

Finally, recent epidemiological studies of measles, both historical and those focusing especially on the experience of African populations, have tended to agree on the check list of common factors influencing mortality and case fatality rates. In the case of London, for example, Hardy has argued that:

Popular attitudes towards measles, continuing high levels of overcrowding, poor facilities for nursing care, and the predisposition of poorly nourished small children with existing respiratory disease to severe respiratory complications, probably explain the failure of the measles death-rates to fall in any real degree before 1916.[24]

[21] See chapter 5, pp. 187–90.
[22] Wilson (1905). Between 1883 and 1902 there were 40,374 reported cases of measles in Aberdeen and 1,346 fatalities.
[23] From table 8.2, 100,000 births a year would generate 1,333 measles deaths under age ten; 100 deaths would be generated by 7,500 births and, assuming a crude birth rate of 35 (a rate typical of early Victorian England and Wales), 7,500 births would require a population of 214,286. None of the 614 districts has a population less than 2,500, but the low population districts have low population densities (districts with populations of less than 10,000 all have population densities less than 100 persons per sq. km) usually with dispersed rather than concentrated settlement patterns.
[24] Hardy (1993), p. 48.

Table 8.2. *Effects of measles attack and fatality rates on 100,000 births illustrated by the case of Aberdeen, 1883–1902*

Age in years	Susceptible to measles infection	Number infected	Measles deaths
0	100,000	422	59
1	99,578	7887	794
2	91,691	7225	248
3	84,466	6225	101
4	78,241	5508	49
5	72,733	5797	38
6	66,936	4712	21
7	62,224	2813	14
8	59,411	1224	5
9	58,187	675	4
10	57,512	391	1

Source: Calculated from Wilson (1905), table 1. See text for explanation.

However, Aaby *et al.*'s comparative work on measles in Guinea-Bissau in the 1970s and the records prepared by Dr Harry Drinkwater of the epidemic in Sunderland in 1885 provides a rather different emphasis within the same list.

The present comparison . . . has suggested that a) previous respiratory infection, b) higher rates of intercurrent infection, and c) a greater load of measles virus may lead to more severe disease.[25]

Aaby *et al.* are less convinced about the role of nutrition. On the basis of Third World studies, they argue that only severe malnourishment may play a complicating role and then it will be alongside respiratory infections, for instance. Their explanation for the varying measles case fatality rate owes far more to exposure to multiple infection and the concept of crowding.

Where many susceptible children stay together, there arise increased risks of intensive exposure as a secondary case not to mention the risk of intercurrent infections. It also seems likely that crowding increases the risk of having had a previous respiratory infection. Crowding patterns may thus help to explain both modern and historical variations in severity of measles infection.[26]

---

[25] Aaby *et al.* (1986), pp. 101–7, quoted from p. 7. Aaby *et al.* use Harry Drinkwater, *Remarks upon the Epidemic of Measles Prevalent in Sunderland. With Notes upon 311 Cases from the Middle of January to the End of March 1885* (Edinburgh: James Thin, 1885). The measles case fatality rate for children under the age of three in Sunderland in 1885 was 10 per cent; for Aberdeen, 1883–1902, it was 8.5 per cent.

[26] Aaby *et al.* (1986), p. 107.

Of course Aaby *et al.*'s concept relates especially to living arrangements within the family and the number of susceptible siblings at any one time, but the idea can also be extended to the wider geographical environment. This is attempted in figure 8.4. It shows the relationship between the Measles early childhood mortality rate (ECMR, ages 1–4) in the 1860s and 1890s and population density among the 614 districts. However, for comparative purposes it also incorporates the Diseases of the Lung ECMR for the 1860s. The scatters illustrate quite clearly just how sensitive Measles mortality was to even small changes in population density; how mortality varied little between the 1860s and the 1890s; and, finally, how close was the association between variations in Measles ECMR and Diseases of the Lung ECMR. The most interesting of these relationships are summarised in table 8.3. For example, it is clear that the association between measles and the respiratory-lung diseases grew stronger between the 1860s and the 1890s, and that population density was even more effective as a predictor of lung disease early childhood mortality than measles.[27] Figure 8.4 and table 8.3 help to define certain specific characteristics of the Victorian disease environment which were due specifically to the aggregation of population – characteristics that were largely stable during the nineteenth century and the cumulative effects of which could only have been exacerbated by population growth and urbanisation.

Table 8.3 also reports the case of scarlet fever which, although an acute childhood infection like measles, had a very different history in the nineteenth century.[28] By all accounts the virulence of the disease declined substantially during the second half of the century, although there is also the suspicion that scarlet fever had become more virulent in the early decades of the century. This means that in the 1850s and 1860s scarlet fever was just another childhood disease alongside measles, whooping cough and diphtheria, and that by the 1890s its aetiology had changed sufficiently for its influence on ECMR to have become modest as figures 7.9 and 7.10 showed. Table 8.3 demonstrates that although there was a highly significant statistical association between scarlet fever and measles ECMR in the 1860s it was not as strong as that between measles and the respiratory diseases. Further, while scarlet fever did vary among the districts with population density at mid-century, although again not as closely as measles or the respiratory diseases, by the 1890s the association was negligible. This point is also emphasised in more dramatic fashion by figure 8.5. Scarlet fever

---

[27] Note that although figure 8.3 has population density on a single log scale, table 8.3 makes a double log transformation in order to maximise the coefficient of determination.   [28] Hardy (1993), pp. 56–79, deals with scarlet fever especially in London.

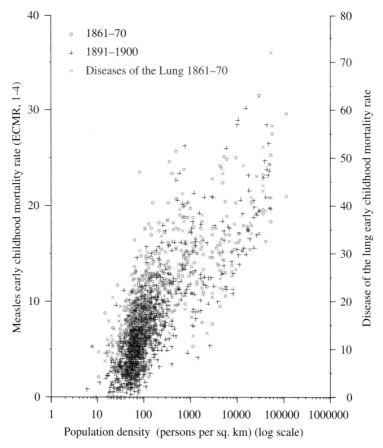

Figure 8.4. Relationship between Measles and Diseases of the Lung
early childhood mortality rate and population density, English and Welsh
districts, 1861–70 and 1891–1900

provides the best example of a disease with a strong and differential
environmental impact, with early childhood mortality four or five times
higher in the densely populated urban places than in the sparsely populated rural areas, where the effects of crowding were critical for easy
contagion, but where the disease itself changed to become essentially
environmentally neutral.[29]

[29] There was a considerable debate among contemporaries about the value of isolation
   hospitals in the case of scarlet fever, but it is now generally accepted that it was the
   disease itself that changed and that, while isolation may have helped, its overall effect
   as a preventive measure was minor in comparison. See Newsholme (1901) and Hardy

Table 8.3. *Associations between selected mortality variables among the 614 districts of England and Wales*

Variable	
Measles ECMR 1861–70	M61
Measles ECMR 1891–1900	M91
Diseases of the Lung ECMR 1861–70	L61
Diseases of the Respiratory system ECMR 1891–1900	L91
Scarlet fever ECMR 1861–70	SF61
Scarlet fever ECMR 1891–1900	SF91
Population density (double log persons per sq. km)	PD

Equation	r^2
$M91 = 0.829M61 + 0.460$	0.617
$L61 = 1.273M61 + 7.579$	0.600
$L91 = 1.248M91 + 10.123$	0.687
$L91 = 0.753L61 + 5.637$	0.606
$M61 = 35.788PD - 2.667$	0.605
$L61 = 61.503PD - 0.777$	0.662
$SF61 = 0.949M61 + 7.576$	0.424
$SF91 = 0.127SF61 + 0.477$	0.141
$SF61 = 43.520PD + 0.370$	0.421
$SF91 = 6.723PD + 0.370$	0.088

In attempting to build up a picture of the influence of environmental factors on Victorian mortality variations and changes, the concept of crowding and the example of measles provide a valuable starting point. They illustrate the direct effects of population aggregation, and indicate what will happen when expansion occurs and medical therapy is largely ineffective. In this case crowding will have demographic consequences over and above the quality of the environment involved. Measles will still be an important killer of children even when, for example, the sanitary environment is of high quality.

Water

One could be forgiven for believing that to Victorians public health meant sanitation: effective sewerage systems, water closets, an uninterrupted supply of pure water piped directly into dwellings and work

(1993), p. 79, 'preventive measures were largely irrelevant to the declining fatality of the disease after 1870'. Eyler (1997), pp. 97–118, takes up this theme in relation to Newsholme's work in Brighton. He points out that Newsholme subsequently recognised that he had over-emphasised the importance of isolation in relation to such diseases as scarlet fever (p. 109).

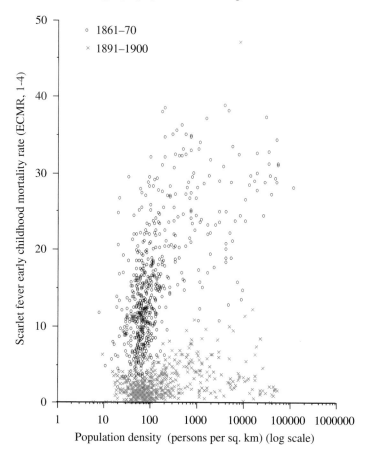

Figure 8.5. Relationship between Scarlet fever early childhood mortality rate and population density, English and Welsh districts, 1861–70 and 1891–1900

places.[30] Although this was not entirely so, sewers–water–excrement provided a clear target for campaigners. It enabled them to focus on the perils that could be clearly seen and smelt in the streets around them, and it benefited all classes but especially the middle class by protecting it from the unclean, the dangerously unhealthy classes. In attempting to assess the contribution of the sanitary revolution and the sanitarists to

[30] This is also the focus adopted in the standard accounts of Wohl (1983), Hassan (1985) and Hamlin (1988, 1998) who argues that 'early Victorians invented one public health among many. Their sanitary movement was not a systematic campaign to eliminate excess mortality. Its concern was with *some* aspects of the health of *some* people: working-class men of working age' (Hamlin, 1998, p. 12).

the improvement in health and the slow rise in life expectancy, considerable attention has been given to the most dramatic water-borne diseases, especially cholera and typhoid, and rather less to diarrhoea and dysentery. Here we shall use mainly Diarrhoea & Dysentery infant mortality to explore the variable quality of the Victorian sanitary environment.[31] Diarrhoea infant mortality has already been examined in figure 7.12 as a means of discounting the effects of the adverse sanitary environment of the late 1890s on the trend of the national infant mortality rate. It is obvious from the case of Birmingham Borough illustrated there – although less clear for London – that diarrhoea deaths could be especially sensitive to annual variations and, where sanitation was inadequate, particularly to higher temperatures in the summer season.[32] Figures 7.9, 7.10 and 8.3 also demonstrate that while Diarrhoea & Dysentery IMRs were similar in the 1860s and the 1890s, the cause-specific mortality rates at older ages declined, although only in childhood (ages 1 to 9) and old age (over 65) could this have had anything other than negligible demographic consequences.

Figure 8.6 shows the relationship between population density and Diarrhoea & Dysentery IMR in the 1860s and the 1890s. In this case, and unlike Measles and Diseases of the Lung, there were districts with high population densities but only moderately high mortality rates. The curve for the 1860s sketches this relationship in which beyond a certain threshold population density (about 100 to 200 persons per sq. km) mortality is likely to increase, but at a far slower rate. The simple point is therefore established: whilst it was usual for the higher population density urban environments to experience high Diarrhoea & Dysentery infant mortality, it was not inevitable. As early as the 1860s and even in the 1890s it was possible in some urban environments for infants to be relatively protected. But which districts and what of mortality at older ages?

Figure 8.7 compares the Diarrhoea & Dysentery IMR with the mortality rate for the 65–74 age group in the 1860s, again relating both to population density. The two age groups are broadly comparable except that for the older one there is a substantial collection of districts having

[31] It will not be assumed that Diarrhoea & Dysentery mortality rates provide an ideal index of the effectiveness of sanitation, merely that of those measures available for districts it is the one that offers the greatest comparative opportunity in terms of age and place.

[32] Hare *et al.* (1981) conclude that 'By about 1920, the previously common excess in death rates, related to summer diarrhoea, had practically disappeared, and summer rates became the lowest of the seasonal rates' (p. 82). Recently van Poppel and van der Heijden (1997) have illustrated just how difficult it is to demonstrate an empirical relationship between the improvement in water quality and the decline of infant mortality.

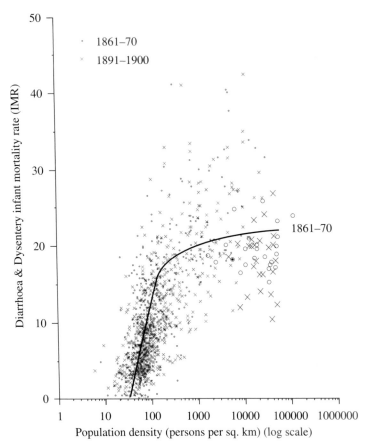

Figure 8.6. Relationship between Diarrhoea & Dysentery infant mortality rate and population density, English and Welsh districts, 1861–70 and 1891–1900
Note: The larger circles/crosses indicate the 25 London districts.

high population densities but experiencing very substantially lower Diarrhoea & Dysentery mortality than would be expected. Figures 8.6 and 8.7 make clear that many of those aberrant districts were in London and that this was especially so in the case of older age mortality, with 20 of the 25 London districts falling well below the curve.[33] These differences between districts are considered in greater detail by figure 8.8. Only the high population density districts are considered and they are

---

[33] The five London districts with higher mortality were: Westminster, Shoreditch, Whitechapel, St George in the East, and Poplar. See also figure 8.8.

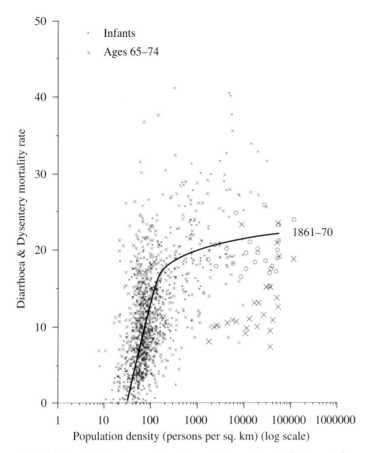

Figure 8.7. Relationship between Diarrhoea & Dysentery infant mortality rate
and mortality rate ages 65–74 and population density, English and Welsh
districts, 1861–70
Note: The larger circles/crosses indicate the 25 London districts.

divided into five categories: London, outer metropolitan districts,
southern towns, northern industrial towns, and the districts of the great
conurbations of the Midlands, the North West, Yorkshire and the North
East. For the Diarrhoea & Dysentery mortality rate at ages 65–74, these
88 districts are numbered 1 to 5, while for the Diarrhoea & Dysentery
infant mortality rate they are simply represented by dots.[34] Figure 8.8
helps to draw the distinction between those urban environments in

[34] The 88 districts contained 39 per cent of the population of England and Wales in 1861
and 45 per cent in 1891.

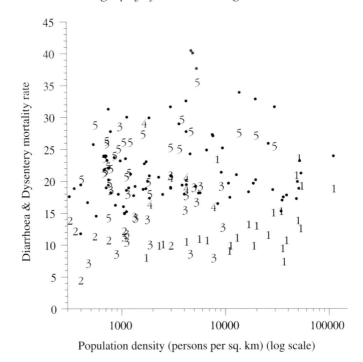

Figure 8.8. Variations in Diarrhoea & Dysentery mortality rates among
high population density districts, England and Wales, 1861–70
Note: The dots represent Diarrhoea & Dysentery IMR; the numbers represent
Diarrhoea & Dysentery mortality rate age group 65–74. 1. London districts,
2. outer metropolitan districts, 3. southern towns, 4. northern industrial
towns, 5. districts in northern conurbations. These 88 districts have been
selected because their population density in either 1861 or 1891 was greater
than 1000 persons per sq. km.

most of London, the rapidly suburbanising metropolitan fringe and the
more stand-alone towns of southern England compared with the rest of
urban England and Wales (1, 2 and 3 versus 4 and 5). In the former it
was possible even in the 1860s for Diarrhoea & Dysentery mortality in
old age to be reduced to a relatively low level, but in the northern urban
districts and some parts of London rates remained high.

The conclusion to be drawn from this brief examination appears to be
that the sanitary environment has several complex components. As far
as Diarrhoea & Dysentery in infancy is concerned, there is some evidence that conditions in certain London districts placed their populations at a distinct advantage compared with those in northern urban
industrial centres and that, even in the 1890s, a handful of those same

London districts were able to sustain lower than might be expected mortality while, in the remainder of the urban system, rates increased.[35] For those in old age the sanitary environment appears to have improved more generally, but because the pace of change varied this also exacerbated differences between urban areas, especially between the north and the south, the inner and outer city. It is not yet possible to explain why these differences should emerge between infancy and old age in terms of such an important cause of death as Diarrhoea & Dysentery. It is possible that water played a relatively minor part in the typical infant diet compared with milk and that the opposite was the case in old age. Since the sanitary revolution was targeted overwhelmingly at water quality and sewerage it is perhaps reasonable to expect its first beneficiaries to be adults and children living in those districts with the earliest and most effective water carriage and purification systems, and where new residential development could take advantage of the most advanced sanitary technology.[36] Clearly, the sanitary environment was being improved during the Victorian era as the direct consequence of human intervention and investment, but the benefits were halting and differential in terms of impact on the mortality experienced by the most vulnerable.

Air

If Measles mortality can be used to represent the effects of crowding and Diarrhoea & Dysentery the effects of sanitation, then mortality due to Diseases of the Lung or Respiratory system may be used to capture something of the variable effects of air quality. Although deaths from bronchitis and pneumonia could occur at any age, in any place and in any season, the most vulnerable were clearly the young and the old who were living and/or working in places with high levels of air pollution. Mortality was also at its worst during the winter months.[37]

Figure 8.9 illustrates the variations in the mortality rate for ages 65–74 due to Diseases of the Lung among the districts. This is set against the mortality from Diarrhoea & Dysentery in the same age group taken from figure 8.7. In the case of the respiratory diseases there is no sign that the London districts were in any sense specially favoured. Indeed,

---

[35] Mooney (1994a) has considered this problem in more detail, while Mooney (1994b) and Luckin and Mooney (1997) also discuss the particular circumstances of London.

[36] See van Poppel and van der Heijden (1997).

[37] Figure 8.2 shows the age profile of Diseases of the Lung for England and Wales in the 1860s. The seasonality of deaths relating to the respiratory system for Birmingham Borough is shown in Woods and Shelton (1997), figure 32.

some of the very highest mortality rates from this group of causes were to be found in the London districts, although the larger northern towns were equally afflicted. Diseases of the Lung were also especially prominent in certain mining districts, particularly those in South Wales and north Staffordshire, where the mortality rate was substantially greater than would be predicted by population density alone. It is also the case that the elderly populations of many of the smaller southern towns experienced far lower mortality from the respiratory diseases than might have been predicted.[38]

It is clear from figures 8.6 to 8.9 that the 25 districts of London occupied an especially interesting and significant position as far as the Victorian disease environment was concerned. Figure 8.10 allows us to explore the differences between London and the remainder of England and Wales in a little more detail. It illustrates the ratio of age-specific mortality rates for Diarrhoea & Dysentery and Diseases of the Lung or Respiratory system. For age groups shown above the horizontal line there was excess mortality in London. While for both groups of diseases London experienced excess mortality in infancy and early childhood, in later childhood and early adulthood England and Wales was consistently in excess, but at older ages Diarrhoea & Dysentery was again lower in London yet mortality from the respiratory diseases was higher in London. In terms of change between the 1860s and the 1890s, London's relative position generally improved although this was most obviously the case for Diarrhoea & Dysentery at ages beyond infancy and early childhood.

The evidence summarised in figure 8.10 helps to support the general argument that the effects of the Victorian public health reforms were partial and selective prior to 1901. London was probably a substantial beneficiary as far as sanitation was concerned, but this could not be said equally of the environmental conditions that fostered the respiratory diseases. In this case not only was there little improvement, but London remained at a disadvantage.

Phthisis

There can be no doubt that pulmonary tuberculosis was one of the most important diseases in the nineteenth century in terms of both its changing demographic impact and the effect that such a debilitating disease could have on the health of the nation and the everyday lives of its

[38] In terms of the equations shown in table 8.3, that between Diseases of the Lung or Respiratory system and population density was: $L61(65–74) = 250.493PD + 32.535$ $r^2 = 0.466$, and $L91(65–74) = 216.497PD + 39.397$ $r^2 = 0.457$.

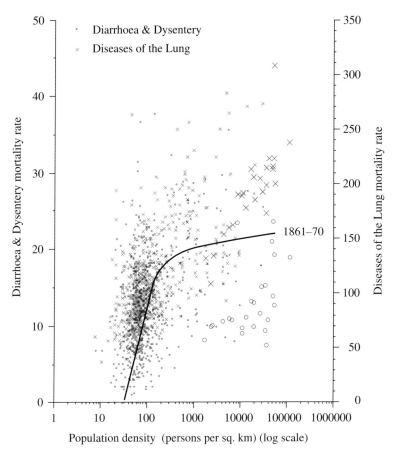

Figure 8.9. Relationship between Diarrhoea & Dysentery mortality
rate and Diseases of the Lung mortality rate ages 65–74 and population
density, English and Welsh districts, 1861–70
Note: The larger circles/crosses indicate the 25 London districts, and the
summary curve for Diarrhoea & Dysentery IMR is shown.

people.[39] Here we are obliged to focus exclusively on Phthisis which is
normally equated with the pulmonary form of tuberculosis. Pulmonary
tuberculosis is a particularly complicated disease to deal with in epidemiological and demographic terms. Certainly it displayed age and

[39] Brownlee (1918, 1922) provides an early twentieth-century summary of the medical statistics while Kayne *et al.* (1939) give a medical survey, Smith (1988) gives the medical
historian's interpretation, Wilson (1990) offers a general review and Sutherland (1976)
summarises recent epidemiological work. Hardy (1993), chapter 8, 'Tuberculosis', and
Bryder (1988) provide excellent introductions.

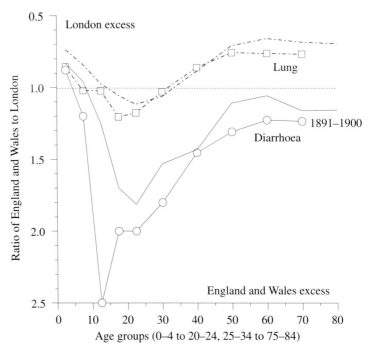

Figure 8.10. Ratio of age-specific mortality rates among females for Diseases of the Lung or Respiratory system and Diarrhoea & Dysentery, England and Wales to those for London, 1861–70 and 1891–1900
Note: See text for explanation.

gender biases which were modified as mortality declined during the second half of the nineteenth century. But it has also been suggested that the decline of phthisis was to some extent offset by the increase in deaths ascribed to respiratory diseases in general. Further, there is uncertainty concerning the extent to which pulmonary tuberculosis was principally an urban disease and whether the decline in mortality with which it was associated was ubiquitous and, if so, what this might imply.

The changing age and sex structure of Phthisis mortality has often been commented on and is illustrated here in figures 8.2 and 8.3.[40] While between the 1850s and the 1900s mortality from Phthisis declined at every age, it did so more for females than for males. However, the shape of the mortality curves also changed so that the rapid increase between ages 10 and 20 so evident at mid-century had become far more muted by the first decade of the twentieth century. This section will focus on

[40] Louis (1831) was one of the first to document the differential using clinical evidence.

the age group 20–34. In general it would appear not only that Phthisis mortality declined, but that there may also have been an element of postponement. Certainly the mortality rate among young adults was much reduced although this should not lead us to conclude that a lower proportion of Victorian 20-year-olds had contracted tuberculosis, simply that it had not yet proved fatal. The effects of 'galloping consumption' became less important, perhaps.

Since tuberculosis attacked the lung it might seem reasonable to classify it as one of the Diseases of the Lung or Diseases of the Respiratory system and this probably did happen especially when the immediate cause of death was pneumonia or bronchitis, and particularly in old age. But the symptoms of pulmonary tuberculosis were quite distinctive as a chronic disease, its age profile was characteristic, as was also its lack of seasonality.[41] While deaths from respiratory diseases follow a strong pattern of seasonal variation, those from phthisis display far less seasonality, although there is some first quarter excess. Phthisis is not a dramatic disease, rather it is insidious in its debilitating effects and inexorable in its ultimate consequence. Its weekly death toll displayed a monotonous regularity.

'The theory that urban areas in particular fostered tuberculosis, and that rural life afforded some protection against the disease, was an important part of nineteenth-century explanations of regional variations in the rates.'[42] Such an interpretation would be far too simple, however. Figure 8.11 shows the relationship between Phthisis mortality rates for 20–24-year-olds against population density for the 614 districts. Clearly, some of the very highest Phthisis rates are in rural districts, but then so are the very lowest rates. The large urban centres experienced only average rates. Unlike infant Diarrhoea & Dysentery and certainly childhood Measles there was no neatly defined association between Phthisis mortality in early adulthood and whether a place was urban or rural.[43] In the 1860s there were groups of districts in East

---

[41] See Hardy (1993), pp. 215–18 and 229–30, but also Bryder (1988), on the problems of using tuberculosis statistics. Farr, *Vital Statistics*, (1885), pp. 266–69, attempted a comparison of phthisis and bronchitis mortality by age for the period 1848–63, but this was largely inconclusive as to the problems of registration. Farr's first wife died from consumption in her early twenties. In general, and especially considering its demographic importance, Farr, and thus the Registrar General, paid relatively little attention to tuberculosis.

[42] Cronjé (1984), p. 93. Using the 45 registration counties, Cronjé concludes that '[t]he statistical data thus bear out the contemporary belief that rural areas escaped more lightly from tuberculosis than urban counties' (p. 94).

[43] It should be remembered that the presence of hospitals, like the Brompton in Kensington which specialised in tuberculosis cases, is likely to distort Phthisis mortality patterns among the London districts. See Mooney *et al.* (1999).

Anglia, the north Pennines and especially west Wales in which Phthisis was particularly high; these were also some of the most rural of areas. It is also the case that none of the urban-industrial areas that we have come to associate with high mortality from virtually every individual cause of death was prominent where Phthisis in early adulthood was concerned.[44]

Of course, what is most interesting about figure 8.11 is that Phthisis mortality appears to have declined in nearly all districts regardless of initial rate or whether the place had urban or rural characteristics. However, it is not a straightforward matter to capture the dimensions of these changes. For example, as a graph of the Phthisis mortality rates in the 1890s against those for the 1860s would show, there is a signifi-cant positive association and the *beta* coefficient is also substantially less than 1. There are many districts in England where Phthisis mortality more than halved between the 1860s and the 1890s and these are wide-spread in parts of the rural North, the south Midlands and East Anglia. But there are also many districts in the north-east and the south-west of both England and Wales where, although there was decline in the early adult age groups (20–24 and 25–34), the relative change in both age groups was far less strong. In North Wales and a scattering of other dis-tricts including several in London, Phthisis mortality in the age group 20–24 declined faster than that in the age group 25–34; and in some dis-tricts (mid-Devon and mid-Kent provide examples of clusters) mortal-ity in the older age group declined faster than in the younger. The patterns suggested by figure 8.11 are not easy to interpret, but there is evidence that clusters of districts existed which experienced similar sorts of patterns of change and that in some of those clusters Phthisis mortality was rather slow to decline at all young adult ages. These dis-tricts were not all rural or urban, rather there were examples of each, but they do show some signs of sub-regional clustering consistent with the maintenance of higher levels of infection among certain geographically distinctive populations.

Since we are not able to distinguish among districts between the Phthisis mortality of males and females from the 1870s to the 1890s, it will not be possible to trace the geographical manifestations of the age and gender shifts in the mortality curve. But we are able to explore the relationship between the Phthisis mortality of males and females at least for the 1860s. While it can be concluded that excess female mortality from Phthisis in the 20–24 age group was experienced mainly in rural districts and that the largest urban centres tended to have excess male

---

[44] See Woods and Shelton (1997), maps 20 and 21.

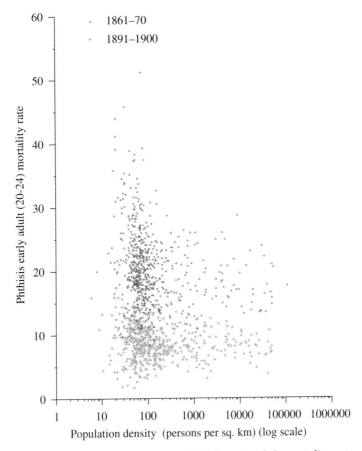

Figure 8.11. Relationship between Phthisis early adult mortality rate
and population density, English and Welsh districts, 1861–70 and 1891–1900

mortality, some rural districts experienced exceptionally high excess
male mortality.[45]

During his time as Medical Officer of Health for Brighton, Arthur
Newsholme prepared a lengthy report on the decline in the phthisis
death rate.[46] He concluded as follows.

Segregation in general institutions is the only factor which has varied constantly
with the phthisis death-rate in the countries that have been examined. It must

[45] See Woods and Shelton (1997), pp. 108–9.
[46] Newsholme (1906b). This is a substantial study which exemplifies Newsholme's
method. Although the importance attached in its conclusion to the significance of one
factor is probably unjustified, the assessment of the relative contributions of other
factors is more convincing. See also Eyler (1997), pp. 142–91.

therefore be regarded as having exerted a more powerful influence on the prevention of phthisis than any of the other factors of which none has varied constantly with the phthisis death-rate.[47]

The other factors to which Newsholme refers are: urbanisation and
industrialisation; 'improved housing and decreased overcrowding' –
'Overcrowding is an important factor of the phthisis-rate but its effect is
usually not strong enough to counteract the influence of other factors';
nutrition – 'The consumption of food per head shows no correspondence with the extent of prevalence of phthisis'; poverty – pauperism is
too heterogeneous a concept in itself, but some of its elements may have
an important influence; improved knowledge of and education about
phthisis – post-dates a well-marked decrease in the disease; and the
introduction of sanatoria – 'insignificant in number relatively to the
amount of the disease.'[48]

Newsholme's principal argument was that the increased treatment of
phthisis cases in workhouses or workhouse infirmaries led to the
removal of infective active cases from the wider community. By the late
1890s and early 1900s up to a third of all phthisis deaths in London
occurred in Poor Law institutions. In Sheffield and Salford the figure
was closer to 25 per cent, in Brighton it was 20 per cent and in Newport
(Monmouthshire) it was closer to 14 per cent.[49] While it is the case that
the percentage of all phthisis deaths occurring in institutions did
increase during the last decades of the nineteenth century (from less
than 15 per cent in the towns in the 1880s to between 20 and 30 per cent
in the early 1900s) and that this would certainly have helped to remove
infectives from the community during the last stages of their illness, it
is not clear whether these percentages are sufficiently high early enough
in the nineteenth century to have made an initial impact on the downward trend of phthisis mortality. It is also unclear from the evidence presented by Newsholme whether the phthisis deaths in institutions
occurred in particular age groups (the aged poor, for example). If they
did, then the strength of his case would be weakened since, as we have
seen in figure 8.3, the reduction in phthisis mortality was mainly
between ages 15 and 50.

There are still many aspects of the historical epidemiology of pulmonary tuberculosis which are not and probably will not be understood. The factors that influenced the duration and intensity of exposure
to infection or reinfection; that led to the active manifestation of the
characteristic symptoms of phthisis, especially the spitting of foul

---

[47] Newsholme (1906b), p. 375. Some of Newsholme's ideas may have been influenced by
Robert Koch's (1906) Nobel lecture of 1905.
[48] Newsholme (1906b), p. 374.   [49] Newsholme (1906b), p. 370.

mucoid sputum and haemoptysis; and the factors that finally led to death from the disease or where pulmonary tuberculosis was an important contributory complication, each need to be distinguished separately. While it is certain that mortality due to pulmonary tuberculosis did decline in the second half of the nineteenth century in England and Wales, that the age and gender profiles changed, and that this had a profound effect on death rates in general and the life chances of young adults in particular, it is still unclear what caused these changes.

The McKeown interpretation holds that the nutritional status of the population improved sufficiently to reduce the risk of dying from phthisis, that the rate of infection did not decline and that therapy before the 1950s was largely ineffective.[50] Although McKeown had no direct evidence for the improvement of nutritional status, more recent work by Floud, Wachter and Gregory using time-series of average heights concludes that 'the fall in mortality in late nineteenth-century England and Wales follows almost exactly the pattern we would expect from the evidence of nutritional status [from the 1860 birth cohort]. The height data make the link between nutrition (although in a wider sense) and mortality which McKeown could only infer.' They go on to state: 'There is little doubt that the second half of the nineteenth century or more precisely the fifty-five years from 1860 to the outbreak of the First World War, saw significant improvements in the nutritional status of the British people and that these improvements were reflected in reductions in mortality and morbidity levels. The evidence of mean heights correlates so well with that of mortality that this inference is fully justified.'[51] F. B. Smith's conclusion is rather more circumspect: 'Better nutrition, housing, nurture, lessening of fatigue, smaller family size acting synergistically in varying permutations through time and place hold the answer, although that answer remains vague because its chronology and linkages are little traced or understood.'[52]

How does the evidence presented in this chapter relate to these arguments? To simplify, suppose we distinguish between the influence of nutrition and that of housing quality, and accept the need to account for

---

[50] McKeown (1976).

[51] Floud *et al.* (1990), pp. 314 and 319. There has been a long and still-active debate on the history of nutrition and the interpretation of height data. See Fogel (1994a, 1994b). Fogel (1994b) argues that 'when final heights are used to explain differences in adult mortality rates, they reveal the effect, not of adult levels of nutrition on adult mortality rates, but of nutritional levels during infancy, childhood, and adolescence on adult mortality rates' (p. 243).

[52] Smith (1988), p. 244. See also Hardy (1993), p. 213: 'The continuing challenge of historical tuberculosis research is to achieve a finer evaluation of the balance of factors driving the decline of the disease.'

both variations and changes in mortality attributed to phthisis. Many of the districts with the highest levels of Phthisis mortality at both 20–24 and 25–34 were in the most remote rural areas little affected by in-migration although experiencing depopulation.[53] Here mortality was high because infection and re-infection rates were high, and housing may have been both poor and overcrowded. But in general the available evidence does not provide support for interpretations that emphasise either changes in nutritional status or the quality of housing or, indeed, some synergistic interaction between the two. Rather, they point towards closer scrutiny of the nature of pulmonary tuberculosis itself and especially its virulence, the effects that health-selective migration might have when such a chronic disease is involved *or* the manner of Phthisis death registration.

The simplest explanation is that the disease became less virulent and that this was the principal reason for a reduction in the risk of the disease developing and leading to early death, that this process occurred slowly and everywhere. This does not mean that registration fashion might not have had a bearing, but this is rather more likely in the early twentieth century, when consumptives were liable to be put away in sanatoria, and after the 1911 National Insurance Act which tended to discriminate against families with a known history of tuberculosis. Nor does it mean that poor nutrition, overcrowded housing and poverty in general did not influence the outcome and its speed once the disease began to develop. However, it does mean that it is no longer necessary to search for substantial and widespread improvements in living standards in order to explain the decline of Phthisis mortality and thus the slow increase in adult life expectancy in the late nineteenth century. Persistent geographical differentiation in the quality of life should be mirrored by tuberculosis deaths; that this was not in this case ought to tell us more about epidemiology than about economic and social history.[54]

---

[53] There is the possibility that selective out-migration of the healthy combined with low levels of in-migration may have affected the disease environments of some especially rural districts. See Welton (1872) and Hardy (1993), pp. 250–53, with respect to London migrants.

[54] This re-emphasis on the disease itself rather than the conditions of vulnerability to the disease becoming active and developing fully requires far greater attention than it has received in recent years. McKeown's (1976) often repeated assertion that '[t]here is no evidence that the virulence of the organism has changed significantly; the disease continues to have devastating effects on populations not previously exposed to it; and the virulence of the bacillus appears not to have diminished during the period when it has been possible to assess it in the laboratory' (p. 83) will need to be countered first. Koch (1906) is, of course, especially informative on the matter of infection. These dangers are at their greatest 'the more uncleanly the [already infected] patients are as regards their sputum, the more lack there is of light and air, and the more closely crowded together the sick live with the hale. The danger of infection becomes especially great when

Composite disease environments

It appears from these brief outlines that the disease environment of Victorian England and Wales was both complicated and multi-faceted. There were certainly some districts in which crowding, poor air and water quality, and tuberculosis combined to create a very hazardous environment in terms of the risks to health and longevity. But equally there would have been other localities hardly affected by any of these influences. In terms of the four principal diseases considered – Measles in early childhood, Diseases of the Lung or Respiratory system in old age, Diarrhoea & Dysentery in infancy and Phthisis in early adulthood – the first three had significant positive associations with population density although there was no sense in which they merely replicated one another, while Phthisis was far less obviously a disease with a strong environmental component.[55] It would be interesting to attempt some combination of these influences in a way that might enable districts to be classified in terms of the composition of their disease environments. For example, was a place more likely to be relatively healthy on all counts except for Phthisis, or relatively dangerous only in terms of the bad effects of air and water?

One way to develop such a district classification would be to create environment–disease variables by averaging Z-scores for selected age- and cause-specific mortality rates.[56] This procedure has been followed in the construction of figure 8.12. It takes Crowding as its starting point

healthy people have to sleep in the same rooms with sick people and even, as unfortunately still frequently happens among the poor, in the same bed' (p. 1449). Koch's lecture is a salutary reminder that even the poorest, most undernourished and badly housed would not die from tuberculosis if they were not first infected by a person with the disease. With notification, a degree of isolation (especially of those in the last stages of the disease) and health education, tuberculosis mortality could be reduced. (Koch regarded bovine tuberculosis as relatively unimportant.) While Koch's account helps to explain the existence of certain differentials in tuberculosis mortality as well as its accelerating decline after the 1880s, it does not help us understand the earlier phase of decline in countries like England and Wales. Brownlee (1918, 1922) also argued the case for a decline in tuberculosis virulence.

55 Scarlet fever, although one of the most interesting of Victorian diseases, has been excluded from further consideration in favour of measles.

56 The variables have been defined in the following way: Crowding – Measles, mean of Z-scores over the 614 districts for Measles early childhood mortality rates (ECMRs, ages 1–4 years) 1861–70 and 1891–1900; Air – Respiratory diseases, Diseases of the Lung 1861–70 and Diseases of the Respiratory system mortality rates 1891–1900 for ages 65–74; Water – Diarrhoea, Diarrhoea & Dysentery infant mortality rates (IMRs for mortality in the first year of life) for 1861–70 and 1891–1900; Phthisis – Phthisis mortality rates for age groups 20–24 and 25–34 for 1861–70 and 1891–1900. Z-scores are commonly used to express deviations from the mean of a distribution in terms of standard deviations. The use of Z-scores and the averaging of two decades not only makes the variables directly comparable, but it helps to remove the effect of change over time in order to focus attention purely on geographical differences.

to which it relates Air, then Water, then Phthisis. At each step the association becomes less significant until, with Phthisis, there is no statistical relationship.[57] By this means we are able to see, albeit in a highly simplified fashion, how the composite disease environment was made up.

Figure 8.13 (colour section, page *n*) shows the distribution of positive Z-scores for the districts of England and Wales focusing on Crowding, Air, Water and Phthisis. There are interesting similarities and differences which warrant detailed scrutiny in their own right, but the principal objective here is to explore combinations of causes of death in disease environments.

Of the 614 districts, 127 had negative Z-scores (O in table 8.4) for all four variables (group 1) while 54 had positive scores (X) for all four (group 2). Of the remaining 433 districts, 213 would have been group 1 but for one positive Z-score (groups 3–6) and 129 would have been group 2 but for one negative score out of the four (7–10). The remaining 94 districts have two positive and two negative Z-scores (11–16). Table 8.4 gives the number of districts in each group, the percentage of the population of England and Wales living in each of the 16 groups of districts and the mean life expectancy at birth in years for each group. Figure 8.14 illustrates the distribution of life expectancy at birth among districts in each group.[58]

The final composite map of the 16 disease environments is illustrated in figure 8.15 (colour section, page *o*). Again, the picture is an interesting one, but far from straightforward. For example, all those districts in group 1 had life expectancies at birth greater than 48 years while all group 2 life expectancies were less than 48. The former were the healthy districts; the latter experienced some of the worst mortality conditions and were in the main urban districts. Groups 1 and 6, on the other hand, were essentially rural in character, with Phthisis in East Anglia and Wales turning many districts that would have been group 1 into group 6. Group 5, those districts that would have been in group 1 but for positive Z-scores for the Water variable, were mainly clustered along a line running north from London to Scarborough where they were joined by members of groups 12 and 13 which also had positive Water Z-scores. Most London and outer metropolitan districts were in group 10; but for negative Phthisis Z-scores they would have been in group 2. They join

---

[57] The r²s are: Crowding–Air, 0.662; Crowding–Water, 0.513; Crowding–Phthisis, 0.012; Air–Water, 0.361; Air–Phthisis, 0.000; Water–Phthisis, 0.036.

[58] The population distribution has been derived by taking the average for the 1860s and the 1890s. The average life expectancy at birth has also been found in this way.

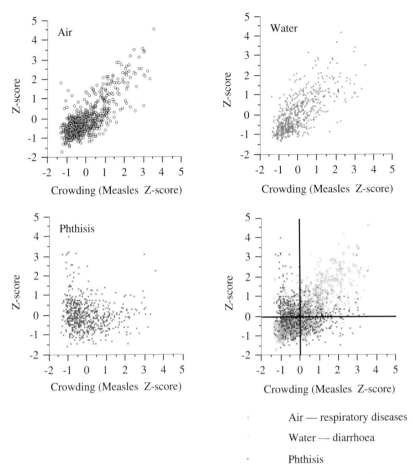

Figure 8.12. Disease environments defined using Z-scores, English and Welsh districts

Note: The bottom right graph shows the combination of each of the three causes with crowding – measles. See text for explanation.

other group 10 districts in the urbanised areas of South Wales, the Midlands and the north of England.

The maps in figures 8.13 and 8.15 (colour section, page o) reveal interesting geographical variations in the disease environments of Victorian England and Wales. They reinforce several long-standing observations regarding the differences between urban and rural places, but they also reflect detailed variations within and between these broad categories. With figure 8.14 these maps illustrate the ways in which cause of death

Table 8.4. *Classification of English and Welsh districts on the basis of disease environments*

	Crowding	Air	Water	Phthisis	Number of districts	Percentage of population	Mean e_0 for group
1	O	O	O	O	127	7.28	51.7
2	X	X	X	X	54	21.86	39.6
3	X	O	O	O	16	1.61	49.5
4	O	X	O	O	17	1.08	49.5
5	O	O	X	O	43	4.59	49.4
6	O	O	O	X	137	9.72	49.9
7	O	X	X	X	7	1.51	44.7
8	X	O	X	X	16	1.99	45.9
9	X	X	O	X	15	2.87	45.0
10	X	X	X	O	88	35.81	43.6
11	X	X	O	O	16	2.36	45.8
12	O	X	X	O	8	0.88	46.2
13	O	O	X	X	18	1.76	48.0
14	X	O	X	O	28	4.43	46.8
15	O	X	O	X	16	1.39	48.0
16	X	O	O	X	8	0.85	48.0

Note:
X = those districts with a positive Z-score; O = those districts with a negative Z-score. See text for explanation.

structures came together to determine different levels of mortality, but also that local disease environments were more often than not like the curate's egg – some good, some bad.

The McKeown interpretation further confounded

It will already be clear from what has been said and illustrated in this chapter that the disease environment of Victorian England and Wales was both diverse and complicated. But how does this now obvious diversity affect our approach to the McKeown interpretation which treats England and Wales as an undifferentiated whole as far as the decline of mortality is concerned? Here we shall consider this problem in some detail, but first it will be necessary to recap on McKeown's method of enquiry. For this we shall take his 1962 paper with R. G. Record as the clearest and most straightforward account of the 'Reasons for the decline of mortality in England and Wales during the nineteenth century'.[59]

[59] McKeown and Record (1962). We have already considered several aspects of the McKeown interpretation as they relate to the general causes of population growth (p.

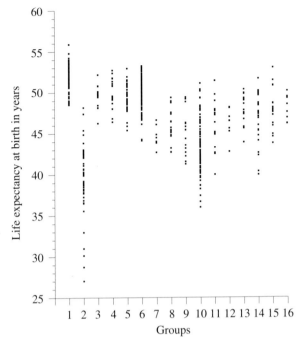

Figure 8.14. Life expectancy at birth among English and Welsh districts
grouped by disease environment
Note: See table 8.4 for definition of groups.

At the heart of the analysis provided by McKeown and Record there
is a table of age-standardised cause-specific mortality rates for England
and Wales which compares 1851–60 with 1891–1900. Because of its
central importance to their subsequent argument it is reproduced here
as table 8.5. They first group causes of death not only to allow for the
recombination of causes which were separated at some stage in the
intervening decades, but also to focus on the infectious diseases since 'it
seems unquestionable that the decline of mortality between 1851–60
and 1891–1900 was attributable almost exclusively to a reduction in the
frequency of death from infectious disease'.[60] Some of this combination
is unavoidable if changes in contribution are to be identified, but

16), infant mortality (p. 248) and tuberculosis (p. 339). Here the issue of uniformity and
diversity is brought to the fore, especially as it relates to the contribution of environmental change. See also Szreter (1988) and Johansson (1994) for important discussion
of McKeown's general approach and especially his arguments in *The Modern Rise of
Population* (1976).   [60] McKeown and Record (1962), p. 103.

Table 8.5. *McKeown's table of the mean annual standardised mortality rates per million living due to certain communicable diseases, England and Wales, 1851–60 and 1891–1900*

Cause	1851–60 *a*	1891–1900 *b*	Difference *a − b*	Difference per cent of total difference $(a-b) \times 100 \over 3085$
Tuberculosis – respiratory	2772	1418	1354	43.9
Tuberculosis – other forms	706	603	103	3.3
Typhus, enteric fever, simple continued fever	891	184	707	22.9
Scarlet fever	779	152	627	20.3
Diarrhoea, Dysentery, Cholera	990	715	275	8.9
Smallpox	202	13	189	6.1
Whooping cough	433	363	70	2.3
Measles	357	398	−41	−1.3
Diphtheria	99	254	−155	−5.0
Other causes	13980	14024	−44	−1.4
Total	21209	18124	3085	100

Note:
Standardisation to age and sex distribution of 1901 population.
Source: McKeown and Record (1962), table 3, p. 104.

McKeown and Record go much further than is necessary and create thereby an enormous 'Other causes' category which contains 63 per cent of all deaths in the 1850s and 77 per cent in the 1890s. From this table they draw the following conclusion.

Of the lives saved the proportions attributable to each of the major diseases (or groups of diseases) were as follows: tuberculosis (all forms), 47.2 per cent; typhus, enteric fever and simple continued fever, 22.9 per cent; scarlet fever, 20.3 per cent; diarrhoea, dysentery and cholera, 8.9 per cent; smallpox, 6.1 per cent; and whooping cough 2.3 per cent.[61]

Later in the paper these percentages are reported as, respectively, 45, 22, 19, 8 and 6 (whooping cough is not mentioned), 'these figures give the percentage contribution of the disease or disease group to the reduction of mortality for which collectively they are responsible'.[62] With the aid

[61] McKeown and Record (1962), p. 103.
[62] McKeown and Record (1962), p. 119 and note 26.

of this quantitative base McKeown moves on to make and justify several by now famous statements about the underlying causes of mortality decline in the Victorian era.

It therefore seems permissible to conclude that a change in the character of these [five] infectious diseases, essentially independent of human intervention, may have been responsible for not less than one-fifth of the total improvement and – as a very rough estimate – for not more than one-third. The remainder must be attributed to environmental change. (p. 119)

These considerations [of the typhus–typhoid and cholera groups] suggest that the specific changes introduced by the sanitary reformers were responsible for about a quarter of the total decline of mortality in the second half of the nineteenth century. (p. 120)

Hence we conclude [mainly because of its association with tuberculosis] that the rising standard of living was the other main influence which accounted for perhaps half of the total reduction of mortality. (p. 120)

To sum up: In order of their relative importance the influences responsible for the decline of mortality in the second half of the nineteenth century were: (a) a rising standard of living, of which the most significant feature was improved diet (responsible mainly for the decline of tuberculosis and less certainly, and to a lesser extent, of typhus); (b) the hygienic changes introduced by the sanitary reformers (responsible for the decline of the typhus–typhoid and cholera groups); and (c) a favourable trend in the relationship between infectious agent and the human host (which accounted for the decline of mortality from scarlet fever and may have contributed to that from tuberculosis, typhus and cholera). The effect of therapy was restricted to smallpox and hence had only a trivial effect on the total reduction of the death rate. (pp. 120–21)

This then is the core of McKeown's account of the reasons for the decline of mortality in England and Wales during the second half of the nineteenth century: 50 per cent of the decline was caused by improvements in the standard of living, but especially by improvements in diet working via the reduction in tuberculosis deaths; 25 per cent was due to improvements in sanitation which made their mark via the typhus–typhoid and cholera group of causes of death; and the final 25 per cent was caused by changes in the diseases themselves, which was especially true in the case of scarlet fever. This account was further elaborated and extended in a series of papers and books, but it was never substantially revised.[63]

At the heart of the problem that McKeown tackles and appears to solve is his ability to measure change and also the contributions to change, and to infer therefrom the ultimate causes with their relative strengths. This is why table 8.5 is so important to the entire approach.

---

[63] McKeown and Brown (1955), the first paper in the series, McKeown, *et al.* (1972), McKeown *et al.* (1975), and McKeown (1976).

Let us attempt the same exercise using the causes of death listed in table 8.1 which are those reported for districts in the *Decennial Supplements*, but on this occasion we shall retain as many comparable categories as possible and compare the 1860s with the 1890s. Table 8.6 illustrates the first step: the combination of causes of death in order to allow comparison between decades. McKeown himself was especially concerned with the problems created by typhus which, until 1869, was reported with typhoid in the Registrar General's returns. But it is obvious that there are many other difficulties, especially in the various 'Diseases of:' as well as the contents of the residual 'Other causes' category. Table 8.6 has many weaknesses which are themselves instructive for a proper appreciation of how McKeown's own work was conducted and table 8.5 formed. Once it is clear what reductionist and *ad hoc* assumptions are necessary merely to consider the extent of cause-specific change at the national level it might well be wiser to conclude that the whole exercise is so flawed that the apparently sound quantitative base of the interpretation is at best spurious and at worst deliberately misleading – in short, a case of constructive misrepresentation.[64]

However, this would probably be to go too far. The approach adopted here will be closer to letting the evidence speak for itself, i.e. using the 19 cause of death categories defined in table 8.6 to indicate the extent of change between the 1860s and 1890s as well as the individual contributions to change. Table 8.7 illustrates different ways of assessing the importance of each cause of death as well as the extent to which change occurs and the contributions to change. It starts (cols. *a* and *b*) by using the method adopted by Preston *et al.* in their survey of international variations in cause of death patterns.[65] Taking the 19 causes in turn it reports the number of years gained in terms of life expectancy at birth if each were to be removed. For example, if there had been no deaths from smallpox in the 1860s then the life expectancy at birth in England and Wales would have been 0.22 years higher (i.e. 41.41 years instead of 41.19). Had there been no smallpox deaths in the 1890s, life expectancy at birth would have improved by 0.02 years from 46.14 to 46.16. Whilst this method offers an extremely effective way of considering the relative importance of individual causes by allowing for the age structure of mortality, it is not ideal for the measurement of contributions to change. Alternative and more realistic methods must be sought.

Column *d* of table 8.7 shows the number of deaths from particular

---

[64] This is close to the line taken by Johansson (1994), for example: 'Even under the best circumstances, some empirically weak but persuasive accounts of the past will be rewarded with acceptance, whether or not they are empirically sound' (p. 120).

[65] Preston *et al.* (1972), pp. 224–47, report cause-specific life tables for England and Wales, 1861–70 to 1901–11, for males and females separately using 12 categories.

Table 8.6. *Combination of causes of death used in the Registrar General's Decennial Supplements for England and Wales*

Label	Code	1861–70	1891–1900
Smallpox	1.	Smallpox	Smallpox
Measles	2.	Measles	Measles
Scarlet fever	3.	Scarlet fever	Scarlet fever
Diphtheria	4.	Diphtheria	Diphtheria
Whooping cough	5.	Whooping cough	Whooping cough
Diarrhoea	6.	Cholera	Cholera
	6.	Diarrhoea & Dysentery	Diarrhoea & Dysentery
Typhus	7.	Typhus	Typhus
	7.		Enteric fever
	7.		Simple continued fever
	19.	Other zymotic diseases	
Cancer	8.	Cancer	Cancer
Scrofula	9.	Scrofula & Tabes mesenterica	
	9.		Tabes mesenterica
	9.		Other tuberculous & Scrofulous diseases
Phthisis	10.	Phthisis	Phthisis
	19.	Hydrocephalus	
		Diseases of:	*Diseases of:*
Brain	11.	Brain	Nervous system
Heart	12.	Heart & Dropsy	Circulatory system
Lung	13.	Lung	Respiratory system
Stomach	14.	Stomach & Liver	Digestive system
Kidneys	15.	Kidneys	Urinary system
Generative	16.	Generative organs	Generative organs
	19.	Joints	
	19.	Skin	
Childbirth	17.		Puerperal fever
	17.	Childbirth & Metria	Childbirth
Violence	18.	Suicide	
	18.	Other violent deaths	Violence
Other causes	19.	Other causes	Other causes
	20.	All causes	All causes

Note:
Based on table 8.1.

Table 8.7. *Alternative approaches to the measurement of changes in cause-specific mortality, England and Wales, 1861–70 to 1891–1900*

Label	Code	Years gained 1861–70 a	Years gained 1891–1900 b	Deaths 1861–70 c	Standardised deaths 1861–70 d	Deaths 1891–1900 e	Total change deaths $e-d$ f	Per cent change $(f/d)\times100$ g	Per cent contribution to change $\dfrac{f\times100}{997920}$ h	Per cent contribution to absolute change $\dfrac{|e-d|\times100}{2000340}$ i
Smallpox	1.	0.22	0.02	34,786	46,713	4,058	−42,655	−91.31	−4.27	2.13
Measles	2.	0.70	0.83	94,099	119,471	126,841	7,370	6.17	0.74	0.37
Scarlet fever	3.	1.57	0.31	207,867	272,437	48,290	−224,147	−82.27	−22.46	11.21
Diphtheria	4.	0.27	0.51	39,454	52,319	80,671	28,352	54.19	2.84	1.42
Whooping cough	5.	0.81	0.74	112,800	140,748	115,670	−25,138	−17.86	−2.52	1.26
Diarrhoea	6.	1.45	0.33	230,201	294,643	226,143	−68,500	−23.25	−6.86	3.42
Typhus	7.	0.36	0.01	189,285	268,467	55,996	−212,471	−79.14	−21.29	10.62
Diarrhoea & Typhus	6+7.	2.80	1.62	419,486	563,110	282,139	−280,971	−49.90	−28.16	14.05
Cancer	8.	0.40	0.96	82,820	119,413	232,178	112,765	94.43	11.30	5.64
Scrofula	9.	0.63	1.15	93,529	121,864	189,782	67,918	55.73	6.81	3.40
Phthisis	10.	3.56	2.16	529,425	777,350	426,224	−351,126	−45.17	−35.19	17.55
Brain	11.	3.75	3.45	595,747	795,075	665,301	−129,774	−16.32	−13.00	6.49
Heart	12.	1.56	2.27	288,447	414,686	507,730	93,044	22.44	9.32	4.65
Lung	13.	4.66	5.82	719,601	971,696	1,044,719	73,023	7.52	7.32	3.65
Stomach	14.	1.17	1.92	209,744	296,120	365,484	69,364	23.42	6.95	3.47
Kidneys	15.	0.31	0.60	63,754	91,828	141,202	49,374	53.77	4.95	2.47

	#	a	b	c	d	e	f	g	h	i
Generative	16.	0.04	0.06	12,506	18,635	14,094	−4,541	−24.37	−0.46	0.23
Childbirth	17.	0.20	0.23	35,254	52,833	46,591	−6,242	−11.81	−0.63	0.31
Violence	18.	1.03	1.03	163,840	283,484	202,363	−81,121	−28.62	−8.13	4.06
Other causes	19.	8.63	6.52	1,091,341	1,435,513	1,082,098	−353,415	−24.62	−35.42	17.67
Total	20.			4,794,500	6,573,295	5,575,375	−997,920	−15.18	100.00	100.00

Note:

For the definitions of causes of death see tables 8.1 and 8.6.

Columns *a* and *b* show the number of years by which life expectancy at birth would be increased if the particular cause of death were to be completely removed.

Column *d* is derived by applying the age- and cause-specific mortality rates for 1861–70 to the population age structure for 1891–1900.

Columns *f* to *i* provide alternative measures of change and percentage contribution to change based on the differences between columns *d* and *e*.

causes that would have occurred if the age- and cause-specific mortality rates for 1861–70 had applied to the age structure for 1891–1900. Column *d* is therefore directly comparable with column *e* which has the actual number of deaths for the 1890s. The remaining columns offer four different ways of measuring change between the 1860s and the 1890s based on the differences between columns *d* and *e*. The total number of deaths declined by 15.18 per cent although there were substantial differences between the individual causes, ranging from a 91.31 per cent decline for Smallpox to a 94.43 per cent increase for Cancer (col. *g*). In column *h*, contributions to change are measured in the way used by McKeown and shown in table 8.5, but column *i* considers contributions to absolute change regardless of whether increase or decrease occurred. The different impressions of change and the contributions to change made by each of the causes of death are further illustrated in figure 8.16 which shows the two approaches to measuring contributions.

Table 8.7 and figure 8.16 offer a rather different perspective on the McKeown interpretation. First, they show that while McKeown was quite justified in stressing the importance of infectious diseases in the nineteenth-century mortality decline, this was done by neglecting the causes to which an increasing number of deaths were assigned: Cancer, Diseases of the Heart, Lung, Stomach and Kidneys, as well as Scrofula. Secondly, the Other causes category takes on a new and altered significance. Because McKeown grouped far more chronic degenerative diseases into the 'Other causes' category it showed an increase between the 1850s and the 1890s, but in table 8.7 'Other causes' is used only as a last resort, it is much smaller and shows a substantial decrease. Thirdly, the causes Phthisis, Diarrhoea & Typhus, Scarlet fever and Diseases of the Brain (Nervous system) account for nearly half of the absolute change whilst dominating the decline. Following McKeown's logic, one might give Phthisis 35 per cent, Diarrhoea & Typhus 28 per cent, Scarlet fever 22 per cent and Diseases of the brain 13 per cent, but once again this would be to simplify and perhaps misrepresent the truly complex changes involved. However, it would seem both rather obvious and reasonable to conclude not only that different methods of forming cause of death categories and of measuring contributions to change have profound effects on the outcome, but also that the contribution of tuberculosis to the general decline of mortality may not have been as large as McKeown would have us believe, while Diarrhoea & Typhus and Scarlet fever were more important. This would encourage even greater emphasis on environmental change including the so-called sanitary revolution as well as other preventive measures. In addition, the autonomous or semi-autonomous epidemiological changes which are

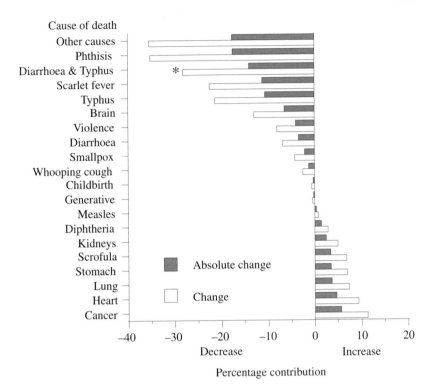

Figure 8.16. Percentage contribution to changes in cause-specific
mortality, England and Wales, 1861–70 to 1891–1900
Note: The causes of death are defined in table 8.6 and the method of
calculation in table 8.7.
* Diarrhoea & Typhus are also treated separately.

traditionally exemplified by scarlet fever could be widened to include
pulmonary tuberculosis. Accounts like McKeown's that stress the
importance of improving nutrition within the context of rising average
living standards during the nineteenth century must therefore come
under renewed attack.

In order to take the discussion a stage further it is important to return
to the principal theme of this chapter: the distinctive nature of local
disease environments in the Victorian era. For example, table 8.7 shows
that in England and Wales between the 1860s and the 1890s age-standardised deaths from Diarrhoea & Typhus fell by 280,971 (col. *f*). But
where were these saved lives located? Was the Victorian experience of
mortality decline an especially localised phenomenon tied to the
amelioration of certain especially hazardous environments? From what

we have seen already this would seem likely in the case of several of the common water-borne diseases, but not the respiratory diseases which did not decline everywhere, or tuberculosis and scarlet fever which did decline in all districts.

One way to approach this problem would be to take those cause of death categories which have already proved to be important contributors to change and to estimate for each district the number of deaths from those particular causes one should expect in 1861–70 if districts had the same population sizes and age structures as in 1891–1900.[66] This involves taking the age- and cause-specific mortality rates for 1861–70 and multiplying them by the age structure for 1891–1900 in a fashion comparable to that used to derive column *d* in table 8.7. The equivalent of column *f* may then be found for each district and thence the relative contribution made by each district to the national change in the selected causes between the 1860s and the 1890s. The causes or groups of causes selected from those listed in table 8.6 are as follows: Scarlet fever (3), Diarrhoea & Typhus (6 + 7), Cancer (8), Phthisis (10), and Diseases of the Brain (11), Heart (12) and Lung (13). Of these, as figure 8.15 shows, Phthisis, Diarrhoea & Typhus, Scarlet fever, and Diseases of the Brain made the most important and consistent contributions to mortality decline, while deaths from Cancer, Diseases of the Heart and Diseases of the Lung increased. Although deaths from Diseases of the Lung increased nationally, they did not do so in every district.

Let us begin by focusing on those causes given special attention by McKeown: Diarrhoea & Typhus, Phthisis and Scarlet fever. Figure 8.17 illustrates two methods of exploring the extent to which contributions to the national decline were geographically concentrated. The curves at *a* show that the contributions of only 14 of the 614 districts gave rise to 25 per cent of the national decline in Diarrhoea & Typhus, for example, while 53 districts contributed 50 per cent. While the *a* curves give each district equal weight, those at *b* weight each district by its average share of the population of England and Wales so that the 14 districts contained 13 per cent of the population and the 53 districts 35 per cent. If each district contributed to the decline in mortality according to its population size then the *b* curves would trace the diagonal from 0 to 1. Phthisis is closest to this position suggesting once again that, in general, mortality from pulmonary tuberculosis declined in a rather uniform fashion, with each district making the contribution relevant to its population size. In the case of Scarlet fever, the *b* curve is biased slightly more towards the smaller districts compared with Diarrhoea & Typhus where the bias is

---

[66] See Kearns (1993) for a parallel approach.

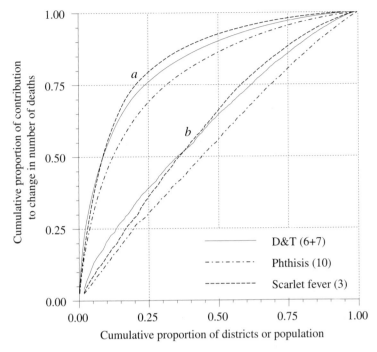

Figure 8.17. Comparison of contributions to mortality decline from three causes of death, England and Wales, 1861–70 to 1891–1900
Note: See text for explanation.

towards a smaller number of populous districts making a large contribution to change. If differences are to be found among the three, Phthisis is the most distinctive although the decline of Diarrhoea & Typhus and then Scarlet fever should illustrate the more interesting geographies.

Let us concentrate on the case of Diarrhoea & Typhus since it is this bundle of causes that is linked to the effects of the sanitary revolution and to public health policy interventions in general. The map on the left in figure 8.18 (colour section, page *p*) labelled Contribution shows the location of the 53 districts that in sum contributed half of the decline in deaths from Diarrhoea & Typhus during the decades from the 1860s to the 1890s. There are several obvious clusters of two or more districts: 13 of the 25 London districts plus West Ham; five districts in Birmingham and the Black Country; three in South Wales, including Cardiff and Swansea; six in and around Manchester; three on Merseyside; four in central Lancashire; six in and around Leeds and Bradford, and around

Sheffield and Rotherham; and five on Tyneside. These were the areas in which Victorian public health reform made its mark to such an extent that national levels of mortality were also affected. While these were the districts making the most substantial contributions they were not necessarily the best performers once their population size is taken into account. For this reason figure 8.18 (Performance) also shows the location of the districts with high positive and low negative residuals from the regression of contribution to decline in deaths from Diarrhoea & Typhus against proportion of population of England and Wales living in the district.[67] Positive residuals will occur where the model under-predicts the level of contribution (districts perform better than their population size would suggest), while the negative residuals pick out those districts that under-contributed to decline. The residuals have been grouped into four broad bands to simplify comparison: high, moderate, as expected and less than expected. They illustrate several interesting points. The largest cluster of high performing districts is to be found in the east Midlands close to a line between London and Scarborough. There are clusters of poorly performing districts in Lincolnshire, Cumbria and north Lancashire, south-west Wales and the West Country.

Finally, figure 8.19 helps to emphasise the point that if sufficient progress could be made in sanitary reform in even a small number of the most populous places its effects might outweigh more substantial advances in places with smaller populations, such as the small towns. The 25 London districts are highlighted in figure 8.19. All but three made substantial contributions to the decline of Diarrhoea & Typhus deaths, but only six (in order: Whitechapel, Islington, St George in the East, Poplar, Stepney and Bethnal Green) also made contributions well in excess of what might have been predicted from their population sizes. The remainder were mainly a little below the expected. Of the 53 districts shown on the map to the left in figure 8.18, a further 13 had high positive residuals and were non-metropolitan (Liverpool and West Derby; Manchester, Salford and Wigan; Newcastle-upon-Tyne and South Shields; Middlesbrough; Leeds; Rotherham; Walsall; Swansea and Neath). These, with the addition of five of the six London districts already mentioned, were the high performing and high contributing areas in terms of Victorian public health initiatives. In sum, these 18 districts contributed nearly 25 per cent of the decline in deaths from Diarrhoea & Typhus.[68]

This reconsideration of local and geographical aspects of the causes

[67] The regression model was of the following form: $\log y = 1.219 \log x + 0.496$ ($r^2 = 0.809$). Figure 8.19 shows the scatter of the residual values.

[68] St George in the East made a rather more modest contribution.

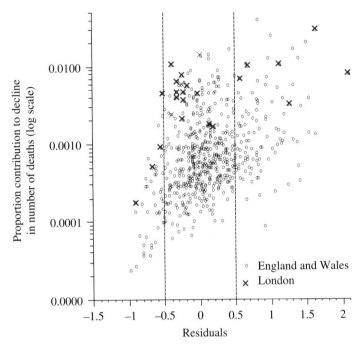

Figure 8.19. Relationship between proportionate contribution to the decline of deaths from Diarrhoea & Typhus (6 + 7) and the residuals from the regression of that proportionate contribution on the proportionate population size among the districts of England and Wales, and London
Note: See text for explanation.

of mortality decline has an important bearing on other recent attempts to assess the McKeown interpretation. For example, Szreter has argued as follows: 'human agency, in the form of a gradual negotiated expansion of preventive public health provision and services at the local level, rather than the impersonal "invisible hand" of inexorably rising nutritional and living standards, should be reinstated at the centre of our attempts to explain the modern mortality decline in Britain', and 'the argument is not that improving nutrition and living standards were entirely unimportant in accounting for the mortality decline, but that the role of a battling public health ideology, politics and medicine operating of necessity through local government, is more correctly seen as the principal causal agency involved'.[69] The analysis presented in this

[69] Szreter (1988), pp. 5 and 36. See also Guha (1994) and Szreter's (1994) reply. Szreter (1997), especially p. 712, rather overstates the case for sanitation and specific public health measures in the late nineteenth century partly because he exaggerates the

chapter goes some considerable way to support Szreter's case, especially when it is set against McKeown's original emphasis on nutritional status and the standard of living, but there are still several important reasons to be wary of simple conclusions.

First, although representing an impressive monument to Victorian medical statistics, the cause of death data published by the Registrar General always need to be treated with care. While much has been learnt from their analysis there are still very considerable problems if one wishes, as McKeown did, to measure contributions to the extent of change over time. This problem is exacerbated to some extent if one also considers local contributions to national change, although the geographical approach does have the great advantage of revealing the diversity of disease environments and of clarifying the extent to which deaths from particular causes were declining or increasing everywhere. Deaths caused by Diseases of the Lung or Respiratory system are a case in point; in some districts they increased between the 1860s and the 1890s, but in many others they declined. There must also be concern about the transfer of deaths between causes and especially the rise in Cancer as a major cause which may to some extent have been at the expense of Diseases of the Nervous system or Diseases of the Respiratory system.[70]

Secondly, although it is clear from figure 8.18 just how important a relatively small number of urban areas were for the decline of deaths in the Diarrhoea & Typhus category, and by implication the importance of the 'battling public health ideology', there still remains a difficulty concerning the persistently high infant mortality rate and its significant Diarrhoea & Dysentery component. Among all age groups except for infancy, the sanitary and other public health improvements of the Victorian age did bear some obvious benefits. Benefits to the very young appear to have been largely excluded before the turn of the century.

Thirdly, while McKeown was surely misguided in placing so much emphasis on the decline of pulmonary tuberculosis and the importance of its inferred causes prior to 1901, Szreter's re-interpretation is rather inclined to play down the significance of Phthisis in order to promote the cause of public health. From what we have seen in this chapter, it would appear that the decline in the number of deaths due to Phthisis

---

footnote 69 (*cont.*)
problem of worsening conditions in the very largest provincial towns in the second quarter of the century, but also because he ignores the problems associated with the measurement of change outlined above.

[70] Mooney *et al.* (1999) have illustrated the importance of deaths in institutions, especially in London, and their potential to distort local analysis of cause of death patterns. This problem also needs to be borne in mind.

was of great significance, particularly because it would have improved the life chances of young adults, those in the prime of life. But it is still not clear what caused the decline. If our suspicions are correct then the disease itself changed in character during the second half of the nineteenth century and this affected tuberculosis death rates everywhere, although variations associated with poverty, overcrowded living conditions and the high incidence of infected people in certain districts shunned by potential in-migrants maintained differences between areas and environments.

Fourthly, while there is little reason to doubt McKeown's analysis of the reasons for the decline of scarlet fever, this very consensus has encouraged commentators to neglect the disease – it is insufficiently controversial. Yet it had an important bearing on the decline of childhood mortality during the late Victorian period, especially deaths above one year of age. It was this decline in early childhood mortality that would have supported, perhaps even stimulated, the reduction in marital fertility which, just like scarlet fever mortality, declined everywhere and quickly.

Perhaps it is time to draw a line under the McKeown interpretation and simply acknowledge that its greatest strength has proved to be its enduring ability to stimulate debate. In terms of the framework provided by figure 1.5, the balance of evidence now suggests that we should think in terms of contributions from b, a, d and then c in the nineteenth century and c plus d in the twentieth.[71]

---

[71] Campbell (1997) provides a valuable corrective for those who remain sceptical about the qualities of Victorian medical statistics and their use in the evaluation of public health reforms and also argues for the local initiatives approach. It should also be noted that not all economic historians are so critical of McKeown's approach to explanation via improvements in standard of living and especially nutrition; see, for example, Millward and Bell (1998) and Bell and Millward (1998).

9

The demographic consequences of urbanisation

Because England and Wales experienced rapid urbanisation whilst also having a strong urban–rural mortality gradient it is likely that mortality rates for the country as a whole would have been adversely affected merely as a consequence of population redistribution above and beyond any deterioration that may also have occurred in the life chances of particular groups of citizens. While the general causes of urban growth and urbanisation are rather well known, the demographic consequences of urbanisation have received far less attention.[1] In an attempt to draw together and summarise some of the salient features of Victorian demography this chapter considers the effects of urbanisation on mortality. It develops a simple model of the consequences for life expectancy of the long-term redistribution of population from rural to urban areas as well as illustrating some of the effects of suburbanisation in and around London.

First, we have to establish the broad pattern of urban growth and urbanisation in nineteenth-century England and Wales. Given the substantial volume of existing published research this should be a relatively simple matter. Tables 9.1 and 9.2 illustrate two complementary versions of what is known. Table 9.1 is based on census data post-1801 and takes a minimum population size of 2,500 for the definition of a town and thus the extent of urbanisation; that is, the percentage of the national population living in urban places. On this definition England and Wales was approximately one-quarter urban by 1751, half by 1851 and three-quarters by 1901. Table 9.2 takes a different line. Here London is treated as a separate category and not simply a town with a population over 100,000, while large towns outside London are defined as having populations in excess of 100,000 and small towns as having populations

---

[1] See, for example, de Vries (1984) and Lawton (1989).

between 10,000 and 100,000. The minimum population threshold for an urban place is set, therefore, at a higher and rather more realistic level considering the nineteenth-century experience of urban growth. Either way, it would be safe to conclude that half the population of England and Wales was living in distinctly urban places by the early 1850s. Here we shall use table 9.2 as the basis for estimating mortality measures for urban and rural settlement categories.[2]

However, it will be obvious that simply taking the size of a place in population terms is a rather arbitrary way of distinguishing between localities that are in functional terms largely non-agricultural and those where agriculture dominates. It is also important to recognise that the choice of spatial units will affect urban–rural classifications and population densities. The latter will vary according to the inclusion of built-up areas within the district or parish. In earlier chapters we have used the 614 districts of England and Wales to show variations in nuptiality, fertility and mortality, and have drawn out some of the differences between urban and rural districts, especially in terms of mortality, by using measures of population density. It would be helpful to use that material again here as a way of assessing the level of mortality in settlements of different sizes. However, as will be clear from figure 9.1, while population density probably offers a simple yet reasonably reliable guide to whether a district was largely urban or predominantly rural it does not correspond exactly with population size. For example, districts with population densities in excess of 1,000 persons per square kilometre may have populations of between 20,000 and 300,000. Although for a substantial majority of the 614 districts there was a close association between population density and size, these tend to be the less populous rural districts, many of which experienced depopulation during the second half of the nineteenth century.

The point is taken a stage further in figure 9.2 which illustrates the associations between population size and population density, and life expectancy at birth among the districts in the 1850s. On this basis one might expect the inhabitants of a non-metropolitan district with a population of 10,000 to have an average life expectancy at birth of 47.8 years and one with a population of 100,000 to have an average life expectancy at birth of 38.5 years at mid-century. In the 1890s the

---

[2] There is an extensive literature on the problems of measuring urbanisation in England and Wales. See Williams (1880) and Lawton (1978). Pooley and Turnbull (1998) provide an excellent summary of recent work on internal migration in nineteenth-century Britain, following up and extending the earlier work of Cairncross (1953) and Friedlander and Roshier (1966).

Table 9.1. *Percentage of the population of England and Wales living in towns and rural areas, 1701–1951*

Year	Towns 2,500–10,000	Towns 10,000–100,000	Towns over 100,000	All towns	Rural
1701	5	2	11	18	82
1751	6	6	11	23	77
1801	10	13	11	34	66
1851	10	19	25	54	46
1901	9	25	44	78	22
1951	1	16	55	72	28

Source: F. M. L. Thompson, 'Town and city', in F. M. L. Thompson (ed.), *Cambridge Social History of Britain, 1700–1950, Volume 1* (Cambridge University Press, 1990), table 1.1, p. 8.

Table 9.2. *Probability distributions of the population of England and Wales among categories of urban places arranged by size*

Decade	London	Over 100,000 Large towns	10,000–100,000 Small towns	Rural residual
1701–10	0.1055	0.0000	0.0262	0.8683
1751–60	0.1084	0.0000	0.0556	0.8360
1801–10	0.1112	0.0125	0.1251	0.7512
1811–20	0.1135	0.0329	0.1280	0.7256
1821–30	0.1170	0.0540	0.1429	0.6861
1831–40	0.1207	0.0761	0.1633	0.6399
1841–50	0.1272	0.1009	0.1840	0.5879
1851–60	0.1359	0.1324	0.1969	0.5348
1861–70	0.1422	0.1647	0.2096	0.4835
1871–80	0.1458	0.1981	0.2251	0.4310
1881–90	0.1464	0.2315	0.2407	0.3814
1891–1900	0.1427	0.2727	0.2515	0.3331
1901–10	0.1324	0.3050	0.2588	0.3038

Sources: 1701 and 1751: based on de Vries, *European Urbanization, 1500–1800* (London: Methuen, 1984), pp. 270–71; 1801–1901: based on C. M. Law, 'The growth of urban population in England and Wales, 1801–1911', *Transactions of the Institute of British Geographers* 41 (1967), p. 141, with the addition of probabilities for London from the *Population Censuses of England and Wales*.

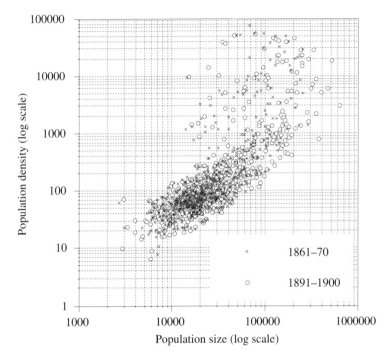

Figure 9.1. Relationship between population density (persons per sq. km) and population size among the 614 English and Welsh districts

equivalent figures would have been 54.1 and 46.3 years.[3] As far as the settlement-size categories defined in table 9.2 are concerned, these estimates can only offer very broad indications of the sorts of mortality levels that might have applied at the time.

In order to derive estimates of the average level of mortality experienced by people living in each of the settlement categories shown in table 9.2 for each of the decades of the nineteenth century it is also necessary to have mortality series for England and Wales and, if possible, direct estimates for some of the individual categories, London perhaps. For the 1840s onwards these can, of course, be based on the Registrar General's *Decennial Supplements*, but for earlier decades whichever mortality measures are selected they are bound to be less exact. Table 9.3 uses life expectancy at birth in years (e_0) and the childhood mortality rate ($1,000_5q_0$, CMR) to measure mortality; the former because it

---

[3] Estimates based on regression analysis over 589 non-metropolitan districts. Table 5.3 gives the regression coefficients for the association between life expectancy at birth and population size for all 614 districts.

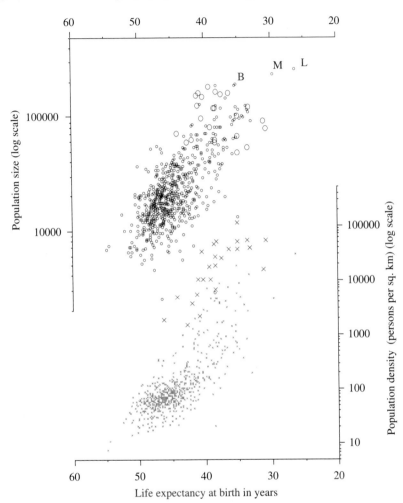

Figure 9.2. Relationship between population size, population density and life expectancy at birth among English and Welsh districts, 1851–60
Note: The larger circles/crosses indicate the 25 London districts. L – Liverpool, M – Manchester, B – Birmingham districts.

provides the best general single number index that is also age standardised and the latter because while childhood mortality is an important component of overall mortality there are known to be interesting differences between their trends which may be expected to have had a bearing on the course of changes in urban–rural mortality differentials.[4]

[4] The quality of the data from which these series were constructed was discussed in chapter 2.

Table 9.3. *Estimates of life expectancy at birth and childhood mortality for England and Wales and London*

Decade	England and Wales		London		
	e_0	CMR	e_0	IMR	CMR
1701–10	38.5	276	*18.5*	*355*	*553*
1751–60	39.0	262	*20.1*	*335*	*530*
1801–10	40.3	261	*35.0*	*190*	*310*
1811–20	41.1	257	*36.0*	*175*	*303*
1821–30	41.0	259	*36.9*	*168*	*285*
1831–40	40.7	264	*36.9*	*160*	*290*
1841–50	40.4	280	36.7	163	317
1851–60	41.1	290	38.0	155	320
1861–70	41.2	289	37.7	162	323
1871–80	43.0	263	40.4	158	282
1881–90	45.3	239	42.6	152	265
1891–1900	46.1	244	43.7	160	261
1901–10	50.9	197	49.4	128	201

Note:
The derivation of the series is discussed in the text. The least reliable estimates are shown in italics.
Source: England and Wales: Wrigley *et al.* (1997), tables 6.1, 6.3 and A9.1 for 1701–10 to 1831–40, and Registrar General's *Annual Reports* and *Decennial Supplements* for later decades.
London: based on Laxton and Williams (1989), figure 7, and Landers (1993), figure 5.3 and table 5.4 for 1701–10 to 1831–40, and Registrar General's *Annual Reports* and *Decennial Supplements* for later decades.

For the period before civil registration, the national estimates have been derived from the most recent run of the inverse projection model reported by Wrigley *et al.*[5] These show that for England and Wales life expectancy at birth changed only slowly during the first half of the nineteenth century, that there was even a nominal decline in several decades, but that after the 1860s life chances began their long-run improvement which accelerated in the early twentieth century and has slowed down only in recent decades. The series of childhood mortality rates for England and Wales rely on the estimates of total infant mortality rates and legitimate early childhood mortality rates (ECMR, $1,000_4q_1$) based on the pooled results of 26 family reconstitution studies. While

---

[5] Wrigley *et al.* (1997), especially chapter 8, 'Reconstitution and inverse projection', and appendix 9. It is assumed that their estimates for England can be used to stand for England and Wales.

the family reconstitution IMR series correspond rather well with those implied by inverse projection as well as matching up with the civil registration series in the middle of the nineteenth century, there is good reason to suspect that ECMR may have been under-estimated for the early decades of the nineteenth century.[6] The CMR series for England and Wales in table 9.3 make some allowance for this, but they still do not have the standing which can now be accepted for the e_0 series. The case of London is very different. There the eighteenth-century Bills of Mortality have been used to estimate infant mortality rates and from these it is possible to make some informed guesses about the prevailing level of both childhood mortality and life expectancy at birth. For example, Landers has estimated that London's IMR for the 1750s was of the order of 335 and that this would correspond to a life expectancy at birth of 20.1 years.[7] Since Model West level 1 ($e_0 = 20.0$) gives an IMR of 366 and a CMR of 532, while Model North gives an IMR of 320 and a CMR of 522 it seems reasonable to conclude that in terms of general demographic experience if IMR is about 330 then CMR will be 530 and life expectancy at birth will be at or about 20 years. By the early decades of the nineteenth century, IMR estimates again based on the Bills of Mortality give far lower rates, as much as half those of a century before. The implication would be that London's life expectancy at birth rose by perhaps 15 years in half a century. Fortunately, these estimates for the 1820s and 1830s tie in reasonably well with the measures based on civil registration data for the 1840s and 1850s as well as Farr's London life table of 1841.[8]

It seems most likely that the mortality estimates reported in table 9.3 will be the subject of revision in the future, especially those for London, but they are nonetheless the most reliable and consistent currently available.[9] Figure 9.3 sketches the timepath for life expectancy at birth and

---

[6] Wrigley *et al.* (1997), p. 259.

[7] Landers (1993), table 5.4, p. 171, and Landers (1996). See also Laxton and Williams (1989), figure 7.

[8] Farr's life table for London in 1841 first appeared in the Registrar General's *Fifth Annual Report for 1841*. Its characteristics and merits were considered in chapter 2; see especially figure 2.12. It seems possible that the 1841 life table for London under-estimated the level of early age mortality, although CMR appears to be at an appropriate level.

[9] The implications of London (with 11 per cent of the population of England and Wales) having such high levels of mortality have still not been fully explored in terms of the demography of the eighteenth century. For example, if London's CMR was 553 in 1701–10 and that for England and Wales was 276 then that for the rural areas would need to be somewhat lower, say about 250. This would mean that for small towns (2.62 per cent of the population) CMR would need to be 22 (using equation 9.1). In fact, York's CMR was closer to 422 and that for Bristol and Norwich was about 405. This would indicate that London's CMR is an over-estimate, the consequence of having to use Bills of Mortality, or that London's experience and importance have not been taken

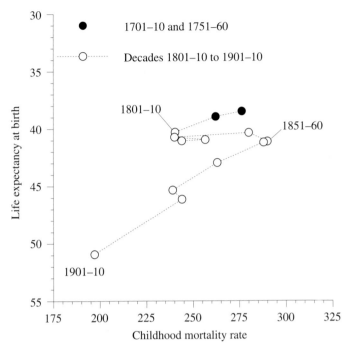

Figure 9.3. Timepath for the changing relationship between childhood mortality and life expectancy at birth, England and Wales, 1801–10 to 1901–10
Source: See table 9.3.

the childhood mortality rate for England and Wales. It offers a simple means of identifying the critical periods of change and stability, and of illustrating the consistency of at least some of the measures given in table 9.3. The most interesting period is that in the middle decades of the nineteenth century when childhood mortality appears to have increased temporarily, but there was also some slow improvement in life expectancy at birth. Thereafter both measures confirm that mortality declined, although there was an increase in childhood mortality between the 1880s and 1890s.

Assuming that the material in tables 9.2 and 9.3 is reasonably reliable, it will also be possible to estimate series of mortality measures for each of the settlement categories by using the weighted mean. The following

fully into account in creating the national series from material in the parish registers of villages and small towns. Largely for this reason, no attempt has been made here to estimate CMRs for the settlement categories in the 1700s or the 1750s. I am grateful to Dr Chris Galley for letting me use his York data; see Galley (1998).

equation may be used to derive mortality measures for large towns (LT), small towns (ST) and the rural areas (R), given some direct estimates of those for London (L) and England and Wales (EW) (from table 9.3) and knowledge of the magnitude of the weights (w_1 to w_4) (from table 9.2). The four weights are probabilities and sum to 1.0.

$$EW = Lw_1 + LTw_2 + STw_3 + Rw_4 \qquad (9.1)$$

A further constraint is provided by the observation that the level of mortality will conform to the progression: $LT > ST > EW > R$. It must be emphasised that this method of component estimation in which the mortality experienced by England and Wales is thought of as the weighted mean of its urban and rural parts can offer little more than a guide to the varying mortality levels experienced by those components. Additional supporting evidence is also needed, although this may only be available for particular periods and for individual, and thus potentially unrepresentative, places.

The first attempt to develop a model of this kind began with the assumption that, on the basis of a comparison of census years rather than decades, life expectancy at birth in England and Wales did not go into decline during the first half of the nineteenth century.[10] The second attempt, this time using decade means, assumed that e_0 was constant at 41 years for six decades between 1811 and 1870.[11] On the basis of new estimates from the inverse projection model and more detailed work with the Registrar General's returns, it now appears more likely that there was some reversal in life expectancy during the middle decades of the nineteenth century. This has been summarised in table 9.3 and becomes the basis for a new run of the weighted mean model. This version also differs from the first in being more tightly constrained by estimates for London and by being more ambitious in considering both childhood mortality and two decades in the eighteenth century.

Table 9.4 reports the results of the model's latest run, and the series for 1801 to 1910 are also illustrated in figures 9.4 and 9.5. It must be remembered that for any one decade, equation 9.1 has three unknowns

---

[10] Woods (1985), especially table 1, p. 646.
[11] Szreter and Mooney (1998). Szreter and Mooney (table 6, p. 104) provide new estimates of life expectancy at birth for the large towns over 100,000 in the decades 1821–30 to 1891–1900 (see table 9.4). For the 1820s and 1830s, they are 35 and 29 taken from the experience of Glasgow estimated for those decades. They assume that, first, the Glasgow estimates are reliable and, secondly, that Glasgow can be permitted to stand for the combined experience of Liverpool, Manchester and Birmingham, the large towns of England and Wales. For the 1840s e_0 is given as 30 years based on a complicated weighting procedure. For the 1850s and subsequent decades Szreter and Mooney's estimates of e_0 converge with those given by Woods (1985), table 3.

Table 9.4. *Estimates of life expectancy at birth and childhood mortality rates for categories of urban places arranged by size, England and Wales*

Decade	Life expectancy at birth				Childhood mortality rate			
	London	Large towns	Small towns	Rural	London	Large towns	Small towns	Rural
1701–10	18.5		26.2	41.3				
1751–60	20.1		27.5	42.2				
1801–10	35.0	32.0	34.2	42.2	310	300	279	250
1811–20	36.0	32.5	35.3	43.3	303	295	268	246
1821–30	36.9	32.7 *35*	36.2	43.5	285	302	275	248
1831–40	36.9	32.6 *29*	36.3	43.5	290	304	281	250
1841–50	36.7	32.0 *30*	36.0	44.0	317	341	310	252
1851–60	38.0	32.3 *34*	37.2	45.5	320	358	320	255
1861–70	37.7	33.0 *34*	38.0	46.5	323	355	310	248
1871–80	40.4	36.6 *38*	41.4	47.7	282	295	277	235
1881–90	42.6	39.0 *40*	44.0	51.0	265	269	249	205
1891–1900	43.7	39.6 *42*	44.8	53.5	261	282	257	196
1901–10	49.4	46.3	50.5	56.5	201	219	198	173

Note:
See text for a discussion of the derivation of the series. Szreter and Mooney's (1998), table 6, estimates are shown in italics.

(LT, ST and R) and that it can only be solved by inserting plausible mortality measures which, when multiplied by the appropriate weights and summed with Lw_1, equal the mortality measure for England and Wales. There are other possible solutions and it is also the case that L and EW could have been misjudged, especially for decades prior to the 1840s.

The simple conclusion drawn from the first run of the model in 1985 was that '[i]t was not necessary for the urban environment to deteriorate in order for mortality decline to be retarded; rapid and substantial urbanisation was sufficient'.[12] In contrast, Szreter and Mooney argue that life expectancy at birth in the large towns of England and Wales declined substantially and that 'during the second quarter of the nineteenth century there was a serious deterioration in the standard of living of the growing proportion of the population recruited into the urban industrial workforce; and furthermore that this trend of deterioration, although halted in the late 1850s and 1860s, was not significantly reversed until as late as the 1870s and 1880s'.[13] Szreter has extended this argument to incorporate what he calls the four Ds of disruption, deprivation, disease and death which are said to be the possible negative consequences of rapid economic growth.

There is, therefore, no doubt as to the basic nature of the relationship between rapid economic growth and the health of the industrial working population in Britain during its classic period of industrialisation. For that ever-increasing proportion of the population directly involved in urban and industrial expansion, despite gradually rising disposable income, there appears to have been a marked deterioration in average life expectancy during the second quarter of the nineteenth century and persisting into the third quarter.[14]

This was a period of 'political and administrative breakdown' which was 'specific to the fast-growing industrial towns and cities, rather than to towns in general', with environmental deterioration related to growing income inequalities, rural immigration and residential segregation.[15]

The new run of the model indicates that these conclusions probably need to be revised. First, there is now more reason to expect urban mortality to have increased during the middle decades of the nineteenth century given that these were the cholera years, the period especially affected by migration from Ireland and, perhaps of greatest significance, the years in which the infectious diseases of childhood appear to have been at their most lethal.[16] Szreter and Mooney are broadly correct in

---

[12] Woods (1985), p. 649.   [13] Szreter and Mooney (1998), p. 110.
[14] Szreter (1997), quoted from p. 701.   [15] Szreter (1997), pp. 701–2.
[16] We have already seen how annual mortality rates increased in the late 1840s and early 1850s (figure 5.7) and how early childhood mortality was at or above the level of infant

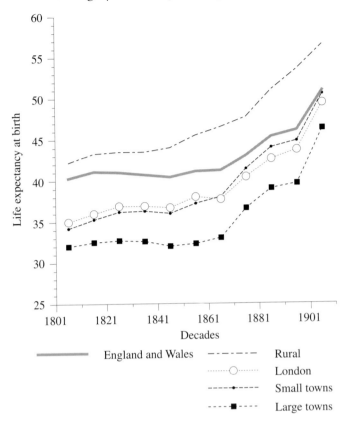

Figure 9.4. Estimates of life expectancy at birth for urban and rural
areas of England and Wales, 1801–1910
Source: See table 9.4.

their view that health conditions deteriorated in at least some of the
large towns, especially Liverpool, Glasgow and Manchester, in the
second quarter of the nineteenth century. But the rise in mortality, which
was probably smaller than their estimates suggest, was due more to
particular circumstances than to general administrative deterioration.

mortality in some years of the 1850s and 1860s (figures 7.1 and 7.2). Both Irish immigration and higher childhood mortality are likely to have affected the large industrial
towns, especially Liverpool, Manchester and Glasgow in the west of Britain. For
Glasgow, Cage (1983) has argued the case for deteriorating living conditions but also
widening income differentials between the skilled and unskilled in the first half of the
nineteenth century. See Neal (1998), but especially ÓGráda (1999), table 3.11, p. 112,
where he attempts an estimate of the consequences of excess mortality due to Irish
immigration in England in the 1840s.

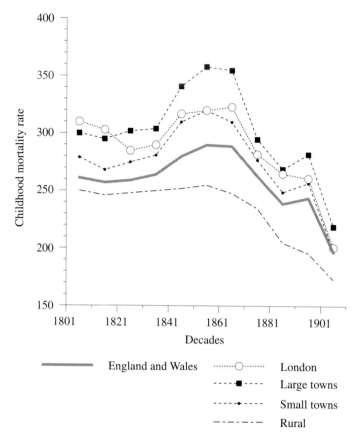

Figure 9.5. Estimates of childhood mortality rate for urban and rural areas of
England and Wales, 1801–1910
Source: See table 9.4.

Secondly, there are more reasons for us to be aware of London's special
position and experience as something more than just a very large town.
Research by urban historians now tends to characterise the metropolis
as a collection of small towns, some of which were inner city slums and
others suburban commuter settlements enjoying all the benefits of
modern sanitary technology and spacious living.[17] Thirdly, and with
particular reference to the interpretation developed by Szreter and

---

[17] This is the picture sketched by Dyos and Reeder (1973), and echoed in Luckin and
Mooney (1997). While these authors are correct to emphasise the importance of residential segregation by social class, the process of selective migration involved need not
necessarily lead automatically to deteriorating conditions in the slums although it certainly will lead to the separation of social groups.

Mooney, economic historians are becoming more cautious about their use of the term 'standard of living' and especially about whether it should include expressions of mortality and morbidity, and thus how measures of mortality like life expectancy at birth might provide indicators of levels of living as well as being associated with more traditional economic measures such as per capita income. For example, is it legitimate to conclude that because mortality in urban areas was increasing then the average living standard of the urban population was deteriorating and vice versa?[18] Finally, there is also a growing interest in health and mortality inequalities and not just levels and trends. Of particular concern here are the changing differentials between the experiences of urban and rural places, more especially the ever-expanding large cities and the depopulation-prone countryside.[19]

The run of the model reported in table 9.4 and illustrated in figures 9.4 and 9.5 suggests that in terms of life expectancy at birth London did indeed experience a level of mortality comparable with that of the small towns, although after the 1860s mortality in the former was higher than in the latter. In the large towns mortality decline stalled and went into reverse from the 1830s to the 1860s; thereafter life expectancy improved considerably, although it stalled again in the 1890s. In the rural areas life expectancy at birth improved decade-on-decade, but here too the pace of improvement was much slower in the 1820s to 1840s. Turning to the childhood mortality rate, we can now see what has helped to create at

[18] This is an intriguing problem. We know that in pre-industrial England medium-term changes in real wages and life expectancy at birth were not closely linked, and that during the past fifty years substantial improvements in life expectancy in Third World countries have occurred even though per capita incomes have not increased. There will be many influences on the level of mortality over and above wages, incomes and the material conditions of everyday life. It is unreasonable, therefore, to use mortality as an index of economic living standards although it is quite proper to include health and mortality in some broader concept such as levels of living. By this means we shall be able to confront the apparent paradox that while levels of living judged by mortality were not only superior in rural England to those in the towns, real wages were also lower in the countryside and subject to decline. In the towns, increases in mortality and real wages could coincide although this would not necessarily mean that reduced life expectancy would indicate a serious deterioration in the standard of living. This problem, aspects of which are more semantic than economic or demographic, is discussed at greater length by Williamson (1990), and most recently by Crafts (1997), Feinstein (1998) and Sen (1998). Hanley (1997) identifies the concept of 'physical well-being' which is closely tied to health and housing, but distinct from standard of living which is associated with income and its distribution (p. 11). As she points out, the two may not always move together especially in the early stages of industrialisation (p. 181).

[19] Some of this concern with inequalities and differentials was inspired by the Black Report of 1980. These issues have been discussed in terms of occupational and social class mortality in chapter 6.

least one important element in the course of the life expectancy trend. Childhood mortality increased in the middle decades of the century, but this was especially pronounced in the case of large towns. In the rural areas childhood mortality increased very slightly until the 1850s, thereafter it went into decline.

There is, of course, no simple way of checking these results other than by reference to inherent plausibility and internal consistency, but there should be a close correspondence between the two mortality measures when equation 9.1 is solved independently for each. Figure 9.6 shows the association between life expectancy at birth and childhood mortality using the Model West pattern as a guide. In general there is a high degree of correspondence. The only possible exceptions are the large towns for the first four decades of the nineteenth century. If the childhood mortality rate has been correctly estimated at 300 then life expectancy at birth might be higher at 35–36; but if the latter is correct at 32–33, then childhood mortality should be higher at 350 in order to match Model West. However, it is more likely that both measures are at about the right order of magnitude and that in the large provincial towns e_0 was being depressed by higher mortality at some ages over five than one might expect from the childhood experience alone.[20]

One of the most revealing ways of examining the results of this exercise is to compare trends in the urban–rural mortality differential measured by the difference in years between the estimated life expectancy at birth for rural areas and for large towns. These series are shown in figure 9.7. It now appears that the original version of the model overestimated the extent to which the gap between the mortality experienced in urban and rural places narrowed during the second half of the nineteenth century. Closer examination of Farr's law in chapter 5 and of disease environments in chapter 8 suggests that there was a general decline in mortality after the 1860s and before 1901, although the urban places did experience faster mortality decline in the early decades of the twentieth century linked especially with the decline of infant mortality. The urban–rural mortality gap was probably greater in the middle decades and in the 1890s than in the first four decades of the nineteenth century. As far as urban–rural inequalities in health and

---

[20] This is pure speculation, of course, but it would be consistent with the heavy mortality of pioneer adult migrants to the large towns. It is also a function of the problems encountered in estimating life expectancy for small areas from decennial census data (the at risk population) and continuous civil registration data (deaths by age); recent migrants who die in the city may be missed by the former, but not the latter. Also, see Woods (1993) for a discussion on the variable relationship between overall mortality and mortality in childhood.

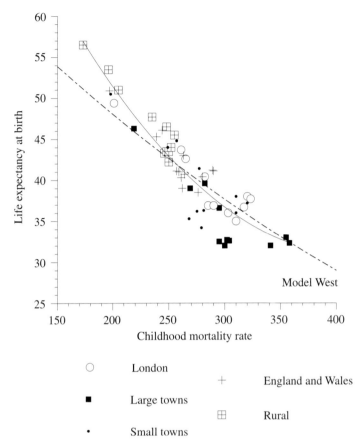

Figure 9.6. Variations in the relationship between life expectancy at birth and childhood mortality rate among estimates for urban and rural areas of England and Wales
Source: See table 9.4.

mortality are concerned, it seems that they either temporarily worsened or were maintained at between 10 and 13 years in terms of life expectancy.

The case of London is especially interesting because of its apparently anomalous low mortality. We have already seen something of this in earlier chapters as well as the differences in terms of nuptiality, fertility and mortality between the 25 districts of London, but it may also be instructive to take the ideas of Welton, Dyos and Reeder a stage further

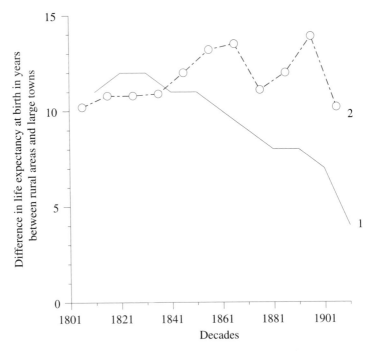

Figure 9.7. Differences in terms of life expectancy at birth between large towns
and rural areas of England and Wales
Source: 1: Woods (1985), table 3; 2: table 9.4.

and to consider the extent to which suburbanisation and mortality
decline were linked in and around the metropolis.[21]

This can be done quite easily by selecting the 25 London districts,
adjacent districts and districts which are in turn adjacent to those plus
a small number of additional districts all lying within 70 kilometres of
the centre of London. By this process 70 districts are chosen. For each
of these the mid-point is identified and its distance from the centre of
London is measured in terms of kilometres from the Temple which lies
on the western edge of the City of London.[22] Measures of population
size and density, and of mortality can thus be ordered purely in terms
of distance. The results of performing this exercise turn out to be
remarkably well ordered and clear-cut.

Figure 9.8 illustrates the process of suburbanisation and the

---

[21] Welton (1872) and Dyos and Reeder (1973). On the expansion of London, see also
Friedlander (1974). Unfortunately, the institutional mortality problem still poses problems for this analysis; see Mooney *et al.* (1999).

[22] See Clout (1991), especially chapter 7, pp. 84–107, on Victorian London, as well as Porter
(1994), especially chapter 9, '"The contagion of numbers": the building of the Victorian
capital, 1820–1890', and Wohl (1977).

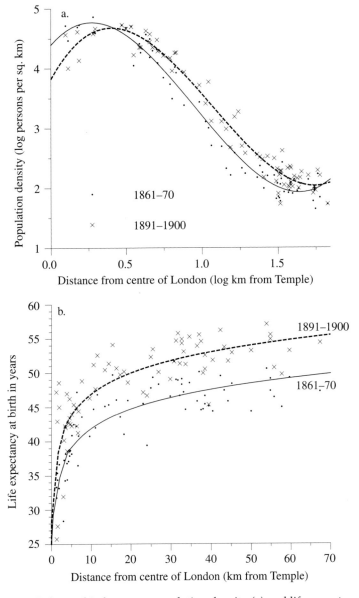

Figure 9.8. Relationship between population density (a) and life expectancy at birth (b) with distance from the centre of London
Note: 70 districts are included, 25 in London itself. All districts are within 70 kilometres of the centre of London.

continuing role of the Victorian metropolis as a 'demographic sink' within its region. Figure 9.8a shows, by comparing curves fitted to the double-log population density–distance relationship, how London's centre became increasingly depopulated between the 1860s and 1890s and the wave of suburban growth moved outwards.[23] From 3 to 50 kilometres from the centre, population density generally increased. Figure 9.8b shows again in strikingly simple terms how life expectancy at birth declined as the centre of London was approached. The districts with the very lowest levels, 35 years and less, were also the ones experiencing depopulation. Out beyond 3 to 5 kilometres, improvement in life expectancy at birth was generally five years and more.

While figure 9.8 gives some impression of population growth and redistribution it does not capture fully the extent of change in the urban system. This is done more effectively in figure 9.9. Here percentage population change and percentage change in life expectancy at birth are both plotted against distance from the centre of London. From this figure it is clear not only that suburbanisation meant the massive shift of population from inner to outer areas of London and beyond, but also that in this case increased population density was accompanied by improvements in life expectancy of 10 per cent on average between the 1860s and the 1890s. What is more, this percentage improvement applied to all districts from 3 to 70 kilometres, and under 3 kilometres there were many examples of districts with far higher percentage improvements. It appears from the evidence summarised in figure 9.9, first, that the average level of mortality experienced by London as a whole would have declined regardless of rapid suburbanisation; secondly, that even if life expectancy at birth had not changed from its 1860s level but suburban expansion into the lower mortality districts had occurred, then average London mortality would also have declined; and, thirdly, that whilst population redistribution and mortality decline operated independently to a large extent, the latter was undoubtedly assisted in the inner districts by the outflow of people and the reduction of housing density.

[23] Clark (1951) attempts to fit the following negative exponential relationship to the density–distance function: $PD_d = PD_0 e^{-bd}$ where PD_d is 'density of residential population outside the central residential zone' at distance d from the centre, PD_0 is interpolated population density at the centre, and b is a constant expressing the slope of the relationship. This function was once the subject of much debate among urban geographers. In passing, Clark shows that in 1801 London did not have a lower population density inner city, but that this had begun to develop by 1841 and was clearly evident in 1871, 1901, 1921 and 1939. Here figure 9.8a uses a third-order polynomial with both population density and distance logarithmically transformed to better capture inner-city depopulation.

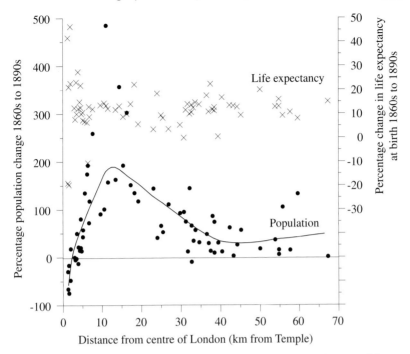

Figure 9.9. Percentage population change and percentage change in life expectancy at birth with distance from the centre of London

Indeed, it would appear that the example of London and its surrounding districts helps to reinforce a general point which this and earlier chapters have often illustrated: namely, that above and beyond the changing economic, social and epidemiological conditions which would affect an area, the flow of population also exerted an especially important influence. The flow from high to low mortality districts that accompanied suburbanisation had just as profound effects, albeit in more limited areas, as the movement from low to high mortality areas which accompanied the initial phase of rapid urbanisation. Even allowing for endogenous changes in those various conditions, it is still legitimate to argue that urbanisation and suburbanisation alone would have exerted profound, and contradictory, influences on the national rate of mortality. It is also necessary to be cautious about the extent to which these conditions were autonomously driven. Was the mid-nineteenth-century increase in urban mortality due more to the vicissitudes of epidemiology than the plight of Irish migrants, or were deteriorating economic conditions chiefly to blame? The balance of evidence presented here favours the epidemiological and the demographic rather than the economic, but the question is clearly a complicated one which will require far more attention before it can be answered fully.[24]

The problem that we have considered in this chapter clearly has a bearing on the wider debate concerning the effectiveness of public health interventions in the late nineteenth century. The mortality gap between the large towns and the rural districts was not narrowed, but life expectancy at birth did improve nonetheless. The Victorian sanitary revolution helped to ameliorate the worst conditions of urban life sufficiently for the water- and food-borne infectious diseases to have been reduced in impact. Had these measures not been put in place, conditions would certainly have deteriorated and the rural–urban gap would have widened even further. Of course, as we saw in chapter 8, the significant decline of such diseases as scarlet fever and pulmonary tuberculosis was not restricted to urban districts, and neither was overwhelmingly the result of preventive public health measures or even an improved standard of living. In these circumstances the sanitary revolution did well to maintain the gap which was not substantially reduced until the twentieth century, although mortality did begin its secular decline.

[24] For example, according to Feinstein's (1998) recent estimates, real weekly earnings in Britain improved by less than 30 per cent between about 1780 and the mid-1850s. Set against this improvement we have the negative effects of greater dependency with increased fertility (minus 10 per cent); the poor housing and inadequate public health associated with the urban way of life (minus 3 to 8 per cent); and reduced poor relief expenditure (minus 2 per cent). 'The combined effect of these three factors would thus reduce any improvement in the standard of living of the average working-class family in the United Kingdom between the 1780s and the 1850s from about 30 per cent to somewhere in the range of 10 to 15 per cent' (p. 650). The jury is still out, but at least it has recognised the importance of evidence on demographic issues especially urbanisation and epidemiology.

10

The transformation of the English and other demographic regimes

Whilst it seems that Adolphe Landry was the first to use the term demographic regime in the 1930s there still exists no simple, formal definition. Those who now use the concept appear to have the following in mind. It is applied to the long-term stability of demographic structures and the different ways in which nuptiality, fertility, mortality and migration may combine to create relatively slow population growth. The analogy is drawn from politics rather than ecology or the stages of development–modernisation; it implies order, stability, continuity, but also suggests variety among regimes that population growth may be regulated in a number of different ways each one of which can produce similar outcomes in terms of growth rates. This form of definition does raise a number of problems, however. Are demographic regimes to be thought of as conscious creations specifically designed to maintain a favourable balance between population and resources in the long term? And, if so, how are the different combinations of regulatory mechanisms created and adjusted, and to whose benefit is the regime ordered? Are some of the components of demographic regimes always more important than others? For example, does mortality set the parameters to which nuptiality and fertility merely adjust? How are demographic regimes transformed? To continue the political analogy, are they subject to revolutionary change, to complete overthrow during short periods of dramatic upheaval which are externally induced perhaps, or is slow internal adjustment more likely?

This penultimate chapter attempts to define some of the key components of the English demographic regime in relation both to other European examples and to some drawn from non-European societies. It also considers the important questions of what may have been unique and what was common about England's regime, and how these influenced its transformation in the nineteenth century. It will also be concerned with the relationship between change and variation, with time and space, as well as returning to the vexed question of whether it is ever possible to draw lessons from the historical experience. But first we must consider in a little more detail the elements that combine to create recognisable demographic regimes.

Table 10.1 provides a check list of the elements of historical demographic regimes.[1] It may be used in the following way. Taking the example of England in the early modern period first, here the marriage pattern was part of the wider structure described by Hajnal as the north-west European marriage pattern, the rules for which were summarised in table 1.1. Marriage (A1–10) is monogamous; it tends to take place in the mid- to late twenties for males and females, with grooms on average two years older than brides; formal divorce is either impossible or extremely rare; remarriage, especially of widows, is common; permanent celibacy among a substantial minority of both males and females is also common. The nuclear or elementary form of family or household arrangement predominates, although many households may also contain living-in servants; residence after marriage is normally neolocal and thus there is a close tie between marriage and the formation of a new and largely independent household. The developmental cycle is of relatively minor importance since co-resident families rarely contain more than one married couple, but they may be multi-generational. Usually the partners themselves make the decision whom to marry, but where property transfers are involved parents may restrict the choice of potential partners and under these circumstances a dowry may be involved. The purpose of marriage is mutual support, the creation of an effective production unit, reproduction and, among the propertied, inheritance.

The birth of children (B1–5) is influenced by the frequency of intercourse, which is unknown, although judging by the considerable extent of bridal pregnancy and the moderate level of illegitimacy, sexual activity is certainly not unknown before marriage. Fecundity appears to have been at least as high as in other west European populations while maternal breastfeeding is the norm for nine to twelve months (and perhaps even longer among a minority). There are no obvious sexual taboos, apart from those relating to incest. There is no particular pattern of reproductive behaviour intended to space or to limit childbearing, and there is no strong gender bias in the preference for children. In terms of effective replacement (C1–5), abortion is not widely practised nor is infanticide, and although children are sometimes adopted or aban-

---

[1] See tables 1 and 2 in Howell (1986) for an alternative approach to population control behaviour.

doned as foundlings these are uncommon events. Childhood mortality is only moderately high compared with societies in which wet nursing is common or breastfeeding is not practised at all.

As for mortality (D1–8), the conditions associated with crisis mortality are rare and their long-term demographic effects are negligible. The background level of mortality is strongly influenced by certain infectious diseases which are especially damaging to the life chances of the young and the old, although between the ages of 15 and 40 tuberculosis is of special importance, and combined with the effects of maternal mortality there is also excess female mortality in this age group. There is a strong and persistent urban–rural mortality gradient with life expectancy at birth as much as twice as high in the villages as in the larger towns and in London. There are also some differences between social groups, but these are not as great as those between environments. Poor nutrition along with the infectious diseases represents a constant challenge to health whilst, in general, morbidity increases with age during adulthood.

Finally, migration (E1–5) is likely to affect all of the other elements. It is especially selective in terms of age, but a majority of young men and women are involved in the circulatory migration associated with service. This is a mobile society with largely unrestricted movement, an active land market, a large landless yet rural population, and rising urbanisation in which the role of the metropolis is especially important. There is also the possibility for trans-Atlantic migration. The reasons for migrating are many and varied, but migration is rarely generated by subsistence crises although labour may be laid off or displaced. Migration for personal betterment or improvement of the household's economic position is dominant.

Outside England, but still within north-west Europe, there were of course distinctly local variations on a similar theme. In northern Scotland, first the clan and afterwards the crofting system, together with the Highland clearances, created and then destroyed a sequence of different demographic regimes. In Scandinavia subsistence crises played a far more prominent part. In the Low Countries, urban growth and high levels of urbanisation also affected the wider level of mortality whilst acting as a magnet for rural migrants. Further afield, but still west of the St Petersburg–Trieste line, other regional societies had their own distinctive variants. In northern France it was common to use wet nurses, and both infant mortality and fertility were consequently higher than in England. In southern Germany infants were either not breastfed or breastfed and weaned very early, and this had similar consequences. In Italy the mean age at marriage for spinsters was less than 20 while for

Table 10.1. *The elements of historical demographic regimes*

A. Marriage	B. Children	C. Effective replacement	D. Mortality	E. Migration
(1)	(1)	(1)	(1)	(1)
• monogamy	• intercourse	• childhood mortality	• 'acute': crises	• selection
• polygyny	(2)	(2)	–war	–age
• polyandry	• fecundity	• abortion	–famine	–gender
(2)	–diet	(3)	–subsistence	–quality
• age/sex	–lactation	• infanticide	–flood	(2)
(3)	(3)	–gender	–drought	• place
• divorce	• sexual taboos	–parity	–natural disaster	–rural
(4)	(4)	(4)	–epidemic	–urban
• remarriage	• spacing	• have adopted	(2)	–distance
(5)	–abstinence	• sell	• 'chronic': endemic	(3)
• celibacy	–postpartum	(5)	(3)	• duration
(6)	(5)	• abandon	• age	–permanent
• form	• stopping		(4)	–temporary
–nuclear/simple	–birth control		• gender	–seasonal
–stem	–family limitation			–circulatory
–joint/grand	–gender/parity ideals			

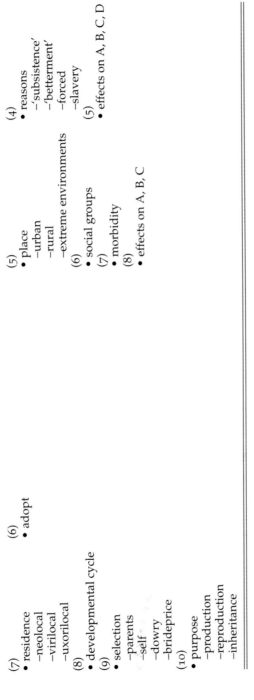

(7)
- residence
  - neolocal
  - virilocal
  - uxorilocal

(8)
- developmental cycle

(9)
- selection
  - parents
  - self
  - dowry
  - brideprice

(10)
- purpose
  - production
  - reproduction
  - inheritance

(6)
- adopt

(5)
- place
  - urban
  - rural
  - extreme environments

(6)
- social groups

(7)
- morbidity

(8)
- effects on A, B, C

(4)
- reasons
  - 'subsistence'
  - 'betterment'
  - forced
  - slavery

(5)
- effects on A, B, C, D

Note:
- contrasts (urban/rural, social hierarchy, ideals, norms, proscriptions, restrictions).

bachelors it was over 25. There was also far greater emphasis on female virginity, a severe social reaction to illegitimates whose fate it was to be abandoned to the foundling hospitals. But despite these regional and local variations, the similarities between the English demographic regime and those of its near neighbours in western Europe were greater than the differences, especially because of the dominance of the former's distinctive marriage pattern and the rules for the formation of households which underpin it.

As we saw in chapter 1, attempts have often been made to compare western Europe, represented by England, with China in the anticipation that an understanding of demographic differences would assist an explanation of differences in economic performance. England had the preventive check with simple structure households and the low pressure demographic system, but China had to cope with the positive check and a high pressure system since there the preventive check could not operate while the joint household prevailed (Hajnal's rules 2a and 2b).[2] Malthus, for example, offers an account in which China epitomises the worst excesses of misery and vice despite the fertility of its soil and the healthiness of its climate. It is the 'extraordinary encouragement to marriage' in China, coupled with the practice of partible inheritance, that has created such a large population and led to its abject poverty. The misery associated with poverty and repeated famines, 'perhaps the most powerful of the positive checks', obliges mothers to expose or destroy many of their children: 'Relative to this barbarous practice, it is difficult to avoid remarking, that there cannot be a stronger proof of the distresses that have been felt by mankind for want of food, than the existence of a custom that thus violates the most natural principle of the human heart.'[3]

We now know a lot more about the demography of China in the Ming and especially the Qing dynasties, and we are now able to sketch the

---

[2] See table 1.1 and footnote 1.25.

[3] Malthus (1993), p. 31 (Malthus's first *Essay* of 1798). See also book I, chapter XII of the second *Essay* of 1803, 'Of the checks to population in China and Japan'. Malthus also remarked on how hard-working the Chinese peasants were, how modest and reserved the women were, and the importance to the preventive check of the considerable number of celibate priests. It is as interesting to trace the sources Malthus used to tell his story of misery and vice as it is to note the means by which it has been perpetuated. For example, Tawney (1932): 'It is true that Chinese habitat and doctrine put a premium on the growth of population, which appears to western eyes unnatural and artificial. Sentiment, hallowed by immemorial tradition, makes it a duty to leave sons, and the communism of the patriarchal family dissociates the production of children from the responsibility for their maintenance. Hence prudential restraints act with less force than elsewhere; and population, instead of being checked by the gradual tightening of economic pressure on individuals, plunges blindly forward, till whole communities go over the precipice.' (p. 104)

broad outlines of traditional China's demographic regime in such a way that it can be compared with that of England in the early modern period, again using the framework provided by table 10.1.[4] In terms of column A, marriage was monogamous, but concubines could be kept by the rich, and divorce and remarriage were possible for men. Marriages took place at an early age, less than 20 years for women, and were almost universal. They were arranged by a go-between acting for the parents, but some element of veto by potential partners may also have been possible. Residence after marriage usually took the virilocal form, but children of either sex could become co-resident upon adoption as prospective partners even prior to betrothal and this may have involved cases of the uxorilocal form. While the joint or grand multi-generational multi-couple family system was regarded as the ideal, it might only be achieved among the rich. The developmental cycle ensured that extended households were always prone to fragmentation so that average household sizes would have been, as in England, rarely over five although there would have been a minority of very large households composed of co-resident kin as opposed to living-in servants. Under column B, fecundity may have been lower than in England, the consequence of a poorer nutritional status among women, and breastfeeding certainly tended to be prolonged, partly in consequence. It is also likely that spacing and stopping behaviour were deliberately practised, but the birth of children may have been spaced partly as an indirect consequence of prolonged lactation and partly as the result of sexual abstinence. Lee and Campbell have estimated the total marital fertility rate for rural Liaoning to be 6.3, that is, 1 to 1.5 children fewer than has been found in England.[5] Gender ideals certainly favoured the birth of sons. As far as columns C and D are concerned, the level of natural childhood mortality appears to have been high, and there were great famines, disastrous floods and devastating epidemics which also kept adult mortality at a high level. The estimates made by Barclay *et al.* for China in 1929–31 give e_5 as 33.5 for males and 33.2 for females, while those for e_6 derived by Lee and Campbell for Liaoning in the mid-Qing suggest 43.8 and 37.2 years.[6] Gender- and parity-specific infanticide was

---

[4] As we shall see, this is neither a simple nor an uncontroversial task. Much of the account has to be based on a relatively small number of studies, especially Barclay *et al.* (1976), Hanley and Wolf (1985), Lee and Campbell (1997), Lavely and Wong (1998), Lee and Wang Feng (1999a, 1999b).

[5] Lee and Campbell (1997), p. 90, Wrigley *et al.* (1997), table 7.1. Barclay *et al.* (1976), table 5, also have an adjusted TMFR of 6.3. Zhao (1997) has found only modest levels of TMFR among women born between 1914 and 1930, leading him to speculate about the long-standing nature of parity and gender fertility control in China.

[6] Barclay *et al.* (1976), table 13; Lee and Campbell (1997), table 4.1. The former use indirect methods of demographic estimation with data from the Land Utilisation of China

certainly practised, but to what extent and under what circumstances remain matters for debate.

For example, Lee and Campbell argue that there were in fact two sets of positive checks in Qing China: the one always associated with Malthus (famine–disease–war), and the other relating to infanticide both in the Imperial Lineage and among the peasants of the north-east. 'The positive check in the Chinese demographic system ... could be an active, rational, individual-level response to changing circumstances, as well as a passive population-level response to exogenous crises, such as famine and disease.'[7] And, 'In rural Liaoning, peasants regarded infanticide as a routine form of post-natal abortion by which they could choose the number and sex of their children in response to a variety of short-term and long-term circumstances.'[8] These two types of positive check were matched by two types of preventive check. Although marriage was early and universal for women, of whom there was a relative shortage, the first birth interval was rather long, four years on average, and the mean age of mothers at their last birth was relatively young, only 34 years in Liaoning. Further, Lee and Campbell point out that if Liaoning did prove to be typical of other rural communities then China's demographic regime would turn out to have been both efficient and complex. Both marriage and effective fertility could be managed in a highly ordered fashion; there would have been far more demographic options than in the English regime where only moral restraint and migration appear possible. But Liaoning is not China, just as Colyton is not England nor Crulai France.

Several points emerge from this brief comparison of the demographic regimes of England and China using table 10.1. First, the framework provided by table 10.1 and the general concept of the demographic regime do offer useful ways of describing the key elements in demographic structures, of focusing on those aspects which are of special

footnote 6 (*cont.*)

Survey, 1929–31. They also give estimates of e_5 for the north of China as 40.0 for males and 36.9 for females. Notestein and Chiao (1937) give estimates of e_5 at 47.6 for males and 47.0 for females in years for China as a whole (table 28). Liaoning is a rural community near Shenyang City in the far north-east of China. In England in the late eighteenth century, e_5 was closer to 48–50 years; see Wrigley *et al.* (1997), table 6.27.

[7] Lee *et al.* (1994), quoted from p. 411. Their analysis suggests that members of the lower nobility may have killed as many as a quarter of their daughters, but that for those who survived, life chances improved considerably during the mid-Qing.

[8] Lee and Campbell (1997), p. 82. These peasants killed a tenth to a quarter of all daughters. As we have already seen, Malthus fully appreciated the potential of infanticide as a positive check although he would have been surprised to find that it was not only a symptom of poverty, but also an active means of family planning used to enhance economic and social position.

importance, and of allowing broad comparisons to be made. It is also possible to use table 10.1 as a way of highlighting those aspects of which we are most ignorant, generally the elements listed under column E. It is now appreciated that just because marriage for women is early and universal this does not necessarily mean that fertility must be high. Similarly, just because the joint family is the preferred type of family structure this does not mean that average household size will actually be greater than in those societies favouring the simple type. Secondly, table 10.1 helps to encourage a sense of diversity and variety in demographic regimes by indicating that equivalent rates of population growth may result from a wide variety of alternative combinations, and that there has been no one simple route to demographic regulation. Thirdly, the comparison of England and China outlined above also allows Malthus's *Principle of Population* to be placed in sharper focus. Its position as a moral principle, as well as an economic and demographic one, is emphasised. If the killing of babies should never be used to control family size and limit population growth then, although China's demographic regime may prove to have been more efficient than England's, in Malthus's language it will always be cast as morally repugnant, founded on vice, and a constant source of misery. Fourthly, in spite of the desire to marry early and to form joint families in complex households, in China other effective means of demographic regulation were widely available, including sexual abstinence and infanticide. The means to check population growth were present, therefore. This should give us reason to question the argument that demographic regulation via nuptiality acted as a powerful and superior means of keeping population growth in balance with resources while encouraging income accumulation and permitting a general rise in living standards. If population control is a precondition for industrialisation and modern economic growth, then China, as well as Europe, should have qualified in the eighteenth century. Effective demographic regulation may have been necessary, but it was not sufficient of itself to stimulate rapid economic growth.[9] Fifthly, and finally, table 10.1 and the comparison of England and China helps to focus particular attention on the elements in column C: effective fertility, or the importance of not only fertility and all its social, economic and proximate determinants, but also mortality

---

[9] In their introduction, Hanley and Wolf (1985), pp. 1–12, speculate using Hajnal's (1965) concept of the European marriage pattern that Japan was essentially European in its marriage pattern and that this was the source of its economic 'take-off', that Japan was to China as north-west Europe was to eastern Europe. This appears to overstate the case, to rely too much on differences in just one element of the demographic regime while ignoring similarities in the cumulative effects of others. Japan's position and the importance of the population control argument are introduced in Smith (1977).

in early life. It encourages the further speculation that the factors controlling effective fertility will hold the key to an understanding of any historical society's demographic regime, and that by focusing on the interplay between fertility and childhood mortality we may also come to a fuller understanding of how those regimes have been or are being transformed. This will be the subject of the remainder of the chapter.[10]

If table 10.1 offers an effective device for describing and comparing the structures of demographic regimes, we now require a means by which their most obvious parameters may be represented, one which will also allow us to trace the course changes have taken. Figure 10.1 offers a simple yet flexible solution. It merely graphs a convenient measure of fertility – the total fertility rate (TFR) – against a measure of mortality, but that particular aspect of mortality capable of establishing effective fertility – the childhood mortality rate for ages 0–4 (CMR). As a guide to population growth it also shows those levels of TFR and CMR which in terms of Model West would generate natural growth rates of 0 per cent (stationary population) and 2 per cent per year. To illustrate its use, figure 10.1 shows the distribution of 129 countries and 53 African provinces in or about 1990.[11] Many Western countries now experience fertility at or below the replacement level while childhood mortality is also exceptionally low, less than 10 in most cases. But even in 1990 all of the 53 provinces of ten countries in East and Central Africa fall above the 2 per cent growth curve because TFR is between 5 and 8 while CMR is still between 50 and 250. It is unlikely that TFR would have been much higher than 8 for substantial periods in the past, but it is quite possible that CMR was above 250 and TFR could have been lower although, even at 6, CMR would have had to be 500 (half of all live born infants would not survive to their fifth birthday) for zero population growth to be reached. Figure 10.1 appears, therefore, to be capable of representing variation and change, and of expressing the effects of a society's position in TFR–CMR space for the rate of population growth it is likely to experience.

It is now possible for us to return to the experience of nineteenth-century England and to examine its position in terms of both the notion

---

[10] The advantages of combining the fertility and early age mortality in the construction of demographic theories is beginning to receive renewed attention in the academic literature; see, for example, Mason (1997) and Reher (1999), especially figure 1, p. 15.

[11] The national data in figure 10.1 are taken from *The State of the World's Children, 1994* (Oxford: Oxford University Press for UNICEF), tables 1 and 5. In many cases TFR and CMR are merely approximations. The data for the 53 African provinces are taken from various Demographic and Health Survey reports. The provinces are: Kenya (7), Uganda (5), Ruanda (5), Burundi (6), Tanzania (7), Malawi (3), Zambia (9), Zimbabwe (7), Botswana (1), Namibia (3).

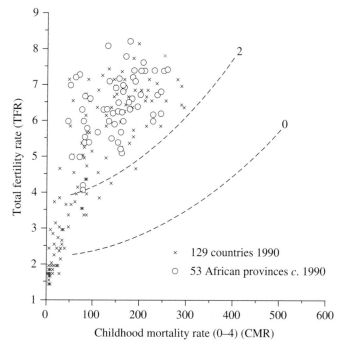

Figure 10.1. Contemporary international variations in fertility and
childhood mortality *c.* 1990
Note: The curves labelled 0 and 2 represent annual natural population
growth rates of 0 and 2 per cent from Model West.

of demographic regimes, and especially effective fertility, and the
graphical framework introduced in figure 10.1. We need to examine
both the timepath of TFR–CMR change in the long run and, as far as is
possible, regional or local variations about the national mean. This is
attempted in figure 10.2. Here we have the TFR–CMR timepath for
England in the decades 1581–90 to 1981–90, with the 11 decades 1801–10
to 1901–10 emphasised, plotted over the distributions for the 614 districts of England and Wales in 1861–70 and 1901–10. Figure 10.2 helps to
combine and re-emphasise three important points raised in earlier
chapters.

Although it is sometimes claimed that England experienced two
demographic revolutions, or even that the revolution began towards the
end of the eighteenth century, figure 10.2 serves to remind us that it was
only in the second part of the nineteenth century that new demographic
territory was entered in terms of lower fertility and lower childhood
mortality. It also focuses attention on the mutually supporting and

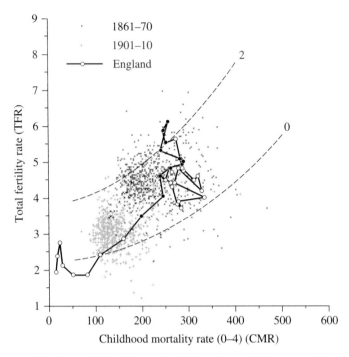

Figure 10.2. Variations in fertility and childhood mortality among the districts
of England and Wales, 1861–70 and 1901–10
Note: The timepath for England shows decades from 1581–90 to 1981–90. The
decades of the nineteenth century have been emphasised. See figure 10.3 for
comparison.

sustained downward movement in TFR–CMR. The causes of their joint
movement hold the key to any full understanding of the transformation
of the English demographic regime. Finally, figure 10.2 also reflects the
importance of variation as well as change. The demographic map of
England and Wales was in some senses more differentiated in the
Victorian era than it was before or since, but nuptiality and childhood
mortality varied especially by locality in ways that are both meaningful
and significant for the course and pace of change.[12]

   The experience of England has often been compared with that of
other European countries, France and Sweden in particular, but as we
have already seen in this chapter broader contrasts may prove more
interesting as a way of highlighting the prominence of the joint downward movement of fertility and childhood mortality in the transforma-

---

[12] See chapter 1, p. 13 and footnote 27.

tion of demographic regimes. While England is unique in having such a long record of demographic series, there are a small number of non-European countries or regions for which demographic measures have been estimated beginning at times sufficiently close to the period in which the 'traditional' demographic regime was in operation for its transformation to be sketched in broad terms. China is of course a candidate, starting from the position outlined by Barclay *et al.* for 1929–31, but Japan post-1920 and Berar (India) post-1881 may also be included.[13] Figure 10.3 traces the four TFR–CMR timepaths, including England. There are some interesting similarities and differences which encourage further speculation. For example, in the cases of Berar and China there is clear evidence that childhood mortality declined while fertility remained largely unchanged and that only in recent decades have both series fallen together. But in England and Japan both series eventually declined together.

For Japan in 1920 we are also able to examine the geographical distribution among the prefectures, and for earlier periods to speculate with some assurance about likely trends. The scatter for the 46 prefectures is shown in figure 10.4. Three – Tokyo, Kyoto and Osaka – lie closer to the 1 or 0 per cent growth curves than the 2 per cent and as such they may provide a clue to the location of the original slow or zero growth position occupied by Japan in the eighteenth and early nineteenth centuries. Hayami, for instance, has argued that the national rate of population growth only began to accelerate after the 1870s and that between the 1820s and 1870s it was closer to 0.3 or 0.4 per cent per year.[14] In earlier decades he suggests that population growth was perhaps 0.2 per cent in western Japan, but that there was stagnation or even decline in the east and north, thus giving a close to zero average for the country as a whole. The large urban centres may also have been subject to stagnation or decline in the mid-nineteenth century. This raises interesting questions about Japan's original position: was it closer to England or to China and Berar? And were there local and regional variations? The balance of evidence suggests that Japan in the Tokugawa period should be located between Berar and England, that childhood mortality was substantially

---

[13] For China: Barclay *et al.* (1976), Banister (1987), especially table 8.2, and Riley and Gardner (1997), especially table 2.3; for Japan, Taeuber (1958), especially tables 90 and 112 (CMR has been estimated from IMR and the timepath shows the years 1920–43, 1947–55 and then 1992); and for Berar, India, Dyson (1989a), especially the appendix pp. 191–96 (annual rates have been converted to decennial means and CMR has been derived from IMR). See also Dyson (1997). It must be emphasised that the comparison of these series is fraught with difficulties and should be regarded as speculative at best.

[14] Hayami (1986).

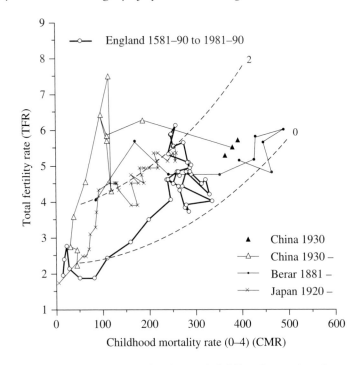

Figure 10.3. Timepaths for fertility and childhood mortality changes in
selected populations
Note: See text for explanation.

higher in Japan than in England although fertility in both was moderate.[15] This would place Japan at about position *a* in say 1820, but if childhood mortality proved to be much higher generally, or in certain places,
then position *b* would be more appropriate.[16]

The case of Berar, now part of Maharashtra State in central India,
which had a population of 2.7 million in 1881 and 6.9 million in 1981 also
merits special attention since its experience may have mirrored that of
India as a whole. Dyson has identified three stages: 1881 to 1921, 1921
to 1947, and post-independence.[17] In the first, mortality was high and

---

[15] See, for example, Jannetta and Preston (1991), Saito (1992) and Cornell (1996) on problems of establishing the background level of natural childhood mortality and thereby
the demographic significance of infanticide.

[16] Jannetta and Preston (1991), table 2, give CMR estimates around 450 for the early nineteenth century and 360 in 1916–35 for their Gifu prefecture villages. Not all Japanese
specialists find these high levels convincing. See Hanley (1997), p. 183, and Saito (1997).
Saito prefers IMR estimates of 176 for the late Tokugawa and 153 for the early Meiji
(table 8.5).　　[17] Dyson (1989b).

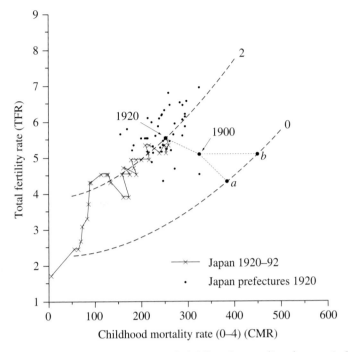

Figure 10.4. Timepaths for fertility and childhood mortality changes in Japan
Note: See text for explanation.

variable with massive mortality peaks in 1900 and 1918 related to famine and influenza, respectively, but after 1921 food was more easily imported into Berar at times of shortage, and certain of the preventive health measures began to have some collective impact in driving child-hood mortality down.[18] Fertility was only moderate – 5.3 live births per woman on average – mainly because breastfeeding was widely prac-tised and prolonged, it was unusual for widows to remarry, and sexual intercourse was avoided during the post-partum period and was likely to be severely curtailed once a woman became a grandmother. If Dyson's analysis is correct then the downward trend of mortality in Berar after 1921 was at least initially exogenously driven by imported food and imported public health measures, but the social and cultural

---

[18] There is still considerable debate about the causes of mortality trends in India gener-ally before 1947. For example, Guha (1991) has suggested that for the inter-war years 'what we observe is not a change of demographic regime but a reversion to normalcy after a period of cataclysms' (p. 384). If this did prove to be the case then, in terms of figure 10.3, 'normal' Berar would be placed even closer to 'traditional rural' China.

practices that affected reproductive behaviour remained in the family domain, locally determined.

The timepaths and patterns of variation sketched in figures 10.2 to 10.4 suggest a number of general observations concerning the structure and transformation of demographic regimes.

The highly appealing notion that there have been high and low pressure demographic systems, both of which achieved low population growth rates – the former because fertility and mortality were both high and the latter because they were both low or at least lower, with the high pressure dominated by the positive check while the low pressure enjoyed the benefits of the preventive check – now needs to be challenged. If anything, our four examples suggest strong similarities in terms of fertility despite their different marriage patterns and household formation rules. Mortality, and especially mortality in childhood, appears to have been the differentiating characteristic. But this was only partly the result of crises – famines, epidemics, wars – and probably had even less to do with population pressure. In China and Japan, infanticide made childhood mortality higher, and in Berar the first decades of British rule together with the increasing commercialisation of agriculture made the population more vulnerable. In other words, in at least two of our examples the high level of childhood mortality was at least partly the consequence of a particular pattern of behaviour, one which was possibly the most efficient regulator of family size and structure. It is no longer reasonable to conclude that only the low pressure system was endogenously controlled or that it was only this system that could take advantage of low fertility and slow long-term population growth to enhance per capita incomes. However, those societies which have been called high pressure would have encountered certain particular problems if childhood mortality was still at a high level when effective sanitary technology and medical science were imported or when government policy took a hand in controlling traditional family behaviour. In either case mortality would respond by declining rapidly, thereby accelerating population growth. Timing, policy and technology transfer are therefore of special importance.

While it is obvious that western Europe, and north-western Europe in particular (including England), did have a unique form of marriage pattern and set of household formation rules, it is now far less clear just how important these were in purely demographic terms. In terms of demographic change the point at which both fertility and childhood mortality began their mutually reinforcing downward course is of special importance. In England this first began in the 1870s and was accentuated during the 1890s and 1900s. To begin with it was largely the result of epidemiological and behavioural changes, although public health policy did have a role; changes were generated in a largely endogenous way. In Japan between the 1920s and late 1940s fertility and childhood mortality kept in balance. Only after 1948–49 and the repeal of the Eugenic Protection Law did they move downward together in a way that affected population growth rates. Government policy, medical technology and the behaviour of individuals combined from that time to establish a very rapid decline. In China the equivalent transformation may be dated from the late 1960s and there too government policy was to the fore. In Berar the course of joint downward change is probably just beginning. What was special about England in demographic terms was its early commencement of the joint decline, largely without policy interventions. Unlike Japan and China this could be achieved without a period in which childhood mortality alone was in decline. If the societies of England and north-west Europe were unique in demographic terms then their lack of dependence on artificially high levels of childhood mortality was surely of at least equal significance compared with their distinctive marriage pattern. Without this dependence the demographic revolution could occur earlier and be initiated without external policy or technical interventions.

For England and Japan the story of massive demographic transformation has drawn to a close although the consequences remain, and in China too the concluding chapter appears to have begun. But, based on past trends, what can we say of the future demographic course of those populations currently experiencing rapid population growth, rates of 2 per cent per year and upwards? The safest answer to this question is very little.[19] Let us take a particular example. Figure 10.5 shows the TFR–CMR timepath for Kenya, 1940–93, set against the distribution for 53 African provinces in or about 1990 taken from figure 10.1.[20] In Kenya

[19] Knodel and van de Walle (1979), reprinted in Coale and Watkins (1986), pp. 390–419, argue a generally positive case especially in terms of the need to recognise the importance of cultural variations for fertility decline and in policy, but in policy terms they counsel the need to promote family planning programmes since the onset and spread of fertility decline in Europe were to an extent independent of socio-economic conditions. There are obvious dangers in attempting to draw lessons from the past, among them 'West was first and must therefore be best'. In their study of high mortality societies, European historical demographers probably learn far more by looking to the well-documented experiences of Asia and Africa today.

[20] The derivation of the TFR and CMR estimates used in figure 10.5 is explained in Brass and Jolly (1993); see also Gould (1995). The estimates for 1940 have been based on the 1948 census.

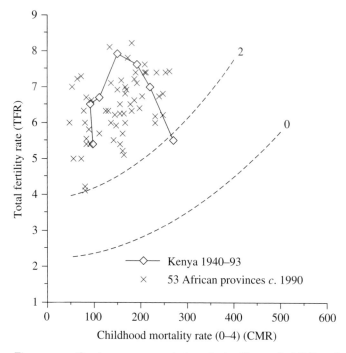

Figure 10.5. Contemporary variations in fertility and childhood
mortality among African provinces and the timepath for Kenya
Note: The timepath for Kenya links estimates for the years 1940, 1960, 1967,
1977, 1987, 1991 and 1993.
Source: Brass and Jolly (1993), table 2.5, p. 20; Gould (1995), table 1, p. 206.

too childhood mortality appears to have gone through a period of
decline since the 1940s, but fertility increased up until the late 1970s and
went into decline thereafter until, by the early 1990s, it had reached the
same level as in the 1940s. Childhood mortality has shown clear evidence of recent increase, the result of HIV/AIDS. Kenya's position in
demographic space in 1940 was similar to England's in the early nineteenth century. Kenya's childhood mortality was brought down largely
by the application of medical knowledge and the establishment of a
basic health infrastructure while fertility has also shown some response
in recent decades to the development of family planning programmes.
On the face of it there would appear to be no shared demographic experience between Kenya and England, but figure 10.3, for instance, might
suggest at least one broad similarity. In both cases there was not, nor

could there be, a demographic revolution with the traditional demographic regime transformed until fertility and childhood mortality declined together. Only in these circumstances can effective fertility be reduced in a sustainable way.[21]

---

[21] It remains to be seen whether, because of HIV/AIDS, Kenya and much of sub-Saharan Africa will experience a new variant of demographic change, but it is unlikely that fertility decline will be sustained for long while childhood mortality continues to increase.

11

Conclusions and unresolved conundrums

In his preface to *Eminent Victorians* Lytton Strachey remarks that 'The history of the Victorian Age will never be written: we know too much about it. For ignorance is the first requisite of the historian – ignorance, which simplifies and clarifies, which selects and omits.'[1] Victorian demography is a similarly vast topic with its own ocean of material; it too is likely to defy the comprehensive survey, the definitive statement. While Strachey's own approach has a certain poetic elegance, a sample of four individuals, even the inhabitants of four counties, would not have been sufficient for us to begin the task of reconstructing the pattern of demographic change during a period of sixty to seventy years in a population which grew from 16 to 36 million, although he is certainly correct about the need for simplification and selection. This concluding chapter is devoted, therefore, to the subject of ignorance and the ways in which it may be better appreciated and used constructively. It begins by considering three problematical areas where recently it has been thought that long-standing demographic conundrums are now resolved, or nearly so.

It still seems most likely that a relatively short-lived upswing in fertility rather than a sharp downturn in mortality was responsible for initiating the modern growth of population in England during the late eighteenth and early nineteenth centuries, and that fertility was responding mainly to a rise in nuptiality. In one sense the principal conundrum in eighteenth-century demography appears to be resolved, but why did this nuptiality-led change occur on such a scale when it did, and why was it a temporary phenomenon?[2] It might be assumed that because there was a close fit, albeit lagged in time, between the reduction in real wages and the decline of nuptiality in the late seventeenth

---

[1] Strachey (1918), p. vii.   [2] See Wrigley (1983, 1998), but also Razzell (1998).

century the rise in nuptiality in the late eighteenth century should be linked to a rise in real wages – i.e., that the economic restraints on marriage were simply relaxed so that more young people could marry and marry younger. But, according to the Phelps Brown and Hopkins real wage index used by Wrigley and Schofield, there was a sharp downturn which reached its nadir in 1801, just at the time when fertility was starting to peak.[3] Similarly, the proletarianisation of the labour force and the consequences of industrialisation in general should have increased the opportunities to marry and thus to form financially independent households, although for most this would also have entailed migration to the towns, but it might not be expected that this process would generate such a medium-term cyclical movement in nuptiality. The essentially geographical, as opposed to temporal, analysis offered in chapter 3 helps to shed some new light on this problem. It emphasises the point that marriage is essentially a local affair; partners generally select from within their community and their choice is affected by availability and by economic and social constraints. The sex ratio among young adults is especially important as are the restrictions imposed by service, whether agricultural or domestic. For national levels of nuptiality to increase substantially the following would be required: (1) a general expansion of economic opportunities especially for men; (2) a reduction of the proportion of young women in service; and (3) balanced sex ratios in most localities. If only (1) applied and this via urban-industrial growth then (3) would certainly be distorted with early and universal marriage for women in some areas, but postponement in many others. If all three applied then in some areas earlier marriages would be encouraged by new opportunities while in others the institutional restraints limiting marriage would be removed. Such an interpretation is complicated by the need to distinguish not only between the experiences of two forms of regional labour markets, but also the circumstances of men and women. This requirement poses special problems for empirical work which has tended to focus on one or other of the geographical extremes – country or parish – and to think of the labour force either as a unified whole, undifferentiated by gender, or as predominantly male. The critical question thus becomes: in England during the late eighteenth and early nineteenth centuries, in a period of declining real wages and labour reorganisation, did young women marry earlier as a way to ensure their survival? We are still some way off answering this question.

Similarly, we are still uncertain as to the reasons for the decline in marital fertility that began during the second half of the nineteenth

---

[3] Wrigley and Schofield (1981), appendix 9.

century and this despite the findings of the Princeton European Fertility Project. But unlike the nuptiality-induced rise in fertility in the late eighteenth century, a phenomenon apparently unique to England, the decline of marital fertility was a secular process which manifested itself on a European scale. Although chapter 4 is primarily concerned with the experience of England and Wales it nonetheless exemplifies the state of our ignorance. For example, we cannot be sure of the means by which fertility was limited, although it seems likely that non-appliance methods, particularly abstinence and *coitus interruptus,* were most important. Spacing and stopping worked together; they were not alternatives and there were many accidents. Now that we are able to trace the variations and changes among the districts of England and Wales, rather than having to rely on the registration counties, it is even more obvious how rapid and widespread the decline of marital fertility was. People living in places with very different economies and local societies – from the remote rural to the metropolitan – appear to have behaved in similar fashions. Certainly there were different starting levels, but by the 1890s a majority of couples must have been engaging in some form of behaviour to reduce the number of children born. The key to understanding this complex of processes is surely the changed attitudes of partners and especially the ability of women to affect their own reproductive behaviour by avoiding pregnancy. This came rather more easily to the liberal-minded Fabians than to the wives of miners, but even here the pattern of lower fertility had been established by the First World War. Arguments still persist over the extent to which this was a fractured and fissured process or a mass movement more akin to an electoral landslide, the extent to which social or neighbour copying was involved, and the roles husbands played in forgoing their conjugal rights.[4] But at least the contours of variation are now far clearer, even though the 'why then?' and 'how?' problems remain.

A third conundrum which may appear close to resolution is concerned with the relative contributions of class and place to mortality and fertility variations.[5] In the case of mortality, chapters 5 and 7 provide numerous examples of how environment affected life chances in the Victorian period, while chapter 8 demonstrates how important the geographical concentration of certain cause of death patterns might be. But the discussion of occupational and social group variations, especially in adult male mortality in chapter 6, also illustrates the fact that there were important differences associated with type of employment. It is also significant that between the 1860s and 1911 the occupational mortality dif-

⁴ Szreter (1996).   ⁵ Garrett *et al.* (forthcoming).

ferentials were, if anything, exacerbated as adult life expectancy improved. The same could be said of life expectancy at birth and infant mortality among the districts. Although mortality began to decline, differentials between places and occupations were not initially reduced. There was also some disparity between the experiences of fathers and their young children, so the level of mortality experienced by one generation cannot be used to predict exactly that in another. This leads us to the conclusion that as far as the relative contributions of place and class are concerned the balance of influence will change with age group. Among infants and young children environment was undoubtedly of greater significance than parental class, although the contribution of the latter, especially as it operated via poverty and knowledge of best child-care practices, was far from negligible. Among adult males, however, the matter of whether type of employment or place of residence was of more significance still remains obscured. For many occupations the latter was virtually determined by the former and we should not be surprised to encounter confounding effects, but for others the trade or profession always exposed people to risk wherever they were conducted. In these cases, dangerous environments simply added another hazard to which all members of the family would be exposed. Two further issues conspire to thwart the place or class debate. First, and as we saw in chapter 6 for members of the medical profession, there would have been considerable differences within many occupations in terms of skill, status, remuneration and exposure to risk, and these would have had a bearing on morbidity and mortality. Secondly, there were aspects of the general process of mortality decline that were place-specific, but as chapter 8 has illustrated there were also at least two important causes of death, scarlet fever and pulmonary tuberculosis, that appear to have declined everywhere. The reduction in tuberculosis mortality in particular had a significant bearing on the decline of mortality in early adulthood in such a way that all occupations and social groups benefited. In taking this discussion further with respect to mortality, we need to be especially sensitive to the multi-faceted nature of the problem in which our perspective on the place and class debate will be affected by the extent to which we focus on variations or trends, children or adults, males or females.

It would, perhaps, be unwise to dwell exclusively on these three areas of continuing ignorance and uncertainty without setting them alongside others about which we can be more confident on the extent to which progress has been made – new knowledge added or old ideas challenged.

First, we should have renewed confidence in the statistical legacy of the Victorian General Register Office. The material published in the Registrar General's *Annual Reports* and *Decennial Supplements,* together with the population censuses, is capable of providing us with a detailed picture of the ways in which demographic patterns varied and changed, but especially those relating to mortality. Of course, demographers of the parish register period are justified in their claim that thanks to family reconstitution studies we now know more about certain aspects of the demographic behaviour of those living in the seventeenth and eighteenth centuries than we do of the Victorians. But it is to the Registrar General's returns that such demographers turn when they wish to check the plausibility of their findings, and it is still a moot point, as Lytton Strachey would readily have appreciated, whether it is better to know a lot about the actions of a few people than it is to know a little about everybody.[6] However, there are some areas in which civil registration lets us down and others where to use what is available requires some act of faith since it is impossible to evaluate its quality. The absence of information on age at marriage and maternal age severely limits our ability to describe in detail the full characteristics of nuptiality or to calculate age-specific fertility rates and their summary indices. This is and will remain a considerable lacuna in our ability to chart the decline of marital fertility. Even when researchers in England and Wales are placed on a par with those working on Scotland's population and given access to substantial numbers of individual birth, death and marriage certificates, it will still not be possible to overcome this problem, although several others might be tackled. The data on cause of death for districts published in the *Decennial Supplements* have now been used extensively both in *An Atlas of Victorian Mortality* and chapter 8. It is to be suspected that the accuracy of these data varied and changed between the 1850s and the 1890s, and was altered again by the introduction of a new nosology in the 1900s, but the source is so rich that it cannot be dismissed on these grounds alone. In chapter 8 it was used to illustrate the complex and varied nature of disease environments experienced by different localities in England and Wales, and to cast further doubt on the McKeown interpretation's emphasis on the importance of nutritional improvements as the prime mover in the secular decline of mortality. Without it we would not have been able to demonstrate just how sensitive the childhood diseases, especially measles, and the respiratory diseases were to variations in population density; how there appears to have been a threshold of population density above which mortality from the major water-borne diseases increased far less

[6] See Wrigley *et al.* (1997).

rapidly; and how mortality due to pulmonary tuberculosis was largely insensitive to the differences between urban and rural environments. Further, and equally important, it would not have been possible to show how geographically neutral was the decline of mortality from scarlet fever and pulmonary tuberculosis, thereby confirming in the case of the former and suggesting in that of the latter the importance of changes to the aetiologies of the diseases themselves rather than their responding to economic developments or policy interventions.

Second, it is now appropriate to question the value of that two-part guiding principle of demographic enquiry – systems and transitions – as it has been applied to England in the nineteenth and twentieth centuries. Although the 'rediscovery' of Malthus's *Principle of Population* has proved extremely important for demographers of the early modern period, its development in the form of ecological systems models which represent homeostatic adjustments has proved far less appropriate for studies of the nineteenth century. Nor can it be said that the demographic transition model and its related theory, at least in the form outlined by Notestein, provides either an accurate description or an adequate explanatory account of demographic change in England and Wales since 1750. For example, the process of industrialisation and urbanisation is more likely to have encouraged mortality to rise than to fall, at least in the short term, and appears to have had at best only a negligible influence on the secular decline of marital fertility. This does not mean that there was no demographic revolution, quite the contrary, but it began during the second half of the nineteenth century and was epitomised by the joint processes of family limitation and reduced childhood mortality. These were new and fundamentally different experiences which exemplify the transformation of the old demographic regime. Chapter 10 offers a brief outline of the varied characteristics of demographic regimes in general as well as providing some preliminary evidence on effective fertility using examples drawn from the experiences of Japan, China, India and Kenya. It argues for a more flexible approach to analysis of long-term demographic change, one that appreciates heterogeneity, cultural diversity, the synergistic relationship especially between fertility and childhood mortality, one that questions Europe's demographic superiority in having a low-nuptiality, low-pressure regime, and one that emphasises the point that there are multiple pathways to change, not just the European route. In terms of the experience of England and Wales, what appears to have been of particular importance was the changing attitudes to reproduction of Victorian women and the influence of certain specific epidemiological changes. The English regime was transformed, initially at least, in these areas which are still relatively neglected by demographic theory.

Third, what were the demographic roles of Victorian women? Chapters 3 and 4 draw particular attention to the critical parts women played in shaping the demography of Victorian England and Wales. This is partly for technical reasons: the measures of nuptiality and fertility used (I_m and I_g) relate exclusively to the behaviour of females and it is these indices that have formed the dependent variables in the various models constructed. In chapter 7 considerable attention was given to the characteristics of mothers, their age and whether they worked, for example, as well as the way they cared for their children, especially the importance of breastfeeding. Chapter 4 also provided some account of the rise in literacy during the nineteenth century, but especially the way in which more and more young women came to acquire some basic education. It demonstrated that there were regional and local variations in literacy at mid-century and that the differences between male and female literacy levels showed interesting geographical variations. It is tempting to attach too much significance to the rise of mass education, but there can be little doubt that it would have had the following consequences: the status and bargaining position of women would be raised in relation to men as the educational level of both rose and converged; the gap between the generations would be accentuated in the short term, with the young, on average, more accomplished, more susceptible to new ideas and behaviour, than the elderly. It is also the case that many demographers of Third World societies now regard investment in the education of females as the single most important measure that could be taken to encourage family planning and one of the most significant contributions to the health and welfare of children.

Fourth, perhaps it will now be possible to give epidemiology a more prominent place in work on the Victorian period. Ever since the publication of Charles Creighton's great compendium of epidemics it has been appreciated how important the comings and goings of epidemic diseases have been to the history of Britain, but only in recent years has it begun to emerge how disease environments were composed in the past, how certain diseases passed through cyclical phases apparently independent of human activity while others were affected by, for example, crowding, direct medical intervention or preventive measures. Several of the childhood infectious diseases were especially sensitive to the crowding effects of urban population growth. There is also strong evidence to suggest that mortality in early childhood passed through a cyclical upswing in the middle decades of the nineteenth century due partly to those effects, but principally to changes in the diseases themselves, especially scarlet fever. Chapter 9 illustrates the importance of this epidemiological wave and suggests that it had its greatest impact in the large towns of England and Wales. It helps to highlight, once again, the lethal nature of the urban environment above and beyond the well-known dangers associated with poor sanitation.

Fifth, what was the role of the State, both national and local, in altering Victorian demography? It is still not clear what the answer to this question should be. One of the State's new roles was outlined in chapter 2: it became increasingly concerned with the need to provide an accurate statistical account of the nation's population, but especially with the need to monitor trends in health and mortality. In large measure this was left to the General Register Office and its excellent Statistical Superintendents, although by the last quarter of the nineteenth century there were also scores of local Medical Officers of Health who were charged with the task of keeping accounts of mortality conditions in their areas. This wealth of data was used by local politicians and their officials to enact policies especially in respect to nuisances, housing and public health. The cumulative effect of these local initiatives has proved difficult to evaluate, but there seems every reason to believe that in London and the other large urban centres, places where mortality was at its worst, direct policy interventions did begin to bear fruit even during the last decades of the nineteenth century and certainly into the early decades of the twentieth century. McKeown, for one, was wrong to undervalue the power of these health and sanitation initiatives. The contribution of the national government is rather less obvious. Certainly it enabled, encouraged and then obliged local administrations to take action. It regulated the medical profession by establishing a national register and thereby raised the standing of doctors and the quality of their formal training. Via the Factory Acts it took halting steps to regulate the dangerous trades, although the effects of this legislation on the occupational mortality patterns shown in chapter 6 are far from clear. With the efforts of Sir John Simon, Sir Arthur Newsholme and Sir George Newman it began to build up its own monitoring and reporting schemes which built on the work of such pioneers as Sir Edwin Chadwick and Florence Nightingale. However, it could also be argued that it was not until 1911 and the National Insurance Act that the British government began to intervene directly in ways that would have a significant bearing on the life chances of its citizens wherever they lived.

Sixth, although there has been a tendency in this and other chapters to dwell on variations and changes in patterns and structures, it is also obvious that at certain key points the actions of individuals significantly changed the course of events or the ways in which we may see them.

The names of some important examples have just been mentioned, but there are others whose contributions were equally significant. Edward Jenner, Joseph Lister, Robert Koch and Louis Pasteur made vital discoveries which, by saving lives, contributed to demographic change. William Farr can be credited not only with overseeing the creation of a particularly large and efficient civil registration system, but also with founding the science of medical statistics through his analysis of the data collected. During his forty years as Statistical Superintendent he developed or refined some of the basic techniques for monitoring health variations, especially by using life tables and by defining healthy districts as a low mortality standard to which all areas might aspire. Farr also appreciated the need to identify differences and to compare environments, occupations and causes of death. Indeed it would be little exaggeration to claim that it is largely because of Farr's endeavours that we are able to create such a rich account of the demography of Victorian England and Wales, and especially the geography of demographic change. It is only to be regretted that he did not turn to the subject of fertility earlier in his career, but left it instead to his last publication.

These six sets of observations help to draw together some of the important points discussed in chapters 1 to 10. They may also help us to focus on certain specific issues that require further attention. These are problems that if they could be resolved would help to advance our demographic understanding in general, and our interpretations of the Victorian period in particular. Here are four examples.

Although the retreat of tuberculosis has been the subject of much research and not a little speculation, there still remain many unanswered questions about the causes of its decline in the nineteenth and early twentieth centuries, as well as its demographic and social impact. If it could be demonstrated conclusively that the disease's case fatality rate declined and that this was associated more with aetiology than improved human resistance then a number of important issues might be resolved or at least considered in a new light. The downward drift of adult mortality, especially between ages 15 and 30, in most occupations and districts could be seen as epidemiological in nature and not the result of improvements in the standard of living, particularly diet and housing. This would in its turn encourage further work on the way in which deaths may have clustered in certain households together with the possible links between maternal and child health. If the virulence of pulmonary tuberculosis among young women declined 'of its own accord' how would this have affected health and survival prospects at the foetal stage and after birth?

The effects of urbanisation and the ways in which demographic behaviour differs between urban and rural places has been one of the most important themes of this book. It was considered explicitly in chapter 9 in terms of how the process of urbanisation is likely to retard the rate of mortality decline in a society with a strong rural–urban mortality gradient. A simple model of the partial effects of population redistribution in these circumstances was outlined and its results compared. It would be interesting to make this model far more sophisticated so that it is capable of replicating a number of alternative situations in terms of the rate and pattern of urbanisation, as well as the shape of the mortality gradient. It would also be important to extend the time frame of the model so that it incorporated at least the eighteenth and twentieth centuries, and for the nineteenth made use of the cause of death data to explore further the underlying causes of the mortality gradient. Once such a model had been developed it could be used to simulate the effects of policy interventions, especially local sanitary and public health initiatives.

Does the process of demographic change, like that of economic growth, necessarily lead to the generation of inequalities? By using the 614 districts and the 71 occupations it has often been possible to observe the extent to which the degree of dispersion in a distribution, measured by the coefficient of variation for example, varied inversely with the mean. That is, as national fertility and mortality rates began to decline so the level of variation increased. This is an old question which while being partly a statistical problem, may also reflect the existence of leaders and followers in the decline of fertility or the presence of other elements of socio-economic inequality, such as access to new knowledge and public health infrastructure, in the case of mortality. Although the variance–mean relationship holds for both fertility and mortality, it may do so for rather different reasons. It is also likely that new enquiries into this problem would be assisted by taking a longer perspective since the level at which convergence begins to take place and inequalities are reduced as averages decline may be of special interest.

Woodrow Borah, the influential historian of native American societies, once gave an address entitled 'America as model: the demographic impact of European expansion on the non-European world'.[7] He was concerned with the creation of a global disease pool by European expansion and its particular impact on isolated populations. An equally convincing case could be made about the impact of the European model of demographic behaviour, especially that of England,

---

[7] Borah (1964).

and the ways it has been used not only as a device to assist understanding, but also as a template for predicting the future of other societies. It should now be appreciated that the demographic experience of Europe, and again especially England, was in most respects not normal. Mortality began to decline without the aid of effective medical intervention and fertility was limited without contraceptives. Drawing demographic lessons from the European past is a hazardous business, therefore. Rather than forcing parallels our enquiries need to focus on differences and their causes. In particular, it will be especially important to emphasise the experiences of women and children, their changing social roles and entitlements to health and security. In this respect at least there is a strong continuity between Victorian England and Wales and the less developed world today.

Bibliography

Aaby, Peter, Jette Bukh, Ida Maria Lisse and Aajon J. Smits, 'Severe measles in Sunderland, 1885: a European–African comparison of causes of severe infection', *International Journal of Epidemiology* 15 (1986), pp. 101–7

Alborn, Timothy L., 'A calculating profession: Victorian actuaries among the statisticians', *Science in Context* 7 (1994), pp. 433–68

Anderson, Michael, 'Marriage patterns in Victorian Britain: an analysis based on registration district data for England and Wales, 1861', *Journal of Family History* 1 (1976), pp. 55–78

Anderson, Michael, 'The social implications of demographic change', in F. M. L. Thompson (ed.), *The Cambridge Social History of Britain, 1750–1950, Volume 2, People and their Environment* (Cambridge: Cambridge University Press, 1990), pp. 1–70

Anderson, Michael, 'Fertility decline in Scotland, England and Wales, and Ireland: comparisons from the 1911 Census of Fertility', *Population Studies* 52 (1998a), pp. 1–20

Anderson, Michael, 'Highly restricted fertility: very small families in the British fertility decline', *Population Studies* 52 (1998b), pp. 177–99

Anderson, Michael and Donald J. Morse, 'High fertility, high emigration, low nuptiality: adjustment processes in Scotland's demographic experience, 1861–1914, Parts I and II', *Population Studies* 47 (1993), pp. 5–25 and 319–43

Anderson, Roy M. and Robert M. May, *Infectious Diseases of Humans: Dynamics and Control* (Oxford: Oxford University Press, 1992)

Angus, John, 'Old and new Bills of Mortality: movement of the population; deaths and fatal diseases in London during the last fourteen years', *Journal of the Statistical Society* 17 (1854), pp. 117–42

Ansell, Charles, *On the Rate of Mortality at Early Periods of Life, the Age at Marriage, the Number of Children to a Marriage, the Length of a Generation, and Other Statistics of Families in the Upper and Professional Classes* (London: National Life Assurance Society, 1874)

Anson, Jon, 'The shape of mortality curves: an analysis of counties in England and Wales, 1911', *European Journal of Population* 9 (1993), pp. 33–54

Antonovsky, Aaron and Judith Bernstein, 'Social class and infant mortality', *Social Science and Medicine* 11 (1977), pp. 453–70

Arlidge, John Thomas, *The Hygiene and Mortality of Occupations* (London: Percival, 1892)

Armstrong, David, 'The invention of infant mortality', *Sociology of Sickness and Health* 20 (1986), pp. 211–32

Bailey, Arthur Hutcheson and Archibald Day, 'On the rate of mortality prevailing amongst the families of the peerage during the 19th century', *Journal of the Institute of Actuaries* 9 (1861), pp. 305–26

Baines, Dudley, *Migration in a Mature Economy: Emigration and Internal Migration in England and Wales, 1861–1900* (Cambridge: Cambridge University Press, 1985)

Bakketeig, Leiv S., Daniel G. Seigel and Phyllis M. Sternthal, 'A fetal-infant life table based on single births in Norway, 1967–1973', *American Journal of Epidemiology* 107 (1978), pp. 216–25

Banister, Judith, *China's Changing Population* (Stanford: Stanford University Press, 1987)

Banks, J. A., *Prosperity and Parenthood: A Study of Family Planning among the Victorian Middle Classes* (London: Routledge and Kegan Paul, 1954)

Banks, J. A., 'Population change and the Victorian city', *Victorian Studies* 11 (1968), pp. 277–89

Banks, J. A., 'The contagion of numbers', in H. J. Dyos and M. Wolff (eds.), *The Victorian City: Images and Reality, Volume I* (London: Routledge and Kegan Paul, 1973), pp. 105–22

Banks, J. A., *Victorian Values: Secularism and the Size of Families* (London: Routledge and Kegan Paul, 1981)

Banks, J. A. and O. Banks, *Feminism and Family Planning in Victorian England* (Liverpool: Liverpool University Press, 1964)

Barclay, George W., Ansley J. Coale, Michael A. Stoto and T. James Trussell, 'A reassessment of the demography of traditional rural China', *Population Index* 42 (1976), pp. 606–35

Bardet, Jean-Pierre and Jacques Dupâquier (eds.), *Histoire des Populations de l'Europe, Volume II, La Révolution Démographique, 1750–1914* (Paris: Fayard, 1998)

Barker, David J. P., *Mothers, Babies, and Diseases in Later Life* (London: BMJ Publishing Group, 1994)

Barker, David J. P. and C. Osmond, 'Inequalities in health in Britain: specific explanations in three Lancashire towns', *British Medical Journal* 294 (1987), pp. 749–52

Basu, Alaka Malwade, *Culture, the Status of Women, and Demographic Behaviour: Illustrated with the Case of India* (Oxford: Clarendon Press, 1992)

Beaver, M. W., 'Population, infant mortality and milk', *Population Studies* 27 (1973), pp. 243–54

Bell, Frances and Robert Millward, 'Public health expenditures and mortality in England and Wales, 1870–1914', *Continuity and Change* 13 (1998), pp. 221–49

Berlin, Isaiah, *The Hedgehog and the Fox* (London: Weidenfeld and Nicolson, 1953)

Berridge, Virginia and Griffith Edwards, *Opium and the People: Opiate Use in Nineteenth-Century England* (London: Allen Lane, 1981)

Bideau, Alain, 'Autoregulating mechanisms in traditional populations', in Nathan Keyfitz (ed.), *Population and Biology* (Liège: Ordina Editions, 1980), pp. 119–31

Bideau, Alain, Bertrand Desjardins and Héctor Pérez Brignoli (eds.), *Infant and Child Mortality in the Past* (Oxford: Clarendon Press, 1997)

Blacker, C. P., 'Stages in population growth', *Eugenics Review* 39 (1947), pp. 88–101

Blacker, C. P. and D. V. Glass, *The Future of Our Population?* (London: Population Investigation Committee, 1936)

Blaikie, Andrew, 'A kind of loving: illegitimacy, grandparents and the rural economy of north east Scotland, 1750–1900', *Scottish Economic and Social History* 14 (1994), pp. 41–57

Bocqet-Appel, Jean-Pierre and Lucienne Jackobi, 'Diffusion spatiale de la contraception en Grande-Bretagne, à l'origine de la transition', *Population* 52 (1997), pp. 977–1004

Bongaarts, John and R. G. Potter, *Fertility, Biology and Behavior: An Analysis of the Proximate Determinants* (New York: Academic Press, 1983)

Bonneuil, Noël, *The Transformation of the French Demographic Landscape, 1806–1906* (Oxford: Clarendon Press, 1997)

Borah, Woodrow, 'America as model: the demographic impact of European expansion upon the non-European world', *XXXV Congreso Internacional de Americanistas, 1962, Volume 3* (Mexico City, 1964), pp. 379–87

Bowley, A. L., 'Death-rates, density, population, and housing', *Journal of the Royal Statistical Society* 86 (1923), pp. 516–46

Boyer, George R. and Timothy J. Hatton, 'Migration and labour market integration in late nineteenth-century England and Wales', *Economic History Review* 50 (1997), pp. 697–734

Brass, William and Carole L. Jolly (eds.), *Population Dynamics of Kenya* (Washington, DC: National Academy Press, 1993)

Brass, William and Mohammed Kabir, 'Regional variations in fertility and child mortality during the demographic transition in England and Wales', in John Hobcraft and Philip Rees (eds.), *Regional Demographic Development* (London: Croom Helm, 1980), pp. 71–88

Brass, William, Ansley J. Coale, Paul Demeny, D. R. Heisel, Frank Lorimer, Anatole Romaniuk and Etienne van de Walle, *The Demography of Tropical Africa* (Princeton, NJ: Princeton University Press, 1968)

Brodie, Janet Farrell, *Contraception and Abortion in Nineteenth-Century America* (Ithaca: Cornell University Press, 1994)

Brownlee, John, 'Historical note on Farr's theory of an epidemic', *British Medical Journal* 2 (2850) (1915), pp. 250–52

Brownlee, John, 'The history of the birth and death rates in England and Wales taken as a whole from 1570 to the present time', *Public Health* 19 (1916), pp. 211–22 and 228–38

Brownlee, John, 'Periodicities of epidemics of measles in the large towns of Great Britain and Ireland', *Proceedings of the Royal Society of Medicine* (Epidemiology Section) 12 (1918–19), pp. 77–120

Brownlee, John, *An Investigation into the Epidemiology of Phthisis in Great Britain and Ireland, Parts I, II and III*, Medical Research Council, Special Reports Nos. 18 and 46 (London: HMSO, 1918 and 1922)

Brownlee, John, 'Notes on the biology of a life-table', *Journal of the Royal Statistical Society* 82 (1919), pp. 34–77

Brownlee, John, 'Density and death-rate: Farr's law', *Journal of the Royal Statistical Society* 83 (1920), pp. 280–83

Bryder, Linda, *Below the Magic Mountain: A Social History of Tuberculosis in the Twentieth Century* (Oxford: Clarendon Press, 1988)

Buchanan, Ian, 'Infant feeding, sanitation and diarrhoea in colliery communities, 1880–1911', in Derek J. Oddy and Derek S. Miller (eds.), *Diet and Health in Modern Britain* (London: Croom Helm, 1985), pp. 148–77

Budin, Pierre, *Le Nourrisson* (Paris, 1900)

Budin, Pierre, 'La mortalité infantile de 0 à 1', *L'Obstétrique* 8 (1903), pp. 1–44

Bull, Thomas, *The Maternal Management of Children in Health and Disease* (London: Longman, Green, Longman, and Roberts, seventh edition, 1861)

Burns, C. M., *Infant and Maternal Mortality in Relation to Size of Family and Rapidity of Breeding* (Newcastle-upon-Tyne, 1942)

Burrow, J. W., *Evolution and Society: A Study in Victorian Social Theory* (Cambridge: Cambridge University Press, 1966)

Cage, R. A., 'The standard of living debate: Glasgow, 1800–1850', *Journal of Economic History* 43 (1983), pp. 175–82

Cairncross, A. K., *Home and Foreign Investment, 1870–1913: Studies in Capital Accumulation* (Cambridge: Cambridge University Press, 1953)

Caldwell, J. C., 'Education as a factor in mortality decline: an examination of Nigerian data', *Population Studies* 33 (1979), pp. 395–413

Caldwell, J. C., *Theory of Fertility Decline* (London: Academic Press, 1982)

Caldwell, John C., 'The delayed Western fertility decline: an examination of English-speaking countries', *Population and Development Review* 25 (1999), pp. 479–513

Campbell, Cameron, 'Public health efforts in China before 1949 and their effects on mortality: the case of Beijing', *Social Science History* 21 (1997), pp. 179–218

Carlsson, Gosta, 'The decline of fertility: innovation or adjustment process?', *Population Studies* 20 (1966), pp. 149–74

Carrier, N. H. and J. R. Jeffery, *External Migration: A Study of the Available Statistics, 1815–1950*, General Register Office, Studies in Medical and Population Subjects No. 6 (London: HMSO, 1953)

Carr-Saunders, A. M., *Population* (London: Oxford University Press, 1925)

Chadwick, Edwin, 'On the best modes of representing accurately, by statistical returns, the duration of life, and the pressure and progress of the causes of mortality amongst different classes of the community, and amongst the populations of different districts and counties', *Journal of the Statistical Society* 7 (1844), pp. 1–40

Chambers, J. D., *Population, Economy, and Society in Pre-industrial England* (Oxford: Oxford University Press, 1972)

Chesnais, Jean-Claude, *The Demographic Transition: Stages, Patterns, and Economic Implications* (Oxford: Clarendon Press, 1992)

Clark, Colin, 'Urban population densities', *Journal of the Royal Statistical Society* 114 (1951), pp. 490–96

Cleland, J. G. and Zeba A. Sathar, 'The effect of child spacing on childhood mortality in Pakistan', *Population Studies* 38 (1984), pp. 401–18

Cleland, John and Chris Wilson, 'Demand theories of the fertility transition: an iconoclastic view', *Population Studies* 41 (1987), pp. 5–30

Cliff, Andrew D., Peter Haggett and Matthew Smallman-Raynor, *Measles: An Historical Geography of a Major Human Viral Disease from Global Expansion to Local Retreat, 1840–1980* (Oxford: Basil Blackwell, 1993)

Cliff, Andrew, Peter Haggett and Matthew Smallman-Raynor, *Deciphering Global Epidemics: Analytical Approaches to the Disease Records of World Cities, 1888–1912* (Cambridge: Cambridge University Press, 1998)

Clout, Hugh (ed.), *London History Atlas* (London: Times Books, 1991)

Coale, Ansley J., 'Factors associated with the development of low fertility: an historic summary', *Proceedings of the World Population Conference, 1965, Volume 2* (New York: United Nations Department of Economic and Social Affairs, 1967), pp. 205–9

Coale, Ansley J., 'The demographic transition', *International Population Conference, Liège, 1973, Volume 1* (Liège: International Union for the Scientific Study of Population, 1973), pp. 53–72

Coale, Ansley J. and Paul Demeny, with Barbara Vaughan, *Regional Model Life Tables and Stable Populations* (Princeton, NJ: Princeton University Press, first edition 1966; New York: Academic Press, second edition 1983)

Coale, Ansley J. and Roy Treadway, 'A summary of the changing distribution of overall fertility, marital fertility, and the proportion married in the provinces of Europe', in Ansley J. Coale and Susan Cotts Watkins (eds.), *The Decline of Fertility in Europe* (Princeton, NJ: Princeton University Press, 1986)

Coale, A. J. and T. J. Trussell, 'Model fertility schedules: variations in the age structure of childbearing in human populations', *Population Index* 40 (1974), pp. 185–258 ('Erratum', *Population Index* 41 (1975), p. 572)

Coale, A. J. and T. J. Trussell, 'Finding the two parameters that specify a model schedule of marital fertility', *Population Index* 44 (1978), pp. 203–13

Coale, Ansley J. and Susan Cotts Watkins (eds.), *The Decline of Fertility in Europe* (Princeton, NJ: Princeton University Press, 1986)

Collis, Edgar L. and Major Greenwood, *The Health of the Industrial Worker* (London: J. & A. Churchill, 1921)

Cornell, Laurel L., 'Infanticide in early modern Japan? Demography, culture and population growth', *Journal of Asian Studies* 55 (1996), pp. 22–50

Corsini, Carlo A. and Pier Paolo Viazzo (eds.), *The Decline of Infant and Child Mortality: The European Experience, 1750–1990* (The Hague: Kluwer, 1997)

Crackanthorpe, Montague, *Population and Progress* (London: Chapman and Hall, 1907)

Crafts, N. F. R., 'A time series study of fertility in England and Wales, 1877–1938', *Journal of European Economic History* 13 (1984a), pp. 571–90

Crafts, N. F. R., 'A cross-sectional study of legitimate fertility in England and Wales, 1911', *Research in Economic History* 9 (1984b), pp. 89–107

Crafts, N. F. R., 'Some dimensions of the "quality of life" during the British industrial revolution', *Economic History Review* 50 (1997), pp. 617–39

Creighton, Charles, *A History of Epidemics in Britain, Volume Two: From the Extinction of the Plague to the Present Time* (Cambridge: Cambridge University Press, 1894; London: Frank Cass, 1965)

Cronjé, Gillian, 'Tuberculosis and mortality decline in England and Wales, 1851–1910', in Robert Woods and John Woodward (eds.), *Urban Disease and Mortality in Nineteenth-Century England* (London: Batsford, 1984), pp. 79–101

Curries, Robert *et al.*, *Churches and Churchgoers: Patterns of Church Growth in the British Isles since 1700* (Oxford: Clarendon Press, 1977)

Daly, C., J. A. Heady and J. N. Morris, 'Social and biological factors in infant mortality. III. The effect of mother's age and parity on social-class differences in infant mortality', *The Lancet* 1 (26 February 1955), pp. 445–48

Das Gupta, Monica, 'Death clustering, mothers' education and the determinants of child mortality in rural Punjab, India', *Population Studies* 44 (1990), pp. 489–505

David, Paul A. and Warren C. Sanderson, 'Rudimentary contraceptive methods and the American transition to marital fertility control, 1855–1915', in Stanley L. Engerman and Robert E. Gallman (eds.), *Long-Term Factors in American Economic Growth* (Chicago: Chicago University Press, 1986), pp. 307–90

Davis, Kingsley, *The Population of India and Pakistan* (Princeton, NJ: Princeton University Press, 1951)

Davis, Kingsley, 'The theory of change and response in demographic history', *Population Index* 29 (1963), pp. 345–66

Del Panta, Lorenzo, Massimo Livi Bacci, Giuliano Pinto and Eugenio Sonnino, *La Popolazione Italiana dal Medioevo a Oggi* (Rome: Editori Laterza, 1996)

Demeny, Paul, 'Early fertility decline in Austria-Hungary: a lesson in demographic transition', in D. V. Glass and R. Revelle (eds.), *Population and Social Change* (London: Edward Arnold, 1972), pp. 153–72

Digby, Anne, *Making a Medical Living: Doctors and Patients in the Market for English Medicine, 1720–1911* (Cambridge: Cambridge University Press, 1994)

Dobson, Mary J., *Contours of Death and Disease in Early Modern England* (Cambridge: Cambridge University Press, 1997)

Douglas, J. W. B., 'The extent of breastfeeding in Great Britain in 1946, with special reference to the health and survival of children', *Journal of Obstetrics and Gynaecology in the British Empire* 57 (1950), pp. 335–61

Douglas, J. W. B., 'Some class differences in health and survival during the first two years of life: the results of a maternity survey', *Population Studies* 5 (1951), pp. 35–58

Douglas, J. W. B., 'Birthweight and the history of breastfeeding', *The Lancet* 267 (2 October 1954), pp. 685–88

Douglas, Mary, 'Population control in primitive groups', *British Journal of Sociology* 17 (1966), pp. 263–73

Drake, Michael, 'Malthus on Norway', *Population Studies* 20 (1966), pp. 175–96

Drake, Michael, *Population and Society in Norway, 1735–1865* (Cambridge: Cambridge University Press, 1969)

Drake, Michael, 'The census, 1801–1891', in E. A. Wrigley (ed.), *Nineteenth-Century Society* (Cambridge: Cambridge University Press, 1972), pp. 7–46

Drever, Frances and Margaret Whitehead (eds.), *Health Inequalities*, Office of National Statistics, Decennial Supplement Series DS No. 15 (London: The Stationery Office, 1997)

Drinkwater, Harry, *Remarks upon the Epidemic of Measles Prevalent in Sunderland. With Notes upon 311 Cases from the Middle of January to the End of March 1885* (Edinburgh: James Thin, 1885)

Dublin, Louis I., Alfred J. Lotka and Mortimer Spiegelman, *Length of Life: A Study of the Life Table* (New York: Ronald Press, revised edition 1949)

Duncan, Jessie G., *Report on Infant Mortality in St George's and St Stephen's Wards*, City of Birmingham Health Department (Birmingham, 1911)

Duncan, Otis Dudley, 'Path analysis: sociological examples', *American Journal of Sociology* 72 (1966), pp. 1–16

Dunlop, James Craufurd, 'Occupation mortalities', *Transactions of the Faculty of Actuaries* 5 (1909), pp. 1–79

Dupâquier, Jacques, *L'Invention de la Table de Mortalité* (Paris: Presses Universitaires de France, 1996)

Dupâquier, Jacques, 'For a history of prematurity', in Alain Bideau, Bertrand Desjardins and Héctor Pérez Brignoli (eds.), *Infant and Child Mortality in the Past* (Oxford: Clarendon Press, 1997), pp. 188–202

Dwork, Deborah, *War is Good for Babies and other Young Children* (London: Tavistock, 1987)

Dyhouse, Carol, 'Working-class mothers and infant mortality in England, 1895–1914', *Journal of Social History* 12 (1978), pp. 248–67

Dyos, H. J. and D. A. Reeder, 'Slums and suburbs', in H. J. Dyos and Michael Wolff (eds.), *The Victorian City: Images and Realities, Volume 1* (London: Routledge and Kegan Paul, 1973), pp. 359–86

Dyson, Tim, 'The historical demography of Berar, 1881–1980', in Tim Dyson (ed.), *India's Historical Demography: Studies in Famine, Disease and Society* (London: Curzon Press, 1989a), pp. 150–96

Dyson, Tim, 'The population history of Berar since 1881 and its potential wider significance', *Indian Economic and Social History Review* 26 (1989b), pp. 167–201

Dyson, Tim, 'Infant and child mortality in the Indian subcontinent, 1881–1947', in Alain Bideau, Bertrand Desjardins and Héctor Pérez Brignoli (eds.), *Infant and Child Mortality in the Past* (Oxford: Clarendon Press, 1997), pp. 109–34

Eaton, Joseph W. and Albert J. Mayer, *Man's Capacity to Reproduce: The Demography of a Unique Population* (Glencoe, IL: Free Press, 1954)

Edmonds, Thomas Rowe, *Practical Moral and Political Economy; or, the Government, Religion, and Institutions, most conducive to Individual Happiness and to National Power* (London: Effingham Wilson, 1828)

Edmonds, Thomas Rowe, *An Enquiry into the Principles of Population, exhibiting a System of Regulations for the Poor; designed immediately to lessen, and finally remove, the evils which have hitherto pressed upon the Labouring Classes of Society* (London: James Duncan, 1832)

Edmonds, Thomas Rowe, 'On the laws of collective vitality', *The Lancet* 2 (605) (1834–35), pp. 5–8

Edmonds, T. R., 'On the law of human mortality; and on Mr. Gompertz's new exposition of his law of mortality', *Journal of the Institute of Actuaries* 9 (1861), pp. 327–40

Elderton, Ethel M., *Report on the English Birth Rate, Part 1. England North of the Humber*, Eugenics Laboratory Memoirs 19 and 20 (Cambridge: Cambridge University Press, 1914)

Elderton, Ethel M., A. Barrington, H. G. Jones, H. Laski and K. Pearson, *On the Correlation of Fertility with Social Value: A Co-operative Study*, Eugenics Laboratory Memoir 18 (London, 1913)

Evans, Richard J., *In Defence of History* (London: Granta, 1997)

Ewbank, Douglas C. and Samuel H. Preston, 'Personal health behaviour and the decline in infant and child mortality: the United States, 1900–1930', in John C. Caldwell *et al.* (eds.), *What Do We Know about Health Transition? The Cultural, Social and Behavioural Determinants of Health, Volume 1* (Canberra: Australian National University, Health Transition Centre, 1990), pp. 116–49

Eyler, John M., 'Mortality statistics and Victorian health policy: program and criticism', *Bulletin of the History of Medicine* 50 (1976), pp. 335–55

Eyler, John M., *Victorian Social Medicine: The Ideas and Methods of William Farr* (Baltimore: Johns Hopkins University Press, 1979)

Eyler, John M., 'The conceptual origins of William Farr's epidemiology: numerical methods and social thought in the 1830s', in Abraham M. Lilienfeld (ed.), *Times, Places, and Persons: Aspects of the History of Epidemiology* (Baltimore: Johns Hopkins University Press, 1980), pp. 1–21

Eyler, John M., *Sir Arthur Newsholme and State Medicine, 1885–1935* (Cambridge: Cambridge University Press, 1997)

Farr, William, 'Vital statistics; or the statistics of health, sickness, diseases, and death', in J. R. McCulloch (ed.), *A Statistical Account of the British Empire* (London: 1837), pp. 567–601, reprinted in Richard Wall (ed.), *Mortality in Mid-19th Century Britain* (London: Gregg International, 1974)

Farr, William, 'The Northampton table of mortality', in Registrar General's *Eighth Annual Report for 1845* (BPP 1847–48/XXV), pp. 290–325

Farr, William, 'Influence of elevation on the fatality of cholera', *Journal of the Statistical Society* 15 (1852), pp. 155–83

Farr, William, 'On the construction of life-tables, illustrated by a new life-table of the healthy districts of England', *Philosophical Transactions of the Royal Society* 149 (1859), pp. 837–78

Farr, William, *English Life Table: Tables of Lifetimes, Annuities, and Premiums, with an Introduction by William Farr, M.D., F.R.S., D.C.L.* (London: HMSO and Longman, Green, Longman, Roberts, and Green, 1864)

Farr, William, 'On infant mortality and on alleged inaccuracies of the census', *Journal of the Statistical Society* 28 (1865), pp. 125–49

Farr, William, 'Mortality of children in the principal states of Europe', *Journal of the Statistical Society* 29 (1866a), pp. 1–35

Farr, William, 'Mr Lowe and the cattle plague', *Daily News* (19 February 1866b), pp. 5–6

Farr, William, 'English reproduction table', *Philosophical Transactions of the Royal Society* 171 (1880), pp. 281–88

Farr, William, *Vital Statistics* (London: The Sanitary Institute of Great Britain, 1885, edited by Noel A. Humphreys)

Feinstein, Charles H., 'Pessimism perpetuated: real wages and the standard of living in Britain during and after the industrial revolution', *Journal of Economic History* 58 (1998), pp. 625–58

Fildes, Valerie, 'Neonatal feeding practices and infant mortality during the 18th century', *Journal of Biosocial Science* 12 (1980), pp. 313–24

Fildes, Valerie, *Breasts, Bottles and Babies: A History of Infant Feeding* (Edinburgh: Edinburgh University Press, 1986)

Fildes, Valerie, 'Breast-feeding in London, 1905–19', *Journal of Biosocial Science* 24 (1992), pp. 53–70

Fildes, Valerie, 'Infant feeding practices and infant mortality in England, 1900–1919', *Continuity and Change* 13 (1998), pp. 251–80

Fisher, R. A., *The Genetical Theory of Natural Selection* (Oxford: Clarendon Press, 1930)

Floud, Roderick, Kenneth Wachter and Annabel Gregory, *Height, Health and History: Nutritional Status in the United Kingdom, 1750–1980* (Cambridge: Cambridge University Press, 1990)

Fogel, Robert W., 'Nutrition and the decline in mortality since 1700: some preliminary findings', in Stanley L. Engerman and Robert E. Gallman (eds.), *Long-Term Factors in American Economic Growth* (Chicago: Chicago University Press, 1986), pp. 439–55

Fogel, Robert W., 'Economic growth, population theory, and physiology: the bearing of long-term processes on the making of economic policy', *American Economic Review* 84 (1994a), pp. 369–95

Fogel, Robert W., 'The relevance of Malthus for the study of mortality today: long-run influences on health, mortality, labour force participation, and population growth', in Kerstin Lindahl-Kiessling and Hans Landberg (eds.), *Population, Economic Development and the Environment* (Oxford: Oxford University Press, 1994b), pp. 231–84

Fox, A. J., P. O. Goldblatt and D. R. Jones, 'Social class mortality differentials: artefact, selection or life circumstances?', *Journal of Epidemiology and Community Health* 39 (1985), pp. 1–8

Frazer, W. M., *Duncan of Liverpool* (London: Hamish Hamilton, 1947)

Friedlander, Dov, 'Demographic patterns and socio-economic characteristics of the coal-mining population in England and Wales in the nineteenth century', *Economic Development and Cultural Change* 22 (1973), pp. 39–51

Friedlander, Dov, 'London's urban transition, 1851–1951', *Urban Studies* 11 (1974), pp. 127–41

Friedlander, Dov, 'Demographic responses and socioeconomic structure: population processes in England and Wales in the nineteenth century', *Demography* 20 (1983), pp. 249–72

Friedlander, Dov and Barbara S. Okun, 'Pretransition marital fertility variation over time: was there deliberate control in England?', *Journal of Family History* 20 (1995), pp. 139–58

Friedlander, Dov and Barbara S. Okun, 'Fertility transition in England and Wales: continuity and change', *Health Transition Review*, Supplement 6 (1996), pp. 1–18

Friedlander, Dov and R. Roshier, 'A study of internal migration in England and Wales', *Population Studies* 19 (1966), pp. 239–79

Galley, Chris, *The Demography of Early Modern Towns: York in the Sixteenth and Seventeenth Centuries* (Liverpool: Liverpool University Press, 1998)

Galley, Chris and Robert Woods, 'Réflexions sur la distribution des décès au cours de la première année de vie', *Population* 53 (1998), pp. 921–46

Galley, Chris, Naomi Williams and Robert Woods, 'Detection without correction: problems in assessing the quality of English ecclesiastical and civil registration', *Annales de Démographie Historique* (1995), pp. 161–83

Galloway, Patrick R., Eugene A. Hammel and Ronald D. Lee, 'Fertility decline in Prussia, 1875–1910: a pooled cross-section time series analysis', *Population Studies* 48 (1994), pp. 135–58

Garrett, Eilidh M., 'Before their Time: Employment and Family Formation in a Northern Textile Town, Keighley 1851–81', unpublished PhD thesis, University of Sheffield, 1987

Garrett, Eilidh M., 'The trials of labour: motherhood versus employment in a nineteenth-century textile centre', *Continuity and Change* 5 (1990), pp. 121–54

Garrett, Eilidh M., 'Was women's work bad for babies? A view from the 1911 census of England and Wales', *Continuity and Change* 13 (1998), pp. 281–316

Garrett, Eilidh and Alice Reid, 'Thinking of England and taking care: family building strategies and infant mortality in England and Wales, 1891–1911', *International Journal of Population Geography* 1 (1996), pp. 69–102

Garrett, Eilidh, Alice Reid, Kevin Schurer and Simon Szreter, *Population Change in Context: Place, Class and Demography in England and Wales, 1891–1911* (Cambridge: Cambridge University Press, forthcoming)

Gibson, J. R. and T. McKeown, 'Observations on all births (23,970) in Birmingham, 1947. I. Duration of gestation. II. Birth weight. III. Survival. V. Birth weight related to economic circumstances of parents. VI. Birth weight, duration of gestation, and survival related to sex. VII. Effect of changing family size on infant mortality', *British Journal of Social Medicine* 4 (1950), pp. 211–33, 5 (1951), pp. 98–112, 177–83 and 259–64, 6 (1952), pp. 152–58 and 183–87

Gillis, John R., Louise A. Tilly and David Levine (eds.), *The European Experience of Declining Fertility: A Quiet Revolution, 1850–1970* (Oxford: Basil Blackwell, 1992)

Gittins, Diana, *Fair Sex: Family Size and Structure, 1900–39* (London: Hutchinson, 1982)

Glass, D. V., 'Changes in fertility in England and Wales, 1851–1931', in Lancelot Hogben (ed.), *Political Arithmetic* (London: George Allen and Unwin, 1938), pp. 161–212

Glass, D. V., 'A note on the under-registration of births in Britain in the nineteenth century', *Population Studies* 5 (1951), pp. 70–88

Glass, D. V., *Numbering the People: The Eighteenth-Century Population Controversy and the Development of Census and Vital Statistics in Britain* (Farnborough: Saxon House, 1973)

Goldblatt, Peter, 'Mortality by social class, 1971–85', *Population Trends* 56 (1989), pp. 6–15

Goldstone, J. A., 'The demographic revolution in England: a re-examination', *Population Studies* 49 (1986), pp. 5–33

Gompertz, Benjamin, 'A sketch of an analysis and notation applicable to the estimation of the value of life contingencies', *Philosophical Transactions of the Royal Society* 110 (1820), pp. 214–94 ('Errata', 115 (1825), pp. 584–85)

Gompertz, Benjamin, 'On the nature of the function expressive of the law of human mortality, and on a new mode of determining the value of life contingencies. In a letter to Francis Baily, Esq. F.R.S. &c.', *Philosophical Transactions of the Royal Society* 115 (1825), pp. 513–83

Gompertz, Benjamin, 'A supplement to two papers published in the Transactions of the Royal Society, "On the science connected with human mortality;" the one published in 1820, and the other in 1825', *Philosophical Transactions of the Royal Society* 152 (1862), pp. 511–59

Gompertz, Benjamin, 'On the uniform law of mortality from birth to extreme old age, and on the law of sickness', *Journal of the Institute of Actuaries* 16 (1872), pp. 329–44

Goody, Jack, 'Comparing family systems in Europe and Asia: are there different sets of rules?', *Population and Development Review* 22 (1996), pp. 1–20

Gould, W. T. S., 'Ideology and data analysis in African population policies: the case of Kenya', *Applied Geography* 15 (1995), pp. 203–18

Greenhalgh, Susan (ed.), *Situating Fertility: Anthropology and Demographic Enquiry* (Cambridge: Cambridge University Press, 1995)

Greenwood, Major, 'On the influence of industrial employment upon general health', *British Medical Journal* 1 (1922): (3200), pp. 667–72; (3201), pp. 708–13; (3202), pp. 752–58

Greenwood, Major, 'Laws of mortality from the biological point of view', *Journal of Hygiene* 28 (1928), pp. 267–94

Greenwood, Major, *The Medical Dictator and Other Biographical Studies* (London: Williams and Norgate, 1936)

Greenwood, Major, 'Occupational and economic factors of mortality', *British Medical Journal* 1 (4086) (1939), pp. 862–66

Greenwood, Major and G. Udny Yule, 'On the determination of size of family and of the distribution of characters in order of birth from samples taken through members of the sibships', *Journal of the Royal Statistical Society* 77 (1914), pp. 179–99

Guha, Sumit, 'Mortality decline in early twentieth century India: a preliminary enquiry', *Indian Economic and Social History Review* 28 (1991), pp. 371–91

Guha, Sumit, 'The importance of social intervention in England's mortality decline: the evidence reviewed', *Social History of Medicine* 7 (1994), pp. 89–113

Guinnane, Timothy W., *The Vanishing Irish: Households, Migration, and the Rural Economy, 1850–1914* (Princeton, NJ: Princeton University Press, 1997)

Guinnane, Timothy W., Barbara S. Okun and James Trussell, 'What do we know about the timing of fertility transition in Europe?', *Demography* 31 (1994), pp. 1–20

Guy, William Augustus, 'An attempt to determine the influence of the seasons and weather on sickness and mortality', *Journal of the Statistical Society* 6 (1843a), pp. 133–50

Guy, William Augustus, 'Contributions to a knowledge of the influence of employments upon health', *Journal of the Statistical Society* 6 (1843b), pp. 197–211

Guy, William Augustus, 'Further contributions to a knowledge of the influence of employments upon health', *Journal of the Statistical Society* 6 (1843c), pp. 283–304

Guy, William Augustus, 'A third contribution to a knowledge of the influence of employments upon health', *Journal of the Statistical Society* 7 (1844), pp. 232–43

Guy, William Augustus, 'On the causes which determine the choice of an employment; being an addition to the essays on the influence of employments upon health', *Journal of the Statistical Society* 8 (1845), pp. 351–53

Guy, William Augustus, 'On the nature and extent of the benefits conferred by hospitals on the working classes and the poor', *Journal of the Statistical Society* 29 (1856), pp. 12–27

Haines, Michael R., *Fertility and Occupation: Population Patterns in Industrialization* (New York: Academic Press, 1979)

Haines, Michael R., 'Inequality and childhood mortality: a comparison of England and Wales, 1911, and the United States, 1900', *Journal of Economic History* 45 (1985), pp. 885–912

Haines, Michael R., 'Social class differentials during fertility decline: England and Wales revisited', *Population Studies* 43 (1989), pp. 305–23

Haines, Michael R., 'Conditions of work and the decline of mortality', in Roger Schofield, David Reher and Alain Bideau (eds.), *The Decline of Mortality in Europe* (Oxford: Clarendon Press, 1991), pp. 177–95

Haines, Michael R., 'Socio-economic differentials in infant and child mortality during mortality decline: England and Wales, 1890–1911', *Population Studies* 49 (1995), pp. 297–315

Hajnal, John, 'Age at marriage and proportion marrying', *Population Studies* 7 (1953), pp. 111–36

Hajnal, John, 'European marriage patterns in perspective', in D. V. Glass and D. E. C. Eversley (eds.), *Population in History* (London: Edward Arnold, 1965), pp. 101–43

Hajnal, John, 'Two kinds of preindustrial household formation system', *Population and Development Review* 8 (1982), pp. 449–94

Hamlin, Christopher, 'Muddling in Bumbledon: on the enormity of sanitary improvements in four British towns, 1855–1885', *Victorian Studies* 32 (1988), pp. 55–83

Hamlin, Christopher, *Public Health and Social Justice in the Age of Chadwick: Britain, 1800–54* (Cambridge: Cambridge University Press, 1998)

Hanley, Susan B., *Everyday Things in Premodern Japan: The Hidden Legacy of Japanese Culture* (Berkeley: University of California Press, 1997)

Hanley, Susan B. and Arthur P. Wolf (eds.), *Family and Population in East Asian History* (Stanford: Stanford University Press, 1985)

Hardy, Anne, *The Epidemic Streets: Infectious Disease and the Rise of Preventive Medicine, 1856–1900* (Oxford: Clarendon Press, 1993)

Hardy, Anne, '"Death is a cure for all diseases": using the General Register Office cause of death statistics for 1837–1920', *Social History of Medicine* 7 (1994), pp. 472–92

Hare, E. H., P. A. P. Moran and A. Macfarlane, 'The changing seasonality of infant deaths in England and Wales 1912–78 and its relation to seasonal temperature', *Journal of Epidemiology and Community Health* 35 (1981), pp. 77–82

Hart, Nicky, 'Beyond infant mortality: gender and stillbirth in reproductive mortality before the twentieth century', *Population Studies* 52 (1998), pp. 215–29

Haskey, John, 'Trends in marriage: church, chapel and civil ceremonies', *Population Trends* 22 (1980), pp. 1–24

Haskey, John, 'Trends in marriage and divorce in England and Wales, 1837–1987', *Population Trends* 48 (1987), pp. 11–19

Hassan, J. A., 'The growth and impact of the British water industry in the nineteenth century', *Economic History Review* 38 (1985), pp. 531–47

Hayami, Akira, 'Population changes', in Marius B. Jansen and Gilbert Rozman (eds.), *Japan in Transition: From Tokugawa to Meiji* (Princeton, NJ: Princeton University Press, 1986), pp. 280–317

Henry, Louis, 'Some data on natural fertility', *Eugenics Quarterly* 8 (1961), pp. 81–91

Henry, Louis, 'Men's and women's mortality in the past', *Population* (English Selection 1) 44 (1989), pp. 177–201

Heron, David, *On the Relation of Fertility in Man to Social Status, and On the Changes in this Relation that have taken place during the Last Fifty Years*, Drapers' Company Research Memoirs, Studies in National Deterioration 1 (London: Dulau and Co., 1906)

Higgs, Edward, *Making Sense of the Census: The Manuscript Returns for England and Wales, 1801–1901* (London: HMSO, 1989)

Higgs, Edward, 'A cuckoo in the nest? The origins of civil registration and state medical statistics in England and Wales', *Continuity and Change* 11 (1996), pp. 115–34

Hinde, P. R. A., 'Household structure, marriage and the institution of service in nineteenth-century rural England', *Local Population Studies* 35 (1985), pp. 201–10

Hinde, P. R. A., 'The marriage market in the nineteenth-century English countryside', *Journal of European Economic History* 18 (1989), pp. 383–92

Hinde, P. R. A. and R. I. Woods, 'Variations in historical natural fertility patterns and the measurement of fertility control', *Journal of Biosocial Science* 16 (1984), pp. 309–21

Hobcraft, John, John W. McDonald and Shea Rutstein, 'Child spacing effects on infant and early child mortality', *Population Index* 49 (1983), pp. 585–618

Hobcraft, J. N., J. W. McDonald and S. O. Rutstein, 'Socio-economic factors in infant and child mortality: a cross-national comparison', *Population Studies* 38 (1984), 193–223

Hobcraft, J. N., J. W. McDonald and S. O. Rutstein, 'Demographic determinants of infant and early child mortality: a comparative analysis', *Population Studies* 39 (1985), pp. 363–85

Holdsworth, Clare, 'Potters' Rot and Plumbism: Occupational Health in the North Staffordshire Pottery Industry', unpublished PhD thesis, University of Liverpool, 1995

Holdsworth, Clare, 'Women's work and family health: evidence from the Staffordshire Potteries, 1890–1920', *Continuity and Change* 12 (1997), pp. 103–28

Holdsworth, Clare, 'Dr John Thomas Arlidge and Victorian occupational medicine', *Medical History* 42 (1998), pp. 458–75

Hope, E. W., 'Observations on autumnal diarrhoea in cities', *Public Health* 11 (July 1899), pp. 660–65

Hope, E. W., *Report on the Physical Welfare of Mothers and Children, England and Wales, Volume 1* (Liverpool, 1917)

Howarth, William J., 'The influence of feeding on the mortality of infants', *The Lancet* 2 (4273) (22 July 1905), pp. 210–13

Howell, Nancy, 'Feedbacks and buffers in relation to scarcity and abundance: studies of hunter-gatherer populations', in David Coleman and Roger Schofield (eds.), *The State of Population Theory: Forward from Malthus* (Oxford: Basil Blackwell, 1986), pp. 156–87

Huck, Paul, 'Infant mortality in nine industrial parishes in northern England, 1813–36', *Population Studies* 48 (1994), pp. 513–26

Huck, Paul, 'Infant mortality and living standards of English workers during the industrial revolution', *Journal of Economic History* 55 (1995), pp. 528–50

Huck, Paul, 'Shifts in the seasonality of infant deaths in nine English towns during the 19th century: a case for reduced breast feeding?', *Explorations in Economic History* 34 (1997), pp. 368–86

Humphreys, N. A., 'The value of death-rates as a test of sanitary condition', *Journal of the Statistical Society* 37 (1874), pp. 437–71

Humphreys, Noel A., 'Class mortality statistics', *Journal of the Royal Statistical Society* 50 (1887), pp. 255–92

Humphries, Jane, '"Bread and a pennyworth of treacle": excess female mortality in England in the 1840s', *Cambridge Journal of Economics* 15 (1991), pp. 451–73

Hunter, Henry Julian, 'Report of Dr Henry Julian Hunter on the Excessive mortality of Infants in some rural districts of England', *Sixth Report of the Medical Officer of the Privy Council for 1863* (BPP 1864/XXVIII), appendix 14, pp. 454–62

Illsley, Raymond and Julian le Grand, 'Regional inequalities in mortality', *Journal of Epidemiology and Community Health* 47 (1993), pp. 444–49

Independent Inquiry into Inequalities in Health: Report (Acheson Report) (London: The Stationery Office, 1998)

Innes, J. W., *Class Fertility Trends in England and Wales, 1876–1934* (Princeton, NJ: Princeton University Press, 1938)

James, Patricia (ed.), *The Travel Diaries of Thomas Robert Malthus* (Cambridge: Cambridge University Press, 1966)

Jannetta, Ann Bowman and Samuel H. Preston, 'Two centuries of mortality change in central Japan: the evidence from a temple death register', *Population Studies* 45 (1991), pp. 417–36

Johansson, S. Ryan, 'Food for thought: rhetoric and reality in modern mortality history', *Historical Methods* 27 (1994), pp. 101–25

Johansson, Sten and Ola Nygren, 'The missing girls of China: a new demographic account', *Population and Development Review* 17 (1991), pp. 35–51

Jones, Gavin W., Robert M. Douglas, John C. Caldwell and Rennie M. D'Souza (eds.), *The Continuing Demographic Transition* (Oxford: Clarendon Press, 1997)

Jones, H. R., 'The perils and protection of infant life', *Journal of the Royal Statistical Society* 57 (1894), pp. 1–103

Kanthack, Emilia, *The Preservation of Infant Life* (London, 1907)

Kayne, George Gregory, Water Pagel and Laurence O'Shaughnessy, *Pulmonary Tuberculosis: Pathology, Diagnosis, Management and Prevention* (Oxford: Oxford University Press, 1939)

Kearns, Gerry, 'Le handicap urbain et le déclin de la mortalité en Angleterre et au Pays de Galles, 1851–1900', *Annales de Démographie Historique* (1993), pp. 75–105

Kertzer, David I. and Tom Fricke (eds.), *Anthropological Demography: Toward a New Synthesis* (Chicago: Chicago University Press, 1997)

Kintner, Hallie J., 'Trends and regional differences in breastfeeding in Germany from 1871 to 1937', *Journal of Family History* 10 (1985), pp. 163–82

Kintner, Hallie, 'The impact of breastfeeding patterns on differences in infant mortality in Germany, 1910', *European Journal of Population* 3 (1987), pp. 233–61

Knodel, John, 'Infant mortality and fertility in three Bavarian villages: an analysis of family histories from the 19th century', *Population Studies* 22 (1968), pp. 297–318

Knodel, John E., *The Decline of Fertility in Germany, 1871–1939* (Princeton, NJ: Princeton University Press, 1974)

Knodel, John, 'Family limitation and the fertility transition: evidence from the age patterns of fertility in Europe and Asia', *Population Studies* 31 (1977a), pp. 219–49

Knodel, John, 'Breastfeeding and population growth', *Science* 198 (16 September 1977b), pp. 1111–15

Knodel, John, 'Natural fertility in pre-industrial Germany', *Population Studies* 32 (1978), pp. 481–510

Knodel, John, 'From natural fertility to family limitation: the onset of fertility transition in a sample of German villages', *Demography* 16 (1979), pp. 493–521

Knodel, John, 'Child mortality and reproductive behaviour in German village populations in the past: a micro-level analysis of the replacement effect', *Population Studies* 36 (1982), pp. 177–200

Knodel, John, 'Natural fertility: age patterns, levels, and trends', in R. Bulatao and R. Lee (eds.), *Determinants of Fertility in Developing Countries* (New York: Academic Press, 1983), pp. 61–102

Knodel, John, 'Starting, stopping, and spacing during the early stages of fertility transition: the experience of German village populations in the eighteenth and nineteenth centuries', *Demography* 24 (1987), pp. 143–62

Knodel, John E., *Demographic Behavior in the Past: A Study of Fourteen German Village Populations in the Eighteenth and Nineteenth Centuries* (Cambridge: Cambridge University Press, 1988)

Knodel, John and A. I. Hermalin, 'The effects of birth rank, maternal age, birth interval and sibship size on infant and child mortality: evidence from 18th and 19th century reproductive histories', *American Journal of Public Health* 74 (1984), pp. 1098–106

Knodel, John and Hallie Kintner, 'The impact of breast feeding patterns on the biometric analysis of infant mortality', *Demography* 14 (1977), pp. 391–409

Knodel, John and Mary Jo Maynes, 'Urban and rural marriage patterns in Imperial Germany', *Journal of Family History* 1 (1976), pp. 129–68

Knodel, John and Etienne van de Walle, 'Breastfeeding, fertility and infant mortality: an analysis of some early German data', *Population Studies* 21 (1967), pp. 109–31

Knodel, John and Etienne van de Walle, 'Lessons from the past: policy implications of historical fertility studies', *Population and Development Review* 5 (1979), pp. 217–45, and in Ansley J. Coale and Susan Cotts Watkins (eds.), *The Decline of Fertility in Europe* (Princeton, NJ: Princeton University Press, 1986), pp. 390–419

Knodel, John and C. Wilson, 'The secular increase in fecundity in German village populations: an analysis of reproductive histories of couples married 1750–1899', *Population Studies* 35 (1981), pp. 53–84

Koch, Robert, 'How the fight against tuberculosis now stands', *The Lancet* 1 (4317) (1906), pp. 1449–51

Kussmaul, Ann, *Servants in Husbandry in Early Modern England* (Cambridge: Cambridge University Press, 1981)

Kussmaul, Ann, 'Time and space, hoofs and grain: the seasonality of marriage in England', in Robert I. Rotberg and Theodore K. Rabb (eds.), *Population and Economy* (Cambridge: Cambridge University Press, 1986), pp. 195–219

Kussmaul, Ann, *A General View of the Rural Economy of England, 1538–1840* (Cambridge: Cambridge University Press, 1990)

Landers, John, *Death and the Metropolis: Studies in the Demographic History of London, 1670–1830* (Cambridge: Cambridge University Press, 1993)

Landers, John, 'Mortality in eighteenth-century London: a note', *Continuity and Change* 11 (1996), pp. 303–10

Landry, Adolphe, 'Les trois théories principales de la population', *Scientia* 6 (3) (1909), pp. 121–47

Landry, Adolphe, *La Révolution Démographique: Études et Essais sur les Problèmes de la Population* (Paris: Librairie du Recueil Sirey, 1934)

Lantz, P., M. Partin and A. Palloni, 'Using retrospective surveys for estimating the effects of breastfeeding and childspacing on infant and child mortality', *Population Studies* 46 (1992), pp. 121–39

Laslett, Peter, Karla Oosterveen and Richard M. Smith (eds.), *Bastardy and its Comparative History* (London: Edward Arnold, 1980)

Lavely, William and R. Bin Wong, 'Revising the Malthusian narrative: the comparative study of population dynamics in late imperial China', *Journal of Asian Studies* 57 (1998), pp. 714–48

Law, C. M., 'The growth of urban population in England and Wales, 1801–1911', *Transactions of the Institute of British Geographers* 41 (1967), pp. 125–43

Lawton, Richard, 'Population changes in England and Wales in the later nineteenth century: an analysis of trends by registration districts', *Transactions of the Institute of British Geographers* 44 (1968), pp. 55–74

Lawton, Richard (ed.), *The Census and Social Structure: An Interpretative Guide to Nineteenth Century Censuses for England and Wales* (London: Frank Cass, 1978)

Lawton, Richard, 'Census data for urban areas', in Richard Lawton (ed.), *The Census and Social Structure: An Interpretative Guide to Nineteenth Century Censuses for England and Wales* (London: Frank Cass, 1978), pp. 82–141

Lawton, Richard, 'Population', in John Langton and R. J. Morris (eds.), *Atlas of Industrialising Britain* (London: Methuen, 1986), pp. 10–29

Lawton, Richard (ed.), *The Rise and Fall of Great Cities* (London: Belhaven, 1989)

Laxton, Paul and Naomi Williams, 'Urbanization and infant mortality in England: a long term perspective and review', in Marie C. Nelson and John Rogers (eds.), *Urbanisation and the Epidemiologic Transition*, Reports from the Family History Group, Department of History, Uppsala University, No. 9 (Uppsala, 1989), pp. 109–35

Lee, James and Cameron Campbell, *Fate and Fortune in Rural China: Social Organization and Population Behavior in Liaoning, 1774–1873* (Cambridge: Cambridge University Press, 1997)

Lee, James, and Wang Feng, 'Malthusian models and Chinese realities: the Chinese demographic system, 1700–2000', *Population and Development Review* 25 (1999a), pp. 33–65

Lee, James Z. and Wang Feng, with contributions by Cameron Campbell, *One Quarter of Humanity: Malthusian Mythology and Chinese Reality, 1700–2000* (Cambridge, MA: Harvard University Press, 1999b)

Lee, James, Wang Feng and Cameron Campbell, 'Infant and child mortality among the Qing nobility: implications for two types of positive check', *Population Studies* 48 (1994), pp. 395–411

Lee, Ronald, 'Population homeostasis and English demographic history', in Robert I. Rotberg and Theodore K. Rabb (eds.), *Population and Economy* (Cambridge: Cambridge University Press, 1986), pp. 75–100

Lee, Ronald, 'Population dynamics of humans and other animals', *Demography* 24 (1987), pp. 443–65

Lee, R. D. and D. Lam, 'Age distribution adjustments for English censuses, 1821 to 1931', *Population Studies* 37 (1983), pp. 445–64

Legge, Thomas, *Industrial Maladies* (Oxford: Oxford Medical Publications, 1934)

Leibenstein, Harvey, 'Socio-economic fertility theories and their relevance to population policy', *International Labour Review* 109 (1974), pp. 443–57

Leibenstein, Harvey, 'The economic theory of fertility decline', *Quarterly Journal of Economics* 89 (1975), pp. 1–31

Lesthaeghe, R. J., 'Nuptiality and population growth', *Population Studies* 25 (1971), pp. 415–32

Lesthaeghe, Ron J., *The Decline of Belgian Fertility, 1800–1970* (Princeton, NJ: Princeton University Press, 1977)

Levine, David, 'Sampling history: the English population', *Journal of Interdisciplinary History* 28 (1998), pp. 605–32

Lewis, Jane (ed.), *Labour and Love: Women's Experience of Home and Family, 1850–1940* (Oxford: Basil Blackwell, 1986)

Lewis-Faning, E., 'A survey of the mortality in Dr Farr's 63 healthy districts of England and Wales during the period 1851–1925', *Journal of Hygiene* 30 (1930), pp. 121–53

Lewis-Faning, E., *Report on an Inquiry into Family Limitation and Human Fertility in the Past Fifty Years*, Royal Commission on Population, Papers, Volume 1 (London: HMSO, 1949)

Lithell, Ulla-Britt, 'Breastfeeding habits and their relation to infant mortality and marital fertility', *Journal of Family History* 6 (1981), pp. 182–94

Lithell, Ulla-Britt, 'Premium weaving in the 19th century parish of Natra. Women, production and reproduction', *Historisk Tidskrift* 4 (1985), pp. 471–90

Livi Bacci, Massimo, 'Fertility and nuptiality changes in Spain from the late 18th to the early 20th century', *Population Studies* 22 (1968), pp. 83–102 and 211–34

Logan, W. P. D., 'Social class variations in mortality', *British Journal of Preventive Social Medicine* 8 (1954), pp. 128–37

Loudon, Irvine, *Death in Childbirth: An International Study of Maternal Care and Maternal Mortality, 1800–1950* (Oxford: Clarendon Press, 1992)

Louis, Pierre Charles Alexandre, 'Note sur la fréquence relative de la phthisie chez les deux sexes', *Annales d'Hygiène Publique* 6 (1831), pp. 49–57

Luckin, Bill and Graham Mooney, 'Urban history and historical epidemiology: the case of London, 1860–1920', *Urban History* 24 (1997), pp. 37–55

Lynch, Katherine A. and Joel B. Greenhouse, 'Risk factors for infant mortality in nineteenth-century Sweden', *Population Studies* 48 (1994), pp. 117–33

McKeown, Thomas, *The Modern Rise of Population* (London: Edward Arnold, 1976)

McKeown, Thomas, 'Fertility, mortality and cause of death', *Population Studies* 32 (1978), pp. 535–42

McKeown, Thomas and R. G. Brown, 'Medical evidence related to English population changes in the eighteenth century', *Population Studies* 9 (1955), pp. 119–41

McKeown, Thomas and C. R. Lowe, *An Introduction to Social Medicine* (Oxford: Blackwell Scientific Publications, 1966)

McKeown, Thomas and R. G. Record, 'Reasons for the decline of mortality in England and Wales during the nineteenth century', *Population Studies* 16 (1962), pp. 94–122

McKeown, Thomas, R. G. Brown and R. G. Record, 'An interpretation of the modern rise of population in Europe', *Population Studies* 26 (1972), pp. 345–82

McKeown, Thomas, R. G. Record and R. D. Turner, 'An interpretation of the decline of mortality in England and Wales during the twentieth century', *Population Studies* 29 (1975), pp. 391–422

McLaren, Angus, *Birth Control in Nineteenth-Century England* (London: Croom Helm, 1978)

Makeham, William Matthew, 'On the law of mortality', *Journal of the Institute of Actuaries* 13 (1867), pp. 325–58

Makeham, W. M., 'Explanation and example of a method of constructing mortality tables with imperfect data; and of the extension of Gompertz's theory to the entire period of life', *Journal of the Institute of Actuaries* 16 (1872), pp. 344–50

Malthus, Thomas Robert, *An Essay on the Principle of Population* (Oxford: Oxford University Press, 1993, first edition of 1798)

Malthus, Thomas Robert, *An Essay on the Principle of Population; . . .* (Cambridge: Cambridge University Press, 1989, second edition of 1803 edited by Patricia James)

Marland, Hilary, 'A pioneer in infant welfare: the Huddersfield scheme, 1903–1920', *Social History of Medicine* 6 (1993), pp. 25–50

Marmot, Michael G., 'Social differentials in health within and between populations', *Daedalus* 123 (4) (1994), pp. 197–216

Mason, Karen Oppenheim, 'Explaining fertility transitions', *Demography* 34 (1997), pp. 443–54

Matthiessen, Poul Christian, *The Limitation of Family Size in Denmark. Part I: Text, with Maps and Figures*, Det Kongelige Danske Videnskabernes Selskab, Historisk-filosofiske Meddelelser 52:1, Part I (Copenhagen: Munksgaard, 1985)

Mercer, Alex, *Disease, Mortality and Population in Transition: Epidemiological-Demographic Change in England since the Eighteenth Century as part of a Global Phenomenon* (Leicester: Leicester University Press, 1990)

Meslé, France and Jacques Vallin, 'Reconstitution of annual life tables for nineteenth-century France', *Population* (English Selection 3) (1991), pp. 33–62

Millman, S. and C. Cooksey, 'Birth weight and the effects of birth spacing and breastfeeding on infant mortality', *Studies in Family Planning* 18 (4) (1987), pp. 202–12

Mills, Dennis and Carol Pearse, *People and Places in the Victorian Census*, Historical Geography Research Series No. 23 (London: Institute of British Geographers, 1989)

Millward, Robert and Frances N. Bell, 'Economic factors in the decline of mortality in nineteenth century Britain', *European Review of Economic History* 2 (1998), pp. 263–88

Milne, Joshua, *A Treatise on the Valuation of Annuities and Assurances on Lives and Survivorships* (London, 1815)

Milne, Joshua, 'On laws of mortality', in *Encyclopaedia Britannica* (Edinburgh, seventh edition, 1842), pp. 544–62

Mitchell, B. R. (ed.), *European Historical Statistics, 1750–1975* (London: Macmillan, second revised edition 1981)

Montgomery, Mark R. and Barney Cohen (eds.), *From Death to Birth: Mortality*

Decline and Reproductive Change (Washington, DC: National Academy Press, 1998)

Mooney, Graham, 'Did London pass the "sanitary test"? Seasonal infant mortality in London, 1870–1914', *Journal of Historical Geography* 20 (1994a), pp. 158–74

Mooney, Graham, 'The Geography of Mortality Decline in Victorian London', unpublished PhD thesis, University of Liverpool, 1994b

Mooney, Graham, Bill Luckin and Andrea Tanner, 'Patient pathways: solving the problem of institutional mortality in London during the later nineteenth century', *Social History of Medicine* 12 (1999), pp. 227–69

Morris, J. N., J. A. Heady *et al.*, 'Social and biological factors in infant mortality', *The Lancet* 1 (12 February 1955), pp. 343–49; (19 February 1955), pp. 395–97; (26 February 1955), pp. 445–48; (5 March 1955), pp. 499–502; (12 March 1955), pp. 554–59

Morse, Donald J., 'The Decline of Fertility in Scotland', unpublished PhD thesis, University of Edinburgh, 1988

Mosley, W. Henry and Lincoln C. Chen, 'Child survival: research and policy', in W. Henry Mosley and Lincoln C. Chen (eds.), *Child Survival: Strategies for Research, Population and Development Review*, Supplement to volume 10 (1984), pp. 25–45

Munro, A. Campbell, 'Measles: an epidemiological study', *Transactions of the Epidemiological Society* 10 (1890–91), pp. 94–109

Neal, Frank, *Black '47: Britain and the Irish Famine* (London: Macmillan, 1998)

Neison, F. G. P., 'On a method recently proposed for conducting inquiries into the comparative sanatory condition of various districts, with illustrations, derived from numerous places in Great Britain at the period of the last census', *Journal of the Statistical Society* 7 (1844), pp. 40–68

Neison, Francis G. P., 'On the rate of mortality in the medical profession', *Journal of the Statistical Society* 15 (1852), pp. 193–222

Newman, George, *Infant Mortality: A Social Problem* (London: Methuen, 1906)

Newsholme, Arthur, *The Elements of Vital Statistics in their Bearing on Social and Public Health Problems* (London: George Allen and Unwin, first edition 1889, third edition 1923)

Newsholme, Arthur, 'The vital statistics of Peabody Buildings and other artisans' and labourers' block dwellings', *Journal of the Royal Statistical Society* 54 (1891), pp. 70–99

Newsholme, Arthur, 'A contribution to the study of epidemic diarrhoea', *Public Health* 12 (December 1899), pp. 139–213

Newsholme, Arthur, 'The epidemiology of scarlet fever in relation to the utility of isolation hospitals', *Transactions of the Epidemiological Society* 20 (1901), pp. 48–69

Newsholme, Arthur, 'Public health aspects of summer diarrhoea', *The Practitioner* (August 1902), pp. 161–80

Newsholme, Arthur, 'Remarks on the causation of epidemic diarrhoea', *Transactions of the Epidemiological Society*, New Series 22 (1902–03), pp. 34–43

Newsholme, Arthur, 'Domestic infection in relation to epidemic diarrhoea', *Journal of Hygiene* 6 (1906a), pp. 139–48

Newsholme, Arthur, 'An inquiry into the principal causes of the reduction in death-rate from phthisis during the last forty years, with special reference to the segregation of phthisical patients in general institutions', *Journal of Hygiene* 6 (1906b), pp. 304–84

Newsholme, Arthur, 'The measurement of progress in public health: with special reference to the life and work of William Farr', *Economica* 3 (1923), pp. 186–202

Newsholme, Arthur, *Fifty Years in Public Health: A Personal Narrative with Comments. The Years Preceding 1909* (London: George Allen and Unwin, 1935)

Nissel, Muriel, *People Count: A History of the General Register Office* (London: HMSO, 1987)

Notestein, Frank W., 'Population: the long view', in T. W. Schultz (ed.), *Food for the World* (Chicago: Chicago University Press, 1945), pp. 36–57

Notestein, Frank W., 'Summary view of the demographic background of problems of undeveloped areas', *Milbank Memorial Fund Quarterly* 26 (1948), pp. 249–55

Notestein, Frank W., 'Economic problems of population change', *Proceedings of the Eighth International Conference of Agricultural Economists, 1953* (London: Oxford University Press, 1953), pp. 13–31

Notestein, Frank W. and Chi-ming Chiao, 'Population', in John Lossing Buck (ed.), *Land Utilisation in China* (Nanking: Nanking University Press; London: Oxford University Press, 1937), pp. 338–99

O'Donnell, Terence, *History of Life Assurance in its Formative Years* (Chicago: American Conservation Company, 1936)

Office of Population Censuses and Surveys, *William Farr, 1807–1883, The Report of a Centenary Symposium held at the Royal Society on 29 April 1983*, OPCS Occasional Paper No. 33 (London: HMSO, 1983)

Office of Population Censuses and Surveys, *Birth Statistics: Historical Series of Statistics from Registrations of Births in England and Wales, 1837–1983*, Series FM1 No. 13 (London: HMSO, 1987)

Ogle, William, 'On marriage-rates and marriage-ages, with special reference to the growth of population', *Journal of the Royal Statistical Society* 53 (1890), pp. 253–89

ÓGráda, Cormac, *Black '47 and Beyond: The Great Irish Famine in History, Economy, and Memory* (Princeton, NJ: Princeton University Press, 1999)

Okun, Barbara S., 'Evaluating methods for detecting fertility control: Coale and Trussell's model and cohort parity analysis', *Population Studies* 43 (1994), pp. 193–222

Oliver, Thomas (ed.), *Dangerous Trades. The Historical, Social and Legal Aspects of Industrial Occupations as Affecting Health* (London: John Murray, 1902)

Olshansky, S. Jay and Bruce A. Carnes, 'Ever since Gompertz', *Demography* 34 (1997), pp. 1–15

Omran, Abdel R., 'The epidemiologic transition: a theory of the epidemiology of population change', *Milbank Memorial Fund Quarterly* 49 (1971), pp. 509–38

Palloni, Alberto and Marta Tienda, 'The effects of breastfeeding and the pace of childbearing on mortality at early ages', *Demography* 23 (1986), pp. 31–52

Pamuk, Elsie R., 'Social class inequality in mortality from 1921 to 1972 in England and Wales', *Population Studies* 39 (1985), pp. 17–31

Pamuk, Elsie R., 'Social-class inequality in infant mortality in England and Wales from 1921 to 1980', *European Journal of Population* 4 (1988), pp. 1–21

Parkes, Alan S., *Patterns of Sexuality and Reproduction* (Oxford: Oxford University Press, 1976)

Pearl, Raymond, *The Rate of Living, Being an Account of Some Experimental Studies on the Biology of Life Duration* (London: London University Press, 1928)

Pearl, Raymond, *The Natural History of Population* (London: Oxford University Press, 1939)

Pearson, Karl, 'The chances of death', in Karl Pearson, *The Chances of Death and other Studies in Evolution, Volume I* (London: Edward Arnold, 1897), pp. 1–41

Peel, J., 'The manufacture and retailing of contraceptives in England', *Population Studies* 17 (1963), pp. 113–25

Perrenoud, Alfred and Patrice Bourdelais, 'Le recul de la mortalité', in Jean-Pierre Bardet and Jacques Dupâquier (eds.), *Histoire des Populations de l'Europe, Volume II* (Paris: Fayard, 1998), pp. 57–101

Political and Economic Planning, *World Population and Resources: A Report by PEP* (London: Political and Economic Planning, 1955)

Pooley, Colin and Jean Turnbull, *Migration and Mobility in Britain since the 18th Century* (London: UCL Press, 1998)

Poppel, Frans van and Cor van der Heijden, 'The effects of water supply on infant and childhood mortality: a review of historical evidence', *Health Transition Review* 7 (1997), pp. 113–48

Porter, Roy, *London: A Social History* (London: Hamish Hamilton, 1994)

Porter, Roy and Lesley Hall, *The Facts of Life: The Creation of Sexual Knowledge in Britain, 1650–1950* (New Haven: Yale University Press, 1995)

Preston, Samuel H., 'The changing relationship between mortality and level of economic development', *Population Studies* 29 (1975), pp. 231–48

Preston, Samuel H. (ed.), *The Effects of Infant and Child Mortality on Fertility* (New York: Academic Press, 1977)

Preston, Samuel H. and Michael R. Haines, *Fatal Years: Child Mortality in Late Nineteenth-Century America* (Princeton, NJ: Princeton University Press, 1991)

Preston, Samuel H. and Etienne van de Walle, 'Urban French mortality in the nineteenth century', *Population Studies* 32 (1978), pp. 275–97

Preston, Samuel H., Nathan Keyfitz and Robert Schoen, *Causes of Death: Life Tables for National Populations* (New York: Seminar Press, 1972)

Price, Richard, *Observations on Reversionary Payments* (London, first edition 1771, fifth edition with notes by William Morgan, 1792)

Ransome, Arthur, 'On the form of the epidemic wave, and some of its probable causes', *Transactions of the Epidemiological Society* 1 (1881–82), pp. 96–107

Razzell, Peter, 'The conundrum of eighteenth-century English population growth', *Social History of Medicine* 11 (1998), pp. 469–500

Reay, Barry, 'Before the transition: fertility in English villages, 1800–1880', *Continuity and Change* 9 (1994), pp. 91–120

Reay, Barry, *Microhistories: Demography, Society and Culture in Rural England, 1800–1930* (Cambridge: Cambridge University Press, 1996)

Reher, David, *Perspectives on the Family in Spain, Past and Present* (Oxford: Clarendon Press, 1997)

Reher, David, 'Back to the basics: mortality and fertility interactions during the demographic transition', *Continuity and Change* 14 (1999), pp. 9–31

Reid, Alice, 'Locality or class? Spatial and social differentials in infant and child mortality in England and Wales, 1895–1911', in Carlo A. Corsini and Pier Paolo Viazzo (eds.), *The Decline of Infant and Child Mortality: The European Experience, 1750–1990* (The Hague: Kluwer, 1997), pp. 129–54

Reves, Randall, 'Declining fertility in England and Wales as a major cause of the twentieth century decline in mortality: the role of changing family size and age structure in infectious disease mortality in infancy', *American Journal of Epidemiology* 122 (1985), pp. 112–26

Riley, James C., *Sick, Not Dead: The Health of British Working Men during the Mortality Decline* (Baltimore: Johns Hopkins University Press, 1997)

Riley, Nancy and Robert W. Gardner, *China's Population: A Review of the Literature* (Liege: IUSSP, 1997)

Roberts, Elizabeth, *A Woman's Place: An Oral History of Working-Class Women, 1890–1940* (Oxford: Basil Blackwell, 1984)

Robertson, John, *Special Report of the Medical Officer of Health on Infant Mortality in the City of Birmingham* (Birmingham, 1904)

Robinson, Alfred, 'The trained midwife and her effect on infantile mortality', *Public Health* 21 (March 1908), pp. 22–27 and 22 (August 1909), pp. 422–25

Rotberg, Robert I. and Theodore K. Rabb (eds.), *Population and Economy* (Cambridge: Cambridge University Press, 1986)

Rowntree, Griselda and Norman H. Carrier, 'The resort to divorce in England and Wales, 1838–1957', *Population Studies* 11 (1958), pp. 188–233

Royal Statistical Society, 'Report of the Special Committee on Infantile Mortality', *Journal of the Royal Statistical Society* 76 (1912), pp. 27–87

Saito, Osamu, 'Infanticide, fertility and "population stagnation": the state of Tokugawa historical demography', *Japan Forum* 4 (1992), pp. 369–81

Saito, Osamu, 'Infant mortality in pre-transition Japan: levels and trends', in Alain Bideau, Bertrand Desjardins and Héctor Pérez Brignoli (eds.), *Infant and Child Mortality in the Past* (Oxford: Clarendon Press, 1997), pp. 135–53

Sargant, William Lucas, 'On certain results and defects of the reports of the Registrar General', *Journal of the Statistical Society* 27 (1864), pp. 170–221

Sargant, William Lucas, 'Inconsistencies of the English census of 1861, with the Registrar General's reports: and deficiencies in the local registry of births', *Journal of the Statistical Society* 28 (1865), pp. 73–184

Sauer, R., 'Infanticide and abortion in nineteenth-century Britain', *Population Studies* 32 (1978), pp. 81–93

Sauvy, Alfred, 'Adolphe Landry', *Population* 11 (1956), pp. 609–20

Schellekens, Jona, 'Illegitimate fertility decline in England, 1851–1911', *Journal of Family History* 20 (1995), pp. 365–77

Schofield, Roger, 'The measurement of literacy in pre-industrial England', in Jack Goody (ed.), *Literacy in Traditional Societies* (Cambridge: Cambridge University Press, 1968), pp. 311–25

Schofield, Roger, 'Dimensions of illiteracy, 1750–1850', *Explorations in Economic History* 10 (1973), pp. 437–54

Schofield, Roger, 'The relationship between demographic structure and environment in pre-industrial western Europe', in W. Conze (ed.), *Sozialgeschichte der Familie in der Neuzeit Europas* (Stuttgart: Klett, 1976), pp. 147–60

Schofield, Roger, 'Review of *The Modern Rise of Population* by Thomas McKeown', *Population Studies* 31 (1977), pp. 179–81

Schofield, Roger, 'Population growth in the century after 1750: the role of mortality decline', in Tommy Bengtsson, Gunnar Fridlizius and Rolf Ohlsson (eds.), *Pre-Industrial Population Change* (Stockholm: Almqvist and Wiksell, 1984), pp. 18–22

Schofield, Roger, 'English marriage patterns revisited', *Journal of Family History* 10 (1985), pp. 2–20

Schofield, Roger, 'Through a glass darkly: *The Population History of England* as an experiment in history', in Rotberg, Robert I. and Theodore K. Rabb (eds.), *Population and Economy* (Cambridge: Cambridge University Press, 1986), pp. 11–33

Schofield, Roger, 'Family structure, demographic behaviour, and economic growth', in John Walter and Roger Schofield (eds.), *Famine, Disease and Social Order in Early Modern Society* (Cambridge: Cambridge University Press, 1989), pp. 279–304

Schofield, Roger, David Reher and Alain Bideau (eds.), *The Decline of Mortality in Europe* (Oxford: Clarendon Press, 1991)

Scott, Susan and Christopher J. Duncan, *Human Demography and Disease* (Cambridge: Cambridge University Press, 1998)

Seccombe, Wally, 'Starting to stop: working-class fertility decline in Britain', *Past and Present* 126 (1990), pp. 151–88

Sen, Amartya, 'Mortality as an indicator of economic success and failure', *Economic Journal* 108 (1998), pp. 1–25

Shorter, Edward, John Knodel and Etienne van de Walle, 'The decline of non-marital fertility in Europe, 1880–1940', *Population Studies* 25 (1971), pp. 375–93

Skinner, G. William, 'Family systems and demographic processes', in David I. Kertzer and Tom Fricke (eds.), *Anthropological Demography* (Chicago: Chicago University Press, 1997), pp. 53–95

Sloggett, Andrew and Heather Joshi, 'Higher mortality in deprived areas: community or personal disadvantage?', *British Medical Journal* 309 (1994), pp. 1470–74

Smith, F. B., *The People's Health, 1830–1910* (London: Croom Helm, 1979)

Smith, F. B., *The Retreat of Tuberculosis, 1850–1950* (London: Croom Helm, 1988)

Smith, Thomas C., *Nakahara: Family Farming and Population in a Japanese Village, 1717–1830* (Stanford: Stanford University Press, 1977)

Soloway, Richard Allen, *Birth Control and the Population Question in England, 1877–1930* (Chapel Hill: University of North Carolina Press, 1982)

Southall, Humphrey and David Gilbert, 'A good time to wed?: marriage and economic distress in England and Wales, 1839–1914', *Economic History Review* 49 (1996), pp. 35–57

Spree, Reinhard, *Health and Social Class in Imperial Germany: A Social History of Mortality, Morbidity and Inequality* (Oxford: Berg, 1988)

Stephens, W. B., *Education, Literacy and Society, 1830–70: The Geography of Diversity in Provincial England* (Manchester: Manchester University Press, 1987)

Stevenson, T. H. C., 'The fertility of various social classes in England and Wales from the middle of the nineteenth century to 1911', *Journal of the Royal Statistical Society* 80 (1920), pp. 401–44

Stevenson, T. H. C., 'The social distribution of mortality from different causes in England and Wales, 1910–12', *Biometrika* 15 (1923), pp. 382–400

Stevenson, T. H. C., 'The vital statistics of wealth and poverty', *Journal of the Royal Statistical Society* 91 (1928), pp. 207–30

Stocks, Percy, 'The effects of occupation and of its accompanying environment on mortality', *Journal of the Royal Statistical Society* 101 (1938), pp. 669–708

Stone, Lawrence, *Road to Divorce: England, 1530–1987* (Oxford: Oxford University Press, 1990)

Strachey, Lytton, *Eminent Victorians* (London: Chatto and Windus, 1918)

Sundt, Eilert, *On Marriage in Norway* (Cambridge: Cambridge University Press, 1980, translated and edited by Michael Drake)

Sutherland, Ian, *Stillbirths: Their Epidemiology and Social Significance* (Oxford: Oxford University Press, 1949)

Sutherland, Ian, 'Recent studies in the epidemiology of tuberculosis', *Advances in Tuberculosis Research* 19 (1976), pp. 1–63

Szreter, S. R. S., 'The genesis of the Registrar-General's social classification of occupations', *British Journal of Sociology* 35 (1984), pp. 522–46

Szreter, Simon, 'The importance of social intervention in Britain's mortality decline c. 1850–1914: a re-interpretation of the role of public health', *Social History of Medicine* 1 (1988), pp. 1–37

Szreter, Simon (ed.), 'The General Register Office of England and Wales and the Public Health Movement, 1837–1914, A Comparative Perspective', *Social History of Medicine*, Special Issue, 4 (3) (1991), pp. 401–537

Szreter, Simon, 'The idea of demographic transition and the study of fertility change: a critical intellectual history', *Population and Development Review* 19 (1993), pp. 659–701

Szreter, Simon, 'Mortality in England in the eighteenth and the nineteenth centuries: a reply to Sumit Guha', *Social History of Medicine* 7 (1994), pp. 269–82

Szreter, Simon, *Fertility, Class and Gender in Britain, 1860–1940* (Cambridge: Cambridge University Press, 1996)

Szreter, Simon, 'Economic growth, disruption, deprivation, disease and death: on the importance of the politics of public health for development', *Population and Development Review* 23 (1997), pp. 693–728

Szreter, Simon and Graham Mooney, 'Urbanization, mortality and the standard of living debate: new estimates of the expectation of life at birth in nineteenth-century British cities', *Economic History Review* 51 (1998), pp. 84–112

Taeuber, Irene B., *The Population of Japan* (Princeton, NJ: Princeton University Press, 1958)

Tawney, R. H., *Land and Labour in China* (London: George Allen and Unwin, 1932)

Teitelbaum, Michael S., 'Birth underregistration in the constituent counties of England and Wales: 1841–1910', *Population Studies* 28 (1974), pp. 329–43

Teitelbaum, Michael S., *The British Fertility Decline: Demographic Transition in the Crucible of the Industrial Revolution* (Princeton, NJ: Princeton University Press, 1984)

Thiele, T. N., 'On a mathematical formula to express the rate of mortality throughout the whole of life, tested by a series of observations made use of by the Danish Life Assurance Company of 1871', *Journal of the Institute of Actuaries* 16 (1872), pp. 313–29

Thompson, F. M. L., 'Town and city', in F. M. L. Thompson (ed.), *The Cambridge Social History of Britain, 1750–1950, Volume 1, Regions and Communities* (Cambridge: Cambridge University Press, 1990), pp. 1–86

Thompson, Warren S., 'Population', *American Journal of Sociology* 34 (1929), pp. 959–75

Tillott, P. M., 'Sources of inaccuracy', in E. A. Wrigley (ed.), *Nineteenth-Century Society* (Cambridge: Cambridge University Press, 1972), pp. 82–133

Tilly, Charles, 'Why birth rates fell', *Population and Development Review* 22 (1996), pp. 557–62

Tilly, Charles, Rudolf Andorka and David Levine, 'Review symposium: *The Decline of Fertility in Europe*', *Population and Development Review* 12 (1986), pp. 323–40

Titmuss, Richard M., *Birth, Poverty and Wealth: A Study of Infant Mortality* (London: Hamish Hamilton, 1943)

Townsend, Peter and Nick Davidson (eds.), *Inequalities in Health* (incorporating the *Black Report*) (London: Penguin, 1982)

Trussell, James and Anne R. Pebley, 'The potential impact of changes in fertility on infant, child and maternal mortality', *Studies in Family Planning* 15 (6) (1984), pp. 267–80

UNICEF, *The State of the World's Children, 1994* (Oxford: Oxford University Press for UNICEF, 1994)

Vallin, Jacques, 'Mortality in Europe from 1720 to 1914: long-term trends and changes in patterns by age and sex', in Roger Schofield, David Reher and Alain Bideau (eds.), *The Decline of Mortality in Europe* (Oxford: Clarendon Press, 1991) pp. 38–67

Vann, R. T. and David Eversley, *Friends in Life and Death: The British and Irish Quakers in the Demographic Transition, 1650–1900* (Cambridge: Cambridge University Press, 1992)

Vernon, H. M., *Health in Relation to Occupation* (London: Oxford University Press, 1939)

Viazzo, Pier Paolo, *Upland Communities: Environment, Population and Social Structure in the Alps since the Sixteenth Century* (Cambridge: Cambridge University Press, 1989)

Vincent, David, *Literacy and Popular Culture: England, 1750–1914* (Cambridge: Cambridge University Press, 1989)

Vries, Jan de, *European Urbanization, 1500–1800* (London: Methuen, 1984)

Wall, Richard, 'The household: demographic and economic change in England, 1650–1970', in Richard Wall, Jean Robin and Peter Laslett (eds.), *Family Forms in Historic Europe* (Cambridge: Cambridge University Press, 1983), pp. 493–512

Wall, Richard, Jean Robin and Peter Laslett (eds.), *Family Forms in Historic Europe* (Cambridge: Cambridge University Press, 1983)

Walle, Etienne van de and John Knodel, 'Europe's fertility transition: new evidence and lessons for today's developing world', *Population Bulletin* 34 (6) (1980), pp. 3–43

Walle, Francine van de, 'Infant mortality and the European demographic transition', in Ansley J. Coale and Susan Cotts Watkins (eds.), *The Decline of Fertility in Europe* (Princeton, NJ: Princeton University Press, 1986), pp. 201–33

Ward, W. Peter, *Birth Weight and Economic Growth: Women's Living Standards in the Industrializing West* (Chicago: Chicago University Press, 1993)

Watkins, Susan Cotts, *From Provinces into Nations: Demographic Integration in Western Europe, 1870–1960* (Princeton, NJ: Princeton University Press, 1991)

Watson, Alfred W., *An Account of an Investigation of the Sickness and Mortality Experience of the I.O.O.F. Manchester Unity during the Years 1893–1897* (Manchester: IOOF, 1903)

Watson, Alfred W., 'The analysis of sickness experience', *Journal of the Institute of Actuaries* 62 (1931), pp. 12–61

Watterson, Patricia A., 'Role of the environment in the decline of infant mortality: an analysis of the 1911 census of England and Wales', *Journal of Biosocial Science* 18 (1986), pp. 457–70

Watterson, Patricia A., 'Environmental Factors in Differential Infant Mortality Decline in England and Wales circa 1895 to 1910', unpublished PhD thesis, University of London, 1987

Watterson, Patricia A., 'Infant mortality by father's occupation from the 1911 census of England and Wales', *Demography* 25 (1988), pp. 289–306

Webb, Sidney, *The Decline in the Birth Rate*, Fabian Tract No. 131 (London: Fabian Society, 1907)

Weir, David R., 'Rather never than late: celibacy and age at marriage in English cohort fertility, 1541–1871', *Journal of Family History* 9 (1984), pp. 340–54

Weir, David R., 'New estimates of nuptiality and marital fertility in France, 1740–1911', *Population Studies* 48 (1994), pp. 307–31

Welton, Thomas A., 'The effects of migration in disturbing local rates of mortality as exemplified in the statistics of London and the surrounding country for the years 1851–60', *Journal of the Institute of Actuaries* 16 (1872), pp. 153–86

Werner, Barry, 'Fertility statistics from birth registrations in England and Wales, 1837–1987', *Population Trends* 48 (1987), pp. 4–10

West, Charles, *Lectures on the Diseases of Infancy and Childhood* (London: Longmans, Green, and Co., seventh edition, 1884)

Westoff, Charles F. and Norman Ryder, *The Contraceptive Revolution* (Princeton, NJ: Princeton University Press, 1977)

Whitelegge, B. Arthur, 'Measles epidemics, major and minor', *Transactions of the Epidemiological Society* 12 (1892–93), pp. 37–54

Williams, Naomi J., *The Occupational Mortality Statistics of the General Register Office, 1861–1911*, Liverpool Papers in Human Geography No. 2, Department of Geography, University of Liverpool, 1990

Williams, Naomi, 'Death in its season: class, environment and the mortality of infants in nineteenth-century Sheffield', *Social History of Medicine* 5 (1992), pp. 71–94

Williams, Naomi and Chris Galley, 'Urban–rural differentials in infant mortality in Victorian England', *Population Studies* 49 (1995), pp. 401–20

Williams, Naomi and Graham Mooney, 'Infant mortality in an "Age of Great Cities": London and the English provincial cities compared, c. 1840–1910', *Continuity and Change* 9 (1994), pp. 185–212

Williams, R. Price, 'On the increase of population in England and Wales', *Journal of the Statistical Society* 43 (1880), pp. 462–508

Williamson, Jeffrey G., *Coping with City Growth during the British Industrial Revolution* (Cambridge: Cambridge University Press, 1990)

Wilson, Chris, 'Natural fertility in pre-industrial England', *Population Studies* 38 (1984), pp. 225–40

Wilson, Chris, 'The proximate determinants of marital fertility in England, 1600–1700', in Lloyd Bonfield, Richard M. Smith and Keith Wrightson (eds.), *The World We Have Gained* (Oxford: Basil Blackwell, 1986), pp. 203–30

Wilson, Chris and Pauline Airey, 'How can a homeostatic perspective enhance demographic transition theory?', *Population Studies* 53 (1999), pp. 117–28

Wilson, Chris and Robert Woods, 'Fertility in England: a long-term perspective', *Population Studies* 45 (1991), pp. 399–415

Wilson, George N., 'Measles: its prevalence and mortality in Aberdeen', *Public Health* 18 (2) (1905), pp. 65–82

Wilson, Leonard G., 'The historical decline of tuberculosis in Europe and America: its causes and significance', *Journal of the History of Medicine* 45 (1990), pp. 49–57

Winikoff, B., 'Issues in the design of breastfeeding research', *Studies in Family Planning* 12 (4) (1981), pp. 177–84

Winter, J. M., 'Aspects of the impact of the First World War on infant mortality in Britain', *Journal of European Economic History* 11 (1982), pp. 713–38

Wohl, Anthony S., *The Eternal Slum: Housing and Social Policy in Victorian London* (London: Edward Arnold, 1977)

Wohl, Anthony S., *Endangered Lives: Public Health in Victorian Britain* (London: Dent, 1983)

Woodbury, Robert M., 'Westergaard's method of expected deaths as applied to the study of infant mortality', *Quarterly Publications of the American Statistical Association* 18 (1922), pp. 366–76

Woodbury, Robert Morse, *Infant Mortality and its Causes* (Baltimore: Williams and Wilkins, 1926)

Woods, Robert, *Theoretical Population Geography* (London: Longman, 1982a)

Woods, Robert, 'The structure of mortality in mid-nineteenth century England and Wales', *Journal of Historical Geography* 8 (1982b), pp. 373–94

Woods, Robert, 'Social class variations in the decline of marital fertility in late nineteenth-century London', *Geografiska Annaler B* 66 (1984), pp. 29–38

Woods, Robert, 'The effects of population redistribution on the level of mortality in nineteenth-century England and Wales', *Journal of Economic History* 45 (1985), pp. 645–51

Woods, Robert, 'Working-class fertility decline in Britain', *Past and Present* 134 (1992), pp. 200–7

Woods, Robert, 'On the historical relationship between infant and adult mortality', *Population Studies* 47 (1993), pp. 195–219

Woods, Robert, 'La mortalité infantile en Grande Bretagne: un bilan des connaissances historiques', *Annales de Démographie Historique* (1994), pp. 119–34 (English version in Bideau *et al.* (1997), pp. 74–88)

Woods, Robert, *The Population of Britain in the Nineteenth Century* (Cambridge: Cambridge University Press, 1995)

Woods, Robert, 'Physician, heal thyself: the health and mortality of Victorian doctors', *Social History of Medicine* 9 (1996), pp. 1–30

Woods, Robert, 'Sickness is a baffling matter. A reply to James C. Riley', *Social History of Medicine* 10 (1997), pp. 157–63

Woods, R. I. and P. R. A. Hinde, 'Nuptiality and age at marriage in nineteenth-century England', *Journal of Family History* 10 (1985), pp. 119–44

Woods, Robert and Nicola Shelton, *An Atlas of Victorian Mortality* (Liverpool: Liverpool University Press, 1997)

Woods, R. I. and C. W. Smith, 'The decline of marital fertility in the late nineteenth century: the case of England and Wales', *Population Studies* 37 (1983), pp. 207–25

Woods, Robert and Naomi Williams, 'Must the gap widen before it can be narrowed? Long-term trends in social class mortality differentials', *Continuity and Change* 10 (1995), pp. 105–37

Woods, Robert and John Woodward (eds.), *Urban Disease and Mortality in Nineteenth-Century England* (London: Batsford, 1984)

Woods, R. I., P. A. Watterson and J. H. Woodward, 'The causes of rapid infant mortality decline in England and Wales, 1861–1921. Parts I and II', *Population Studies* 42 (1988), pp. 343–66; and 43 (1989), pp. 113–32

Wrigley, E. A., 'Demographic models and geography', in Richard J. Chorley and Peter Haggett (eds.), *Models in Geography* (London: Methuen, 1967), pp. 189–215

Wrigley, E. A., *Population and History* (London: Weidenfeld and Nicolson, 1969)

Wrigley, E. A. (ed.), *Nineteenth-Century Society: Essays in the Use of Quantitative Methods for the Study of Social Data* (Cambridge: Cambridge University Press, 1972)

Wrigley, E. A., 'Births and baptisms: the use of Anglican baptism registers as a source of information about the numbers of births in England before the beginning of civil registration', *Population Studies* 31 (1977), pp. 281–312

Wrigley, E. A., 'Marital fertility in seventeenth-century Colyton: a note', *Economic History Review* 31 (1978), pp. 429–36

Wrigley, E. A., 'Age at marriage in early modern England', *Family History* 12 (91–92) (1982), pp. 219–34

Wrigley, E. A., 'The growth of population in eighteenth-century England: a conundrum resolved', *Past and Present* 98 (1983), pp. 121–50

Wrigley, E. A., *People, Cities and Wealth* (Oxford: Basil Blackwell, 1987)

Wrigley, E. A., 'The fall of marital fertility in nineteenth-century France: exemplar or exception?', in E. A. Wrigley, *People, Cities and Wealth* (Oxford: Basil Blackwell, 1987), pp. 270–321

Wrigley, E. A., *Continuity, Chance and Change: The Character of the Industrial Revolution in England* (Cambridge: Cambridge University Press, 1988)

Wrigley, E. A., 'How reliable is our knowledge of the demographic characteristics of the English population in the early modern period?', *Historical Journal* 40 (1997), pp. 571–95

Wrigley, E. A., 'Explaining the rise in fertility in England in the "long" eighteenth century', *Economic History Review* 51 (1998), pp. 435–64

Wrigley, E. A. and R. S. Schofield, *The Population History of England, 1541–1871: A Reconstruction* (London: Edward Arnold, 1981; reprinted Cambridge: Cambridge University Press, 1989)

Wrigley, E. A., R. S. Davies, J. E. Oeppen and R. S. Schofield, *English Population History from Family Reconstitution, 1580–1837* (Cambridge: Cambridge University Press, 1997)

Wynne-Edwards, V. C., *Animal Dispersion in Relation to Social Behaviour* (Edinburgh: Oliver and Boyd, 1962)

Xie, Y. and E. E. Pimental, 'Age patterns of marital fertility: revising the Coale–Trussell method', *Journal of the American Statistical Association* 87 (1992), pp. 977–84

Yule, G. U., 'On the changes in the marriage and birth-rates in England and Wales during the past half century, with an inquiry as to their probable causes', *Journal of the Royal Statistical Society* 69 (1906), pp. 88–132

Yule, G. U., *The Fall in the Birth Rate* (Cambridge: Cambridge University Press, 1920)

Yule, G. Udny, 'On some points relating to vital statistics, more especially statistics of occupational mortality', *Journal of the Royal Statistical Society* 97 (1934), pp. 1–84

Zelinsky, Wilbur, 'The hypothesis of the mobility transition', *Geographical Review* 61 (1971), pp. 219–49

Zhao, Zhongwei, 'Deliberate birth control under a high-fertility regime: reproductive behavior in China before 1970', *Population and Development Review* 23 (1997), pp. 729–67

Index